RUSSIA AND THE SOVIET UNION

FIFTH EDITION

RUSSIA AND THE SOVIET UNION

An Historical Introduction from the Kievan State to the Present

John M. Thompson

A Member of the Perseus Books Group

Copyright © 1990, 1994, 1998, 2004 by Westview Press, A Member of the Perseus Books Group

Published in 1998 in the United States of America by Westview Press, 5500 Central Avenue, Boulder, Colorado 80301–2877, and in the United Kingdom by Westview Press, 12 Hid's Copse Road, Cumnor Hill, Oxford OX2 9JJ

First published in 1986 by Macmillan Publishing Company

Library of Congress Cataloging-in-Publication Data
Thompson, John M.
    Russia and the Soviet Union : an historical introduction from the Kievan state to the present / John M. Thompson. — 5th ed.
        p.   cm.
    Includes bibliographical references and index.
    ISBN 0-8133-4145-0 (pbk. : alk. paper) —
    ISBN 0-8133-4146-9 (hardcover : alk. paper)
    1. Russia—History.   2. Soviet Union—History.   3. Russia (Federation)—History.   I. Title.
DK40.T48 2004
947—dc21

                                                                        2003006397

The paper used in this publication meets the requirements of the American National Standard for Permanence of Paper for Printed Library Materials Z39.48–1984.

10   9   8   7   6   5   4

Contents

Preface

Events have again outpaced earlier revisions of this book made in 1990 and 1994. Developments in Russia, particularly the political ups and downs of Boris Yeltsin, the reformers' struggle to improve everyday life while reining in "crony capitalism's" worst excesses, the tussle between the West and Russia over NATO expansion, and ongoing changes in Russia's social and cultural life prompted me to rewrite completely Chapter 15, which covers the period since the collapse of the Soviet Union in 1991. In that chapter of the third edition I had sought to provide brief, capsule treatments of each of the fifteen successor states to the USSR. Now their separate histories are sufficiently unfolded and complex that I decided to focus Chapter 15 on Russia alone, treating the other fourteen states only as neighbors and as key elements in Russian foreign policy.

For this edition I also rewrote a few sections of Chapter 14 on the Gorbachev "revolution," attempting to incorporate new evidence and interpretations. Overall, however, I decided that the earlier account had so far withstood the test of time and required no changes in its major conclusions about the man and the era.

Throughout the book I corrected a few errors brought to my attention by students and colleagues. I also revised and added new books to the suggestions for "Further Reading" at the ends of chapters.

As in previous editions, my goal remains to provide students and general readers with a clear, concise treatment of the dramatic history of this significant region and its long-suffering and talented peoples.

John M. Thompson

Preface to the First Edition

This book grew out of dissatisfaction with longer, more detailed histories of Russia that my students and I experienced at the University of Hawaii in spring 1983, when I taught a survey course treating the entire history of Russia in one semester. Such a course, difficult in the best of circumstances, becomes almost impossible for both instructor and students when the latter must try to master in fourteen weeks the complex material of a six-hundred-page textbook designed for a two-semester course. In my view, there is no up-to-date, clear, short history of Russia that gives approximately equal attention to earlier Russian history and to the modern period since 1801. This is the book I attempted to write in the hope it will fill a need for teachers and students at the upper secondary and college levels.

At the same time, I was aware of the interest in Russia and its past on the part of many individuals not enrolled in courses in Russian history—those in other fields or with a general curiosity about foreign cultures or international affairs. Friends of my children, acquaintances, members of the audience at public lectures I give, and others frequently ask me, "I would like to learn something about Russia and its history; is there a good short book I can start with?" Unfortunately, I cannot recommend any single book as an introduction to the subject. Consequently, although I wrote this volume primarily for students, I also had in mind general readers, with the goal that this brief account might both provide them basic information and whet their appetites for further reading and study of Russian history.

To some extent this book is also the outgrowth of my career as a student and teacher of Russian history for almost forty years. The story of the Russian people—their tribulations and courage, their tragedies and triumphs, and their remarkable contribution to world culture—remains just as fascinating to me today as when I first encountered it in 1946 in the undergraduate classroom of Professor E. Dwight Salmon of Amherst College. I hope that the personalities, excitement, and drama of Russian history can be glimpsed even in this introductory account.

A work of this circumscribed compass has obvious limitations. In this preface and throughout the book I occasionally use the term *Russia* or *Russian* to mean the whole territory and collection of peoples in the tsarist empire or the Soviet Union. The reader needs to keep in mind that this terminology is for brevity and convenience, that in fact Russia is only part of a much larger state, and that Russians are barely half the population of the

Soviet Union. Although the book tries to make clear that the tsarist empire was multinational from at least the 1600s and that non-Russians made important contributions to Russian and Soviet history, a longer volume would be needed to provide adequate treatment of the non-Russian aspects of this story.

Similarly, a number of significant topics, such as religious history, could be dealt with only cursorily, and no subject could receive full and definitive treatment. Moreover, many questions in Russian history are still matters of lively historiographic debate. Although I have tried to note the most significant of these disputes, lack of space made it infeasible to present contending positions in detail or to take account of the Marxist views of Soviet historians as fully as is probably warranted.

The book is designed for the introductory survey course that treats Russian history from Kiev to the present in one semester or fourteen weeks. If the instructor desires, one chapter can be assigned for student reading each week. Since the chapters are short, averaging about twenty-five pages, the instructor can require corollary reading as well. The book can also be used in two-semester survey courses, in which the instructor wants students to acquire a basic chronological structure and framework of information from a textbook but also seeks to expand their acquaintance with Russian history and culture by asking them to read primary sources, selected articles, contemporary documents, or fiction (poetry, short stories, novels, plays). To assist both students and general readers who wish to delve more deeply into a topic that interests them, a brief list of recommended readings in English follows each chapter. Maps and illustrations have been chosen to relate directly to the text.

This history is predominantly a straightforward narrative. Its aim is to give the reader a logically organized, lucid, unembellished account of the main events and developments in the history of Russia from its origins to today. No particular theory about the evolution of Russia is espoused; no special or novel interpretations are advanced. Within the limits of space the reasons why important events happened are analyzed, and for certain questions readers are challenged to think through their own answers. Whenever a conclusion is put forward that is not widely accepted among Western scholars or that represents a new point of view, I have noted it as my own opinion.

DATES AND NAMES

Beginning in 1700 and continuing until February 1918, dates in Russia were calculated according to the Julian calendar, or in the Old Style (O.S.). In the eighteenth century that calendar was eleven days behind the Gregorian calendar (New Style [N.S.]) used in the West; in the nineteenth century it was twelve days; and in the twentieth century, thirteen days. Because students are familiar with Western dates, I have given all dates in New Style, or according to the Gregorian calendar.

Since some Russian names are familiar to Western readers (Nicholas for the last tsar, Leo Tolstoy for the novelist), it would be confusing to transliterate all names according to strictly followed rules. I have tried to use common sense, seeking clarity and trying at the same time to avoid excessive anglicization.

ACKNOWLEDGMENTS

I am indebted to my first graduate teachers of Russian history, Professors Philip E. Mosely and Geroid T. Robinson, for providing the enthusiasm and insights on which I began to build my own understanding of Russia and the Soviet Union. My students at the University of Hawaii and my colleagues there, Professors Don Raleigh and Rex Wade, empathized with my complaints about the difficulty of the course I was teaching and the lack of suitable text material for it, and all of them strongly encouraged me when I was seized by a determination to try to write the book I needed. My employer, the Universities Field Staff International, generously released me half-time between May and September 1984 so that I could begin this book. My first editor, Alex Holzman, reacted enthusiastically when I first suggested this volume and assisted me with heartening support in the initial stages of planning and writing it.

Invaluable help was furnished by Professor John T. Alexander of the University of Kansas, a distinguished scholar of seventeenth- and eighteenth-century Russia, who acted as my consultant and meticulous first reader. He not only caught many errors and awkward expressions but was willing to discuss with me points of befuddlement and interpretation. I am most grateful for his cheerful assistance. Needless to say, he is in no way responsible for whatever mistakes and infelicities remain.

This book was written at home, and I thank my wife warmly for her constant support and understanding.

J.M.T.
September 1985

I

Ancient Russia and the Kievan State

THE RUSSIAN LAND

Most Americans, even those accustomed to the transcontinental reach of their own country, find it difficult to comprehend the vast expanse of territory encompassed in the old Russian empire, which became the Union of Soviet Socialist Republics (USSR) after the Bolshevik Revolution of 1917. This huge area is now home to the new Russian Republic and to fourteen other states that emerged from the collapse of the Soviet Union in 1991. We may be aware of a few numbing facts: that this enormous region covers one-sixth of the land surface of the entire earth and that the old Russian state and its Soviet successor stretched, at least since the late 1600s, all across Eurasia from "sea to shining sea," from the Pacific Ocean on the eastern border to the Baltic Sea, an arm of the Atlantic Ocean, on the western boundary (see Map 1). But it requires a specific experience to make concrete the great sweep of the Russian land.

For me, this realization came one evening in the 1960s, when I boarded a train to travel from Kiev, an ancient city in the then Soviet republic of Ukraine, to Moscow, the old and present capital of Russia. I would travel only overnight, but I found occupying at least 80 percent of the space in the Pullman compartment I had been assigned a large and voluble Soviet woman (sleeping cars on Russian trains traditionally accommodate both sexes) accompanied by what seemed like a hundred suitcases, bundles, packages, and even a small trunk. Friendly conversation soon revealed that her husband was a colonel in the Soviet air force stationed in Vladivostok, a main port and base on the Pacific Ocean. She had been home visiting relatives in Ukraine and had stocked up on a few supplies to make her life on the distant frontier of the Soviet Far East a bit more comfortable. As I tried to wedge myself in among the boxes and bags, I asked her how long a trip she would have. When she replied, "Eight nights and seven days," my jaw dropped and I stared at her. Seeing my surprise, she admonished me, "Yes, it *is* a big country, much bigger than yours." (And, in fact, the USSR was bigger than the United States and Canada combined.)

RUSSIA AND OTHER POST-SOVIET STATES

MAP 1

Six thousand miles and eleven time zones from east to west, 3,000 miles from north to south, with the world's longest coastline (much of it on the frozen Arctic Ocean), the expanse of the Russian empire and the former Soviet Union contained every sort of terrain: deserts, semitropical beaches and fruit groves, inland seas, sweeping semiarid plains, rugged mountains, fertile treeless agricultural fields (the famous steppe), thick forests, long rivers, and the ice-locked tundra of the far north.

The size of the Russian empire and of the USSR created special challenges for the people living there. How could such a huge territory be managed and its riches extracted and used efficiently? How could its inhabitants stay in touch with one another and develop a sense of common identity and purpose? How could power be exercised and the state administered over such vast distances? What should be the balance between control from the center and local decision making? Should new industry be developed where a majority of the people lived but where there were few resources, or where lots of raw materials existed but there were few inhabitants?

In addition, the great extent of the Russian land mass had important strategic consequences. Paradoxically, Russia was both hard to conquer and hard to defend. The Russian people at various times had to cope with enemies on three, four, and occasionally even five fronts. Thus, the Russian government always had to allocate much of its effort and resources to defending its large territories. But for their part, Russia's opponents often had trouble invading and occupying the country. Although the Mongols succeeded in conquering and ruling most of Russia from the 1200s to the 1400s, the Poles, the Swedes, the Turks, the French under Napoleon, and the Germans twice in the twentieth century had less luck, turned back in part by the enormous distances to be traversed.

In assessing the influence of Russia's natural environment on its history, we find that its location is as important as its size. For example, if you lived in Washington, D.C., and were suddenly transported by magic to a city in the former Soviet Union with a comparable location, where do you think you would end up—in Moscow? Kiev? Not at all. You would miss the area entirely because it lies in latitudes parallel to those of Canada and Alaska. St. Petersburg (Leningrad in the Soviet era), for example, is just a bit farther north than Juneau, Alaska.

This northerly position on the earth's surface causes recurring hardships for Russia's citizens. In most of the country, winters are long and cold, and the growing season for food is short. Besides, much of the land is so far north that it cannot be farmed, and living there is unpleasant and expensive. Consequently, Russia and the Soviet Union were never rich agriculturally, despite their huge size.

Although situated in the northern part of the great Eurasian land mass, the Russian empire stretched south, east, and west so that it touched most of continental Asia, the Middle East, and Europe (see Map 1). As a result, the region was always a crossroads of cultures and ideas. Russia was affected by European, Asian, and Islamic civilizations and absorbed something from all of them. In turn, and increasingly in the past two centuries, the Russian empire and the Soviet Union influenced and on occasion dominated their neighbors.

In the 1930s an elaborate theory of "geopolitics" concluded that Russia was ideally located to rule the world. Although such a notion is clearly rubbish, there is no doubt that the central location of the country in Eurasia has contributed strongly to the mix of cultures and values in it today and to its important role in contemporary world affairs. Even though it is linked to both Asia and the West, Russian society has evolved in distinct and complex ways. It need not be characterized as exotic, Asian, or "Mongol"; nor should it be interpreted as a stunted offshoot of Western civilization. It has had a unique history that has produced a modern society unlike any other. The region must be understood on its own terms.

Without venturing into geographical detail, we need also to note the effects on Russia's historical development of several topographical features of the Russian land. Partly because of its northerly location and partly because it is situated far from the major oceans, Russia has a forbidding climate in most regions: very hot and dry in the summer, and bitterly cold in the winter, with a spring marked by deep mud that makes travel on unpaved roads almost impossible. Since most of the rain comes across Europe from the Atlantic Ocean, it peters out as it moves over the Russian agricultural plain from west to east. Some of the best soil receives insufficient rainfall, and almost all the farming in Central Asia requires irrigation. The result is that less than 15 percent of Russia's land is used for growing food, another feature that limits the country's agricultural potential and strength.

In some ways the Russian empire was well protected, especially in the north by the frozen expanse of the Arctic Ocean and in the southeast by some of the highest mountains in the world (see Map 1). Yet, along its borders in the east, the southwest, and the west, Russia had virtually no natural defenses and at different times suffered invasions from all these points of the compass.

Moreover, the heart of the Russian empire was one vast plain, broken only by the Ural Mountains, which are not very high and which in any case do not reach all the way to the Caspian Sea. The impact of this plain on Russia's development was two-edged. Russia often lay open to attack across this terrain, but the extent of the plain made it easy for Russians, and the Russian state, to expand and to bring surrounding nationalities under Russian rule. Thus, when I flew for the first time from Moscow to Tashkent in Soviet Central Asia, looking down hour after hour at endless semidesert, or when I took the train from Czechoslovakia to Moscow and gazed for almost two days across rolling Russian steppe, I could easily visualize Asian horsemen, Russian traders, and modern armies moving back and forth across the flat expanses.

But Russians historically traveled as much by water as by land. Although the Russian empire was largely landlocked and had limited access to the sea—the Arctic shore opens primarily on ice, and the Baltic and Black seas and the Sea of Japan in the Far East lead to the Atlantic and Pacific oceans only through narrow straits subject to closure by enemy military action—Russia possessed a widespread system of interconnecting rivers, "the roads that run," as folk wisdom puts it. Up to the last one hundred years, when railroads, motor vehicles, and planes appeared, Russians moved extensively by boat, up and down the rivers, which generally flow in a north-south or south-north direction, or on the tributaries that touch each other along an east-west axis. Thus, the earliest inhabitants, using river routes, traveled to and traded with Europeans and Vikings in the northwest, Greek Christians of Byzantium in the southwest, and Asian merchants and artisans in the south. Later, Russia's expansion across Siberia, led by fur trappers and traders, was carried out primarily by water. Even in modern times river transport played an important role in moving goods and people throughout the region (see Figure 1).

Modern Russia and the Soviet Union possessed rich natural resources, but much of this wealth, such as oil, natural gas, and other abundant minerals, was exploited only recently. For most of its history, Russia was a very poor country, its people struggling to survive and improve their way of life while supporting, with limited resources, a government-organized defense against recurrent enemies. Unfortunately, carrying the burden of the state and the army often meant that the people lived in harsh poverty. Since World War II, progress in raising the quality of life has been made, and the resources exist for citizens of the region to live more comfortably in the future.

Nevertheless, a major dilemma remains. The most important and abundant natural resources lie in the eastern part of the country, where the fewest people live and where the climate is generally inhospitable. It is expensive to transport these raw materials to factories in western Russia and other parts of the former Soviet Union, where the bulk of the population lives. Yet it is unlikely that many people, even with attractive material inducements, will be persuaded to move permanently to Siberia.

THE PEOPLES OF RUSSIA

The most striking fact about the population of the Russian empire and the USSR was its great diversity: in the twentieth century some 125 nationality groups, of which over twenty included more than one million people, inhabited the area. In the Soviet period school textbooks were printed in over fifty languages, and a wide variety of religions and cultures coexisted within the USSR's borders. Jews, who numbered about 2.5 million people, generally spoke Russian and lived intermixed throughout European Russia

Figure 1. *Barge traffic in the 1890s on the Volga River, an important commercial artery in Russia from earliest times.*

(the 1991 states of Russia, Ukraine, and Belarus). The other large non-Slavic nationalities in the Russian empire and the former Soviet Union spoke their own languages, lived in geographically separate regions, had their own republics within the federal state of the Union of Soviet Socialist Republics, and formed independent states after 1991. In the twentieth century the non-Russian groups developed a sense of ethnic identity and growing nationalist aspirations, which created the pressures that led to the USSR's collapse in 1991.

To review the size of the various ethnic groups in the region, we will use figures from the 1989 Soviet census. Except for some increase in the Muslim population, the flight of refugees from fighting in Azerbaijan and Georgia, emigration of several hundred thousand Jews, and the movement of Russians from non-Russian areas to the new Russian state, these totals are still fairly accurate in 1994. In 1989 the Soviet Union contained 286.7 million people. The largest groups were:

1. Eastern Slavs: 207 million (72 percent)
    A. Great Russians: 150 million (52 percent)
    B. Ukrainians: 48 million (16+ percent)
    C. Belarusans: 9 million (3 percent)
2. Turkic and Tatar Peoples (Bashkirs, Azerbaijanis, Uzbeks, Turkmens, Kazakhs, and others): 48 million (16+ percent)
3. Caucasian peoples (Armenians, Georgians, and others): 11 million (4 percent)

Figure 2. *A typical non-Russian citizen of the former Soviet Union: a Kazakh visitor from Central Asia in Red Square in front of the Kremlin. (Courtesy of the United Nations)*

4. Finno-Ugric peoples (Estonians and Karelians): 5.5 million (2 percent)
5. Baltic peoples (Latvians and Lithuanians): 4–5 million (1+ percent)
6. Jews: 2.5 million (less than 1 percent)
7. All others: 10 million (3 percent)

The Great Russians formed the core of the Russian state established in northeastern Russia in the 1100s, and largely dominated the government and society of the Russian empire and the Soviet Union. They make up 83 percent of the population of the post-1991 Russian state, which extends from the northwest part of European Russia across the great Eurasian plain and Siberia to the Sea of Japan. The Ukrainians are descendants of the Slavs who formed the first Russian state based at Kiev, and they have their own Slavic language akin to Russian. The Ukrainians had their own republic in the southwest of the Soviet Union and in 1991 set up an independent state. The Belarusans, who live in the western part of European Russia bordering Poland, speak a form of Russian. They, too, created a separate state in 1991, based on a former republic of the Soviet Union.

Ethnic diversity created linguistic, religious, and cultural differences as well. The majority of the population who practiced religion were Russian Orthodox Christians, an estimated fifty to sixty million people. Most of the Turkic and Tatar peoples were Muslims, some forty million believers (see Figure 2). Roman Catholic and Protestant Christians, largely in the Baltic area, totaled several million each.

Only in the past three hundred years did Russia develop as a predominantly multinational society. The Muscovite state founded by the Great Russians in the 1300s expanded to incorporate the Ukrainians in the 1600s and the other major non-Russian nationalities between 1700 and 1850. With the rise of nationalistic and religious feeling among these groups in the past one hundred years, their place in the Russian empire before 1917 and in the Soviet Union after 1917 created special problems. In recent decades, because of a higher birthrate, the number of Central Asians increased rapidly. The total population of Slavs grew more slowly, as their birthrate declined. In post-1991 Russia the birthrate dropped sharply, and deaths outnumbered births. Parents apparently did not want to have children in the unsettled economic and political conditions of the first years of Russian independence.

As this short overview has indicated, geographic and demographic factors influenced the development of Russian society. A word of caution is in order, however. History is made by individuals in a society interacting with each other and with their neighbors. Thus, it would be a misleading oversimplification to conclude that Russian institutions, such as a centralized authoritarian system of government, or Russian values, such as a concern for the group rather than the individual, resulted primarily from the harsh conditions of Russia's natural environment.

Even worse, it is utter nonsense to predetermine the future of the peoples of the region on the basis of their past. To say that history has made the Russians inherently "subservient" or insensitive to the rights of individuals or naturally militaristic is as silly as the old axiom "Scratch a Russian; find a Mongol." Certainly no American would accept the conclusion that because the history of the United States is filled with instances of discrimination against Native Americans and blacks, our institutions and our values condemn us to a future of racial bias and oppression. Consequently, as we begin to trace Russia's historical evolution, we need constantly to bear in mind that this society is a complicated product of the interplay over a thousand years among the land, the people and outside influences. We will not look for simplified, pat answers but will instead seek sympathetic and broad understanding of who the Russians are and how they came to be that way.

THE SLAVS COME TO RUSSIA

Archeology helps explain the past, but there is a lot it cannot tell us. In the past few decades excavations in the southern part of European Russia have revealed that early human settlements were well established there by at least 3500 B.C. These ancient inhabitants of the steppe farmed and kept domestic animals, but who they were and how they organized their society remain largely unanswered questions.

In the centuries just before the birth of Christ, the region north of the Black Sea (today Ukraine) was dominated by two talented and well-organized partly nomadic peoples who migrated there from Central Asia: Scythians, who ruled the area from 700 to 200 B.C., and Sarmatians, who held sway from 200 B.C. to A.D. 200. They were only the latest in a succession of loosely organized "steppe empires." The Scythians, who were in contact with the Greeks, were master artisans and created exquisite gold jewelry, which has hardly been matched since. A highlight of any trip to Russia is a visit to the Treasure Room of the Hermitage Museum in St. Petersburg, where original pieces of this lovely and delicate Scythian jewelry are displayed.

The Scythians and Sarmatians were linked by language and culture to the Persians, and both groups established militarized states. At the same time they maintained cultural and trading ties with Greek colonies on the north shore of the Black Sea so that the influence of classical civilization reached the territory that was to become Russia as early as it did western Europe.

A series of nomadic invasions disrupted the evolution of this region for almost five hundred years, from about A.D. 200 to the 700s. As was to occur later in Russian history, the invaders came from all directions, first the Goths from the northwest, then the Huns and Avars from the east, and finally the Khazars, who from their bases southeast of Russia extended their control over the northern Caucasus, as well as the area around the lower part of the Volga River and nearby stretches of the great steppe.

Two important characteristics of Khazar civilization influenced the birth and early development of the first East Slav state at Kiev. First, the Khazars were active and successful traders, maintaining lively commercial contacts with the Arabs, the Greek civilization of Byzantium, and various Asian societies to the east and south of them. Second, the Khazars seem to have been open to and tolerant of a variety of cultural and religious influences. Their leaders eventually adopted Judaism, but Christian, Islamic, and pagan ideas circulated widely in the Khazar state. In a similar fashion Kievan society depended heavily on trade and plunder and was in contact with a range of European and Asian societies.

In fact, it seems quite clear that the Kievan state was multinational. It included descendants of previous occupiers of the region north of the Black Sea, as well as Finns and Vikings from Scandinavia, together with a majority of Eastern Slavs. We are not sure, however, where the Slavs came from or how long they had been there. Some specialists in prehistory make the case that Slavs had lived on the plains of European Russia hundreds of years before the historic state of Kiev was founded, and they may be right. One difficulty is that the term *Slav* is a linguistic one; it designates a group of people who speak a common language, one of a family of languages called Indo-European, which are today spoken from India and southwest Asia all across Europe to England and the Americas (in the transported languages of English, Spanish, and Portuguese). *Slav* itself probably comes from *slovo,* meaning in the Slavic language "word"; thus, the Slavs were all those who spoke a common word or language. By contrast the original Slavic term for foreigners apparently was *nemtsy,* meaning "those who are mute": who could not speak the word. (Today *nemtsy* in the Russian language means "Germans.") We know that in modern times speakers of Slavic languages are distributed from Yugoslavia (Serbs, Croats, and Slovenes) in southeastern Europe through the southern Balkans (Bulgarians and Macedonians) to central Europe (Czechs, Slovaks, and Poles: the Western Slavs) and European Russia (Russians, Ukrainians, and Belarusans: Eastern Slavs). But exactly how each group got to its present location and whether they all started from some central point remains a mystery.

The archeological remains of villages in southern Russia unfortunately cannot tell us what language the inhabitants spoke. Nevertheless, by about A.D. 600 references by Gothic, Byzantine, and Arabic authors make it clear that Slavic tribes formed a considerable part of the population north of the Black Sea and that these tribes paid tribute to the Khazars. Putting the written and archeological evidence together, we know that these early Slavs had well-developed agriculture, raised cattle and bees, fished and hunted, and knew how to weave and make pottery. Yet we know little about their social structure, government, customs, or beliefs. Unfortunately, no traveler, no early Marco Polo, penetrated the region, which was on the fringe of the great civilizations of the Mediterranean basin and of Asia, to leave us a detailed description of Slavic life at the time.

THE FORMATION OF THE KIEVAN STATE

The first East Slavic state was founded in the 800s, making Russian civilization just over a thousand years old. It was centered briefly on the northern city of Novgorod, then for several hundred years on Kiev, a city on the Dnieper River in south Russia, and it was soon known as the state of Kiev Rus'. But, as with the origins of the Slavs, how the state was established and the meaning of the word *Rus',* from which Russia derives, are obscure. The key point of uncertainty is the role of Swedish Vikings, known as Varangians in the first Slavic chronicles, in forming the state and in their relations with the predominant Slavic population of the region.

The most detailed historical source, *The Primary Chronicle,* compiled by monks in the eleventh century, recounts that since there was no order among the Slavic tribes, they invited a Scandinavian named Riurik and his two brothers to come and rule over them. But this chronicle was written several hundred years later, partly for the purpose of legitimizing the claims to power of Riurik's alleged descendants, making the story suspect in itself. In addition, there is a growing body of archeological and other evidence to suggest that the role of the Vikings, or Varangians, in Russia was a good deal more complex than the picture the chronicle paints.

In this period long-distance trading flourished, and the Vikings participated in it. They certainly knew that silver and gold, as well as other valuable articles, existed in Asia and were traded by the Khazars and by Arabs. They were also well acquainted with the trading route from Scandinavia to the advanced Byzantine (formerly Greek) civilization at Constantinople ("the road from the Varangians to the Greeks," as it was called) that passed through Russia, primarily down the Dnieper River and across the Black Sea. Finally, the Vikings' travels into Russia, primarily by boat across the Baltic Sea and then via lakes and rivers, were motivated in part by their recognition of the value of the furs, honey, and wax that existed in the areas of Slavic settlement.

Consequently it is quite clear that the Vikings, though occasionally plundering and conquering as they did in western Europe a short time later, entered Russia primarily as traders and mercenaries. It seems logical to assume that in these roles they worked closely with local Slavic leaders to increase order and security, to protect trade routes, and to encourage regular payment of tribute by rural peoples to the commercial and military leaders of the towns in Russia. Thus, although in certain times and places Slavs and Varangians undoubtedly clashed, and even on occasion Vikings may have attempted to assert political control over Slavic groups, much more often the Varangians and the local leaders almost certainly cooperated in pursuit of common objectives. The most sensible conclusion is, not that they set up a state for the hapless Slavs, but that they worked with Slavic chieftains to create a stable government and state system.

Even this interpretation does not entirely satisfy many historians in Russia who, for understandably patriotic reasons, would prefer to have the role of the Vikings downgraded to insignificance and the contributions of the Slavs highlighted. In a similar vein Russian writers are unhappy with the theory that the word *Rus'* is of Scandinavian origin. Another explanation links it to a place name in southern Russia. Since the evidence is scanty and inconclusive, we will probably never know where the word came from. But we are certain that it was applied to the first state at Kiev, and that from it came *Russia* and *Russian*.

This first state is important to an understanding of Russian civilization for several reasons. In Kievan Russia the fundamental characteristics of Russian culture and religion took root. The Kievan state also introduced basic and lasting political ideas and social institutions. Finally, it created the tradition of Russia as a major force in international affairs and as a linkage point between Europe and Asia, between East and West.

HOW DID KIEVAN RUSSIANS MAKE A LIVING?

Kiev Rus' lasted from the 800s to the early 1200s, considerably longer than the history of the United States to date. At its largest the Kievan state was long and skinny. It stretched in the 1000s from the Baltic Sea on the north to the Black Sea on the south, including a band of territory of varying width both east and west of its main axis on the Dnieper River (see Map 2). Educated guesses put its maximum population at about seven or eight million, of whom fewer than a million lived in towns and cities. The largest cities, like Kiev, probably contained tens of thousands of people, but in most of the over two hundred fortified centers that have been identified the population was undoubtedly less than five thousand.

Over 85 percent of the people lived on the land as farmers, hunters and trappers, beekeepers, and herdsmen. Most of the farming was small-scale and used primitive implements, such as wooden plows and harrows (though some iron plows existed). Agriculture was often carried out by the slash-and-burn method: when old, cleared ground lost its fertility, a new area of trees and undergrowth was cut away and then burned, with the ashes providing nutrients for the new crops planted there.

Most of what people produced they ate. But some of the output was delivered (or seized) as tribute or taxes to political and military leaders, first representing clans or tribes and later based in towns within the Kievan state. These goods included, besides crops used to feed soldiers and townspeople, furs, honey, hides, and wax, all of which could then be traded to outsiders, primarily to the Byzantine Empire. Since there were frequent military campaigns to collect tribute and recurring wars with outsiders, captives were taken and were often sold or traded as slaves, a convenient commodity since they could walk to market.

Because individual farmers or even farming families of the sort we are accustomed to in Europe and the United States could not muster sufficient labor power to grow crops in the difficult conditions and with the poor methods of that era, most rural people in Kievan Russia banded together in communes. A farming commune, known in Russian as *obshchina* (ohb-shcheena), usually consisted of several extended families, although some apparently included individuals who were not near relatives. The *obshchina* lasted over a thousand years, down to the Bolshevik Revolution of 1917. In 1929 Stalin instituted the Soviet collective farm, a modified form of the *obshchina*. Members of both the collective farm and the *obshchina* pooled labor and tools to accomplish heavy agricultural tasks. They shared not only the work but the products of their labor. Throughout Russian history these institutions, dominated by patriarchal elders, embodied joint responsibility for taxes and military recruits. They also fostered attitudes of egalitarianism and collectivism that have continuously influenced Russian society.

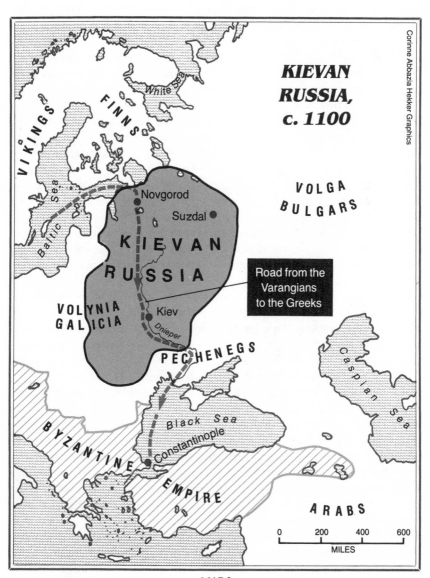

KIEVAN RUSSIA, c. 1100

Corinne Abbazia Hekker Graphics

VIKINGS

FINNS

White Sea

Baltic Sea

VOLGA BULGARS

Novgorod

Suzdal

KIEVAN RUSSIA

VOLYNIA GALICIA

Kiev

Dnieper

Road from the Varangians to the Greeks

PECHENEGS

Caspian Sea

BYZANTINE

Black Sea

Constantinople

EMPIRE

ARABS

0   200   400   600
MILES

MAP 2

After the 1917 Revolution, Soviet histories argued that the economic, social, and political system of the Kievan state was feudalism. This term derives from Karl Marx's *historical materialism,* or laws of historical development, so applying it to Kiev corresponded with the basic tenets of the Soviet Union's official ideology, Marxism-Leninism. Other historians have denied that Kievan Russia was a feudal society. For our purposes the technical issues in this debate are largely irrelevant. The important conclusion is that the Kievan system was distinctive, quite different in various ways from feudalism in western Europe or feudalism in Japan.

At the same time it is useful to note several aspects of Kievan society related to feudalism that influenced later Russian history. In the first place the system of tribute (and later taxes) did lead to continuing obligations by peasant farmers to various sorts of social, religious, and political overlords. Although in the Kievan period these obligations were not usually in the form of labor nor tied to land ownership (*obshchinas* generally possessed their own land), later on they took the form of service to a particular lord in return for certain use rights to land. Thus, in Kievan Russia a pattern of obligation developed that in later centuries and under different economic and political conditions would help turn essentially free peasants into serfs.

Second, the Kievan state did incorporate concepts of service that resembled some aspects of the relationship between lord and vassal in western Europe. In particular, fighting men in Kiev, who came to be known as *boyars,* served particular princes, although the terms and duties of such service are rather unclear. This service concept later reappeared as a major principle in Russian society at the time of the development of the Muscovite state.

Finally, a key ingredient of European feudalism was largely lacking in Kievan society: the idea of mutuality. In the European relationship between lord and vassal, the lord had definite responsibilities to his subordinate vassals; in return the vassals owed obligations to the lord. Some writers have argued that this sense of a contract, of a mutual responsibility, is a crucial element in the development of representative government and civil rights in Western civilization. Whether they are right or not, the principle of mutual obligations hardly existed in Kiev, and this may have contributed later to the ease with which the Russian tsars were able to assert unlimited authority over all the people, lords and peasants alike.

Not only feudalism has sparked historiographic controversy about Kiev. Historians have also argued whether agriculture or trade predominated in the Kievan economy. The commonsense answer is that although most of the people farmed and most of what they produced were agricultural and forest goods, trade and commercial activity also played an important role, especially in the life of the towns. Their location favored the Kievan Russians in this regard. Situated between northern Europe and Byzantium and midway between central Europe and Asia, they could carry on a lively commerce in several directions.

There were, of course, risks. Small nomadic groups, such as the Cumans and Pechenegs, often attacked trading parties, particularly at rapids, where boats and goods had to be portaged. Terms of trade with the Byzantine Empire were not always favorable, and Kiev sent several military expeditions against Constantinople to compel the opening of better trading opportunities and contracts. Thus, military activity, including the collection of tribute, and trade went hand in hand. As a result, warriors and merchants—often the same persons—ranked high on the Kievan social scale.

The importance of trade to Kievan society was not only in economic benefits. Because the Russians traded with neighbors on all sides, in Byzantium and in Asia, they were exposed to a wide range of ideas, technology, and cultural influences. Kievan Russia was not a "closed" society at all and interacted effectively with Christian Europe, with the Hellenic empire of Byzantium, and with the Islamic civilization of the Arabs. Only later, after the Mongols conquered it, did Russia become more isolated. In Kievan times it was in the mainstream of world history.

KIEVAN SOCIETY

Because rigid class divisions do not exist in the United States, it is hard for Americans to imagine societies in which every group has a place clearly defined by custom and law. Yet most societies in the world are structured in such a fashion; ours is the exception, not the rule. No evidence exists to tell us when class differentiation began in Russian society, but by the time of the first Russian law codes, compiled in the eleventh and twelfth centuries, the lines were sharply drawn. Russian society remained divided into classes down to the Revolution of 1917, and some observers would argue that even in the allegedly classless Soviet society that followed, class distinctions remained.

Depending on how you define a distinct class, there were as many as eleven classes stipulated in Kievan law. But these can be allocated among seven main categories: princes, *boyars* (nobles), merchants, artisans, *smerdy* (peasants), semifree persons, and slaves. At the top of the ladder were the princely families. These were allegedly descendants of the legendary Riurik and his brothers, and they exercised military, judicial, and administrative power over most Russian towns and territories. As we shall see shortly, relations among the princes were complicated, and their struggles for political preeminence led to civil war and greatly weakened the Kievan state.

At first each prince had his own band of military servitors, of whom many in the beginning were probably Vikings. But soon they merged with already existing groups of Slavic warriors, and by the 1000s a Slavicized upper class of lords, called *boyars,* had been formed. Their numbers were always small, but their role was crucial since they carried out military service on behalf of prince, town, and state and also assumed administrative and governing responsibilities. Some of them certainly engaged in commerce as well.

In this role they blended with a separate merchant class, the origins of which undoubtedly go back before the formation of the Kievan state. The merchants, though of lower rank than the princely families and the boyars, had considerable influence because of their importance to the economy of Kievan Russia and because in some towns they exercised political power as well. The merchants were among the chief consumers of the goods they imported from Asia and Byzantium: silks, spices, wines, fruits, metals, and jewelry.

Most people in towns were free and fell into a broad group of artisans and workers. Their equivalent in the countryside were peasants, who bore the colorful designation *smerdy* (best translated "smelly ones"). Some were dependent on princes or boyars, but apparently most were free. Through debt or other circumstances both artisans and peasants could fall into a semifree class: people who were bound to another through some sort of obligation.

At the bottom of the social ladder were slaves. How important they were to the Kievan economy is not clear. Some may have been semifree individuals who fell into complete bondage, but a majority were apparently captured in war, and many were therefore not Slavic. In the earlier years of Kievan rule, slaves formed an important item of trading.

RELIGION AND CULTURE IN KIEVAN RUSSIA

The single most important event in the history of Kiev was the state's official adoption of Christianity in A.D. 988. Although pagan beliefs and practices and earlier cultural attributes of Kievan society persisted long after the conversion, the acceptance of Christian religion fundamentally altered Russian civilization ever after. Adopting Christianity affected not just religious beliefs and practices but also law, education, literature, the arts, attitudes and feelings, and even the political system. To grasp the overriding significance of this conversion you need only think about how completely different the history of Russia would have been if the rulers of Kiev had chosen Judaism or Islam, options open to them and that they apparently considered. Or think about how the United States would have turned out if Hindus from India or Buddhists from China had discovered the New World.

An extremely significant aspect of Russia's conversion was that Christianity came to Kiev from the Byzantine Empire, which practiced what is today called Eastern or Orthodox Christianity. When the Russians were converted, the Christian or Holy Catholic (that is, universal) Church was united, although there were already considerable differences between its western wing based in Rome and its eastern wing centered on Constantinople. A short time later, in A.D. 1054, these divisions became irreconcilable and the Christian Church split in two: the Latin or Roman Catholic Church, which dominated in western Europe, and the Greek or Eastern Orthodox Church, which was prevalent in the Balkans, the Middle East, and Russia.

This separation had three important consequences: first, the development of Christianity took quite a different form in Russia from that in western Europe. Second, as the hostility between the two main branches of Christianity heightened, Russians were put at odds with their nearest neighbors to the west: Poles, Lithuanians, and later German settlers along the shores of the Baltic Sea, all of whom were Catholic. Finally, Russia's intellectual and cultural contacts with west European societies were curtailed for five or six hundred years, almost into modern times when religious differences became much less important. It is true that the Mongol conquest of Russia in the 1200s also acted to sever Russia's ties with central and western Europe, but religious difference was a formidable barrier and a source of suspicion and hostility.

As early as 955 the first woman ruler of Russia, the Regent Olga, chose Christianity for herself, but another three decades elapsed before Vladimir, one of Kiev's ablest princes, decided to adopt Christianity as an official religion for the whole state and all its subjects. To make sure everyone got the message he had the pagan idols smashed and arranged a mass baptism in the Dnieper River for all the inhabitants of Kiev, according to the *Chronicle*.

We do not know Vladimir's reasons for choosing Eastern Christianity but can surmise fairly safely that the close commercial and political ties with Byzantium that Kiev had developed in the preceding hundred years were an important factor. Vladimir (who was later made a saint in recognition of his decision and whose magnificent statue looks out over the Dnieper River in present-day Kiev) was probably also influenced by the fact that two Christian monks, Cyril and Methodius, had developed a written language that, though based on Greek, transcribed quite well the spoken Slavic language. This new literary language meant that people did not need to learn Greek or Latin to become Christians and the average person could understand the mass and other church services. Russian is still written in the Cyrillic alphabet, named in honor of one of those inventive monks.

Finally, geographic and political factors undoubtedly weighed heavily in Vladimir's choice. If he selected Judaism, its nearest adherents, the Khazars, were some distance away to the southeast, and their power was already in decline. If he chose Islam, the Arabs were even farther away, and he would be drawn into wars against their continuing enemy, the Byzantine Empire. As regards Latin Christianity, it had spread only recently to northern Europe and must have seemed quite insignificant to Vladimir, in comparison to the nearby might and magnificence of Orthodox Christianity with its seat at Constantinople.

The Christianity Vladimir adopted had several important characteristics that were reinforced by Russian conditions and that later differentiated it sharply from Western Christianity, particularly after the Latin Church split in the 1500s into Protestant and Catholic branches. One was the almost mystical concern in Orthodox Christianity with the collective spirit of the whole congregation. In the religious service itself and in the spiritual outlook of the faithful the focus is on the group of believers, rather than on individual souls and their salvation. This attitude, called *sobornost'*, or "spirit of the congregation" (*sobor* may also mean "cathedral"), fitted well with the collective sense of the community that had already been developed among the Russians through the peasant institution of the *obshchina*.

Another aspect of Orthodox Christianity that was strongly implanted in the Russian Church was an emphasis on outward forms of religion: the church buildings and decorations, the icons (paintings on wood of holy figures and saints), and the structure and ritual of the mass itself. To stress these visible signs of devotion made it easier to wean the East Slavs away from pagan idols and customs and to convert an illiterate population, but; together with the concept of *sobornost'*, it encouraged a rather routine and passive practice of the new religion rather than engaging individuals directly in the process and stimulating personal commitments of faith and belief. Later, in Western Christianity, particularly after the Protestant Reformation, individualism in religion (and later in other matters) gained ground while collectivism continued to predominate in Russian Orthodox Christianity.

Finally, Byzantine Christianity was quite otherworldly, stressing asceticism, the importance of a communal monastic life, and the rewards in the hereafter. Again, this tendency was strengthened in its transplantation to Russia, and later it militated against the Russian Orthodox Church's taking an active role in everyday life as a force for social betterment.

For a long time Christianity was only thinly superimposed on the basic animistic beliefs and customs of the Slavic population of the Kievan state. Many old pagan rites and practices were continued or even adapted to the new religion. As a result, some historians say, many Russians never fully understood the new faith and accepted it only superficially. Only the educated few in the upper classes of society were fully committed to Christianity.

At the same time there is no doubt that the introduction of Christianity raised the general level of culture, learning, and artistic expression in Kievan Rus'. Well-educated monks and priests entered Russia, monasteries were established, churches were built, and artisans were trained. By the middle of the eleventh century, Kievan civilization, though modeled on Byzantine achievements in most fields, had reached a height of cultural and artistic splendor that was not to be equaled in Russia again until some five hundred years later. As the most renowned Soviet historian of Kiev, B. D. Grekov, has recounted:

> There is no need to list all the treasures of Kiev, Novgorod, Chernigov, Polotsk, Galich and other ancient cities of Rus'. Even without such a recital one is struck not only by the high level of Russian culture of the 10th–11th

centuries, but also by its wide diffusion over the tremendous expanses of Eastern Europe.[1]

The introduction of a written language, Old Church Slavonic, meant that books were produced and circulated (usually copied or composed by monks). To be sure, only a tiny fraction of the population was literate, but this upper crust was quite sophisticated, aware of intellectual currents and developments in both Byzantium and Europe. In addition, Byzantine masters taught Russians the art of painting icons and introduced church music to them. A magnificent cathedral in Byzantine style, St. Sophia, named after the main church in Constantinople, was built in Kiev and decorated by Russian craftsmen. Russian artisans, who had developed great skill in working with indigenous materials, particularly wood, modified Byzantine forms into a distinctive and charming style. Unfortunately, because almost all the buildings they erected were made of wood and were subsequently destroyed in the frequent fires that plagued early Russian towns, we have descriptions or examples of only a few of their striking architectural achievements.

Education, scholarship, art, architecture, and music were all predominantly religious in motivation and theme. Naturally all these aspects of cultural life followed Byzantine precepts and models. But Russian artists soon introduced local subjects and techniques and in icon painting they before long surpassed their Byzantine masters, creating some of the most moving and beautiful religious painting in the world.

Nonreligious, primarily folk, art also developed, particularly in songs and stories. The first secular piece of literature, *The Tale of the Host of Igor,* is a stirring pagan saga of the adventures of a Kievan prince and his followers in fighting an array of enemies in order to defend their homeland. In the words of the *Tale:*

Igor leads his warriors to the Don.
The birds in oak trees portend his misfortunes
The wolves howl of the menace in the ravines
The eagles with their clatter summon beasts to a bony feast

The foxes yelp at the crimson shield.
O Russian land! You are so far behind the mountains. . . .
With their shields the Russians have divided the great field
Seeking honor for themselves and glory for their prince.[2]

Considered as a whole, Russian culture and civilization in the 1000s and 1100s was probably at a higher level than Western European civilization at the same time. The Russians were definitely not a backward "strange" race in the panoply of world peoples. Moreover, the upper classes in Kievan society interacted with the elite of central and western Europe. In addition to the contacts and travels between Russian and European merchants, the princely families in Kiev intermarried with noble and royal families in the Germanies and in Scandinavia.

POWER AND POLITICS IN KIEVAN RUSSIA

The impact of Byzantine civilization was felt not only in religion and culture but also in thought, values, and attitudes. These influences were made tangible in Kievan law codes of the eleventh and twelfth centuries and in the political order. Yet in politics Byzantine ideas could never quite overcome more traditional concepts and institutions and therefore had their greatest impact quite a bit later, in the Muscovite period of the tsars.

For example, in Byzantine the state was a clearly defined geographic area over all of which the emperor and his administration exercised control. But the concept of state and sovereignty in the Kievan system was much less clear. Authority derived originally from the person of the prince, and his jurisdiction ran along trade routes, over scattered areas that paid him tribute, and in certain fortified centers, rather than over a specific contiguous territory.

Moreover, although eventually it was recognized that the prince at Kiev was the senior prince and therefore head of the state, princes in other towns had rights of their own. They also felt free to contest for the headship with the Kievan prince. Certain towns, particularly the important northern trading and administrative center of Novgorod, also seem to have had autonomous rights. In general, therefore, the Kievan state was much looser and more disjointed than our modern state. The princes at Kiev possessed little centralized authority or direct administrative and political control but rather led a fluid federation of towns and tribes.

In the middle of the Kievan period, Iaroslav (1019–1054), one of the ablest Kievan princes, tried to set up a system of rotation of rulership under which younger brothers to the prince of Kiev held power in towns designated according to their seniority. When the ruler at Kiev died, everyone moved up one notch. This system was designed to avert the bitter and bloody struggles for succession that had plagued the politics of the Kievan state over the preceding hundred years. But such a complicated system, requiring great self-restraint by all the players, soon broke down in practice, and the succession to the princedom at Kiev continued to be settled on most occasions by force and strife.

This meant that the Kievan prince had to spend a good part of his reign fighting off rival claimants to the throne, who were usually jealous brothers or nephews. In addition, he had to defend the state from external enemies on all sides and, particularly, to protect the trade routes to Byzantium from nomadic attacks originating in the southeast. A further major military obligation was to keep sufficient pressure on the Byzantine emperors so that they would grant political concessions and favorable commercial privileges to the prince, his warriors, and merchants. As if all this were not enough, the prince was frequently called upon to wage military campaigns against recalcitrant subjects or neighboring tribes who refused to pay taxes or deliver tribute.

It is little wonder that a good part of a prince's life was spent in warfare. One of Kiev's most successful military leaders, Sviatoslav, who ruled from 962 to 972, is described in the *Chronicle* as follows:

> Stepping light as a leopard, he undertook many campaigns. Upon his expeditions he carried with him neither wagons nor kettles, and boiled no meat, but cut off small strips of horseflesh, game, or beef, and ate it after roasting it on the coals. Nor did he have a tent, but he spread out a horseblanket under him, and set his saddle under his head; and all his retinue did likewise.[3]

When the princes were at home, they faced other obstacles to their rule. Two political-administrative institutions existed in Kievan Russia to represent the interests of the upper classes: the boyars' *duma* and the *veche*. The *duma* was a body of the highest-ranking nobles advisory to the prince. How much power it had and how regularly he consulted it are not clear. Before major military campaigns and during succession struggles over title to the head principality at Kiev, it behooved the prince to get as much support from the boyars as possible, and he probably used the *duma* for that purpose.

The *veche*, a town council dominated by merchants, had considerable influence, particularly in towns in the north of Russia, where it had a stronger and longer tradition. In a few places, such as Novgorod, the *veche* on occasion exercised full political authority and administered the town and surrounding territory. But in other towns it had only a minor advisory role.

As with any series of rulers, the princes of Kiev varied greatly in ability, persistence, and success. The first few were Vikings, though quite Slavicized; all the rest for over two hundred years were Slavs. In our effort to understand the complex nature of politics in Kievan times, three outstanding princes can serve as example of the challenges Russia's early rulers faced and the victories they won.

Although the legendary credit goes to Riurik, Prince Oleg was the actual founder of the Kievan state. A Varangian from Novgorod, he saw the advantages of linking as many towns as possible along the main trade route from the Baltic Sea to the Black Sea, and he united Novgorod and Kiev by force. Moving his base to Kiev around A.D. 880, he established the primacy of that city, "the mother of Rus towns," which lasted until 1132. In 907, Oleg attacked Constantinople. As a result of his victories, he was able to negotiate an effective commercial treaty with Byzantium in 911. Oleg also merged his Viking and Slavic warriors into a single upper class and established greater control over the Slavic tribes along both sides of the Dnieper River.

Almost a hundred years after Oleg had established and begun to consolidate the state, Vladimir, who ruled from about A.D. 980 to 1015, made remarkable strides in extending its authority east, south, and west and in raising the level of culture and sophistication in Kievan society. As we saw earlier, he adopted Christianity as the official religion and at the same time encouraged and supported the arts and education.

Yet Vladimir's sons fought over the succession, and civil war weakened the state for two decades. Strong leadership was restored under Iaroslav the Wise, who reigned from 1036 to 1054. He extended Kievan authority over new areas and was able to put an end for some time to the constant harassing attacks of the Pechenegs in the east. He also supervised compilation of the first Russian law code and encouraged the building of St. Sophia and other important churches. But within a few decades of his death, interprincely fighting was again widespread, and except for a brief resurgence in the first quarter of the twelfth century Kievan power and cohesion declined steadily in the next one hundred and fifty years.

THE FALL AND SIGNIFICANCE OF KIEVAN RUSSIA

Various reasons have been advanced for the decline of Kiev. As is so often true in explaining major events in history, not one cause but many produced the collapse of the Kievan state. Perhaps the most important was its political weakness. Not effectively centralized nor cohesive in the best of times, by the late 1100s under weaker princes Kievan Russia increasingly disintegrated into rival princedoms and towns that spent more time fighting each other than their common external enemies. As we saw earlier, no institutionalized central government existed, and the struggle to become grand prince became increasingly divisive. For example, between 1139 and 1169 the throne changed hands seventeen times. The loose federation that was the Kievan state gradually fractured into its component parts.

A second major factor in the decline of Kiev was its loss of economic strength. The goods it traded became less valuable, and at about the same time Europeans established new trade routes to the Near East and Asia, while the position of the Byzantine Empire weakened. As a result, the trade routes across Russia became less important, and the Kievan economy declined.

However important political, economic, and commercial reasons for Kiev's demise were, in the end external factors played the decisive role. Throughout its history Kiev had struggled, with limited resources, against foreign foes, particularly various nomads from Asia who constantly attacked the state from the southeast. In the 1100s this effort became increasingly a losing fight, and Kievan Russia was much weakened by recurring battles against the Cumans (also called Polovtsy). These latest nomadic invaders succeeded on various occasions in cutting the trade route to the Black Sea and caused much damage, as well as loss of life. Moreover, in 1169 Andrei Bogoliubskii, prince of Vladimir-Suzdal, an area in the northeast, sacked Kiev and then chose to reign as grand prince at Vladimir instead of Kiev. In the thirteenth century the Mongols arrived to administer the *coup de grace* to the Kievan state.

Although Kievan Russia was overrun and conquered, Kievan civilization was not. The state disappeared but left a powerful legacy on which much of subsequent Russian civilization was built. Kiev had succeeded in drawing together and blending four elements: the ancient indigenous population, the imprint of successive steppe empires, the influence of the Varangians/Vikings, and the powerful impact of Byzantium.

A major bequest of Kiev was the tradition of Slavic political unity and glory. Even today Russians look back on Kiev as a "golden age," an era of power and accomplishment when Russia occupied a significant place among the world's societies. It was indeed a civilization of which to be proud. It was multinational yet tolerant for its time. It was stratified but not unduly oppressive. It produced beautiful art and architecture but was not vainglorious.

The most significant concrete gift Kiev bestowed on subsequent generations was Orthodox Christianity. As we shall see, the Orthodox Church and faith played a quite different role in Russia than Christianity did in Western history, but its importance in the development of Russian society cannot be denied. After the Bolshevik Revolution of 1917, the Soviet government attempted to eliminate religion, but it failed. More than 50 million Christians still practiced their faith in 1991, when the Soviet Union collapsed.

Because the Christianity of Kievan Russia came from Byzantium, it developed in Russia quite differently from Latin Christianity in the West. At the same time Byzantine culture, learning, law, and the arts accompanied it. Consequently, Russian civilization developed from the very beginning as a compound of indigenous Slavic values and forms and Byzantine borrowings. The result was quite distinct from Western European civilization.

At the same time it would be a dreadful mistake for a reader to conclude at this point, "Ah, the poor Russians, so that is where they began to go astray, to diverge from the good things that were about to happen in the West. They fell under the influence of Byzantium, with its rather mystical obscurantist religion and its rigid, formal culture." The rejoinder of course is that, indeed, the Russians began to go their own way, to build their own civilization, borrowing to some degree from the Byzantine experience, but what was being formed was not worse or better, only different. A foundation had been laid, but it was only a beginning. Much more, and much of it traumatic, was to happen to the Russians as they struggled to build their unique civilization and future.

FURTHER READING

Geography and Peoples

Chew, Allen. *An Atlas of Russian History.* New Haven, Conn.: 1970.

Hubbs, Joanna. *Mother Russia: The Feminine Myth in Russian Culture.* Bloomington, Ind.: 1988.

Levin, Eve. *Sex and Society in the World of the Orthodox Slavs, 900–1700.* Ithaca, N.Y.: 1989.

Lydolph, P. E. *Geography of the USSR.* New York: 1964.

Milner-Gulland, Robin. *The Russians.* Oxford: 1997.

Pushkareva, Natalia. *Women in Russian History from the Tenth to the Twentieth Century.* Armonk, N.Y.: 1997.

Ancient and Kievan Russia

Boba, I. *Nomads, Northmen and Slavs.* Wiesbaden and The Hague: 1967.

Cross, Samuel H., ed. *The Russian Primary Chronicle.* Cambridge, Mass.: 1953.

Franklin, Simon, and Shepard, Jonathan. *The Emergence of Russia, 750–1200.* London: 1996.

Grekov, B. *Kiev Rus.* Moscow: 1959.

Martin, Janet. *Medieval Russia, 980–1254.* Cambridge: 1995.

Mongait, A. L. *Archeology in the USSR.* London: 1961.

Noonan, Thomas. "Kievan Russia." In *Modern Encyclopedia of Russia and the Soviet Union,* Vol. 16, pp. 230–245. Gulf Breeze, Fla.: 1980.

Philipp, Werner. "Russia's Position in Medieval Europe." In Lyman Letgers, ed., *Russia: Essays in History and Literature.* Leiden: 1972.

Riasanovsky, Nicholas. "The Norman Theory of the Origin of the Russian State." In Sidney Harcave, ed., *Readings in Russian History* (Vol. 1). New York: 1962.

Rybakov, B. *Kievan Russia.* Moscow: 1989.

Sawyer, P. H. *Kings and Vikings.* London and New York: 1982.

Shchapov, Ya. N. *State and Church in Early Russia.* New Rochelle, N.Y.: 1995.

Vernadsky, George. *Kievan Russia.* New Haven, Conn.: 1948.

2

Russia Divided and Conquered, 1054–1462

In the twelfth century internal dissension gravely weakened Kievan civilization. In the thirteenth century Mongol conquest delivered a crushing blow to it. To be sure, some features of the old society persisted and were incorporated into the new Muscovite state that arose in the fourteenth century. But the new civilization was different in a number of ways, many of which resulted from the devastating psychological, economic, and political effects of Mongol invasion and domination.

It is difficult for Americans to comprehend the long-term impact of internal strife and foreign conquest on a society and people. In the past one hundred and forty years we have been spared both. The Civil War between the North and the South was divisive and disruptive, yet five generations later those wounds have largely healed. Imagine, however, what the effect would have been had a foreign power, say, Great Britain or Mexico, invaded and occupied most of the United States shortly after the Civil War and were still ruling the country today. That is what happened to the Russians 750 years ago.

For Russians living in the thirteenth and fourteenth centuries the overriding need was for security. This was at the very time when Europeans, as they emerged from the Middle Ages, were both enjoying increased protection from feudal in-fighting and external attack and benefiting from rising economic well-being provided by improved agriculture and reviving trade. Yet Russians lived under Mongol domination and were forced to deliver tribute and sometimes conscripts to the Mongols. Trade and handicraft production languished, and agriculture remained primitive. Consequently, the Russians' efforts to protect themselves and to create a stable society were hampered by limited resources. Moreover, the Russians' enemies maintained continuing pressure on the newly forming state. Russian civilization struggled to rise from the ashes of the Mongol conquest in conditions that were far from ideal.

RUSSIA DIVIDED

Despite brief periods of strong, unifying rule by able princes the Kievan state from A.D. 1054 to the Mongol invasion in A.D. 1237 was characterized primarily by internal dissension and political weakness. As we saw in Chapter 1, this was partly because the Kievan state system was inherently unstable, based as it was on rotating authority among princely families and lacking the concept and practice of a homogeneous, centralized territorial government. It was also due to the relentless pressure of foreign enemies, particularly the nomadic tribes to the southeast.

As the unity of Kiev disintegrated, the average citizen reacted in two ways: many fled from the open exposed plains of southern Russia to the thick protecting forests of the north. Although we have no precise numbers, we know that a considerable population shift took place in the eleventh through thirteenth centuries, from southern Russia to the northeast in particular. Mixing with the people already there, the immigrants formed a new strand of the Russian line, called Great Russians.

Second, people throughout Russia sought security from the depredations of outside foes and neighboring princes by placing themselves under the protection of a local boyar, monastery, or prince. This marked a significant ste ɔ toward development of a social system characterized by privileges for the upper classes and obligations for the lower classes. But a considerable period of transition occurred before Russian serfdom and the Russian service state emerged.

In political terms, when the grand prince at Kiev could no longer command tribute and allegiance from all the towns and tribes over whom Iaroslav the Wise had ruled, the system began to break up into separate principalities and city-states. At the height of this process of disintegration European Russia was divided into dozens of such small units, many of which fought each other. Although only a rough generalization, one can say that different forms of government tended to predominate in three main areas of Russia:

- The southwest (Volynia and Galicia): aristocratic (rule by boyars)
- The northwest (Pskov and Novgorod): democratic/oligarchic (rule by the *veche*)
- The northeast (Suzdal and Moscow): monarchic (rule by a prince)

There were exceptions to this pattern, and in many principalities all three institutions—boyars' duma, *veche*, and prince—coexisted although one was dominant. That Russians developed and practiced each of these systems belies the misleading aphorism that harsh autocratic rule is natural to, and needed by, the Russian people.

To look at each of these areas in turn, the southwest encompassed the territory stretching west and northwest of Kiev to the northern slopes of the

Carpathian Mountains and including present-day Belarus. It contained two important principalities, Volynia and Galicia, and was probably the richest area agriculturally. It had excellent prospects of emerging as the center of a revived Russian state, the logical successor to Kiev, with close ties to Europe. Strategically, the principalities of Volynia and Galicia had certain advantages. They were far enough away from the eastern borders of Russia to be spared the incursions of the Cumans. They were next door to Poland and Hungary, two strong European states of the time, with which Volynia and Galicia had lively commercial and cultural intercourse.

On the other hand, their location created certain disadvantages for these southwestern states. Their trading partners, Hungary and Poland (and later Lithuania), were larger and more powerful and soon began to covet the resources of neighboring Volynia and Galicia. Moreover, Hungarians, Poles, and Lithuanians were all Latin Catholics and looked upon the Orthodox Russians to their east as ripe for reconversion into the fold of true Christianity. Finally, although these small states were on the western border of European Russia, they were, alas, not far enough west to escape the Mongols, who overran and briefly occupied the region in the 1240s.

Another liability to the potential of the southwest's forming the nucleus of a restored Russia was that state power in Volynia and Galicia was quite unstable. Wealthy boyar landholders contended with aspiring princes for political control, and it was the only area of Russia down to the 1500s in which a boyar had the audacity to claim a princely throne. During the period of Mongol overlordship boyar power and prestige continued to grow, and it seems likely that Volynia and Galicia would have ultimately had a full-fledged system of aristocratic rule, had the two territories not been absorbed by Lithuania and Poland, respectively, in the 1300s.

A second area that could have shaped and led a resurrected Russian state was the northwest. As we saw in the first chapter, this was probably where the first towns and organized government were established, even before the founding of Kiev. Its largest town, calling itself Lord Novgorod the Great, had a population of over thirty thousand and ranked in splendor and culture with the major towns of Europe. Any visit to Russia is incomplete without a side trip from St. Petersburg to Novgorod, where one can stand amid the beautifully restored ancient churches and, eyes closed, easily imagine the bustle, excitement, and relative magnificence of the squares and streets of the twelfth-century city.

Novgorod, a city-state, controlled a considerable hinterland from which it drew forest and agricultural products. It traded extensively with Scandinavia and the north German towns of the Baltic Sea, exchanging Russian furs, wax, honey, and timber for grains, woolens, wine, metal, and sweets. It also served as a major storage and transshipment point for trade to south Russia down both the Volga and Dnieper rivers. At the same time, small manufacturing and craft work were almost as important to Novgorod as commerce. The town was well known for talented artisans who created not only practical items like tools and corduroy (log-paved) streets but intricate wooden decorations and tall, elegant churches in a distinctive, northern style.

The people of Novgorod were cultured, energetic, and decidedly independent-minded. Despite a number of threats, the Novgorodians preserved their independence for six hundred years, a remarkable record in those times. As we shall see in Chapter 3, they finally succumbed to the rising state of Moscow after A.D. 1470.

It is of course an oversimplification to call Novgorod democratic, just as it is misleading to label ancient Greece a democracy (or the United States in 1776, for that matter). Like those other societies, Novgorod did not permit women, slaves, and certain other classes in society to vote. But most freemen could, so it was a republic in form and provided a considerable degree of representative government. Voters elected both an all-city government and district administrations in five boroughs. For the first few hundred years there was a prince, though with strictly limited powers. In 1136 the *veche* began to elect the prince, who "reigned but did not govern." After the 1290s the post of prince was abolished altogether.

There was also a complex and quite enlightened judicial system as well as an autonomous church, whose archbishop was elected by the townspeople (though confirmed by the highest official of the Orthodox Church in Russia, the metropolitan of Kiev).

The *veche*, a town meeting of all freemen, was summoned by the ringing of a special bell. In the 1470s, when Moscow conquered Novgorod, the bell was carried back to Moscow as a symbol of Novgorod's loss of freedom. In the beginning the *veche*, besides electing officials, decided major issues of policy. Later an elected council, or executive committee, acted in its stead on most matters. Also the wealth, education, and influence of the leading merchants and landowners meant that increasingly they controlled the government and affairs of Novgorod. It became more an oligarchy than a democracy.

As in most medieval towns, disease, famine, and fire regularly ravaged Novgorod. Moreover, the *veche* was supposed to act unanimously, and when there were strongly opposing viewpoints, quarreling in the *veche* could turn into fisticuffs and brawls. Finally, as the gap between the boyars (upper-class merchants and landowners) and the rest of the population widened, social strife would occasionally erupt, as *The Chronicle of Novgorod* for A.D. 1418 makes clear:

> And again they [the common people] became enraged like drunkards, against another boyar, Ivan Yevlich . . . and on his account pillaged a great many boyars' houses, as well as the monastery of St. Nikola in the Field, crying out: "Here is the treasure house of the Boyars." And again the same morning they plundered many houses in the Lyudgoshcha Street, calling out: "They are our enemies. . . ." And they began to ring throughout the whole town, and armed men began to pour out from both sides as for war, fully armed, to the great

bridge. And there was loss of life, too. Some fell by arrows, others by arms . . . and a dread fell on the people on both sides.[1]

At its height Novgorod controlled a good part of northern Russia, including the satellite town of Pskov, as well as colonized territories to the northeast, along the shores of the Arctic Ocean. By acknowledging Mongol suzerainty and paying tribute to the Mongol khan, it averted direct Mongol attack or occupation. This strategy permitted Novgorod to fend off enemies to the west, including Sweden, Teutonic knights who occupied the area along the eastern shore of the Baltic Sea, and finally Lithuanians. But Novgorod was not basically a warrior state, and its decentralized system of government made it an unlikely candidate to lead the restoration and unification of the Russian lands.

The honor was to fall instead to the area of the northeast and, ultimately, to a small and obscure principality that was not even founded until the middle of the twelfth century: Moscow. Although the northeast contained old and important cities, such as Suzdal and Rostov, it had fewer resources than either the southwest or Novgorod. The balance of power began to shift there, even before the Mongol invasions, for two reasons. First, it was a relatively secure area, entirely in the forest zone and fairly far removed from Russia's western and southeastern foes. Second, it developed a tradition of princely rule that permitted the beginnings of centralized authority and effective government.

Thus, when the tradition that the most powerful prince should be based at Kiev broke down, his seat was moved to Suzdal, then to a newer town in the northeast, Vladimir. Later, the metropolitan, the chief official of the Orthodox Church in Russia, also migrated from Kiev to the northeast. In this way the tradition of Russian unity was preserved in the states of that region, including eventually that of Moscow.

Moreover, as trade declined and land became a more important resource, the princes of the northeast, dependent primarily on agriculture, were better able to mobilize the limited wealth of the country and to establish viable state power. But before they could do so, they had to endure the sudden smashing intrusion of the Mongols.

THE MONGOL SCOURGE

In the woods, glades, and towns of northeastern Russia A.D. 1237 must have seemed like any other year. The seemingly endless winter had at last suddenly erupted into green and luxuriant spring growth. The crops had been sown, tended, and harvested; winter pelts and hides were prepared for market; traders had come and gone; and quarrels among the region's princes had been no worse nor more harmful than customary. To be sure, people still passed about rumors of a new and ruthless band of nomads who had routed the Russian army fourteen years earlier southeast of Kiev, but neither hide nor hair of the intruders had been seen since (see Figure 3).

Figure 3. *A painting of Mongol warriors like those who conquered Russia. (Courtesy of the Freer Gallery of Art, Smithsonian Institution, Washington, D.C. Attributed to Chao Lin, A.D. 1360)*

The autumn had been spent accumulating food and fuel for winter, repairing houses and town walls, and hunting and trapping. No one was prepared for what suddenly occurred in mid-December, as reported, no doubt with some exaggeration, in chronicles and other early sources:

> With irresistible vigor and astonishing speed, the Mongols made their way through the forests of Penza and Tambov, and appeared before the beautiful city of Riazan. For five days they discharged a ceaseless storm of shot from their ballistae [military catapults] and, having made a breach in the defenses, carried the city by assault on the 21st of December, 1237. The prince, with his mother, wife [and] sons, the boyars and the inhabitants, without regard to age or sex, were slaughtered . . . some were impaled, some shot at with arrows for sport, others were flayed or had nails or splinters of wood driven under their fingernails. Priests were roasted alive, and nuns and maidens ravished in the churches before their relatives. No eye remained open to weep for the dead.[2]

Who were these cruel and indomitable despoilers? Today we know much more about the Mongols than the bewildered and hapless citizens of Riazan in the thirteenth century, although the origins of the Mongols—where they first lived and who their cultural forebears were—remain obscure.[3] In any case, they emerge into history in the 1100s, clearly in the same mold as earlier nomadic horsemen, from the Scythians through the Huns, who attacked the main centers of civilization and who invaded Europe, trampling over the Slavs north of the Black Sea as they passed westward from inner Asia.

MAP 3

The Mongols, however, differed from their predecessors in two important respects. First, their impact was even more devastating, both materially in loss of life and physical destruction of towns, churches, and dwellings, and psychologically, in terrorizing their opponents and subjugating them. Second, the Mongols were extremely well organized and disciplined, characteristics that permitted them to establish the largest empire in history. At its height the realm of the Great Khan of the Mongols stretched 5,000 miles from the China Sea to the Adriatic Sea in the Balkans and from the frozen wastes of Siberia in the north to the Persian Gulf in the south. The Mongols soon withdrew from Europe, and this huge empire, as a unit, did not last very long. Nevertheless, the Mongols conquered and ruled China and Russia, affected India and Islam, and threatened western Europe (see Map 3).

Moreover, they did all this with a relative handful of warriors and administrators; several hundred thousand Mongols held sway over more than one hundred million people in Eurasia.

It is an astounding record and it was due largely to the inspired (or half-mad) genius of one man, Genghis (more accurately, Chingiz) Khan. He was born as Temuchin, around 1165, the son of a minor chieftain among some nomadic tribes living in present-day Mongolia. Reputedly a skilled horseman and archer by the age of eleven. Temuchin worked unceasingly as a young man to unite the quarreling Mongol tribes. Finally, in 1206 at a solemn conclave of tribal leaders, he was proclaimed "mighty ruler," or

Genghis Khan. He apparently believed he had a divine mission to rule the world. After subduing neighboring regions, he conquered north China, almost all of central Asia, and part of Persia. After his death in 1227, his three sons and his grandson, Batu Khan, extended the empire by overrunning most of the Russian principalities, the Caucasus, southwest Asia, and the rest of China.

The dazzling military success of the Mongols depended on four qualities that characterized almost all their campaigns: surprise, mobility, organization, and discipline. Applied together, these traits permitted the Mongols to overrun armies that were often twice as large as their forces. The Mongol generals were carefully selected and trained, usually by the Great Khan himself. They relied on stealth and tactical and strategic surprise to catch the enemy unaware and to confuse him in battle. The army was organized on a decimal basis into units of ten, one hundred, one thousand, and ten thousand, and strict discipline was enforced from the lowliest soldier to the highest general reporting to the Great Khan.

The soldiers were outstanding horsemen and highly skilled with the bow and arrow. They wore cloth, leather, or metal armor and could travel incredible distances, as this account by Marco Polo, who worked at the court of Kublai Khan, shows:

> [The Mongol soldiers] are also more capable of hardships than other nations; for many a time, if need be, they will go for a month without any supply of food, living only on the milk of their mares and on such game as their bows may win them. Their horses also will subsist entirely on the grass of the plains, so that there is no need to carry store of barley or straw or oats....[4]

Finally, the Mongols were skillful adapters. By the time they invaded Russia, they had learned from the Chinese how to use catapults and other siege weapons.

Between the attack on Riazan in 1237 and 1241–1242, when their armies pushed through central Europe to the Balkans, the Mongols overran and destroyed most of the Russian cities. Those in the northwest were spared direct conquest. A few towns that offered no resistance were bypassed, but the usual pattern was to raze a town's main buildings, to slaughter or enslave up to a quarter of the population, and to demand future subordination to Mongol rule. Princes and boyars who knuckled under were tolerated, as was continuation of the activities of the Orthodox Church. Even after the Mongols were converted to Islam in the latter part of the thirteenth century, they made no attempt to force the Russians to become Muslims.

After the death of Genghis Khan in 1227, his empire was divided among three surviving sons and a grandson. The western territories fell to the grandson, Batu Khan, who planned and executed the invasion of Russia and western Europe. In the spring of 1242 his forces unexpectedly withdrew from the Balkans, and he returned to his headquarters at Old Sarai, a town north of the Caspian Sea along the Volga River. It is unclear whether this voluntary withdrawal occurred because Batu believed he was overextended militarily and politically; because he lost interest in Europe, not finding anything there to justify permanent Mongol occupation; or because he was anxious to be near the center of Mongol power in Asia so that he could participate in the selection of a successor to the Great Khan, his uncle Ugedei, who had died a few months before. Perhaps all of these considerations influenced him.

Whatever his reasons, one result of Batu Khan's pulling back was to consolidate his authority in a western Mongol state that soon became virtually independent and was known as the Khanate of the Golden Horde. (Apparently called *Golden* from the gold-leaf decorations that adorned the felt tents of Batu Khan and some of his leading lieutenants.) Batu Khan and his successors established for the Russian lands a system of indirect rule. Russian princes had to recognize the suzerainty of the Khan but were allowed to continue to administer their principalities. For example, Alexander Nevskii, a Russian national hero because he defeated the German order of Teutonic Knights, was permitted to rule Novgorod and assume the title of grand prince as long as he acknowledged Mongol overlordship. The princes had to go regularly to the Khan's capital at Sarai to pledge submission and to receive a *yarlyk,* or charter of authority. The Golden Horde collected taxes among the Russian principalities, based on a crude census of the population that the Mongols carried out. Later, the Mongols permitted Russian administrators to assess the taxes for them.

Occasionally the Mongols also demanded Russian recruits for their armies, but such levies were relatively infrequent. The Mongol overlords interfered little in the Russians' daily life and tolerated the Orthodox Church. If, however, any Russian town or group resisted their dominion, the Mongols, reacting swiftly, wreaked terrible vengeance on the rebels, leveling villages or towns and killing or enslaving most of the inhabitants.

The Mongols ruled the Russian lands in this fashion until the latter part of the fourteenth century, for about 140 years. Because of Mongol decline and growing Russian strength, as we shall see in the next chapter, after 1380 the Russians, although still obliged to recognize Mongol suzerainty and subject to sporadic depredations by Mongol troops, were increasingly independent.

THE IMPACT OF THE MONGOLS

The Mongol invasion of Russia nearly 800 years ago may seem far removed from the hostile relations between the West and the Soviet Union that marked the 1980s. Yet I vividly recall the final argument of a young Soviet history professor at that time, as we discussed enthusiastically but politely the course of Russian and Western development: "How can the

United States fear us? The Russians saved Western civilization in the thirteenth century by taking the brunt of the Mongol onslaught. And look what it cost us!"

As we have seen, there is little truth to this assertion that somehow the Russians, despite being overrun, blunted the Mongol sweep westward toward the Atlantic Ocean, thereby sparing most of Europe the horrors of Mongol conquest and occupation. In fact, the forces of Batu Khan rather easily defeated a Polish-German army and then the Hungarians in 1241, and it is difficult to see who could have stopped them, had they wished to seize all of Europe. The fact that they did not do so and shortly withdrew to their headquarters in southeastern Russia had almost nothing to do with the Russians, who were prostrate and benumbed after the Mongol incursion. Thus, we can hardly accept the reasoning that Russia "saved" the West, although, as we shall see much later in this book, Soviet historians sometimes made an analogous argument concerning the Soviet Union's contribution to the defeat of Hitler and the Nazis in World War II.

That leaves unanswered, however, the more complex and intriguing question raised by the last part of the young Soviet scholar's comment: "And look what it cost us!" As with the role of the Vikings in the founding of the first Russian state, the impact of the Mongols on Russian civilization is a touchy issue. Some writers sympathetic to Russia are anxious to blame characteristics of Russian development since the thirteenth century that they disapprove of, such as autocratic government and serfdom, on the poor example and punishing harassment of the Mongols. Otherwise, they claim, Russia might have evolved democratically, as the West did.

Some Russian scholars, although eager to discount Mongol influence on Russian society, are nevertheless happy, like the young historian quoted previously, to ascribe Russia's early struggles in Muscovite times and its relative backwardness compared to European civilization to the destructiveness of Mongol rule. Finally, some observers, basically critical of both the tsarist and Soviet systems, argue that the Mongols simply reinforced and brought out negative traits already inherent in Russian civilization before the thirteenth century: cruelty, repression, militarization, and expansionism.

As so often in historiographic debates, a middle ground seems the sensible answer. The Mongols certainly affected the course of Russian history. It would be difficult to dismiss their devastating invasion and two centuries of domination as counting for naught. But it would be equally foolish to decide that Mongol precepts, values, and institutions completely shaped the Muscovite state that emerged in the fourteenth century. In the first place, Mongol rule was indirect; the Mongols made no effort to mold Russia exactly in their image. In the second place, the new Russian society grew organically out of the traditions and three-hundred-year experience of the Kievan state and the conditions and challenges of its times. The Muscovite leaders tried not to imitate Mongol society because the Mongols were thoroughly detested for what they had done to Russia and because they were pagans and infidels.

To see how this middle-of-the-road conclusion about the impact of the Mongols works out in practice, we will examine some of the areas in which the Mongols did have some influence and then note those in which they had almost none. In my view, the most important effect of the Mongol conquest was economic. In three key ways, the Mongols' defeat and subjugation of Russia led to severe economic losses: first, and perhaps least important, was the immediate physical destruction—the leveling of towns and villages, the seizing of goods and crops, and the killing of large numbers of people. This was certainly a setback, but these costs were shortly recouped, and after Mongol dominion was established and acknowledged by most Russian princes and towns, subsequent physical devastation was not extensive.

Second, the Mongols seriously weakened the productive capacities of Russian society. In those preindustrial times most production was agricultural, but there was also a significant output of household goods, clothing, tools, implements, buildings, and other handicrafts by artisans, who, though limited primarily to using human power, displayed a high degree of skill and ingenuity. Most of these goods were consumed locally, in towns and villages, but some were traded regionally and a few internationally. In the Kievan period Russia, like other European and Asian societies, had developed this kind of production to a moderate level. Although the evidence is not clear whether artisan work in Russia had already begun to decline before the Mongols' arrival, as part of a general weakening of the Kievan economy, it is patent that the destruction associated with the Mongol invasion was a serious setback to this sector of Russian economic life. Not only were workshops and tools destroyed; skilled artisans were killed or sent as captives to work at the Mongol capital of Sarai. It was not so easy for Russian society to bounce back from losses of that sort.

Finally, although the Russians apparently profited by their secondary participation in the extensive international trade carried on by the Mongols, this was more than offset by the Mongols' expropriation—mainly through a fairly efficient system of taxation—of most of the surplus the Russians produced. In colloquial terms, they skimmed the cream off the Russian economy. This was a serious blow because early agricultural societies such as that of Russia had, even in the best of times, little surplus. To have the Mongols take most of it each year left the Russians struggling to survive, with little opportunity for economic growth.

Moreover, it is likely that the drain that Mongol taxation represented also thwarted Russia's potential for economic growth, although this is difficult to prove since we do not know what might have been and since economic data from that period are sparse. Even though recent studies suggest that Russian trade and economic activity under the Mongols were less curtailed than was once believed, the essential point is that without the Mongol conquest, the Russian economy might have gone through—and indeed been an eastern-most part of—the same economic upsurge that western Europe experienced in the fourteenth century and that undergirded Europe's commercial revolution and subsequent worldwide expansion. An important part of this economic boom was the accumulation of capital (or surpluses) from the production and trading of agricultural and handicraft goods. This stimulated the growth of towns and a wide range of social and political changes in Western civilization. Yet Russians under the Mongols had limited opportunities to expand production, increase trade, and accumulate capital. Whatever surplus was built up, the Mongols took.

At this point you might well say, "but the conditions for this sort of economic expansion didn't exist in Russia anyway, regardless of the Mongols," and you would certainly be right to some degree. We must leave, however, to the next chapter a full consideration of why by the 1400s the Russian economy lagged behind that in the West. The point here is that it seems fair to say that Mongol exactions certainly didn't help.

A somewhat less complex but still quite tangled issue is the political effects of Mongol rule. Some have argued that the Russian princes borrowed Mongol political ideas, particularly the concept of the unlimited, unchallengeable authority of the Mongol Khan, and melded these into the theory and practice of absolute rule in the Muscovite state. Yet this view is not entirely convincing: the Russians had both indigenous and Byzantine models of autocratic power exercised by a single ruler on which to draw. And these were what they referred to when they wanted to justify the autocracy.

It has also been suggested, even less convincingly, that from the Mongols the Russians took the goal of establishing a universal world empire, that the messianic mission of Slavic (or later Communist) world dominion had its misty origins in Genghis Khan's belief that he was divinely anointed to conquer the universe. But, again, it is much easier to trace the origins of such ideas, as we will do in a subsequent chapter, to the later concept of a special Christian mission for the Russian people and state, rather than to try to find Mongol roots for them.

In fact, in my view, the Russians took little directly from the Mongol political system. They borrowed in some administrative areas, for example, in fiscal matters, in setting up tax and postal systems, and possibly in military organization and technology, but otherwise adopted little else.

To be sure, many policies of the early Muscovite princes were a *reaction against* the Mongol overlordship, designed first to survive and then to overthrow the Mongol yoke. Consequently, in this indirect sense, as we shall see in Chapter 3, the Mongols greatly influenced Moscow's political actions and institutions—but directly, not very much.

An important way, related to politics, that the Mongols affected Russia was psychologically, although such an influence is almost impossible to substantiate. The notion that because of the Mongol yoke and the fact that

Russian princes had to humble themselves at the court of Khan, Russians became inherently servile and craved strong rule is of course utter rubbish. But that Russians were shocked, humiliated, and grief-stricken by the suddenness, fury, and cruelty of the Mongol onslaught makes excellent sense. And this certainly made them extremely, if not obsessively, concerned with their own safety and with the security of their society and state. Russians had been battling various foes and invaders throughout the previous four hundred years of their recorded history, but the Mongol conquest was an experience at an entirely different and traumatic level. It is no exaggeration to say that the excessive fear of the outside world that Russians displayed over the past five hundred years—and especially under Stalin's rule—can be traced in part to the nightmarish devastation of their society in 1237–1241 at the hands of the Mongols.

Finally, it is certainly true that the Mongol conquest affected Russian development by making it more difficult for the Russian principalities to stay in close touch with Byzantium and with the states of central and western Europe. Recent research has shown that Russia was not as totally cut off and isolated as we once believed, that some trade and cultural contacts persisted throughout the period of the Mongol yoke. But, obviously, personal, intellectual, and commercial ties were much attenuated by Mongol rule at the very time when Europe was beginning to change in a rapid and revolutionary way. The Russians might well have been as suspicious of the culture of Roman Catholic Europe as they were of the culture of the Islamic Golden Horde. Nevertheless, as we saw earlier, there were close links between Kiev and Europe in the preceding centuries, and it is logical to assume that the intellectual, social, and economic stirrings and excitement of the High Middle Ages and, particularly, of the Renaissance would have had some spillover and impact in Russia, had Russia not been first under the Mongols' thumb and then bending all its energies to overthrow the Mongol yoke.

It is important to note that the Mongol domination, although perhaps not causing division of the Russian lands, at least accelerated this process. Such a fragmentation would probably have occurred anyway, but the Mongol conquest strengthened the centrifugal tendencies already at work. In west Russia, where Mongol domination lasted only one hundred years, Volynia and Galicia were absorbed by Lithuania and Poland. This marked a point of no return in the branching of the Russian peoples into Belarusans in the east, Ukrainians in the southwest, and Great Russians in the northeast. At the same time the Mongol invasion undoubtedly facilitated the occupation of the lands along the Baltic Sea by Germanic knights and later by Swedes, so that these territories remained outside Russian control for several hundred years.

The list of areas in which the Mongols' rule had little or no effect is much shorter than that just discussed, but it encompasses important aspects of Russian society. First, as we have already noted, because the Mongols governed indirectly, through Russian princes, the daily life of the Russians who survived the first assault and whose princes did not defy the Mongols changed little. Their customs and patterns of living were not affected. Local social and political arrangements and institutions were basically not altered. The peasant commune, the village, the town, the principality, all remained pretty much as before.

Most important, the beliefs and culture of the Russian people persisted unchanged. This continuity permitted gradual reestablishment of a distinctly Russian society and emergence of an autonomous and finally independent and expanding Muscovite state. The Orthodox Church, which the Mongols left untouched, was able to preserve and transmit the essentials of earlier Russian civilization through the period of Mongol domination: religion, education, literature, and values all survived. In the hardest times the people were able to look to and rally around the Church. It carried forward the tradition of unity and uniqueness, on which a resurrected civilization could be built. Consoler and protector, the Church played an indispensable role in preventing the people from abandoning themselves to despair and in holding the society together. Later, with the prince, the Church was able to induce the people to support a new political system that eventually liberated them from the Mongol yoke (though, some would argue, enslaving them to indigenous institutions).

Thus, by retaining their religion and with it the essential attributes of their culture, which was undoubtedly at a higher level than that of the Mongols, the Russians, though set back economically and subjugated politically, were able to outlast their conquerors and rebuild their own state and civilization.

THE DECLINE OF MONGOL POWER

The Russians collapsed under the Mongol onslaught in part because they were divided and had no viable state system. In an ironic turnabout, the Russians were finally able to rid themselves of the Mongols because the latter became disunited and failed to build an effective state structure. The huge Eurasian empire put together by Genghis Khan and his successors split into several parts by the end of the 1200s. And in the 1300s and 1400s the Khanate of the Golden Horde, its westernmost unit and Russia's overlord, gradually weakened as a result of struggles for power among the descendants of Batu Khan and as internal dissension among its component tribes increased. The result was that although nominal Mongol suzerainty over Russia continued until 1480, Mongol power could be brought to bear only sporadically, and the Russian principalities gradually acquired autonomy.

One factor undermining Mongol authority was that although they had developed a discipline, organization, and system of rule that was well suited to expansion and conquest, they did not have a well-developed social or religious system that would enable them to hold together disparate peoples and societies. The Mongols constituted a thin overlay on existing cultures, and they did little to fuse their domains into an integrated civilization. Without linguistic, religious, or cultural unity the Khanate of the Golden Horde could not develop a strong political structure, and the centrifugal tendencies within it gradually began to pull it apart. In the 1400s separate khanates were established at Kazan and Astrakhan and in the Crimea; this fragmentation made the task of the Russian princes striving for independence a good deal easier.

Though divided, the Mongols, or Tatars as their descendants were now called, were still formidable foes. Mongol rule over Russia did not collapse of its own weight. The Muscovite princes and the Lithuanians worked hard to overturn it and succeeded only after a long struggle, as we shall see shortly.

CONCLUSION

In assessing the Mongol period of Russian history it is important neither to dismiss it nor to overplay it. Looked at from the broadest perspective, the Mongol era left three significant legacies for future Russian civilization. First, it heightened a deep sense of insecurity among Russians and within Russian society. The fear of being overrun and subjugated might eventually have faded from the consciousness of ordinary Russians and their leaders, except that subsequent events, as we shall see, kept those anxieties boiling. Thus, time and again in Russian history the people and state struggled, with limited resources, to ward off foreign intruders and to ensure their own safety and security.

Second, the Mongol invasion made unity and cohesiveness a high-priority value in Russian society and the Russian state. The Russians had had no chance against the Mongols, in part because they were divided, with each prince and his followers trying to fend for themselves. Out of that experience and the necessity of building a strong state to overthrow the Mongol yoke came an emphasis on the strength to be found in a common religion, Orthodoxy, and in a common allegiance to the grand prince (later the tsar). Without the Mongols a Russian state or empire might eventually have been formed out of the disparate pieces into which Kievan civilization had separated, but it is at least equally possible that the Russians would have remained divided and would have been absorbed by their powerful neighbors: Poles, Lithuanians, and others.

Finally, whatever specific effects the Mongols had in draining the Russian economy and terrorizing the population, a highly significant fundamental outcome of their rule was to spur the divergence of Russian civilization from the West. As we have discussed, Russia was bound to emerge as a unique society, but at least in Kievan times it was developing along a track parallel to that of western Europe and its Latin Christian civilization. But after the Mongols the distance between them had perceptibly widened, and Russian society evolved along more distinctly different lines than it had a few centuries earlier. As a result, serfdom emerged in Russia just as it was disappearing in western Europe. Trade and commercial capitalism flourished in Europe but languished in Russia. Europe bubbled over with intellectual ferment and social fluidity, particularly during the Renaissance. Thought in Russia remained quite traditional, even stagnant, as Russian society became increasingly rigid and stratified. To be sure, this is not to argue that, but for the Mongols, Russia would have turned out (happily in our view) much like the West. It is simply to underscore that the Mongol era made certain that Russian civilization would follow a markedly different course from that being traversed by Western civilization.

FURTHER READING

Halperin, Charles J. *Russia and the Golden Horde*. Bloomington, Ind.: 1985.

Kollman, Nancy Shields. *By Honor Bound: State and Society in Early Modern Russia*. Ithaca, N.Y., and London: 1997.

Martin, Janet. *Medieval Russia, 980–1584*. Cambridge: 1995.

Morgan, David. *The Mongols*. Oxford: 1986.

Presniakov, A. E. *The Formation of the Great Russian State*. New York: 1971.

Tikhomirov, M. N. *The Towns of Ancient Rus*. Moscow: 1959.

Treadgold, Donald. "Russia and the East." In Donald Treadgold, ed., *The Development of the USSR*. Seattle, Wash.: 1964.

Vernadsky, George. *The Mongols and Russia*. New Haven, Conn.: 1953.

3

Moscow and "The Gathering of the Russian Lands," 1328–1533

A bird's-eye view of European Russia in the mid-1300s would have revealed four major centers of power and civilization: the Mongols in the southeast; the emerging Lithuanian or Lithuanian-Russian state in the west; Novgorod in the northwest; and two contending princely states in the northeast: Tver and Moscow. Any one of these had the potential to become the heir of the Kievan state and the unifier of Russia. Yet by the early 1500s Moscow, which 150 years earlier was the smallest and least promising contender, had emerged as the dominant power. In the words of the *Chronicle*, it "gathered the Russian lands" under its rule and established a loosely centralized state. In five generations Moscow defeated all its nearby rivals, such as Tver and Novgorod; threw off the Mongol yoke forever; and seized much of the territory of the Lithuanian state, pushing it westward and into union with Poland.

This remarkable development, almost as sweeping and dramatic as the Mongol conquest itself, also had fateful consequences for the future course of Russian history. In the first place, Moscow's expansion set the emerging society on a course of imperial domination of neighboring lands that would make it five hundred years later the largest and longest-lasting territorial empire in modern history. The burgeoning Muscovite state included at an accelerating pace many non-Slav ethnic groups, cultures, and religions, making for a diverse and complex society. Second, Moscow's victory meant that the principle of obligatory service to the ruler, a policy that was key to Moscow's success, became a central tenet of Russian society from that time forward. Third, the triumph of Moscow ensured that of the three political concepts that coexisted in Kievan times—princely or autocratic rule, republican or democratic government, and boyar or aristocratic domination—the autocratic system would prevail in the new Russian state. Finally, the rise of Moscow meant that the reemergent Russian civilization would have a strong religious orientation, that of the Orthodox faith, and would be dominated by Great Russians. If, for example, the Lithuanian state had won instead, the resulting society would have been Latinized and subject to Roman Catholic influences and would have had an aristocratic system of governance. Thus, the triumph of Moscow set firmly in place characteristics of a Russian society that would last more than five centuries, down to 1917.

THE ODDS AGAINST MOSCOW

Certainly if you had been sent to Russia as an objective observer in the early 1300s and asked to predict which among the contending factions were destined to unify Russia, you would hardly have picked the tiny principality of Moscow. You might have concluded that other northeastern princedoms, like Suzdal-Vladimir or Riazan or Tver, had a better chance. Moscow's disadvantages were several. It was, to begin with, an upstart. First mentioned in the *Primary Chronicle* for the year 1147, it was fortified in 1156 but remained a minor principality and was then ravaged by the Mongols in 1237. Even in the early 1300s as its significance began to grow, Moscow was still small and "second-class" compared to its long-established and more powerful rivals.

Second, the Moscow princes had to fight against the dominant principle of post-Kievan Russian society, the *udel* or *appanage* system. In medieval Russia appanages were princely holdings of land, or territories, from which the prince and his family were expected to draw economic sustenance and over which the prince exercised considerable administrative, judicial, and political rights. In a sense it was the private property of the prince, but he controlled it for public purposes as well. It is important to note that *primogeniture,* or the inheritance of property by the eldest son, did not operate in post-Kievan Russia. Thus, a prince's appanage and title were divided among all his sons, a system that produced more and more princes with smaller and smaller holdings from generation to generation. Moreover, *boyars,* the aristocratic servitors of the princes, who held *votchinas* (vóht-cheena), that is, hereditary estates for which they owed no service, also divided their lands among their heirs. As a result, the overriding tendency in Russia of the thirteenth and fourteenth centuries was for territory to be cut up constantly into bits and pieces. The princes of Moscow had to reverse that trend, or at least make it work for them.

Third, the Muscovite rulers had to contend with the Kievan tradition of senior or grand princes and the rotation of people in that office. The princes of Moscow, as we shall see, first had to claim and solidify the title of grand prince and then make sure it was passed on only to their eldest sons.

Fourth, the founders of the Muscovite state had only extremely limited resources with which to defeat powerful rivals. Theirs was not a particularly rich town, they had little accumulated wealth, and they possessed no tangible assets to give them an advantage over others. Consequently, they had to scrimp and save and then to mobilize and manage what little was available to them more efficiently than their competitors.

Finally, the Muscovites had a level of technology and culture that was certainly no better, and perhaps even lower, than their enemies. To be sure, they had the great spiritual advantage of the support of the Orthodox Church, as we shall shortly see, but otherwise they had no great tradition, no well-educated servitors or general population, no special skills or weapons, no knowledgeable and wealthy merchants or intellectuals, and no ideas or precepts, at least in the beginning, that gave them any edge over other contenders for power in Russia.

MOSCOW'S ADVANTAGES

In spite of its liabilities, Moscow also had a number of assets that help explain its rapid ascent to dominion over the Russian lands. Some of these were circumstances that benefited the Moscow princes but over which they had no control. Others resulted from the conscious actions and policies of the princes. We will examine this latter set of advantages for Moscow first.

Security and Internal Order

From our smug modern perspective it is easy to say, "How could the Russians have acquiesced so abjectly in the building of a state and society that was based on absolutism and that soon instituted an oppressive social system, serfdom?" Yet if we imagine ourselves back in those times, we can at once see how attractive the policies of the growing Muscovite state were for the inhabitants of the Russian lands. For almost three hundred years the people had been buffeted by civil war, invasions, and finally conquest. Their towns and villages had been overrun and razed many times. Apart from the usual medieval disasters of famine, fire, and disease, their lives were in constant danger, and they were afraid and insecure most of the time.

It is not surprising, therefore, that when the Moscow princes said, "Here you will be safe," people flocked to the territory and willingly served the Muscovite rulers. The Russian people were happy to trade freedom for protection. It is true, of course, that the Moscow princes could not absolutely guarantee security and tranquillity; for example, the Mongols sacked the city in 1382. Moreover, many Muscovites were engaged in fighting external foes of the principality: rival princedoms, the Mongols, and the Lithuanians. Nevertheless, within the territories controlled by Moscow, a rapidly expanding area, peace and order reigned most of the time. In my view, which is based on that of V. O. Kliuchevsky, the leading Russian historian before the 1917 Revolution, the ability of the Moscow princes to provide security for the people was their greatest asset.

Organization and Management

Although sufficient information for making precise judgments obviously does not exist, it seems fair to conclude from what we do know that the Moscow princes were on the whole skillful administrators and proprietors of their domain, probably abler in this regard than most of their rivals. We have already noted that they did not have much to work with, but they made the most of their limited resources. They encouraged agriculture and helped colonize and develop new lands. They built up the city of Moscow and established other towns. They handled their military campaigns adroitly and succeeded in balancing their fiscal base with their military expenses. They were successful tax collectors and merchants, and they encouraged commerce among the population. It is appropriate that one of the first princes, who ruled from 1327 to 1341, was called Ivan Kalita, or John the Moneybags.

The Moscow princes were also generally successful in avoiding civil war within the princely family. Only once during the two centuries of Moscow's climb to preeminence was there protracted quarreling and strife over the succession to the throne. Finally, they managed to minimize the division of the Muscovite lands among heirs each time a prince died. Although younger sons at times inherited territories of Moscow, every effort was made to ensure that before long these reverted to the larger Moscow state of the senior son, or grand prince.

Diplomatic Skill

The princes of Moscow displayed remarkable ability in dealing with an array of foreign foes. Toward the Mongols they were submissive and helpful at those times, particularly in the fourteenth century, when the Mongols were still strong and could easily crush the fledgling Muscovite state. As a reward for their obedience and cooperation, the princes of Moscow were empowered to serve as tax agents for the Mongols and received Mongol assistance against the rival principality of Tver. Yet, when Mongol power declined in the latter half of the 1300s, the Moscow princes were quick to seize the opportunity to turn against their masters and to lead a virtual crusade against Mongol domination. In 1380 the Moscow prince Dmitrii Donskoi (so called because his victory over the Mongols took place on the Don River) became a hero to many Russians by opposing Mongol rule. Over time the Moscow state emerged as a symbol of resistance to Mongol oppression and marauding, thus giving it a further advantage in its struggle to unify the Russian lands.

The Moscow princes, usually cited for their skill in handling relations with the Mongols, were equally adept in dealing with the Lithuanians, the principality of Tver, and the leaders of Novgorod. On most occasions the Muscovites out-maneuvered their opponents and thus were able to expand their domain at less military cost than would otherwise have resulted.

Identification with the Orthodox Church

An important advantage for the Moscow princes was their close cooperation with the Orthodox religion and Church. In this way Moscow was able to draw directly on the tradition of Kiev and to act as the logical successor of a great and unified Russian state and civilization.

The Orthodox Church played an increasingly important role in the Russian territories at this time. Pagan practices and attitudes persisted, many Russians still believing in powerful natural forces and spirits that acted in unpredictable and perverse ways. Nevertheless, the church provided a symbol of unity and continuity for the Russian people. When all else was in confusion and upheaval, the Church served as a refuge for and consoler of the people. The rituals of the Church were familiar and comforting, and its doctrine promised eventual salvation. Moreover, it was a faith and a practice that all Russians, no matter in whose territory they lived, shared.

The Church was also important economically. By the 1500s one quarter of all the land in Russia belonged to the Church and its monasteries, much of it bequeathed by devout parishioners. The monasteries were often active in establishing outposts and havens in the forested wilderness and in colonizing new territory in the north. Many peasants worked on Church land, probably under slightly better conditions than peasants on private or princely estates.

Finally, the Church was the main center of artistic and cultural life throughout this period. Under the Mongol occupation the Church attempted to preserve scholarship and education, but only a few people were literate, and most of the boyars and even many of the clergy could not read or write. Moreover, the emphasis in Russian Orthodoxy was on the church services and rituals, rather than on intellectual training and rational inquiry. The other strand of Church activity, represented in the monasteries and in the work of the revered Russian monk, St. Sergius (1322–1392), focused on asceticism and a denial of this world. Consequently, the Orthodox Church did not play the important scholarly, educational, and intellectual role that the Roman Catholic Church did in western Europe during this same period. Nevertheless, it remained the center of the learning and culture that persisted under Mongol rule.

Almost all the written literature of the time was religious: chronicles of events, lives of saints, sermons. It was quite stylized and traditional, and there were few secular writings to match the lyricism and vigor of the earlier *Tale of the Host of Igor.*

The glory of medieval Russian culture was in religious art and architecture. As we saw in Chapter 1, Kievan Russians had learned icon painting from Byzantium but had already begun to develop it in their own style. Because icons are not familiar to most Westerners (icons were banned in the Latin Church), their significance and beauty are sometimes not fully appreciated. In viewing and understanding an icon, it is important to remember that each icon served two crucial purposes. It was designed both to educate and to inspire the illiterate and bowed-down worshipper who gazed upon it (originally only in churches, later in most Russian homes). Thus, it had to be clear and articulate on the one hand, conveying a simple but powerful

Figure 4.   *The beautiful* Holy Trinity *icon by Rublev,
painted in the early fifteenth century. (Courtesy of Sovfoto/
Eastfoto)*

message about the Bible or the life of Christ or the lives of saints. Yet on the
other it had to dazzle and uplift so as to provide an important spiritual experience for the humble churchgoer.

In the 1300s Russian icon painters began to elevate their work to a plane
considerably beyond anything that Byzantine masters had achieved, and in
the icons of Andrei Rublev, who died in 1430, this art form reached its
apogee. Rublev's masterpiece, the *Old Testament Holy Trinity* (see Figure
4), is one of the world's great paintings, combining perfect composition and
harmony with warm feeling and exquisite grace. Its rich and soft colors are
an important part of the painting, so a black-and-white reproduction unfortunately cannot do it full justice.

A final, significant contribution of the Church to medieval Russian life
was in architecture. Some of the finest churches were built in this period.
Many of them, particularly the wooden churches in the north Russian
style, have not survived, but those that have impress the observer with
their clean, utilitarian but graceful lines and with their superb decorations and cupolas. The major stone churches in Moscow, although built

Figure 5.   Interior of the Church of the Assumption in the Moscow Kremlin, showing the icons painted on the pillars and before the altar.

under the supervision of imported Italian architects, remain today as complex, impressive monuments to the Russians' creativity in fusing the Byzantine style with indigenous expression. No trip to Russia makes sense unless you can spend at least a day and a half enjoying at a leisurely pace the four glorious cathedrals and the palace of the Moscow Kremlin (see Figure 5).

As this quick overview has indicated, the Church occupied a central position in medieval Russian civilization. The Moscow princes must have recognized this, for from the beginning they associated themselves closely with the Church and worked with the Orthodox hierarchy continuously in the monumental task of defending and unifying the Russian lands. The political benefits were enormous since the Moscow princes could claim not only the mantle of Kiev and the most glorious Russian traditions but also the blessing of the Church leaders and through them of God Himself. As we shall see shortly, there were also some strains in relations between the princes and the Church, but overall Moscow's identification with Orthodoxy helped it to gain power and set the basic tone of Russian civilization for generations to come.

Other advantages that Moscow enjoyed as it grew and expanded were more fortuitous, having relatively little relation to the policies of the princes.

Moscow's Location

One does not have to accept geographical determinism in history to conclude that Moscow happened to be extremely well situated. The city grew up in the middle of northeastern Russia, almost equidistant in every direction from the borders of the traditional Russian "lands." This site served it well in two ways: the city was strategically placed so it could move easily outward in absorbing the other Russian principalities, yet it was far enough away from its external enemies, such as the Mongols and the Lithuanians, that they could not easily attack Moscow.

Moscow's Commerce

As a corollary to its location, Moscow developed as an important trading center. Two main commercial routes crossed in Moscow, one from the northwest to the southeast, that is, from Novgorod to the Black and Caspian Seas via the Don and Volga rivers; and the other from the south up the Dnieper River to the cities northeast of Moscow, such as Rostov and Suzdal. Situated on the Moskva (Moscow) River, the city's merchants had easy access by tributaries to the three main rivers of European Russia: the Dnieper, the Volga, and the Don. Although Soviet historians have stressed the agricultural basis of Moscow's economy, and although the importance of trade had certainly declined since Kievan times, recent evidence suggests that commerce was well developed in Moscow and contributed notably to its success.

Luck

One of the fascinations of history is that time and again the historian comes across a significant incident or factor that can only be ascribed to accident or chance. In this case the princes of Moscow were just plain lucky. They lived much longer than most of their contemporaries and consequently had long reigns. For example, Ivan III (Ivan the Great) ruled for forty-three years from 1462 to 1505, providing remarkable stability and continuity for the state at a crucial period in its development. Between 1389 and 1584, almost two hundred years, the Muscovite state had only five rulers, an incredible record for its time.

This meant that the uncertainty, and often the civil war, that had customarily marked each succession in Kievan times recurred infrequently. Moreover, each prince, beginning with Dmitrii in 1359, ruled long enough to consolidate his position and the power of the state, as well as to carry out a set of consistent policies designed to expand the realm and to strengthen it.

Had the throne been in contention every five or ten years, with new princes struggling to assert their authority, the Muscovite state could hardly have grown and prevailed in the way that it did. Although several of the princes of Moscow took power in their teens, their long reigns are still remarkable in an era of high infant mortality and frequent epidemics. They may have been hardy but they were also lucky.

THE UNIFICATION OF RUSSIA, 1328–1533

To see concretely how the Muscovite princes overcame their liabilities and took advantage of their assets, we will survey briefly the most important events that marked the "gathering of the Russian lands." Moscow's rise was both rapid and dramatic, with surprisingly few setbacks along the way. In the first 150 years, from the early fourteenth century to the middle of the fifteenth century, Moscow grew from a tiny principality smaller than the state of Rhode Island to a major state the size of Connecticut and Massachusetts combined.

Founded in the mid-1100s, Moscow was not at first a significant town in northeast Russia. Its larger neighbors, boasting of princes as colorfully named as George the Long-Arm and Dmitrii Big Eyes, were more powerful and politically influential. In the late 1200s and early 1300s the princes of tiny Moscow took a first step down the road of expansion by incorporating territory along the Moscow River into their principality. They also began what was to be a bitter, almost two-hundred-year-long struggle with the older and better known principality of Tver northwest of Moscow.

An important prize in this rivalry was the title of grand prince. Traditionally associated with Kiev, the office of grand prince had been transferred to the northeastern town of Vladimir in 1169, when Kiev was much weakened. In the early 1300s the princes of Moscow and Tver claimed it at various times, but finally around 1331 Ivan I (Ivan Kalita) of Moscow, who also ruled Vladimir, was recognized as grand prince, and the important title was associated with Moscow from then on.

A second significant event at the same time was the move to Moscow of the metropolitan, the highest official of the Orthodox Church in Russia. To some extent chance favored the Muscovites on this occasion. The seat of the metropolitan, originally in Kiev, had been transferred to the northeast in the twelfth century. In 1326 an extremely popular and talented metropolitan, Peter, died while visiting Moscow. He was later canonized, and Saint Peter's name became associated with Moscow. In 1328 his successor decided to reside in the city. From that time on the metropolitans of the Orthodox Church worked closely with the grand princes of Moscow to oppose the infidel Mongols (converted to Islam in the preceding century) and the heretic Lithuanians (predominantly Roman Catholic after 1386), as well as to bring together the Russian principalities in a unified state (see Map 4).

GROWTH OF
MOSCOW
to 1533

0   400
MILES

White Sea

FINNS

Semidependent

Colonies

SWEDEN

N. Dvina

Lake
Ladoga

Ustiug

Reval   Narva

ORDER

Novgorod

Beloo
zero

Baltic   Sea

Yaroslavl

KHANATE

LIVONIAN

Riga

Pskov

Rostov

Kazan

W.

Dvina

Tver

Vladimir

OF   KAZAN

PRUSSIA

Vilna

Smolensk

Moscow

Riazan

Kaluga

LITHUANIA

Oka

Tula

BOUNDARY OF
LITHUANIA,
1462

Warsaw

Orel

Dnieper

POLAND

Chernigov

Voronezh

Volga

Kiev

GOLDEN HORDE

Belgorod

Don

Sarai

Donets

HUNGARY

MOLDAVIA

Dnieper

KHANATE
OF ASTRAKHAN

Azov

Danube

CRIMEAN

BULGARIA

KHANATE

Caspian

OTTOMAN

Black   Sea

CAUCASUS

Sea

Constantinople (to Turks, 1453)

EMPIRE

Corinne Abbazia Hekker Graphics

▓ Moscow, c. 1300	▨	To 1462: Vasili I, Vasili II
▒ To 1389: Ivan I - Dmitrii	▓	To 1533: Ivan III, Vasili III

MAP 4

The reign of Ivan I is important in one other way. An able ruler, he instituted policies that came to be associated with Moscow's success. Ivan made Moscow more secure, managed its resources effectively, and encouraged commerce. He acted as tax collector for the Mongols and minimized Moscow's share of what was paid them. Finally, he bought up territories adjacent to Moscow as one method of extending his domain.

The long reign of Dmitrii Donskoi from 1359 to 1389 was marked by continued expansion and consolidation and by Moscow's recurring struggles with the Lithuanians and the Mongols. From the fourteenth to the sixteenth century the Lithuanian state played an important role in Russian history, and a few words about it are needed. The Lithuanians are a Baltic people with an ancient and distinct language and culture. In medieval times they lived in the forests of northwest Russia and along the southeastern shores of the Baltic Sea. In response to pressure from crusading German knights who occupied much of the Baltic littoral and threatened northwest Russia in the 1200s, the Lithuanians organized their own state. In the 1300s the Lithuanian state expanded rapidly southeast from the Baltic, occupying Russian territories until it encompassed much of western Russia. At its farthest advance the Lithuanian state included such important Russian cities as Kiev, Chernigov, and Smolensk, as well as the territory of Volynia, and reached all the way to the Black Sea.

Because the Lithuanians were few in number, they fused with the local Russian nobility as they expanded. Hence some historians prefer to call their empire a Lithuanian-Russian state. The dominant language was a distinct form of Russian known today as Belarusan. This state could clearly claim to be an heir of Kiev and acted as a formidable rival to Moscow for control of the Russian lands.

In 1386 the Lithuanian ruler married a Polish princess and began to convert his people to Latin Christianity. As a result of this personal union with Poland, Catholic and Polish influences in Lithuania-Russia grew. The union also strengthened the state, and, though checked by Moscow in the east, Lithuania defeated the Germans in the famous Battle of Tannenberg in 1410 and soon extended its suzerainty southwestward toward the Balkans. In 1569 by the Union of Lublin Lithuania and Poland were formally joined. The resulting state was predominantly Polish and continued to contend with Moscow.

Although the most that Dmitrii Donskoi could accomplish against the Lithuanians was to check their expansion eastward into the heart of Russia, he did win an important and famous victory over the Mongols at the Battle of Kulikovo Field in 1380. The *Primary Chronicle* has left us a stirring, colorful, and somewhat exaggerated description of that encounter:

There never was such a mighty Russian Army, for all forces combined numbered some 200,000. . . . A week later, on September 6, they reached the River Don. Then he [Dmitrii] received a letter from the Reverend Abbot Sergei urging him to fight the Tatars. Dmitrii, however, ordered his troops to put on their native garments while he himself waited for a long time, contemplating. . . . Early Saturday morning, September 8, he told his troops to cross the river and go to the meadow. At first there was a heavy fog but when it later disappeared everyone crossed the Don; there was a real multitude of troops as far as one could see. . . .

At six o'clock in the morning the godless Tatars appeared in the field and faced the Christians . . . and when these two great forces met they covered an area thirteen versts [eight miles] long. And there was a great massacre and bitter warfare and great noise . . . and blood flowed like a heavy rain. . . . At nine o'clock God took mercy on the Christians; many saw an angel and saintly martyrs helping the Christians. . . . Shortly thereafter the godless fled and the Christians pursued them . . . to their camp where they took all of their wealth and their cattle, killing many and trampling others.[1]

This defeat was the beginning of the end for the Mongols, even though two years later they counterattacked and burned Moscow.

Dmitrii's successor, Vasilii I (1389–1425), built up the economic strength of his domain and expanded Moscow's holdings. When he died, a struggle for the throne broke out, and a period of political turmoil ensued. In the fighting the eldest son, Vasilii II (1425–1462), was blinded. After finally establishing himself securely in power, he ruled successfully and in 1452 refused to pay any further tribute to the Mongols, although he left it to his son, Ivan III, formally to renounce Mongol suzerainty over Russia in 1480.

During the reign of Vasilii the Blind, the Russian Orthodox Church took an important step toward becoming an independent institution. With the Byzantine Empire gravely threatened by the Turks, the Greek Orthodox Church had reached a tentative reconciliation with the Roman Catholic Church in the political hope of ensuring European assistance against Turkish attacks. The majority of the clergy in Russia repudiated this agreement and in 1443 established a separate church administration. Moreover, in 1453 the Turks captured Constantinople, and the Russian Church was on its own in any case.

In the course of the long reigns of Ivan III (the Great) and Vasilii III from 1462 to 1533, the Muscovite state and system took nearly final form, and many of the basic institutions that characterized Russian civilization down to the 1700s were firmly established. It was also the period of the maximum expansion of Moscow: it grew from a still relatively small principality in northeastern Russia to a major European power stretching hundreds of miles in every direction from its capital (see Map 4). Ivan the Great (1462–1505) in particular brought to their fullest development the four basic methods used by his predecessors to "gather the Russian lands": inheritance, colonization of unoccupied areas in the north and east, purchase, and conquest.

The defeat by Ivan of the republic of Novgorod in the 1470s brought under Moscow's control Novgorod's vast holdings in the north, as well as its trade contacts through the Baltic with Europe and Scandinavia. Novgorod fell at last, after over one hundred years' opposition to Moscow, because it was a badly divided society. The elite looked to Lithuania for help against Muscovite encroachments, but the majority of the people, resenting the boyars and merchants anyway, objected to allying with Catholics and fought Ivan's forces only halfheartedly. The Novgorodians were defeated first in 1471 and then in 1478, after further resistance, were completely humiliated. The *veche* bell, Novgorod's symbol of freedom, was seized and taken to Moscow, and its lands were annexed to the Muscovite state. In 1485 a similar fate befell Moscow's old competitor, Tver. Thus, Ivan the Great both absorbed Moscow's nearest rivals and formally liberated Russia from the Mongol yoke. Only Lithuania-Russia remained to challenge Moscow for leadership of the lands of the former Kievan state.

Under Vasilii III (1505–1533) Moscow further extended its sway, particularly westward against Lithuania, and the important cities of Pskov and Smolensk were annexed. Vasilii also exerted pressure against Moscow's main enemy to the east, the Khanate of Kazan, ruled by descendants of the Mongols.

The extensive expansion under these two important rulers was accompanied by important political and social changes. Although in many respects the Muscovite rulers still ruled the state much as if it were their private domain, state administration became both more complex and more institutionalized. At the same time as the power and authority of the rulers increased, grander and more prestigious symbols and trappings were adopted. One reflection of this was the marriage in 1472 of Ivan III to Zoe Paleologus, a niece of the last Byzantine emperor. At about the same time the title of grand prince was superseded by the designation of *autocrat* or *tsar*, both borrowed from Byzantine practice. *Autocrat* in its Russian translation meant literally the self-wielder of power but was increasingly interpreted as the holder of unlimited authority. *Tsar* (derived from the Latin *caesar*) also connoted complete and absolute power. Finally, in 1493, Ivan the Great took for himself the appellation *Gosudar* (ga-sóo-dar), or Sovereign, of All the Russian Lands.

The new grandeur of titles was complemented by adoption of a new symbol, the two-headed eagle used by both the Byzantine emperor and the Holy Roman Emperor in Europe, which lasted down to 1917, and by development of elaborate court ceremonials, including the formal anointing and coronation of the tsar in a Kremlin cathedral. As a reflection of his new status, Tsar Vasilii III opened diplomatic relations with the Holy Roman Emperor and the Pope in Europe and with the Turkish sultan in Constantinople.

The most important political development, however, was the growth of the concept of state service. In the past the majority of the prince's warriors, administrators, and servitors had been boyars. Customarily each boyar had his own hereditary estate, or *votchina*, and on it he exercised almost total authority, without interference from the prince or the state. He contracted with the prince to perform specific duties in return for certain rewards and was free to leave the prince's service at any time (and to sign on with another prince if he wished). In short, the prince had relatively little hold over a boyar, except to offer him money, trade, or protection that he could not obtain on his own. During the course of the rise of the Muscovite state and as the princes of Moscow saw the territory seized by them grow, they naturally tried to set up a system of land tenure and service over which they would have more control.

Increasingly, they took on servitors who were not boyars (or who were sometimes impoverished or landless boyars) and who in return for service received a grant of land to support them. This land was called a *pomestie* (pa-més-tye), and at first it was allotted to the servitor only for the duration of his service. Later, the *pomestie*, like the *votchina*, became hereditary. Clearly, these men of service were much more under the thumb of the prince or tsar, and Vasilii III tried to prevent both boyars and servitors from leaving his service. There was even discussion that such an act was treasonous. In retrospect, it is surprising how quickly the concept of obligatory service to the state emerged in the fifteenth and early sixteenth centuries. In the next chapter we will see how important it became.

There were obviously significant social implications of this idea of service. One was that it began to be applied to other groups in the population, especially the peasants. An assumption that the peasants too owed an obligation to the state and that this could best be met by service to the landlord, whether prince, monastery, boyar, or servitor, arose. Moreover, as a money economy grew with the expansion of the state, peasants became more indebted to landlords, and the terms of loans and of sharecropping arrangements became increasingly burdensome. As a result, although serfdom (the binding of the peasant to the land) did not develop fully until some decades later, by the early 1500s the peasant's right to move to other land or to the service of a different lord had been restricted to a two-week period in the fall, after the harvest was in.

Commerce remained a significant part of economic life in Muscovy. One of the first European travelers to report his observations of the city, Ambrosio Contarini, an Italian diplomat en route home to Venice from Persia, passed through Moscow in 1476. He described the Moscow market as follows:

> By the end of October the river which passes through the city is frozen over, and shops and bazaars for the sale of all sorts of things are erected on it, scarcely anything being sold in the town. They do this, as the river, from being surrounded on all sides by the city, and so protected from the wind, is less cold than anywhere else. On this frozen river may be seen daily numbers of cows

and pigs, great quantities of corn, wood, hay, and every other necessary, nor does the supply fail during the whole winter. . . . [Cows and pigs] are frozen whole, and it is curious to see so many skinned cows standing upright on their feet. . . . Horses run on the river when it is frozen, and a good deal of amusement takes place. Sometimes, also a neck is broken. . . . A great many merchants frequent this city from Germany and Poland during the winter for the sole purpose of buying pelts such as the furs of young goats, foxes, ermines, squirrels, wolves, and other animals. . . .[2]

The tsar engaged actively in trade, and as in other areas of Muscovite society, he did his best to control the commercial life of the city.

Concomitant with the increase in the power of the grand prince and tsar, the authority, wealth, and importance of the Russian Orthodox Church grew. After 1453, when the Turks seized Constantinople, the Russian churchmen concluded that the tasks of defending Orthodox Christianity and ensuring the purity of the faith had fallen to them. This gave rise to the theory of the Third Rome, which, put most simply, declared that the first Rome had fallen because of heresy within the church, that the second Rome (Constantinople) had succumbed to the infidel Turks, and that Moscow was the Third Rome, the new center of true Christian belief—and a fourth Rome there would not be.

This was primarily a religious explanation of secular events and did not produce, as some Russophobes have contended, a Muscovite plan for expansion and for conversion of the non-Orthodox world. But the outlook reflected in the Third Rome idea certainly did make the Russian Orthodox Church (and therefore much of tsarist society) overly defensive and quite intolerant of ideas and influences from outside, including those from the Catholic (and later Protestant) West. To some extent the strong streak of xenophobia that kept surfacing in Russia in subsequent centuries can be traced back to the self-righteous commitment to protect the one true faith inherent in the theory of the Third Rome.

An important issue for the Orthodox Church in medieval Russia, as occurs frequently in organized religions when they expand and become rich, was the proper role and function of the Church in society. In the latter part of the 1400s and the first half of the 1500s, a group of reformers, called the Trans-Volga Elders and led by the monk Nil Sorskii, challenged the Church leadership, urging renunciation of worldly goods and pursuit of a simple monastic life. The reformers wanted the Church to give up its landholdings and other wealth and to emphasize instead contemplation and the striving for moral perfection. In the long run the reformers were defeated. As a result the Russian Church became even more focused on ritual and tradition and less concerned with intellectual innovation and the welfare of the people.

The challenge of the Trans-Volga Elders to established Church policy posed a dilemma for Tsars Ivan III and Vasilii III. In the past relations between the Church and state had seldom been a contentious issue. The met-

ropolitans of Moscow had worked hand in hand with the Muscovite
princes to advance their shared interests, the expansion of state and
Church. On a few occasions, the metropolitans had virtually ruled the principality when a prince was very young or when there was a succession
struggle. By the end of the fifteenth century, however, the tsars began to
look greedily upon the vast landholdings of the Church. The tsars could use
more land, both to support their court and to parcel out as *pomestie* to
their growing body of servitors.

Consequently, when the reformers first called for the Church to give up
its estates, Ivan III was sympathetic to their position, apparently hoping
that the state would acquire these holdings. On the other hand, the Trans-
Volga Elders also insisted on the complete separation of church and state,
demanding that the tsar and his government stay completely out of religious affairs. This plank of their platform was clearly less attractive since
victory for the reformers would have ended the close, mutually beneficial
cooperation between the secular power and the religious authority that had
been so instrumental in the rise of Moscow.

The Church leaders, in opposing Nil Sorskii and his followers, argued
that the interests of the Orthodox Church and the Muscovite state were
closely linked and that the Church should support and obey the tsar. This
fitted well the emerging concept of state service, and finally, after some wa-
vering, both Ivan III and Vasilii III backed the church hierarchy in condemning the reformers.

CONCLUSION

By the mid-1500s, well before the founding of the first colonies in North
America, the forerunner of the modern Russian state had been formed and
many of its basic policies and institutions established. In the course of its
formation several key principles had predominated, and were to continue
to do so.

In the first place, the Muscovite state arose out of a need in the forested
wilderness of northeastern Russia for security and for unity. The core of the
state-building experience was the constant struggle against first the Mongols and other princes and then the Lithuanians, the Novgorodians, and the
Mongols' descendants, the Tatars. Because the Moscow princes were talented and long-lived, they were better able to provide protection and to ensure cohesion in their own domains. But in return they demanded service to
them and to the emerging state. Assertion of the rights of boyars, or merchants, or peasants could lead to disunity and insecurity. Pluralism was not
encouraged, and traditional privileges were slowly eroded and finally were
largely abolished.

A second tenet on which unification of the Russian lands rested was a belief in the worth of the community, of the people as a whole. It was not
only that group or individual rights were a threat but rather that society

valued highly the preservation and cohesion of the community. This view, dating back to Kievan times in the concept of *sobornost'* in the Orthodox Church and in the collectivity of spontaneously formed peasant communes, was now reaffirmed in a new form: the common purpose and significance of the society as a whole as represented in the Muscovite state.

A third important view that predominated in Moscow was a sense of inferiority and of the need to overcome inherent liabilities. To survive and to expand, limited resources had to be husbanded and used efficiently. Surrounded on all sides by powerful enemies, the Moscow rulers were driven to mobilize the people and the society in order to prevail. Everything had to be subordinated to the effort to equalize the balance of forces and to restore the Russian state and civilization.

At the same time the people also benefited from the gathering of the Russian lands. Christianity and other important elements of Kievan civilization were preserved and transmitted. A reasonable degree of internal peace was achieved, and economic recovery from the Mongol period began. Russia reestablished extensive relations with the West in the 1400s, and divergent views and patterns still existed in Muscovite society. Yet in the next one hundred and fifty years, the state steadily strengthened its position, imposing increasingly heavy burdens on the bulk of the Muscovite population.

FURTHER READING

Fedotov, G. *The Russian Religious Mind*. Cambridge, Mass.: 1966.

Fennell, J. L. *Ivan the Great of Moscow*. London: 1961.

_____. *The Emergence of Moscow, 1305–59*. Berkeley: 1968.

_____. *The Crisis of Medieval Russia, 1200–1304*. London: 1983.

Florovsky, G. "The Problem of Old Russian Culture." *Slavic Review,* 21 (1962), 153–164.

Kaiser, D. *The Growth of Law in Medieval Russia*. Princeton, N.J.: 1981.

Kollman, Nancy Shields. *Kinship and Politics: The Making of the Muscovite Political System, 1345–1517*. Stanford, Calif.: 1987.

Martin, Janet. *Medieval Russia, 980–1584*. Cambridge: 1995.

Medlin, W. K. *Moscow and East Rome*. Geneva: 1952.

Thompson, M. W. *Novgorod the Great*. New York: 1967.

Vernadsky, George. *Russia at the Dawn of the Modern Age*. New Haven, Conn.: 1959.

Voyce, Arthur. *The Art and Architecture of Medieval Russia*. Norman, Okla.: 1964.

4

Ivan the Terrible and the Time of Troubles, 1533–1618

The unification of Russia under Moscow had laid the foundations of state and society, but the events of the next one hundred and fifty years built up and completed the structure, as we shall see in this chapter and the next. Political changes in the eighty years from the death of Vasilii III in 1533 to the election of Michael Romanov as tsar in 1613 marked a major turning point in Russian history, equal in importance to the reign of Peter the Great in the eighteenth century or to the Bolshevik and Stalinist revolutions in the two decades after 1917 (see the chart on p. 60).

Ivan IV (1533–1584) was known as *groznyi* in Russian, a word that is poorly rendered by the English *terrible*. It is more correctly translated as *awesome* or *inspiring reverential dread*. Nevertheless, because it is so well known, we will use the customary term in English-language writing, "Ivan the Terrible," hoping that the reader will bear in mind that Russians of his time and later viewed Ivan with both admiration and fear.

Ivan the Terrible sought, however irrationally at times, to expand considerably the borders of Muscovy and to increase central authority and control. The latter effort meant smashing the privileges of the boyar elite. The social conflict and oppression this generated, combined with an economic crisis and the huge cost of major foreign wars, brought state and society to near collapse and temporary anarchy. Russia narrowly missed dissolution again into petty principalities and was nearly conquered by Sweden and Poland. Yet by an extraordinary effort, foreign enemies were repulsed, civil war ended, and state and society rebuilt. And making these turbulent times even more dramatic, love, hate, madness, deception, and heroism all figured significantly in the events of this era.

THE PERSONALITY AND CHARACTER OF IVAN THE TERRIBLE

Everyone agrees that Ivan the Terrible was violent and cruel and acted at times in a paranoiac fashion. Some historians go further and believe he had a severe personality disorder bordering on madness. Others argue that al-

TSARS OF RUSSIA, 1547–1917

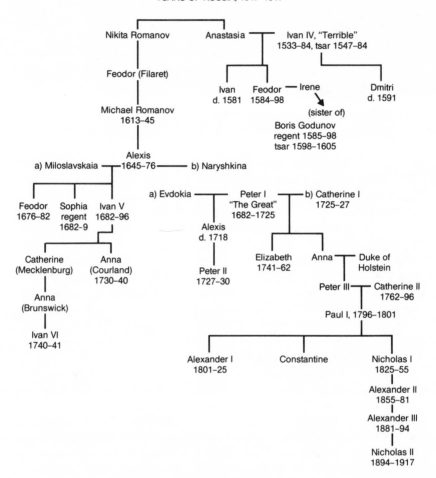

though he certainly behaved irrationally on occasion, he displayed consider-able method in his "madness" and was most of the time an intelligent, far-sighted ruler driven to extreme measures by scheming and implacable oppo-nents both at home and abroad. One interesting historical-medical analysis, drawing on eyewitness descriptions of the tsar's person and behavior, con-cludes that Ivan was suffering from syphilis (which spread rapidly through Europe in the sixteenth century). This disease progressively affected his brain as he aged, causing near insanity and finally death. Naturally this can-not be proved, but such a theory explains rather well certain aspects of Ivan's behavior, although it fails to account for the extraordinarily long pe-riod, over twenty years, that he acted unpredictably and outrageously.

There is some dispute as well about his general level of ability and intelligence. Traditionally, Ivan has been viewed as well educated for his time, widely read, and possessing some skill as a writer and thinker. Recently it has been alleged that letters attributed to him were forgeries and that in fact he was quite unlettered and was altogether a rather crude and uncultured person. In my view, he was certainly literate and whether or not he actually wrote the pieces bearing his name, he was a clever and unusually able leader, though obviously unstable emotionally.

Without getting into a complex Freudian analysis, it is clear that Ivan the Terrible's childhood and upbringing distorted his personality, his values, and his outlook on the world. His father, Vasilii III, died when Ivan was only three. For another five years his life was reasonably normal, with Ivan as a child ruler and his mother serving as regent, in concert with her advisers. Unfortunately, the most powerful boyars resented her position, and when she died (perhaps poisoned) in 1538, a bloody, no-holds-barred struggle for power between two prominent boyar families, the Shuiskiis and the Belskiis, broke out. Ivan, caught in the middle and alternately ignored and abused, witnessed beatings, torture, and murder. Apparently a sensitive boy, Ivan was undoubtedly made suspicious and resentful by the intrigues and violence surrounding him. This atmosphere is melodramatically portrayed in the film *Ivan the Terrible,* made in the 1940s by the great Soviet movie director Sergei Eisenstein.

Ivan also developed at this time a streak of cruelty and suppressed rage and a deep-seated determination to revenge himself on those responsible for his mistreatment and humiliation. Though perhaps exaggerating, Ivan later in life wrote:

> But when I had entered upon my eighth year of life and when thus our subjects had achieved their desire, namely to have the kingdom without a ruler, then they did not deem us, their sovereigns, worthy of any loving care, but themselves ran after wealth and glory.... How many boyars and well-wishers of our father ... did they massacre! And the courts and the villages and the possessions of our uncles did they seize....

But not only the usurpation of power and wealth irked Ivan; petty harassments aroused his indignation as well:

> they began to feed us as though we were foreigners or the most wretched servants. What sufferings did I [not] endure through [lack of] clothing and through hunger! For in all things my will was not my own....[1]

As he entered his teens, Ivan began to assert his rights, and in 1547, when he was sixteen, he had himself crowned tsar and married Anastasia, a member of the well-liked boyar family, the Romanovs. Even though it was a political marriage, it turned out well, and Ivan lived happily with Anastasia

Figure 6.   Russian boyars in the 1600s; some of their dress reflects Polish stylistic influence. (Courtesy of the British Library)

until her death thirteen years later. Many historians believe she was a beneficent influence on the tsar, and it is certainly true that his more unorthodox and violent behavior began after Anastasia died.

THE REFORMS OF IVAN IV

In 1547, the year of Ivan's coronation, extensive rioting occurred in Moscow, and social disorders broke out in other parts of the country. These were symptomatic of major problems that were coming to a head about the time Ivan ascended the throne. The most general was that the Russian state, including by now about nine or ten million people and having expanded too rapidly, possessed an insufficient resource base to support it and too small and antiquated an administration and social system to manage it well. Ivan attempted both to build up the strength of Russia and to rationalize and improve its governance. The first task led him into conflict with aggressive foreign foes—Tatars, Swedes, and Poles—and the second, into a remorseless and violent struggle with the most powerful single group in Russia: the aristocracy of princely families and boyars (see Figure 6).

At first Ivan the Terrible's reforming efforts went well. He surrounded himself with a group of able advisers, including Macarius, metropolitan of the Orthodox Church; Sylvester, a well-educated priest; and Adashev, a talented servitor. These men and Ivan's other close collaborators came to be known as the Chosen Council, although it is unclear whether the council ever existed as a formal body. Ivan did not directly challenge the *boyar duma*, the ancient consultative body to the Russian princes, trying instead to work around it. In 1549 he convened a much broader advisory group, known eventually as the *zemskii sobor* (assembly of the land), representing not only the boyar elite but gentry (servitors), Church officials, townspeople, and on one occasion, a few state peasants (from estates owned by the tsar or the government). Information on the composition and actions of this *zemskii sobor* is lacking, but probably Ivan discussed with it the various reform measures he was about to undertake. Several times in later years he called together and consulted with *zemskii sobors*.

A high priority for Ivan was to improve the fighting capacity of the army. The top commands were held by the highest-ranking boyars, regardless of ability, and this system often created serious leadership deficiencies. Although Ivan could not abolish the boyar-defended system of command by elite birth or rank, he managed to institute rules that permitted exceptions under special circumstances. In this way he was able, for certain campaigns and battles, to advance the best officers to top posts. Ivan also regularized the terms of military service: how long a boyar or member of the gentry had to serve, what he received and contributed, and what his responsibilities were. Finally, he accelerated and strengthened earlier efforts to form specialized military units of musketeers (called *streltsy*), artillerymen, and contract cavalry, all of whom were especially useful in manning the growing number of forts and outposts along Russia's continuously expanding frontier.

Second, Ivan supervised collection and codification of the laws and a reform of local government. Both were important to a more orderly and equitable administration of the state, especially when linked to his efforts to build up a core of efficient central administrators in Moscow. Improvement of local government was greatly needed since governors and other local officials were often corrupt and systematically exploited the local population. The new system did not end all abuses but was a step forward at least.

Third, Ivan convened a major council of the Orthodox Church, which came to be known as the Council of the Hundred Chapters (from the number of charges given to it). It clarified a number of issues in internal Church administration, endorsed strongly the close tie between the tsar and the Church, and limited the right of the Church to acquire more land.

Finally, Ivan the Terrible made a strong effort to strengthen Russia's ties with Europe. He invited European specialists to Moscow to help improve the army, to erect new buildings and churches, to introduce new technology, and to practice medicine. Only a few came, but they were instrumental in introducing new ideas and techniques to Muscovite society. In the 1570s Ivan established a special suburb of Moscow for foreign residents, and by the 1600s many of them were performing important services for Ivan's suc-

Figure 7. *St. Basil's Cathedral in Red Square in Moscow. Although built by Ivan the Terrible in the 1500s, today it is still a dazzling sight, with its multicolored cupolas and facades. (Courtesy of the United Nations)*

cessors. Ivan also ordered construction of St. Basil's, the wonderfully ornate and colorful cathedral in Red Square. No tourist dares go to Moscow without being photographed in front of this splendid building with its many octagons and shimmering bulbous domes (see Figure 7).

Through good luck Ivan also established friendly and profitable relations with England. In 1553 Richard Chancellor, an English explorer searching for a northern route to the Orient, happened into the White Sea in north Russia. He went on to Moscow, where Ivan cordially welcomed him, and an important trade grew out of this chance encounter. Some English specialists also came to Russia in the latter part of the 1500s.

IVAN VERSUS THE ARISTOCRACY

In none of these early successes of his reign did Ivan confront head-on the basic issue of Muscovite politics: could the tsar exercise unlimited authority, or was his growing power restricted by the customary privileges of princely families and boyars? In this contest the aristocracy had several advantages. First was tradition. From the very founding of Russia they had been the senior warriors and administrators of the state and the closest advisers of the grand princes of Kiev and Moscow. It was unthinkable that the tsar could act and the state function without their close cooperation and full support. Second, they wielded considerable power: they owned the largest estates, could provide the greatest numbers of armed men for the tsar's army, and had almost total control over the population on their lands. Third, the boyars had institutionalized access to power through the *boyar duma* and through holding most of the top positions in the army and in the government.

At the same time the boyars, particularly when compared to the landed nobility of Europe, were quite weak. They were few in numbers, probably less than two hundred families in the 1500s. They had no corporate identity and indeed could not rely on any extensive body of custom or law that gave them privileges and rights as a class (instead of as individuals). Moreover, they were deeply disunited, quarreling endlessly over precedence and rank and resorting to intrigue and brutality in their internecine struggles, instead of uniting against the tsar. Finally, their position had been gradually undercut by the rise over the preceding century and a half of gentry, or men of service. The latter, originally considered a clearly inferior class, at first held their estates only as long as they served the grand prince, and they were clearly dependent on the tsar; the boyars, however, had hereditary title to their land and in theory could leave the tsar's service at any time. Gradually but steadily in the 1500s the distinctions between boyars and gentry disappeared: Both held their land on a hereditary basis and both owed obligatory service (though some boyars fled to Lithuania to escape this burden).

The tsar also had certain advantages in an open struggle with the boyars. He had the backing of the Church as an institution, no matter what individual prelates and priests might feel. Second, the theory and aura of autocracy—of unlimited rule—inherited from the Byzantine empire and nurtured under Ivan III and his successors, although not fully accepted in Muscovite society of the mid-1500s, served to strengthen the claim of Ivan the Terrible to absolute authority. Finally, he could count on the support of the gentry, who of course stood to gain much from diminution of the boyars' position. Ivan, however—unlike his contemporary absolute monarchs in the West, such as Henry VIII—did not have a strong merchant class or autonomous towns on which to draw for financial and political backing.

In retrospect, we may view the fierce struggle between Ivan the Terrible and the boyars that broke out in the 1560s as an unnecessary and even tragic contest, with neither side taking account of how much the struggle endangered the state. In the end, although the power of the boyars was not totally broken, the principle of state service and the growing authority of the tsar were confirmed and enhanced. But at the time it was far from clear what the outcome would be, and the resulting bloodshed and disruption very nearly brought down the Muscovite regime altogether. Had Ivan not won, the nature of Russian society and the subsequent course of Russian history would certainly have been quite different.

Although the evidence is contradictory, two developments seemed to have triggered the bloody showdown between Ivan the Terrible and the boyars. One was an unlucky event, the serious illness of the tsar in 1553. At that time he asked his privileged subjects, including top government officials and boyars, to swear allegiance to his son Dmitrii as heir to the throne. Some did, but many at first refused, apparently because Dmitrii was still a child, and because they feared another period of minority rule marked by internal strife and weakness as had occurred in Ivan's boyhood. The incident infuriated and frightened Ivan, who, when he recovered from his illness, apparently marked down for future retribution those boyars whom he believed had wanted to usurp his family's right to the throne.[2]

The second event that brought on domestic discord in Moscow was disagreement over foreign policy. Although the Muscovite state had formally thrown off the Mongol yoke in 1480, the descendants of the Mongols continued to harass Russia from the south and east in the 1500s. Deciding that bold measures were needed, Ivan in 1551 launched a campaign against Moscow's nearest enemy, the Tatar Khanate of Kazan. In 1552 after a long siege Kazan itself, a city on the Volga River east of Moscow, was captured, and by 1557 the Russians had annexed the whole khanate. In 1556 Ivan also succeeded in capturing the Khanate of Astrakhan at the mouth of the Volga and adding it to his domain (see Map 5, next chapter). These conquests brought mainly non-Slavs into the expanding Russian state and added to the considerable diversity of Muscovite society. However, the Tatars of the Crimean khanate remained independent, and they, backed by the Ottoman Turks, launched major attacks against Ivan on several occasions throughout his reign and were not finally subdued by the Russians until more than two hundred years later.

In addition to security against the Muslim Tatars, Ivan had an important foreign policy goal in the other direction, toward Europe. Ever since Ivan III's absorption of Lord Novgorod the Great, the Muscovite state had had a toehold on the shore of the Baltic Sea. Ivan the Terrible wanted to increase Russia's territory on the Baltic coast and to expand trade with northern and central Europe. Blocking his way were the Livonian order of Germanic knights, who held what is today Estonia and Latvia, and to their south the Polish-Lithuanian state (see Map 4). In 1558 Ivan launched what came to be known as the Livonian War and at first met with great success. By the early 1560s the Livonian order had been destroyed and some territory captured from Lithuania. It was, however, a bloody and expensive war, and it meant that Russia was fighting on two fronts at the same time. It required higher taxes and more recruits for the army. Not only was there popular grumbling, but some of Ivan's advisers, including members of the Chosen Council, warned against getting too deeply involved in a costly military struggle in the west.

In 1560 as the policy dispute over the Livonian War was heating up, Ivan's first wife, Anastasia, died suddenly. Whether removal of her loving and calming influence was a factor in Ivan's subsequent irrational behavior is unclear, but in any case Ivan shortly launched an extraordinary vendetta against his friends and against the leading boyar families. Accusing his trusted colleagues Sylvester and Adashev of conspiring to poison his wife,

Ivan sent Sylvester into remote exile and threw Adashev into prison, where he died. Ivan then turned against their circle of friends and began, mercilessly and without trial, to have them tortured and executed. There seemed no rhyme or reason to his actions, and during this reign of terror a number of prominent officials and boyars fled to Lithuania. Ivan the Terrible immediately branded these flights as treason and increased the fury of his persecution against those who remained.

One bizarre episode followed another until suddenly and without explanation the tsar left Moscow in late 1564 with the treasury and withdrew to a monastery in a remote area some distance from the city. This action created bafflement and uncertainty, and since no one knew what to do, emissaries from Moscow begged the tsar to return. Finally, several months later, he reappeared, looking haggard and distraught. He agreed to resume his position as tsar only if his authority to punish traitors and evildoers as he saw fit were confirmed and he were allowed to set up a separate and autonomous area within the Muscovite state entirely under his control, conditions that the leading officials accepted.

Thus originated the strange institution called the *oprichnina* (uh-préech-neena), literally, "the area set apart." This area was under Ivan's personal rule and consisted of scattered territories and estates, many of which were seized from the princely families and boyars. The *oprichnina* included some of the best land, as well as districts of several cities. The rest of the country was left under regular administration. In 1572 Ivan, apparently convinced that he had broken the back of the opposition, ended the *oprichnina* and reunited the Muscovite tsardom.

Because the documents and memoirs from this period are sketchy, it is difficult to evaluate precisely the purpose and significance of the *oprichnina*. There is, however, little doubt that Ivan the Terrible considered it first and foremost as a weapon in his struggle with the boyars and princely families. To administer the *oprichnina*, he appointed ambitious and obedient servitors who did not hesitate to take harsh actions against his enemies and whom he rewarded with land grants and wealth. Ivan ignored or degraded the regular officials and boyars, and he confiscated the estates of many as a means both of punishing them and of undermining their economic and social position. At times the tsar was subject to fits of paranoia and rage against his imagined persecutors. He personally participated—and according to some accounts delighted—in the torture and murder of individuals and groups. On one occasion he killed his favorite son during a furious outburst. At other times he repented of his deeds and sought solace and atonement in contemplation and prayer.

The *oprichnina* as an institution, combined with Ivan's unbridled anger and violent oppression, succeeded in weakening and demoralizing the boyars, and for the last twenty years of his reign Ivan encountered little opposition to his half-mad rule. But the cost was enormous. The division of the state into two parts wrecked the administration and seriously damaged the economy. The aura of terror and suspicion made normal social or political life impossible, and educated Muscovite society became paralyzed and cowed. Ivan the Terrible, with no one to gainsay him, plunged ahead with the draining Livonian War, exhausting the country and sapping its resources. Moreover, the fortunes of war turned against him, and when peace was finally made in 1583, after twenty-five years of wasting struggle, he had lost almost everything originally gained, and Russia was back where it had started. Or perhaps the country was worse off, because in the course of the war the Swedes had entered the fray and were now allied with the Poles as deadly enemies of Moscow.

What did it all mean? Clearly Ivan the Terrible was mentally and emotionally disturbed, at the very least, and we need only look to the recent past in our own "modern" century, to the case of Adolf Hitler, to appreciate how terrible can be the consequences when an intelligent person with a pathological personality wields absolute power, even for a brief time. Yet it would be a mistake to write off Ivan as simply deranged. His struggle with the aristocracy was also a contest for control of the state, and although his opponents were perhaps less serious a threat than he imagined, the outcome confirmed the supreme power of the tsar. The shape of the full absolutism that was to take final form in the 1600s and 1700s was clearly presaged in the tsardom of Ivan the Terrible.

At the same time the cost was exorbitant. The people were oppressed and squeezed, the economy ravaged, and the society nearly torn apart by civil persecution and unrelenting terror. Although Ivan succeeded in securing Russia's eastern frontier, his grand design for the Baltic collapsed, and he was unable to subdue the Crimean Tatars in the south. Most significantly, the fears and tensions of his rule, as well as the near ruination of the country, set the stage for one of the most sensational and dramatic periods in Russian history, aptly named the Time of Troubles.

THE TIME OF TROUBLES, 1598–1613

Three main issues characterized the tumultuous era of the Time of Troubles: a struggle for political power, a widespread social revolution, and a national movement to prevent foreign domination of Russia. These themes were closely intertwined and were often being played out simultaneously. Nevertheless, to make comprehensible the confused events of the Time of Troubles, we will consider each of them in turn.

Struggle for Political Power

The main thread of Muscovite history into the 1500s was the extension of the personal power and authority of the grand prince-tsar from his own estate to the larger principality and finally to the unified Russian lands. Facilitated by the continuity of a dynasty descended from Kiev, this process had culminated in the expansionist and absolutist rule of Ivan the Terrible. Tradition and the God-given status of the tsar glued the diverse Muscovite holdings together and shored up state power. Moreover, as we saw, Moscow was fortunate in having long-lived rulers and few succession problems. Thus, when Ivan's successor, the weak and sickly Feodor, died in 1598 without an heir, this event not only provoked a major crisis but very nearly led to the complete dissolution of the state that had been laboriously built up in the preceding 250 years.

The bitterness and resentment still felt by the upper classes as a result of their forcible subjugation by Ivan the Terrible exacerbated the turmoil that followed the end of the dynasty. The great boyar families were determined to recoup their fortunes and recapture their dominant political position in Muscovite society. The gentry, who had benefited from Ivan's *oprichnina* but were suffering economically, were no less determined to advance their own interests by seizing as much political power as possible. The merchants, who had not fared particularly well under Ivan and who were considered second-class citizens by the others, believed a golden opportunity to improve their position was at hand. The stage was set for a maximum amount of political strife.

The prologue was provided by a twenty-one-year period, from 1584 to 1605, during which the talented Boris Godunov dominated the political life of Russia. A minor boyar who participated in the administration of Ivan the Terrible's *oprichnina,* he was the brother-in-law of Tsar Feodor. Through his sister, Boris Godunov acquired a commanding position in affairs of state early in Feodor's reign. Beginning in 1587, he served as regent and was in fact the ruler of Russia, while Feodor, who was extremely devout, concentrated on religious affairs. Godunov was talented and just, attempting to settle the country down domestically and to patch up the quarrels with Sweden and Poland. He skillfully helped engineer establishment in Moscow of a patriarchate, the highest administrative unit in the Greek Orthodox Church, and had his friend Metropolitan Job named the first patriarch. This arrangement permitted enlargement of the church hierarchy and enhanced Moscow's international prestige because the other patriarchs in the Orthodox Church were located in areas under Turkish rule.

Nonetheless, Boris Godunov had two strikes against him. Although he promoted trade and ties with the West, he could do little to overcome Moscow's fundamental economic problems: declining agriculture and huge losses caused by Ivan's wars. He also had no legitimate claim to the throne. As a consequence, his enemies spread rumors that Godunov had been involved in a 1591 conspiracy that resulted in the death of Ivan the Terrible's youngest son, Dmitrii (a story dramatically told in Mussorgsky's great opera, *Boris Godunov*). In any case, in 1598, when Feodor died childless, Boris Godunov clearly aspired to be his successor.

In this unprecedented situation a *zemskii sobor* of some five hundred representatives of the boyars, gentry, clergy, and townspeople was convened. For the first time in the history of Moscow no natural heir to the throne existed. Moreover, there was no law of succession. Because of the powerful position he had developed over the preceding decade and because he undoubtedly was the most suitable candidate available, Boris Godunov was elected tsar in 1598.

His reign began auspiciously, but before long events over which he had little control undermined his position. First, in 1601–1603 Russia suffered a terrible drought and famine. Despite extraordinary efforts by the government to relieve the misery, people were reduced to eating fodder and bark and even, on occasion, to cannibalism, as this contemporary account makes clear:

> But I swear by God that in Moscow I saw, with my own eyes, people who rolled in the streets and, like animals, ate grass during the summer and hay during the winter. . . . Human flesh, finely ground, baked in pies (a kind of pastry), was sold and consumed like beef. . . . Daily, on the Tsar's orders they collected hundreds of corpses and carried them outside the city in wagons—an undertaking which was awesome to observe. Specially appointed people washed the dead, wrapped them in a white cloth, put red shoes on them, and wheeled them to the church to be buried.[3]

Second, beginning in 1603 rumors began to spread that Ivan's last son, Dmitrii, had not died in 1591; it was whispered that he not only still lived but was preparing to assert his rightful claim to the throne. Despite his best efforts Tsar Boris was unable to squelch these allegations. Moreover, stories also began to circulate that Godunov was a murderer and usurper and that Russia was being punished by God for Godunov's sins. How much Boris's boyar opponents were behind these stories is unclear, but there is no doubt that the boyars fanned the flames of slander, some because they were jealous of Godunov's position, others because they had been slighted or oppressed by his policies.

The upshot was that in the fall of 1604 a major rebellion against Tsar Boris broke out, headed by a pretender to the throne known retrospectively as the first False Dmitrii. Allegedly a former monk, he deluded himself into believing that he was indeed the lawful heir to the throne. His supporters included a group of Polish nobles, who were patently using him to further their own ends, and a motley collection of discontented Russians, some of whom were convinced he was in fact Dmitrii and others who didn't care about his claims as long as they could channel their grievances against the government through him.

The challenge of this first pretender opened eight years of chaotic and complex maneuvering for political supremacy among the boyars, gentry, and merchants, who backed first one candidate to the throne and then another. At the nadir of this unseemly contest, there was no tsar at all, and it seemed the vaunted Muscovite autocracy would disappear altogether. Greatly complicating the political struggle was the eruption of a major social revolution shortly after the appearance of the first False Dmitrii.

Social Revolution

Although a number of fringe and semicriminal elements participated, the main groups involved in the widespread social revolution that broke out in Russia in 1605–1606 were peasants, cossacks, slaves, and runaway serfs. As we will see in the next chapter, by the early 1600s *serfdom,* the binding of peasants to the land, had developed quite far though the process was not yet complete. In the last part of the sixteenth century an agricultural depression and the exactions accompanying Ivan the Terrible's *oprichnina* and his wars had made the situation of the rural population grave, and the drought and famine of 1601–1602 made it desperate. As a result, almost all groups in the countryside, particularly in central and southern Russia, whether they were still free peasants, were loosely bound to the landlord by debts, were fully enserfed, or had run away from their obligations and their lords, could unite against the upper classes and the government. And since symbolism and superstition were important in their lives, so much the better if they could believe their rebellious fury was being expended in support of the "true" tsar and the righting of a dynastic wrong.

The cossacks need a special word of explanation. The name *cossack,* originally derived from a warlike, nomadic group of horsemen in Central Asia, began at this time to be applied to bands of independent frontiersmen who lived on the southern and eastern borderlands of the Russian state. Some cossacks were mainly freebooters and brigands; others were farmers and herders. Cossack bands frequently included escapees from authority, such as tax evaders, runaway serfs, and fugitives from the lord's or the tsar's justice. Proud of their skills as horsemen and fighters, determined to remain free, and fickle in their political loyalties during the Time of Troubles, the cossacks were an effective but volatile force in both the struggle for power and the social revolution. On a number of occasions they switched sides unexpectedly, tipping the balance in favor of one faction or another. As we shall see, they continued to play a significant role in subsequent Russian history.

When the first False Dmitrii invaded Russia in October 1604 with his Polish supporters, the first to rally to his cause were cossacks. But other dissatisfied rural elements soon swelled his ranks, and in the spring of 1605, after the unexpected natural death of Boris Godunov, Dmitrii's forces captured Moscow, and he was installed as tsar. Ugly and ungainly in appearance, he tried to placate the boyars and the general populace, but his idiosyncratic habits and the haughty conduct of his Polish entourage soon alienated the Muscovites. Having used Dmitrii to dislodge Tsar Boris, the boyars and princely families were now quite prepared to discard the pretender. New rumors, that Dmitrii was an impostor, began to spread. After he had been on the throne less than a year, the first False Dmitrii was unseated and killed in a coup led by the boyar Prince Vasilii Shuisky, who then arranged to have himself proclaimed tsar. Dmitrii's ashes were supposedly loaded in a cannon and fired back toward Poland.

With Shuisky on the throne, it seemed the boyars had won the political contest. The new tsar was compelled to provide the boyars guarantees against arbitrary treatment and punishment, and his policies reflected their interests. Though his "election" as tsar had been enthusiastically endorsed by the Moscow mobs, who were particularly incensed against the Polish clique that had dominated the city during the brief reign of the first False Dmitrii, Shuisky could offer them little once he was enthroned. As a result, they soon turned against him and joined a countrywide revolt to overthrow the boyar tsar.

With the central authority tarnished and weakened by the dynastic struggle and the successive coups, the country began to dissolve into anarchy. Local governors rebelled, as did non-Russian groups who opposed Muscovite repression. Most important, the lower classes of southern Russia rose in a massive conflagration that raged throughout 1606 and 1607. The rebels' leader was Ivan Bolotnikov, a colorful and extremely able demagogue of obscure origins, who roused and organized the masses to fight for their own interests and needs and to destroy the boyars and landlords.

During this period various new pretenders emerged, including one who claimed to be the son of Tsar Feodor, even though the record was clear that Feodor had had no sons. Finally, in August 1607, a second False Dmitrii appeared and quickly gathered a considerable following. Nicknamed the "Brigand of Tushino" for the Moscow suburb where he established his headquarters, he soon rallied all the anti-government forces. Although neither he nor his close advisers took his claim to the throne seriously, many were happy to follow his banner in the hope of seeing order restored and obtaining what they wanted. In two bizarre episodes the mother of the real Dmitrii, now a nun, declared the second False Dmitrii her son, and the Polish wife of the first False Dmitrii recognized him as her husband and bore him a son, the "Baby Brigand." As the social revolution burned itself out during 1608 and with neither the boyar tsar, Vasilii Shuisky, nor the second False Dmitrii able to defeat the other, a stalemate developed.

Movement for National Defense

At this juncture a new theme was introduced: a struggle against foreigners meddling in Russian affairs. This had been presaged in the resentment against the Polish followers of the first False Dmitrii, but it became a major element in the Time of Troubles in early 1609, when Tsar Vasilii, with his back to the wall, turned to Sweden for help. In return for territorial concessions along the Baltic and a promise Russia would ally with Sweden against Poland, the Swedes provided troops who helped Vasilii Shuisky's army put the second False Dmitrii to flight.

To counter this outside assistance for Shuisky, some of the second False Dmitrii's supporters appealed to the king of Poland, Sigismund III, for help. Sigismund, anxious to extend his influence in Russia and to thwart a Russo-Swedish alliance, invaded Russia and agreed to have his son placed on the Russian throne. But, most historians agree, Sigismund really wanted to rule Russia himself, and he apparently saw to it that negotiations over the conditions under which his son would become tsar broke down. Polish forces occupied Moscow, the Swedes attacked in the north because the Russians had allied with the Poles, and the second False Dmitrii reappeared in the southeast to make another try for the throne. In the midst of these disasters, Tsar Vasilii was deposed and sent to a monastery.

This was certainly the low point in the fortunes of the Muscovite state: with no tsar, the capital occupied by Poles and the northwest by Swedes, and a pretender stirring up trouble in the countryside, its chances for survival seemed slim. Yet the very gravity of the situation sparked an upsurge of national (or at least antiforeign) feeling and a determination to restore Russia's independence and some semblance of order. Soviet historians emphasized the breadth of popular participation in this national movement, but in fact the upper classes seem to have played the dominant role, for good reason. They had the most to lose under Polish domination and continuing civil disorder and the most to gain by resurrection of the Muscovite state of the 1500s, albeit without the arbitrary persecutions of Ivan the Terrible. Moreover, the effort at national regeneration began in the towns of north Russia, which had been least affected by the social revolution and which could still command enough economic resources to support the drive to expel the foreigners.

There was also a strong religious element in the national revival. The Catholic Poles, the main enemy, were considered heretical, and the head of the Russian Orthodox Church, Patriarch Hermogen, played an important role in initiating the national resistance movement. In all likelihood, many illiterate but devout Russians, bewildered by the kaleidoscopic events of the preceding few years, were delighted to be told at last who the true enemy was: the heretical Poles.

In 1612 two remarkable individuals, a butcher named Kuzma Minin, and an experienced general, Prince Dmitrii Pozharsky, combined their organizational, fighting, and inspirational talents to form a national army that liberated Moscow from the Poles by the end of the year. The army was supported by large contributions made by citizens of many towns, and there is little doubt, despite some exaggeration by Soviet historians, that this national movement represented a determined effort by Russians to take their destiny back into their own hands.

It is significant that once the Poles had been driven out, the first step of the leaders of the national resistance was to restore tsarist rule. A *zemskii sobor* was convened in early 1613, and after considerable deliberation it chose Michael Romanov as tsar, establishing a family that was to rule Russia for over three hundred years, down to 1917. Michael was only sixteen and thus had not been compromised in the earlier political machinations of the Time of Troubles. He was a grand-nephew of Anastasia, Ivan the Terrible's "good" wife, and thus indirectly related to the old dynasty. Perhaps most important, the Patriarch Hermogen backed him (although Hermogen died before the actual election), and Michael's father, the Metropolitan Filaret, was a popular and influential churchman and former boyar.

CONCLUSION

The new government of Tsar Michael was weak, and disorder and civil strife continued until at least 1618, which marks the beginning of firm rule and the end of the Time of Troubles. The most important direct results of this period were that the foreigners and Catholics were driven out, the Muscovite state and the purity of the Orthodox Church saved, and the tsardom restored. But equally significantly, under the surface the upper classes had salvaged their position (even though the boyars' effort to seize power was defeated), the lower classes succeeded only in postponing the day of their final enserfment, and development of autocratic rule could be resumed.

The most interesting question is why absolutist authority first expanded greatly under Ivan the Terrible and then, despite the wracking crisis of the Time of Troubles, survived to become the dominant political institution of modern Russian history? Although any answer must be speculative, four main factors explain this phenomenon, in my view.

In the first place, given the weak economy of Russia, strong central government was needed to mobilize the resources and people for the tasks of unification, growth, and defense. Since centralizing monarchs, fulfilling analogous goals, existed about the same time in western Europe, the Russian experience was hardly unique. But the power of the tsar to command obedience, sanctified by Byzantine tradition and theory and fortified by observation of Mongol practice, was crucial to the further development and expansion of the Muscovite state.

Second, the tsar became a symbol of unity and security in a fragmented and hostile world. This role, enhanced by memories of the glorious days of Kiev under the grand prince, had first taken shape when the prince was simply proprietor of an enlarged private estate turned into a principality; it had been expanded in the struggle to throw off the Mongol yoke and to gather the Russian lands. It is significant that during the Time of Troubles one common thread was the search for the "true" tsar, and again and again the people, both upper and lower classes, rallied around a pretender, no matter how flimsy his claims. Moreover, their first action to reunite the divided society was to elect a new tsar.

Third, the autocracy emerged, flourished, and survived because from the earliest days, first in Kiev and then in the 1300s in Moscow, it was linked with the Orthodox Church. In our secular era it is all too easy to overlook or forget the powerful hold of religion on people. Russians of this period may have understood little of Christian theology or of the ideas and politics of the patriarchs, metropolitans, and archbishops, but they devoutly believed in the rituals and physical presence of the Russian Orthodox Church. Thus, when state and church supported each other and the tsar acted as defender of the true faith as well as ruler of the Muscovite state, this association greatly reinforced his authority and his influence over the population.

Finally, it is important to remember that the tsars prevailed in part because no other group or institution in Muscovite society seemed capable of organizing society and building the state. We will see later how, just when classes and institutions competitive with the king were growing stronger in Europe, they were declining in Russia; in fact once Ivan the Terrible had undercut the power of the boyars, no group existed in Moscow to challenge seriously the growing absolutism of the tsar. The people could resist, individually or in the mass, as they did during Ivan the Terrible's depredations and during the Time of Troubles, but such resistance was either isolated defiance or disorganized rebellion. Even to make revolt coherent it was necessary to raise the standard of a false tsar or a boyar tsar. Group fought group, the masses struck out blindly at the government and their economic oppressors, landlords and merchants, but no alternative basis for organizing society was propounded.

As a result, Russia entered the seventeenth century, the era of the founding of the American colonies, with a battle-scarred but well-entrenched system of tsarist autocracy. What form it would take, how it might be shaped and even restrained in practice, and how the average Russian fared under it are questions to which we will turn in the next few chapters.

FURTHER READING

Barbour, Philip. *Dmitry Called the Pretender, 1605–06.* Boston: 1966.

Fennell, J. L., ed. *The Correspondence Between Prince Kurbsky and Tsar Ivan IV of Russia, 1564–1579.* Cambridge, England: 1955.

Hellie, Richard. *Slavery in Russia, 1450–1725.* Chicago: 1982.

Keenan, Edward. "Muscovy and Kazan." *Slavic Review*, Vol. 26, pp. 548–558. December 1967.

_____. *The Kurbsky-Groznyi Apocrypha.* Cambridge, Mass.: 1981.

Longworth, P. *The Cossacks.* New York: 1970.

Platonov, S. *The Time of Troubles*. Translated by J. T. Alexander. Lawrence, Ks.: 1970.

Skrynnikov, R. G. *Ivan the Terrible*. Translated by Hugh F. Graham. Gulf Breeze, Fla.: 1981.

_____. *The Time of Troubles: Russia in Crisis, 1604–1618*. Gulf Breeze, Fla.: 1988.

Vernadsky, George. *The Tsardom of Moscow, 1547–1682* (Part 1). New Haven, Conn.: 1969.

5

The Molding of Russian Society,
1613–1689

Forenoon prayers had not quite ended when Tsar Alexis heard a great hubbub outside the church. It was a hot summer morning, July 25, 1662, and the tsar, perturbed at this unexpected interruption of his daily devotions, called loudly to attendants in the courtyard beside the church, demanding to know what the commotion was all about. He soon learned that a mob was clamoring to see him, insisting that they be allowed to present their grievances to the tsar in person.

Alexis acted decisively and courageously. Ordering his wife and children, as well as some of the officials against whom the mob was railing, to take refuge in his nearby summer palace, the tsar walked out of the church to deal with the protesters. He was unaware that earlier that morning in Moscow, some ten miles from his summer retreat, riots had broken out over high taxes and allegations of corruption and that the crowds had accused several of his closest advisers of treasonous support of the king of Poland, with whom Russia was at war. A few hotheads had persuaded the mob to march out of the city to find Tsar Alexis himself.

To approach the tsar directly was unprecedented. He was ordinarily a remote and haughty figure, with whom only a few high officials, clergy, and court attendants were permitted to communicate. Nonetheless in this crisis Alexis listened to the rancorous and sometimes profane complaints of the mob's leaders. They demanded a lowering of taxes and the surrender to them of the officials and merchants they had accused. According to historian Joseph T. Fuhrmann, the tsar handled the situation masterfully:

> Alexis spoke to the rioters in a quiet way, hoping to calm them and persuade them to leave. He promised after mass to return to Moscow, to conduct a personal investigation, to right all wrongs. Several of the crowd grabbed Alexis by the buttons of his coat, shouting, "Whom do you believe—the traitors or us?" Alexis swore before God that his faith was in his subjects, and one member of the crowd stepped forward to seal this covenant by shaking the tsar's hand.[1]

Later that same day the tsar behaved quite differently. When a second mob approached him just as he was setting out for Moscow in accord with the promise he had made earlier, Alexis ordered loyal troops who had rallied round him in the interim to disperse the crowd by force. Over one hundred of the rioters were driven into a nearby river and drowned. Thousands were captured and flogged on the spot. In the next few days several hundred ring-leaders were hanged publicly, and several thousand rioters were exiled to southeast Russia and to Siberia. At the same time the tsar richly rewarded the officers and troops who supported him. Somewhat later he undertook a few of the reforms the Moscow mobs had clamored for.

This major disturbance in Moscow in 1662 was preceded by citywide riots in the capital in 1648 and by uprisings in other cities and in scattered rural areas. Subsequently in 1667–1671 a major rebellion broke out in southeast Russia that mustered an armed force of over twenty thousand men and threatened to topple the government. It was led by Stenka Razin, a colorful and energetic Don cossack, who roused the poorer cossacks and the lower classes in the south against all officials and authority with a vague but appealing cry for freedom and an end to taxes. Much to the relief of Tsar Alexis, who had personally trained the troops to be sent against the rebels, some rich cossacks betrayed Stenka Razin in the spring of 1671 and turned him over to the government. He was tortured and executed in Moscow in June 1671. But Stenka Razin remained a hero to the oppressed masses and passed into folk legend and song as a romantic Robin Hood capable of extraordinary feats in defending the poor from the depredations of the rich.

As melodramatic as some of these instances of popular unrest in the 1600s were, they served merely to underscore the overall helplessness of the people under the dominant institutions of Russian society that took shape in that century. During the reigns of three tsars and a regent—Michael (1613–1645), Alexis (1645–1676), Feodor (1676–1682), and Sophia (1682–1689)—a major effort to secure and expand the Russian state and to build a viable military and governmental system was made. It largely succeeded, but because Russia's physical and economic resources were limited, the average subject had to bear most of the burden. By 1690 some fifteen million people were struggling to support a huge state that stretched from the Pacific Ocean into eastern Europe.

In this chapter we will examine three chief pillars of tsarist society: the system of serfdom that lasted to 1861, the institution of the autocracy that was reestablished and refined in the 1600s and persisted until 1906 (and with minor modification to 1917), and the nature and function of the Orthodox Church, which has changed little till the present day, although its role in the Soviet period was much diminished. In the last two parts of the chapter we will look at the territorial expansion of Russia in its continuing search for security and at the development of closer relations with the West, which had a portentous initial impact on Russian thought and society.

SERFDOM

Human bondage is an ancient phenomenon, dating back at least to early recorded history and persisting in some parts of the world until about fifty years ago. Yet it emerged in Russia late, soon took an unusually widespread and oppressive form, and lasted for over two hundred years, down to 1861 (about as long as slavery in the United States). The details of how and why serfdom developed in tsarist society are still being debated among historians, but the overall pattern of its evolution is reasonably clear.

As we saw in Chapter 1, most people who farmed in Kievan times were free. Many were organized in communes or *obshchinas* and possessed their own land. Nevertheless, even then some peasants had begun to incur obligations to others, usually large landholders. In return for assistance— seed, tools, money, use of more land—a peasant would agree to do a certain amount of work for the lord or to pay back a given sum, in cash or in kind. When these debts were paid, the peasant was free once more. Until they were, the peasant could not leave the land and the obligations he had accepted.

In this way some peasants were moving toward being enserfed. During the decline of Kiev, the civil strife that followed, and the invasion of the Mongols, many peasants found making ends meet difficult. Crops were seized, fields and tools destroyed, and villages burned. Moreover, storms, drought, and pests could wipe out any year's harvest. Finally, taxes imposed by the Moscow grand princes and tsars made it even more difficult to subsist without falling into debt. For example, scattered evidence indicates that during the last half of the 1500s there was a serious agricultural crisis, probably caused by a combination of bad weather and the exactions resulting from Ivan the Terrible's *oprichnina* and his foreign wars. By 1601 a terrible famine had gripped Russia. Clearly, many peasants were being driven by economic necessity to take on obligations they had little hope of ever repaying. Thus, their bondage was becoming permanent, and serfdom was spreading in Russia.

But it might never have become so extensive had not state policy at this very time acted to bolster and intensify the natural economic trend toward serfdom. To unify and defend Russia the tsars had to finance their armies and reward their servitors. Although they earned some profits from trade in furs and other commodities, the most valuable resource available to the Ivans and Vasiliis of the fifteenth and sixteenth centuries was land: land whose products could be requisitioned or taxed and land that could be given fighting men in return for service. Yet neither sort of land was valuable without peasants to work it. If peasants could run away to the frontier or escape to the cossacks, the land became worthless and the tsars and their state bankrupt.

As a consequence the tsarist government followed several policies that helped fasten serfdom on the Russian countryside. First, they gave many

grants of land *(pomestie)* to servitors; most of these grants included peasants with the land, peasants who owed service to the tsar's servitor in return for their continued right to use the land.

Second, the tsars began to interfere in the customary rules that had governed obligations between lord and peasant. Traditionally, peasants who
paid their debts (sometimes their debts were paid by another lord, who
wanted their labor) were free to leave the land and the lord's service at the
end of the harvest season, during the two weeks before and after St.
George's Day (usually falling in November). But beginning in the latter part
of the 1500s the state now and then decreed a "forbidden" year, that is,
abolished in a given year the right to move during the period around St.
George's Day. Before long every year was "forbidden" and the peasants
were prohibited from leaving at any time. De facto they were bound to the
land and, after a while, personally to the lord.

Third, the government, at the urging of major landowners, made it more
and more difficult for peasants to run away, to escape their obligations by
flight. By long custom if the lord could not recapture a fugitive serf within a
certain period of time (in Western Europe it was "a year and a day"), the
serf had won his freedom. In Russia the tsars kept extending the length of
time in which a lord could recover a fugitive serf, first to three years, then
to five, and finally indefinitely. Thus, an individual, even if he escaped, was
always subject to reenserfment. As an additional support for the
landowner, the government decreed increasingly harsh penalties against
those who aided or harbored runaway serfs.

In these ways state policy and economic necessity reinforced each other
in transforming most Russian peasants into serfs. The process was a gradual one, over approximately two centuries, but it culminated distinctly in
the *Ulozhenie,* or Law Code of 1649. Its provisions forbade serfs to leave at
any time and gave landowners unlimited time and rights in reclaiming runaway serfs. From that time on the position of the serf deteriorated. Landlords not only required labor or payments in cash or produce in return for
the serfs' right to use the land but also began to exercise judicial and administrative control over their serfs (see Figure 8). By the end of the 1600s
the serf had become the personal chattel of the landlord and was approaching the status of a slave (but, unlike in the United States, of the same culture
and race as his owner).

What happened to the peasant commune in this process? Interestingly, it
was preserved as the peasant passed from free person to serf to near slave.
The sense of the community was maintained, and decisions in the *obshchina* continued to be taken fairly democratically, that is, by a consensus
of the heads of all the households participating. The lord used it as an administrative device, making the commune responsible for the peasants'
obligations to him, and later the government also exacted taxes and recruits for the army through the instrumentality of the commune.

Figure 8. *Russian nobles had judicial authority over their serfs, including the right to punish them by flogging. (Courtesy of the British Library)*

Not all peasants became serfs of private landowners, though 60 to 70 percent of the population were in this status by the end of the seventeenth century. The remainder were predominantly state peasants or church peasants. They lived on land holdings of the tsar, the state, or the Orthodox Church, and they owed obligations, usually in kind or in cash, less often in labor, to their respective institutional overseers. Their conditions of work and service were generally less onerous than those of serfs belonging to private landowners. Finally, a small number of peasants remained entirely free, especially those on the eastern and southern frontiers of the vast country.

Why did serfdom come to Russia so late, and why did it become such an extensive and long-lasting institution? One answer is summed up in the aphorism "Serfdom is the price paid by Russians for the sake of survival." In other words, the tsars, ruling a poor country but determined to build the Russian state and to defeat Russia's enemies on several fronts, could only mobilize the required resources by demanding service from the whole population. The gentry provided military and administrative service and were paid with land. The peasants, in return for order and protection, served at first by paying taxes and providing recruits for the army. Later, however, they served by supporting the gentry so the latter could in turn serve the tsar and the state. They made the gentry's land valuable either by working a certain number of days per week on it or by paying the lord (usually in produce) to use the land. In essence, Russian society, excluding townspeople, was a simple pyramidal structure, as shown in the chart above.

Yet the question remains: why did serfdom emerge in Russia at the very moment it was disappearing in western Europe? European kings were also trying to unify their territories and set up centralized systems of government, but they did not have to resort to enforced service. The simplest answer is that in attempting similar tasks the Russian tsars and the European kings commanded quite different resources. The latter could draw on the accumulated wealth of towns and merchants who had been engaged in profitable local, regional, and international trade for some time, as well as on an increasing agricultural surplus generated by new farming techniques and technology developed in the High Middle Ages. In Russia, by contrast, agriculture remained at a low subsistence level and there was little commercial surplus concentrated in towns and in the hands of rich merchants. As we saw earlier, the Mongols had appropriated the few resources of the country during their rule, and under the Muscovite tsars trade and towns had grown only slowly. No capital had been amassed on which Russian rulers could draw in their long struggle to consolidate and strengthen the state. Service (and serfdom) had to substitute for capital.

Perhaps if Russia had not been cut off from European technology in the 1200s and 1300s; perhaps if Russia had participated with the Europeans in the overseas discoveries and rich trade with the Americas, Africa, and Asia that occurred in the 1400s and 1500s; perhaps if the early grand princes and tsars had tried more actively to improve agriculture and promote commerce; perhaps if Russia had not been strained by long wars with its neighbors, like Ivan the Terrible's Livonian War, the Russian economy would have flourished without serfdom. But history is not made up of "ifs." None of those things happened, and we will never know whether Russia might have escaped serfdom under different circumstances. Instead we know that serfdom became the dominant social institution of Russia in the 1600s and persisted for over two hundred years.

This system influenced Russia's future development in several important ways. First, it meant that the Russian economy remained predominantly agricultural, that the level of productivity remained low, and that trade, towns, and the merchant class all grew rather slowly. Second, it created a deep and virtually unbridgeable split in Russian society: the great mass of the population (the lower classes, the people, or in Russian the *narod*) who were serfs and second-class citizens of the state, with many obligations and few rights, versus a tiny upper elite who were privileged and mostly conservative. Finally, almost from the beginning serfdom created a great moral dilemma in Russia. How could one justify subjugating millions of one's fellow-Russians? That they were also Christians, also subjects of the tsar, simply made their degradation more stark, the situation more indefensible. These economic, social, and moral dimensions of serfdom became persistent issues throughout the eighteenth and into the nineteenth centuries.

THE AUTOCRACY

As we saw in the previous chapter, the autocracy, the unlimited rule of the tsar, nearly disappeared in the turmoil and upheavals of the Time of Troubles. Yet the tsar's importance as the symbol of the state and the focus of Russian unity was shown in the repeated attempts during those stormy years to put forward a pretender to the throne and in the decision of the *zemskii sobor* of 1613 to elect a new tsar, young Michael Romanov.

For the first part of his reign Michael ruled in concert with boyar advisers and from 1619 together with his father, Patriarch Filaret. After the latter's death in 1633, Michael ruled alone until he died in 1645, a reign of thirty-two years. His successor, Alexis, also had a long reign, thirty-one years, to 1676. The very length of the rule of these first two Romanov tsars contributed significantly to restoring stability and authority to the tsardom. Moreover, both Michael and Alexis were moderately capable, if not particularly brilliant or far-sighted.

More important in resurrecting the autocracy, however, was the failure of any alternative system or center of power to develop. Certainly in 1613, at the accession of Michael, it seemed probable that the *zemskii sobor,* or assembly of the land, that had played such a key role in the national resurgence against the Swedes and Poles and that had been ruling the country for some months, would emerge as either an executive body coequal to the tsar or at least as an institutionalized advisory council representing the interests and views of the upper classes in Russian society. And, indeed, in the first years of Michael's rule the *zemskii sobor* was in almost continuous session. It was also convened on the occasion of major foreign policy or domestic crises in the 1630s, 1640s, and 1650s. Yet it met infrequently after mid-century and had died out by the end of the 1600s.

No definitive explanation for the demise of the *zemskii sobor* can be affirmed, but we can speculate about two possible reasons. The first is a paradox: its very success in sharing power with the tsar led to its curtailment. It helped Michael and Alexis to rebuild the tsarist state and overcome foreign and domestic challenges by rallying support from the upper classes of Muscovite society. But once the autocratic system, with assistance from the *zemskii sobor,* had recovered from the ravages of the Time of Troubles and the state had begun to grow and expand again, Tsar Alexis hastened to discard any restraints on his authority and gladly let this institution fall into disuse.

Second, unlike the parliaments of western Europe that began to develop about the same time, the *zemskii sobor* had no legal, theoretical, or ideological basis on which to build an ongoing role as a political institution. In an emergency the tsar had convened it to rally support behind him and to give him advice. It was an ad hoc device and never developed an independent position in the Moscow state structure. Consequently, when the tsar no longer needed it and stopped convening it, the *zemskii sobor* disappeared.

In a larger sense the dying out of the *zemskii sobor* reflected the weak political position of the upper classes whose representatives made up the *zemskii sobor.* If the boyars, the high clergy, the gentry, and the rich townsmen had had independent power positions, as separate classes, they might have acted to limit the growing absolutism of the tsar. But the boyars, who during the Time of Troubles had made a remarkable recovery from the setbacks they had suffered at the hands of Ivan the Terrible, were still unable in the 1600s to act together as a class or to assert political rights against the tsar. They continued to squabble over rank and position, they were often venal and narrow-minded, and Tsars Michael and Alexis were able to keep them under control. Moreover, as the historian Robert Crummey has shown, their ranks were swelled greatly in the 1600s by marriage and by appointments of servitors essentially loyal to the tsar. They became an elite of privilege and wealth but posed no threat to the autocracy.

During the Time of Troubles high Church officials had worked closely with other national leaders to save the country, and in the 1620s Patriarch Filaret had been virtual co-tsar with his son Michael. But the overriding tradition of the Orthodox Church was to support the autocracy and to work closely with it, rather than to challenge it. As we shall see shortly, one churchman later in the seventeenth century did defy the tsar's authority, but his bid to share power was quickly quelled. By the end of the century, the Russian Church, weakened by internal dissension, was politically helpless and wholly dependent on the tsar, a position quite different from that of many Protestant and Catholic Churches in western Europe.

The gentry and the townspeople had even less chance to limit the burgeoning autocratic power. The gentry were essentially the tsar's men. Even though, by the end of the 1600s, they had achieved considerable status and the hereditary rights to their lands, the gentry, like the boyars, did not consider themselves or act as a class, with group interests to be defended or rights to be asserted. Although in the 1700s the gentry did show some po-litical muscle, they were then in a stronger position than they had been in the seventeenth century.

The townspeople of Russia had almost no political influence, partly be-cause they lacked clear status as a class, but most importantly because Russian towns were mainly administrative centers, extensions of the au-thority of the tsar, whereas in western Europe they were commercial-finan-cial centers with autonomous charters and independent wealth. The tsar himself was the richest merchant, and although some Muscovites became wealthy in commerce and production, there was no autonomous merchant or financial class. There were no guilds, banks, or companies for the accu-mulation of capital, the protection of economic privilege, and the eventual assertion of political influence.

It is therefore hardly surprising that the autocracy grew and flourished during the seventeenth century to become the overriding political institu-tion of tsarist Russia for almost three hundred more years. To be sure, the tsar's power was limited, but not by individuals, classes or institutions. First, it was limited in spiritual terms: the autocrat was to rule according to God's will, and it would have been impossible for the tsar to act in a way that directly contravened the Orthodox faith and belief of his people. In fact, as we shall shortly see, Tsar Alexis had to face just such a crisis, during which many hundreds of thousands of his subjects rejected his authority over a religious issue.

Second, the tsar's absolutism was tempered by the sheer size of his realm and the magnitude of the task of governing it. No tsar could do everything. Each tsar had to depend to a considerable extent on his military and civil-ian advisers and officials. Thus, beginning earlier but accelerating in the 1600s, the tsar's army and civil service grew rapidly. The tsar set general policies and even made final decisions on relatively small matters, but obvi-ously the day-to-day business of administration—keeping order, making judgments, collecting taxes—was left to an increasing number of clerks and bureaucrats. The local self-government established under Ivan the Terrible had disappeared during the Time of Troubles, so the first Romanovs relied heavily on military governors to manage local and regional affairs. Corrup-tion and harassment of the people were widespread, and some historians believe that the urban riots in Moscow and other cities in the 1600s and even the great rebellion of Stenka Razin were sparked largely by resentment against the venality and petty oppressions of local officials rather than by any broad rejection of the tsarist system.

Drunkenness and random violence also played a role in these outbursts, as the provincial governor of Khotmyshsk reported in October 1648:

At prayer gatherings, weddings, christenings and at relatives' homes they drink themselves drunk and fight and struggle in their stupor. Having fought, they make [political] denunciations against [one another].[2]

Before judging Russians of the seventeenth century too harshly, we should bear in mind that their behavior was not outrageous according to the standards of *that time*. We also need to remember that our own "civilized" century has seen the worst violence and killing in human history (in two world wars, Stalin's purges, and the Holocaust).

THE ORTHODOX CHURCH

In the 1600s as the restored autocracy increased its centralized power, so also the might and authority of the Russian Orthodox Church expanded. But two events, occurring about the same time in the third quarter of the century, greatly weakened the Church and prepared the way for its complete subjugation to the state by Peter the Great in the early 1700s. Both events were associated with one imposing, talented, and strong-willed individual, Patriarch Nikon, head of the Church from 1652 to 1667.

Unlike most high clergy, Nikon was not from the upper classes but was of peasant descent. Extremely bright and well educated, Nikon had come to the attention of young Tsar Alexis early in the latter's reign. Nikon's powerful personality and erudition soon exerted considerable influence over the tsar. Nikon, apparently partly through ambition and partly through his interpretation of the role of the Church in the Byzantine system, asserted in the late 1650s that the Church was independent of, or even in some respects superior to, the state. He demanded to share authority with the tsar. This action flew in the face of longstanding Russian tradition and soon provoked a political storm. The tsar finally broke with Nikon, and in 1666–1667 a high Church council, including prelates from other parts of the Orthodox world, rejected Nikon's claims, unseated him as patriarch, and exiled him to a remote monastery. That was the last time in Russian history that the spiritual power attempted to challenge the secular authority of the tsar.

Of even more long-lasting consequence, however, was Nikon's other major action: a thoroughgoing reform of Russian Orthodox texts and rituals. What seemed a perfectly reasonable proposition—to correct errors that had crept into liturgical materials and church services over the centuries—soon turned into a major struggle that divided the Russian Orthodox Church irrevocably and sparked social conflict leading to thousands of deaths.

To us the issues may appear obscure, or even ridiculous: for example, whether the sign of the cross should be made with three fingers or with two, the correct spelling of Jesus' name, in which direction around the church the procession that makes up part of the Orthodox Mass should go. But to both sides in the mounting controversy such questions were connected with the fundamental question of what was the true Christian faith. Moreover, each side was led by a powerful, determined, and eloquent individual: the reformers by Patriarch Nikon and the defenders of the old forms

by the Archpriest Avvakum, whose autobiographical account of his suffer-
ings is a major work of Russian literature.

The whole affair, known as the Schism (*Raskol* in Russian) because it
split the Church, began innocently enough as a byproduct of the expansion
and increasing sophistication of the Russian Church. Early in Nikon's
tenure as patriarch, well-educated and scholarly clergy, some of whom
came from the Ukraine, which had recently been added to the Church's jurisdiction, called to Nikon's attention that certain parts of the Russian liturgical texts and rituals did not correspond with Greek versions. The latter
were considered more "correct" since they were closer to the original
sources, and it was alleged that errors in translating materials into Russian
had occurred at various times during the long period since Russia's conversion to Orthodoxy. Nikon, who was anxious to upgrade and improve the
Russian Church in various ways, soon accepted this point of view and began an intense campaign to eliminate the errors and to reform the ecclesias-
tical books and the Mass accordingly.

To his surprise and then anger, a number of high prelates disagreed with
him and refused to accept the proposed changes. Before long hundreds of
thousands of parishioners had joined the opposition. After some indecision
Tsar Alexis and the government as a whole backed the reforms and soon
began to use force against those who opposed the changes. Nikon was determined to impose the reforms on the whole church, but his opponents
were equally adamant in rejecting them. As a consequence the Russian
Church was torn apart, and those who opposed the reforms went their own
way, known thenceforth as Old Believers. Paradoxically, the same high
Church council that deposed Nikon for his political ambitions fully endorsed his reforms in 1667.

Both the Church and the government exerted great moral pressure and
even physical coercion in an effort to bring the Old Believers back into the
fold. But few returned. And some, perhaps as many as twenty thousand,
convinced that the changes presaged the end of the world, burned themselves to death. Others defied the government, and Old Believers at the
Solovetskii Monastery in northern Russia held out against repeated military assaults for eight years from 1668 to 1676.

The Archpriest Avvakum was imprisoned and then burned at the stake in
1682 as part of a general persecution of opposition leaders. Nevertheless,
the Old Believers survived to become a significant religious and social force
in eighteenth- and nineteenth-century Russia, numbering some ten or
twelve million adherents in 1900. Some Old Believers exist today in Russia,
and a few schismatic sects persist among Russian emigrants in Canada and
the United States.

What led the Old Believers to resist so fiercely what were after all superficial changes, emendations that did not touch basic doctrine and tenets of
faith? In part it was a commendable devoutness, a profound emotional and

intellectual passion to preserve what they believed was the purity and sanctity of true Christianity, as this appeal of Archpriest Avvakum makes clear:

> Come, Orthodox people, call upon the name of Christ, stand in the midst of Moscow, make the sign of the cross of Christ our Savior holding two fingers as we learned it from our Holy Fathers. The Kingdom of God is born in this land.
> ... Do not falter. I, together with ye, am ready to die for Christ. Although I have not much understanding—I am not a learned man—yet I know that the church, which we have received from our Holy Fathers, is pure and sacred. As it came to me so shall I uphold my faith until the end. It was established long before our time, and thus may it remain for evermore.[3]

An innate conservatism, bordering on superstition, was also a factor in the position taken by the Old Believers. Illiterate and insecure for the most part, they feared change and became convinced that altering the mass or correcting the texts could only be the work of the devil, designed to bring God's wrath down on them. For some schismatics xenophobia may also have played a role: the changes came from Greek-trained or Greek-oriented scholars and threatened true Russian practices. The purity of the faith could only be preserved by rejecting these influences from the outside.

Finally, there may have been an element of sociopolitical protest in the Old Believer movement. Some of the schismatics were extremely poor and may have used the religious issue as a way of expressing their opposition to the government and the existing order. In any case, once the tsar and his administration sided with the church hierarchy, many Old Believers moved willingly to open rebellion against all authority, religious and civil, and waged guerrilla warfare against both the established church and the state. It marked a major crisis in the reign of Tsar Alexis, one that he barely overcame before his death in 1676.

The Schism seriously weakened the Russian Orthodox Church. As the prerevolutionary Russian historian Paul Miliukov argued, the church lost some of its ablest leaders and some of its most devout and vital congregations. Moreover, the triumph of the reformers meant that form won out over content, ritual over feeling and ideas. As a result, Orthodoxy became increasingly formalistic and stultified, with less and less intellectual, social, and political influence in Russian society.

A corollary effect was that Russian life became more secularized. After the Schism the role of religion and the church at the Russian court and among the upper classes was reduced, a change that helped pave the way for Peter the Great's Westernization program forty years later.

THE EXPANSION OF RUSSIA

The seeker of patterns in Russia's historical development could reasonably argue that before the 1600s the growth of the principality of Moscow and the expansion of the tsarist state were essentially defensive in nature, necessary to consolidate power and territory and to secure Russia's borders against a host of enemies on three sides. But after 1600 it is harder to maintain that the additions to Russia's lands were primarily for self-protection. The tsars now appeared more interested in aggrandizement, power for the sake of power, and territories that would benefit Russia economically. Moreover, prior to the seventeenth century the state annexed lands that were predominantly inhabited by other Russians, except for Finno-Ugric groups in the north and Tatars and indigenous non-Slavs in the conquered khanates of Kazan and Astrakhan. Yet in the 1600s and after, most of the peoples who fell under Russian rule were either distant cousins, like the Ukrainians, or not Russian at all (Balts, Caucasian peoples, Asians). Russia became a multinational state, but Great Russians continued to rule and dominate it.

In the 1600s the two main directions of Russian expansion were eastward and southwestward (see Map 5).

The former, a push all across the Eurasian continent to the Pacific Ocean, added an enormous sweep of territory to the Russian state but had little political or strategic significance at the time. The latter, which brought part of Ukraine, including Kiev, into the tsars' realm, involved only a small amount of land but was very important politically and strategically.

Expansion across the Ural Mountains and into Siberia had begun in the latter part of the previous century but advanced eastward in the 1600s another three thousand miles. By the 1640s Russian explorers reached the Pacific Ocean, and one expedition even sailed through the Bering Strait. The Russian advance was checked only when it ran up against the outposts of the large Chinese empire. By the Treaty of Nerchinsk in 1689 Russia's eastern border was established short of the Amur River.

In some respects the Siberian expansion resembled the westward movement in the United States two centuries later. In both cases traders, fur trappers, adventurers, and military officers led the way, motivated by a combination of curiosity, greed, daring, and civic pride. Settlement, government, and taxes soon followed, though in both Siberia and the American West there was for a time a greater degree of freedom and individual initiative on the frontier than in the older, more "civilized" sections of the country. For example, serfdom was never established in Siberia.

At the same time the two movements differed considerably in important respects. The tsarist government played a larger direct role in exploring, colonizing, and reaping the economic benefits (primarily furs) of Siberia than the United States government did in the American West. The Russians treated the indigenous Asian peoples they conquered considerably better than the settlers treated the Native Americans. Finally, Siberia remained thinly settled and rather unimportant until recent times, whereas the American West was soon thickly inhabited and rapidly became an important section, politically and economically, of the United States.

For a long time the acquisition of furs was the major advantage of Siberia for the Russian state. But in the past one hundred years extremely

Corinne Abbazia Hekker Graphics

EXPANSION OF MUSCOVY & RUSSIA, 1533-1801

Muscovy in 1533

Expansion, 1533 - 98

Expansion, 1598 - 1689

Expansion, 1689 - 1801

ALASKA

KAMCHATKA

S I B E R I A

U R A L   M O U N T A I N S

0   600

MILES

Archangel

St. Petersburg, 1703

Moscow ★

Pskov

Kazan

Astrakhan

Azov

Kiev

Baltic Sea

SWEDEN

POLAND

LIVONIA

LITHUANIA

CRIMEAN TATARS

Black Sea

Caspian Sea

OTTOMAN EMPIRE

PERSIA

MAP 5

valuable mineral resources, including gold, petroleum, and natural gas, have been discovered in Siberia, and today it is of great economic significance for Russia. Ever since the 1600s migration and colonization in Siberia have developed rather slowly, mainly because of the distances and the harsh climate, but Siberia did offer a chance to escape the oppressive conditions of life in central Russia, and it attracted some peasants and serfs soon after it was opened up. Moreover, on its southeastern borders the Russian state consistently spurred colonization in order to extend its frontiers against Asian nomads and Muslims. Fortified towns and outposts were built farther and farther toward Central Asia, and Russian settlers were given attractive incentives to man them.

Russia's acquisition of the eastern half of Ukraine between the 1640s and the 1660s was closely connected with the tsars' continuing struggle against Poland, which in the seventeenth century was a more powerful country than Russia. After the Polish effort to conquer Russia during the Time of Troubles had been rebuffed, relations between the two Slavic states remained strained, though a peace treaty was finally signed in 1634 after another inconclusive war. The situation was complicated because the Poles faced increasing difficulty controlling the population on Poland's eastern and southeastern lands, territory that had been part of the Kievan state and that was now known as Ukraine. Most of the people were peasants and belonged to the Orthodox Church, whereas a majority of the landowners were Polish Catholics. The Ukrainians considered themselves oppressed socially and religiously by their Polish overlords. In the late sixteenth century the Poles had helped establish a special branch of the Catholic Church called the Uniate Church, which acknowledged the authority of the Pope in Rome but had Orthodox liturgy and used Slavic language in the Mass. Although some Orthodox Ukrainians accepted the new church, the majority did not and the religious division in Ukraine was further exacerbated.

The Poles were also having trouble with a special group living in Ukraine, the Dnieper cossacks. The Polish government gave them limited support and permitted some continuation of traditional cossack autonomy, but the cossacks could not be won entirely to the Polish cause since they were Orthodox in religion and had close ties with the Ukrainian people as a whole. By dint of ruthless repression and at considerable cost, the Polish government was able to keep a lid on the situation until 1648, when the Ukrainians, led by a great national hero, Bogdan Khmelnitsky, started a broad-scale rebellion against Polish rule.

Although the Ukrainians achieved considerable success against much larger Polish forces, it was clear that in the long run they would need outside help. They turned naturally to their coreligionists in Moscow. At first Tsar Alexis and his advisers were reluctant to aid the Ukrainian rebels, since it certainly would mean war with Poland, an expensive and risky proposition. Finally, in 1653–1654, with the approval of a *zemskii sobor,* Alexis responded favorably to the Ukrainians' request for assistance, in return for which the Ukrainians swore allegiance to the Russian tsar. As a result of the ensuing war with Poland, territorial settlements were finally reached in 1667 and 1686, by which all the lands on the left or eastern bank of the Dnieper River, plus the cities of Smolensk and Kiev, became part of Russia.

Ukrainian historians and nationalists have strongly criticized Russia's absorption of Ukraine, but it is hard to see how an independent Ukraine could have survived, sandwiched as it would have been between Turkey, Poland, and Russia. On the other hand, the Russians, though also Slavic and Orthodox, soon proved stern masters. They failed to respect the autonomy of Ukraine as stipulated in the arrangements of 1654 and 1667, and before long they imposed serfdom on much of its territory. Later, as we shall see, they also tried to suppress the development of an independent Ukrainian literature and culture.

RELATIONS WITH THE WEST

Although in the 1300s and 1400s Moscow had some contact with central and western Europe through Novgorod and Poland-Lithuania, the emerging Russian state was largely isolated from the West during the period of its unification and rapid expansion. Increasingly in the 1500s and 1600s relations were reestablished. Not only did trade expand, but ambassadors were exchanged, a few Russians visited the West, and several thousand Westerners traveled or lived in Russia. These contacts stimulated intellectual intercourse, first in religious matters and technology but later in secular knowledge and general culture.

The tsarist state benefited from closer ties with the West in several important ways: First, the trade, though not extensive, was an important source of revenue and brought to Russia a variety of goods and finished products that otherwise would have been unavailable. Second, the Romanov tsars drew on Western military ideas and technology as they built up their army. Finally, Western artisans and entrepreneurs played a significant role in developing early Russian mining and manufacturing enterprises, for example, in glass-making and iron working.

In the long run the deepest impact of the West on Russia was in the realm of ideas. Part of this intellectual stimulation was a byproduct of religious competition between the Orthodox Church and the Catholic and Uniate Churches. Orthodox leaders recognized that if they were to prevent the influx of Catholicism in Ukraine and other western borderlands of Russia, they needed better-educated clergy. Spurred by the model of Metropolitan Peter Mogila's educational institution in Kiev, the authorities encouraged schools in Moscow staffed largely by learned monks from Ukraine. These efforts culminated in the opening in the 1680s of a Slavonic-Greek-Latin Academy, which taught not only those languages but rhetoric, philosophy, grammar, and theology, a curriculum common to most of Europe since the sixteenth century.

At the same time some secular literature modeled on Western forms began to appear, and the first theater was established under the patronage of Tsar Alexis. Not only the tsar himself but elite Russian society displayed a growing interest in things Western. European dress, food, tobacco, furniture, and baroque architecture all were in vogue among upper-class Muscovites, and smoking spread rapidly through all levels of the population.

In short, by the third quarter of the seventeenth century, there was a growing receptiveness to thought, manners, and institutions of the West, an attitude that certainly prepared the ground for Peter the Great and his all-out effort to Westernize Russia in the early eighteenth century.

The psychological side effects of this openness to European civilization must not be overlooked, on the other hand. Because the Europeans were richer, thanks to the agricultural and commercial revolutions they were experiencing and to their profitable overseas trade, and because they were more advanced technologically, some Russians felt inferior to the West and were anxious to push Russia to catch up. This led some to criticize their own society as backward and barbaric, a view shared by several Europeans who traveled in Russia and published detailed accounts of this "strange and exotic" land. Yet it is important to remember that in some respects Russians possessed a more advanced society than their Western neighbors; for example, they had a centralized effective state when the Italians and Germans still lived in a motley collection of city-states, tiny principalities, and chopped-up feudal fiefdoms. They enjoyed a common religion and relative peace at a time when Europe was rent with religious strife and recurring warfare. The Russians were certainly different in many respects, but whether they were better or worse off is a moot point.

CONCLUSION

In many ways the seventeenth century was a transitional period in the development of Russian society. The state, after a long period of growth and after nearly breaking apart in the Time of Troubles, was consolidated and centralized. Nevertheless, despite some reforms and an expansion of the bureaucracy, it had an archaic outlook and administration. The role of the tsar remained highly personalized, and government was not very efficient. At the same time the Russian economy developed only slowly while the western European countries were accumulating wealth and laying the basis for the Industrial Revolution that would begin in the next century. Russia's expansion into Ukraine added important territory as well as several million fellow Slavs and coreligionists. On the other hand, Russia's expansion eastward brought Asians under tsarist rule and had economic and strategic significance only much later.

In the 1600s class divisions in Russia hardened, and in particular a large proportion of the peasants became permanently enserfed and sank toward the level of slaves. The institution of serfdom widened the gap between a small elite and the bulk of the population and created a major social and moral issue for the next two centuries. The Schism weakened the Russian Orthodox Church, with a large minority of dedicated "outcasts" breaking away from the established religion.

In the largest sense the seventeenth century was a bridge between medieval Russia of the late Kievan, Mongol, and early Muscovite periods and the Russian empire of the 1700s and 1800s that was thrust precipitously into modern times. The 1600s cracked the door to the entry of Western science, technology, and thought, and Russia has been struggling with the impact of modernization ever since.

FURTHER READING

Avvakum, S. *The Life of the Archpriest Avvakum by Himself.* London: 1924, 1968.

Blum, Jerome. *Lord and Peasant in Russia from the Ninth to the Nineteenth Century.* Princeton, N.J.: 1961.

Bushkovitch, Paul. *Religion and Society in Russia: The Sixteenth and Seventeenth Centuries.* New York: 1992.

Crummey, Robert O. *The Old Believers and the World of AntiChrist.* Madison, Wisc.: 1970.

_____. *Aristocrats and Servitors.* Princeton, N.J.: 1983.

Fuhrmann, Joseph. *Tsar Alexis: His Reign and His Russia.* Gulf Breeze, Fla.: 1981.

Fuller, William C., Jr. *Strategy and Power in Russia, 1600–1914.* New York: 1992.

Hellie, Richard. *The Economy and Material Culture of Russia, 1600–1775.* Chicago: 1999.

Keep, John. "The Decline of the Zemsky Sobor," *Slavic and East European Review* 36 (December 1957), 100–122.

Kivelson, Valerie M. *Autocracy in the Provinces: The Muscovite Gentry and Political Culture in the Seventeenth Century.* Stanford: 1996.

Lantzeff, George. *Siberia in the Seventeenth Century.* Berkeley: 1943.

Longworth, P. *Tsar Alexis.* London: 1984.

Philipp, Werner. "Russia: The Beginning of Westernization." In F. S. Carsten, ed., *New Cambridge Modern History* (Vol. 5). Cambridge, England: 1961.

Platonov, S. F. *Moscow and the West.* Hattiesburg, Miss.: 1972.

6

Peter the Great and Westernization, 1689–1725

The thud of axes slicing into wood resounded through the walls of the small log house on the riverbank. Peter, tsar of Russia, stirred in his sleep, then sat up quickly. Seeing daylight under the door, he cursed himself and jumped out of bed, throwing on his clothes as he hastened outside. He liked to be first on the job, but already carpenters were perched on top of and around the frames of several large ships nearby. After momentarily warming his hands over a fire alongside several just arisen workmen, Peter picked up his own hammer and axe. Energetically he clambered up the scaffolding surrounding a galley under construction and threw himself into the work. Peter looked supremely happy. As he wrote in a letter at that time, "we are eating our bread in the sweat of our face."

No one seemed surprised to see his tsarist majesty, the autocrat of all the Russians, the "most pious father of his people," laboring as hard as any peasant in the shipyard. Most of his co-workers were already accustomed to the unorthodox ways of the young tsar, and they respected him for his skill as a shipwright and his willingness to tackle the toughest jobs. On this occasion, in March 1696, both Peter's talents and his leadership were being tested to the fullest. Reigning tsar for only two years, he had suffered a serious defeat at the hands of the Turks the previous summer, and there was already considerable grumbling against him in Moscow. In 1695 Peter had tried to capture the fortified town of Azov, which commanded the entrance to the Sea of Azov, at the mouth of the Don River (see Map 5). Peter's army besieged Azov, but because Peter had no support ships on the river, the Turks were able to relieve the garrison with reinforcements and supplies brought in by sea. Peter finally had to retreat.

Undaunted, Peter, as soon as he returned to Moscow in December, decided to resume the attack the following summer, but with a Russian fleet to control the river. That meant he had to build from scratch the armada he needed in only five months: twenty-five sea-going galleys and over a thousand barges for troops and supplies, an almost impossible task even under the best of conditions! Yet Peter had little to work with. It was win-

ter, with numbing cold, ice, and shortened days; there was no shipyard anywhere in south Russia; no one in that region knew how to build large ships;
and there was no prepared timber or other supplies for ship construction.
As a recent biographer of Peter observed:

> Peter's plan, then, was to build the shipyards, assemble the workmen, teach
> them to mark, cut and hew the timber, lay the keels, build the hulls, step the
> masts, shape the oars, weave the ropes, sew the sails, train the crews, and sail
> the whole massive fleet down the Don River to Azov. All within five winter
> months![1]

Despite bad weather, delays in the arrival of skilled craftsmen, and the
desertion of many conscripted laborers, Peter, to everyone's astonishment,
drove the project through to completion. In early May he sailed down the
Don at the head of his mininavy, which compared favorably with Turkish
and Western ships of the time, and by the end of July he had captured Azov.
In the triumphal procession several miles long that entered Moscow the following October to celebrate this important Russian victory, Tsar Peter
walked on foot, among other captains of the Russian galleys, wearing a
plain black uniform with only a white feather in his hat indicating he had
any special status.

As this episode illustrates, Peter the Great was determined to use modern
techniques and weapons to strengthen his country and unstintingly applied
his considerable energy to this task. Russia had already begun to change
under the impact of new ideas and increasing contact with Europe, as we
saw in Chapter 5, and doubtless, even without Peter, Russia would have
eventually been transformed into a more modern society. What Peter did
was to accelerate this transition greatly. At the same time, because he forced
the pace of change, he widened the gulf between Westernized and old Russia. In their hearts many Russians refused to accept the reforms Peter insisted on.

Moreover, in some respects Peter the Great failed. On the surface, to be
sure, Russian society, or at least the upper classes, appeared to adopt European ideas, technology, and attitudes, but in retrospect the result can be
seen as a rough and uneven patchwork of the new and the traditional, with
many anomalies and incongruities. Even today, 300 years later, it is apparent that Russian society still suffers from a split personality, with part of the
national outlook secular, rational, and tolerant and part zealous, emotional, and xenophobic.

Russia, as with all traditional societies that have come in contact with
Western science, technology, and power, really had no choice but to modernize. To ignore or reject Europe's influence meant isolation, backwardness, and eventual subjugation. Peter saw this clearly and did everything
possible to propel Russia into the modern era. He competed successfully
with his nearest and powerful Western neighbors, Sweden and Poland, and

he greatly increased Russian security and prestige. He also set in motion far-reaching changes in almost every sector of Russian life. Yet he did not tamper with the institution of serfdom, which meant that societywide modernization could not develop in Russia until after the liberation of the serfs in 1861.

Peter's impact was muted for two related reasons. First, unlike the west European nations, Russia lacked the resources to move quickly to a basic overhaul of its institutions and way of life. It had a relatively small population of about 15 million, and as we have seen, at the end of the 1600s it was still a poor country, with low agricultural productivity, few cities, limited trade, and no substantial surplus. For Peter even to make headway in establishing Russia's place in the European state system and in raising the level of culture in the country required a ruthless mobilization of Russia's available means and heavy exactions on the population.

Second, again differing from the West, Russia lacked many of the institutions and attitudes that could help carry out modernization. In the West a reforming church, an entrepreneurial class, a developed higher educational system, and well-established guilds and other associations all stood ready to assist any king or group of leaders who proposed modernizing techniques and changes. But in Russia Peter and his advisers had to act almost alone: the established church was apathetic and the Old Believers hostile; the merchants weak and the nobles as a group divided, indifferent, and recalcitrant; education almost nonexistent; corporate bodies absent; and the bulk of the population a conservative opposition. It is no wonder that many believed Peter to be the Anti-Christ and that only by compulsion and through his astounding energy and will could progress be made.

PETER'S COMING OF AGE

Peter, like Ivan the Terrible, did not have a happy childhood, punctuated as it was by fights among noble families vying for power and by periods when the boy tsar was isolated and ignored. Peter was born in 1672, the first son of the second wife of Tsar Alexis. His mother, Natalia Naryshkin, a member of a prominent family, was politically ambitious but traditional and conservative. As a young man Peter quickly rejected her position and point of view.

On his death Tsar Alexis was succeeded by Feodor, his eldest surviving son by his first wife, Maria Miloslavsky. After a reign of six years Feodor died in 1682, without an heir. A hundred years earlier a similar succession crisis had opened the door to the Time of Troubles, but this time the Naryshkins quickly had Peter, a boy of ten, proclaimed tsar. Their claim was almost immediately contested, however, by the Miloslavsky faction, backed by special army regiments known as the *streltsy*, or musketeers. During the subsequent fighting Peter saw some of his mother's supporters murdered. It was finally agreed that Ivan, Peter's elder half-brother, would be senior tsar and Peter junior tsar. An older daughter of Alexis, Peter's half-sister Sophia, ruled as regent, with some effectiveness, until 1689, when a disastrous military campaign in the south against the Crimean Tatars led to her political downfall. Sophia was packed off to a convent, and Peter, who seemed uninterested in exercising power, permitted his mother and her family and supporters to manage affairs of state. After five years his mother died, and in 1694, at the age of twenty-two, Peter began to direct policy. In 1696 the sickly co-tsar Ivan died, and Peter assumed full authority.

In the 1680s, when Sophia was in charge, Peter had been shunted off to a village outside Moscow called Preobrazhenskoe, where he was largely left to his own devices. As a result he had little formal education but did a great deal to educate himself, particularly in practical matters about which he was intensely curious. Moreover, he was able to choose his own companions and develop his own interests. He surrounded himself with a motley crew of Russians and a few foreigners. These were selected not because of birth or position but because Peter liked them or because they had talents Peter wanted to tap. As recreation Peter was allowed to form his own "play" army, with which he first displayed his love of organization and his genius at military tactics. These young playmate-soldiers later formed the core of the first guards regiment in Russia, military units that lasted till 1917.

PETER'S PERSONALITY AND CHARACTER

Gargantuan is an adjective frequently used to describe Peter the Great, and it is indeed apt. Physically he was huge and very strong. Having read often that Peter was "nearly seven feet tall" and suspecting this to be sheer exaggeration, I hastened on one of my first visits to Moscow to the military museum in the Kremlin, where I knew a uniform Peter wore was preserved. When no one was looking, I stretched my six-foot five-inch frame alongside the display case holding a dummy of Peter decked out in rather faded but still impressive battle dress. To my surprise Peter towered comfortably above me, certainly not seven feet in height but probably a commanding six feet seven inches. Living in an era when most people were only a little over five feet tall, how Peter must have dominated any meeting or gathering!

His energy; his appetite for food, drink, and work; his enthusiasm and intellectual curiosity were all virtually boundless. He wanted to do everything, know everything, see everything. He drove his officials, soldiers, and people hard, but he drove himself harder. He was determined to make Russia stronger and better; he worked as single-mindedly for education and science as he strove fiercely for victory in battle. He cajoled and goaded his countrymen, and when all else failed, he coerced them, down the path of modernization.

Darker sides to his personality and character should not be overlooked. He was often rude and inconsiderate. He was frequently ruthless and cruel.

He personally participated in the torture and execution of some members of the *streltsy* who had rebelled against his rule, as this eyewitness account makes clear:

> [On 27 October 1698] . . . two rebels, brothers, having had their thighs and other members broken in front of the castle of the Kremlin, were set alive upon the wheel. . . . Their miserable cries had struck the Tsar [Peter] as he was being driven past. He went up to the wheels, and first promised speedy death, and afterward proffered them a free pardon, if they would confess sincerely. But when upon the very wheel he found them more obstinate than ever, and that they would confess nothing . . . the Tsar left them to the agonies of death, and hastened on to the Monastery of the Nuns, in front of which monastery there were thirty gibbets erected in a quadrangular shape, from which there hung two hundred and thirty *streltsy*.[2]

Like so many extremely talented and determined people, Peter tried to do too much. He took on more than he could manage; as a result, some of his actions were haphazard and some of his reforms uncoordinated and incomplete. Nonetheless he accomplished more than a dozen others could have.

Characteristic of his outlook and behavior was the extended trip to western Europe Peter undertook early in his reign. As a youth he had absorbed from specialists residing in the foreigners' quarter of Moscow information and techniques in a wide range of civil and military trades. Peter was particularly fascinated with shipbuilding and navigation. Although he had helped establish shipyards and construct vessels for the first Russian navy in 1694 and 1695, Peter wanted to learn still more and looked naturally to the West. In addition, he hoped that in the course of visiting European nations he might enlist their support in his continuing struggle against the Ottoman Turkish empire.

Consequently he set out in the spring of 1697 as part of a delegation of over two hundred Russians. Peter attempted to travel incognito as simply a member of the group, but his size made him easily identifiable. Moreover, as the first tsar to travel in Europe, he was the center of attention not only among European governments but among the general public as well. Besides his diplomatic purpose Peter wanted to learn as much as he could about the West, to absorb as much technical knowledge as possible, and to recruit foreigners to serve in Russia. He spent almost a year and a half abroad, visiting Holland, England, and the Hapsburg empire and was about to continue to Italy when political turmoil in Russia compelled him to return home.

His "grand embassy" was largely successful. Peter spent most time in Holland, acquiring a great deal of information about seafaring and boat building and actually working in a shipyard. He hired a number of Dutch specialists to work for him back home. He learned a great deal there and in the other countries about European attitudes, customs, and education, although his own rowdy behavior at times shocked the Europeans. He did not succeed in forging an alliance against the Turks, but he established personal ties with European officials that were useful in his later diplomatic pursuits. Most of all he returned to Moscow with his head crammed with ideas about ways to modernize his tradition-bound homeland.

PETER IN WAR AND DIPLOMACY

Peter greatly changed Russian society but not Russian foreign policy. He consistently pursued objectives abroad that were very like those of his predecessors as far back as the fifteenth century. He viewed Russia's needs and interests as an independent state in a traditional way, in much the same light as earlier tsars had. Of highest priority was securing the vulnerable borders of Russia, particularly in the south and the west. Next came the task of expanding Russia's contacts and territory, especially in ways that would liberate Russia from its long isolation as a landlocked country. Finally, Peter, like Ivan the Terrible and the first Romanov tsars, encouraged exploration and expansion in Asia in a search for new opportunities and trading partners.

The main threat to Russia in the south came from the Crimean Tatars, descendants of the Mongols who periodically attacked the tsarist state from their well-defended khanate based on the Crimean peninsula in the Black Sea. Since the late 1400s the Tatars had been under the protection of the Ottoman Turks, and the Ottoman Empire was therefore the target of Peter's first campaign. In 1695, shortly after assuming full authority as tsar, he attacked Azov, finally subduing it in 1696 with the help of his newly constructed southern fleet, as we saw at the start of the chapter.

Later on, after a second war against the Turks in which Peter narrowly escaped a major defeat, he had to give back Azov and dismantle his Black Sea fleet. Nevertheless a precedent for Russian expansion to the Black Sea had been set, and by the end of the eighteenth century Russia had established a firm foothold along the northern shore of that important inland waterway.

As we saw in Chapter 3, Ivan the Terrible made a major effort to reach the Baltic Sea but was ultimately defeated. In the Great Northern War, which lasted the greater part of Peter's reign, from 1700 to 1721, the modernizing tsar renewed this struggle. His two main objectives were to break the power of Sweden, at that time the dominant country in north central Europe, and to open trade and contact directly with Europe via the Baltic Sea, his "window to the West." Although partners in the anti-Swedish coalition shifted with the fortunes of war, Poland and Russia were Sweden's main opponents during most of the Great Northern War.

When the war began, Sweden seemed at a disadvantage: not only had most of the states of the region allied against her, but Sweden's new king was a youth not yet twenty, Charles XII. Charles, however, proved to be a formidable adversary, an energetic and talented leader and a military genius. Before his death on the battlefield at the age of thirty-seven, he had conducted some brilliant campaigns and won a number of major victories.

One of his first triumphs was the defeat of Peter and a much larger Russian army at Narva in the Baltic region in late 1700. Dismayed but not discouraged, Peter began at once to rebuild and reorganize his whole military establishment, including training methods, artillery, and supply. As we shall shortly see, civil government was also mobilized completely behind the war effort.

Luckily for Peter, Charles XII, although he probably could have forced Russia's withdrawal from the war had he pursued an offensive toward Moscow, turned his attention southward against Poland, which he considered the main enemy. Peter the Great took maximum advantage of this respite, expanding and reshaping his army and beginning a fleet for use in the Baltic Sea. Beginning in 1701, the Russians captured most of the territories of Estonia and Livonia (present-day Latvia) along the Baltic shore, and in 1703 Peter founded a city strategically located in the northeastern corner of the Baltic Sea at the mouth of the Neva River (see Map 5). Soon named St. Petersburg (after the saint, not the tsar), it served as one of the two capitals of Russia from 1713 until 1918.

Charles XII finally defeated the Poles and thus could focus fully on the Russians. In 1708 he and his army crossed into Russia from Poland, but instead of heading directly for Moscow, the Swedes turned south into the Ukraine, hoping to win over the cossacks and to establish a firm base there. Several thousand cossacks did join forces with Charles XII, but the majority of Ukrainians remained loyal to Peter. After a preliminary battle in which Peter was able to capture some reinforcements and relief supplies intended for Charles XII, the main struggle between the Russians and the Swedish forces was joined in July 1709 at Poltava. Outnumbered almost two to one, the Swedes fought heroically but finally suffered a crushing defeat:

At 9 o'clock . . . the Swedish army turned and moved south to get into a position parallel to that of the Russians. . . . Opposite . . . [were] two packed lines of Russian infantry . . . supported by seventy field guns. . . . The Russian first line of twenty-four battalions was 10,000 strong, the second (of eighteen battalions) 8,000. . . . The enemy superiority in numbers was terrifying. So was their superiority in firepower.

The Swedes attacked first to gain a moral advantage. [Swedish General] Lewenhaupt led a charge with *armes blanches* [bared swords] by the Swedish right wing which made the Russians fall back and gave the Swedes some field guns to turn against their enemy. But a gap appeared between the elite regiments of the right and those of the left, which could not keep up the same pace. Russian troops poured into the gap and widened it. Panic gripped men whose colonel was wounded and the Swedish line began to give way. Even Lewenhaupt when he came on the scene could not make the men stand. "I rode up and down in front of them," he later reported, "I begged, threatened, cursed, and hit out. All was in vain, it was as if they neither saw nor heard me."

Within half an hour the battle was over. The Swedes were either casualties of the battle or . . . fled to the safety of the baggage and reserve regiments at Pushkarivka.

Charles XII on his stretcher [from an earlier wound] had been at the head of the right infantry wing. When the panic spread to that sector of the thin line, his cry of "Swedes, Swedes" went unheeded. His stretcher was hit by musket bullets and destroyed. It looked as if the king would become a prisoner of the Russians. . . . Lewenhaupt's call that the king was in danger brought, however, a front of soldiers willing to delay the enemy by laying down their lives for his. Charles forced himself on to a horse, the bandages on his foot came undone, and blood dripped from [his] wound that opened with the unwonted activity. The horse was shot under him and was replaced. . . .

The Russians did not pursue the Swedes. The fight had been one between infantry in the main, and the foot soldiers of Tsar Peter were nearly as shaken as those of Charles. . . . The Swedes had left some 10,000 on the battlefield, 6,901 dead and 2,760 prisoners of the Tsar. Russian losses were relatively light: 1,345 killed and 3,290 wounded.[3]

Charles managed to escape southwest into Turkish territory. But Russia's reconstructed army had acquitted itself well under Peter's personal leadership, and Peter had every reason to be proud of the progress his Europeanizing program had achieved. He quickly followed up the victory at Poltava, capturing the Baltic coast from Riga to southern Finland in 1710, which secured his new city, St. Petersburg.

Shortly thereafter, however, he became embroiled with the Ottoman Empire again, and the war with Sweden, though essentially settled at Poltava, dragged on over a decade longer. Peter made further gains along the Baltic shore and finally the Peace of Nystadt in 1721 brought the Great Northern War to an end. Russia's possession of what are today the countries of Estonia and Latvia and of territory between St. Petersburg and Finland was confirmed. Russia at last had secure access to the Baltic Sea and through it to western Europe. Even more important, Russia replaced Sweden as the dominant power in north central Europe and was able to concentrate its energies during the rest of the century on a contest with Poland for supremacy in eastern Europe. As British historian B. H. Sumner succinctly summed up the outcome: "Peter made Russia a power in Europe and all three knew it." From the Great Northern War to the present, Russia has been a major player in the game of European power politics, and its influence in Europe seems likely to continue into the foreseeable future.

In recognition of his success Peter was given the titles *Great* and *Emperor,* and from that time on the tsarist state was known as the Russian Empire. Moreover, by adding Balts and Finns, Peter extended the multinational character of the empire, a feature that persisted to 1991. Finally, it can be argued, Russia reached the geographic limits, at least in the west, of any expansion dictated by security considerations. But in fact the expansion of the empire continued steadily into the 1860s.

Although Peter's main concerns in foreign affairs were his wars with Turkey and Sweden, he had a continuing interest in and curiosity about Asia. He maintained relations with China, encouraged explorations and contacts in the Pacific and with Mongolia and Central Asia, and occupied Persian territory along the Caspian Sea (though it was returned shortly after his death). He even planned an expedition to establish ties with India. Peter, a leader of vision, clearly understood that because of Russia's location in Eurasia, it was bound to have increasing intercourse with the Asian peoples and cultures lying to the southeast. Besides, he was curious; he wanted to know more about these other societies, and he encouraged Russians to study them.

PETER'S REFORMS

In undertaking major changes in Russian society and government, did Peter have a grand design? Or was he driven helter-skelter from one reform to another by necessity, by the need to keep his war machine going? Proponents of the latter view point out that Russia was at peace only a little over two years during the whole period of Peter's reign and that in a society as little developed economically as Russia the major wars Peter waged demanded an all-out effort and overshadowed any other purpose or activity. On the other hand, those who believe Peter had a plan can point to his own justifications for the changes he made and to reforms he undertook that were quite unrelated to the military mobilization of Russia.

As in so many historiographic controversies, the answer seems to lie some-where between the two positions. Peter certainly had a definite purpose: he intended to introduce into Russia modern ideas, technology, methods, and institutions he had learned about or had observed on his mission to Europe. These, he was convinced, would both make Russia stronger and improve the welfare of his people. On the other hand, Peter certainly did not have a carefully worked out and consciously timed scheme for Europeanizing the country. He often did things impulsively and in an uncoordinated fashion. And certain measures were clearly related directly to the war effort and to the support of his new army and navy.

Though not a philosopher or theoretician, Peter the Great had a practical sense of the sort of state and society he was trying to shape. His models were the European nations of his time: monarchies with effective bureaucracies and commercial economies. Peter accepted completely the concept of autocracy, the idea of centralized absolutism. The governmental reforms he carried through were designed not to limit the tsar's rule but to make it more effective. The one change in the ideology of autocracy he did try to make was to secularize and depersonalize the tsar's role. The tsar was to remain an absolute ruler, but not for his own sake, or even for God's. Instead the tsar-emperor was to serve the state, as everyone else did. Peter wanted the people to obey not the tsar as a person or a patriarch but as a symbol of sovereignty, as the first servant of the state. The bulk of the population, however, continued to see the tsar as both a "father" and a ruler anointed by God.

Consonant with his view of the tsardom was Peter's belief that all should serve the state. Neither religion nor wealth nor birth should exempt one from fulfilling a primary obligation to the state. Civil and military service were the highest callings, and everything should be done to ensure that the army and the bureaucracy were efficient, honest, and just.

So also should economic life benefit the state. Peter accepted the ideas of *mercantilism,* then the dominant economic theory in Europe, that production should be stimulated and trade managed in such a way as to accrue maximum advantage to the state. At the same time the state should encourage and support science, technology, and education, which were needed for effective governance and for expanding the economy.

As already noted, Peter carried out a complete overhaul of the Russian army and founded the Russian navy in order to be better able to wage war against the Ottoman Empire and Sweden. In his military reforms Peter changed almost everything, from *A* to *Z,* from the design, production, and procurement of weapons and ships; through recruitment, training, and supply of enlisted men and officers; to transport, deployment, and battlefield tactics. From Peter's time on Russia had a professional army and navy that rivaled those of any European power.

To ensure the manning and command of his armed forces (and his civil service as well) Peter required that everyone serve. To be sure, this was a principle established earlier by the Muscovite tsars, but Peter made it universal and life-long and saw that it was enforced. Nobles served with their units as long as they were fit and peasant recruits were drafted for life (reduced to twenty-five years later in the 1700s). Peter also decreed that appointment and advancement in civil and military service would be according to ability and merit, not through privilege, birth, or "pull." To this end he set up the *Table of Ranks,* fourteen parallel grades in the civil and military service. Peter provided his own best example, working his way up in both the army and navy until he became a general and later an admiral. Peter encouraged upward social mobility. A person who attained the eighth rank of the civil service, for example, automatically became a noble (see Figure 9).

Moreover, Peter chose his own closest advisers not primarily from the old boyar and gentry families but from all classes in society, selecting individuals he thought had special skills or unusual ability. Alexander Menshikov, Peter's most trusted confidant, whom he later made a prince, was of humble origins and reputedly worked as a street vendor in Moscow before

Figure 9. *A noble's house in Moscow about 1790. (Courtesy of the Board of Trustees of the Victoria and Albert Museum)*

becoming the tsar's orderly and rising to prominence. Other high officials in Peter's reign included several Swiss, Scots, and Germans, a former serf, a shepherd, and a clerk. At the same time one of his ablest generals was a member of an old noble family.

Peter did not, however, alter serfdom. He seemed unaware that it was probably not an efficient system of agricultural production, apart from the moral issues it raised. Yet in other areas of economic life Peter did his best to stimulate activity and output. He established hundreds of small manufacturing enterprises, most, to be sure, primarily to supply the armed forces, and he introduced a number of new products and trades into Russia. He provided subsidies to promote exports and assisted native Russian artisans. Because of the heavy costs of his wars, however, the Russian economy hardly flourished in the Petrine era, and some estimates suggest that Russia was worse off at the end of his reign than at the beginning.

There is certainly no doubt that the average citizen carried a heavy fiscal burden under Peter's rule, the state budget more than doubling between 1700 and 1725. Peter and his advisers were ingenious at devising new taxes, including some intended to discourage traditional practices, such as those on beards and Old Believers. A reform of lasting significance was Peter's decree changing the basis of taxation on the peasantry from the household to the individual. It was suspected, probably correctly, that peasants were crowding together in ever larger households in order to spread the burden of the steadily increasing exactions levied by the central government. In order to prevent this and to make sure everyone paid, Peter's government carried out a crude census and then decreed a "soul tax" that assessed each adult male. There is some speculation that this led to the setting up of new households and eventually to a marked rise in fertility and population later in the century. In any case, since both serfs and household slaves were counted and taxed, without distinction, Peter's fiscal policies further erased any lingering distinction between serfs and slaves: all became the movable property of their owners.

In a related fashion a reform of Peter designed with another purpose in mind helped eliminate the difference between estates held for service and those that were hereditary without any legal obligation for service. In a decree of 1714 (abrogated after his death) Peter attempted to end the traditional practice of dividing an estate among all the male heirs since it resulted in ever smaller and less efficient landholdings. The new single inheritance (or primogeniture) law required designation of one son as sole heir, with the eldest male child receiving title if no one were named. At the same time the decree made no distinction among estates, assuming that all were hereditary and that all estate owners owed service.

Peter's desire to make the tsarist system work better led to much tinkering with government institutions and procedures. The result was a patchwork of the old, the adapted, and the European. Because he was frequently away campaigning, Peter originally established the Senate, a senior council of about a dozen officials, to rule in his absence. After a while the Senate came to have considerable administrative and judicial power and turned into a permanent institution of the empire. Peter ceased appointing boyars, and the boyar duma and *zemskii sobor* both disappeared. Peter thoroughly reorganized the central bureaucracy, setting up a series of "colleges" to handle such matters as foreign affairs, the army, the navy, justice, finance, mining, and commerce. Modeled on Swedish institutions, the colleges were to be run by a council or collegial group. In theory this system would prevent abuse of power by one individual and would provide a wider range of experience and judgment in making important decisions. In practice the colleges were quite unwieldy but nevertheless lasted for almost a century.

In provincial and municipal government Peter took some bold initiatives, but his reforms were largely unsuccessful. As the Russian empire grew, it became harder and harder to manage and govern, a problem that not only Peter but his successors failed to overcome.

Though Orthodox, Peter engaged at times in drunken and blasphemous parodies of Church rituals and celebrations while relaxing with his friends. As in other fields he called freely on the talents of several educated and able clerics, but he saw little role for the traditional Church in the modernized Russia he was trying to mold. Since the general thrust of his policies was to secularize society, he tried to minimize the role of the Church in Russia. To make sure the Church would be subservient to the state, Peter left the patriarchate vacant when Patriarch Hadrian died in 1700. Later he abolished the post, replacing it with the Holy Synod, a body of high clerics supervised by a lay official, the ober-procurator of the Holy Synod. This arrangement lasted until 1917 and permitted the government to keep tight rein on Church activities and policies. Not yet recovered from the turmoil of the Schism, the Church could do little to resist its subjugation by Peter.

Peter was an enthusiastic supporter of education. Training schools for the armed services naturally received high priority, but Peter also encouraged lay schools. He was particularly eager to advance the sciences and technology and laid plans for a national Academy of Sciences, which came into being shortly after his death. He established the first general hospital and surgical school at Moscow in 1706. Later he reorganized medical affairs under the Medical Chancery headed by a foreign-educated imperial physician.

To make education more accessible to the average citizen he oversaw a simplification of the Old Church Slavonic alphabet. To disseminate culture he sponsored the first newspaper and greatly expanded printing in Russia. The number of titles issued annually rose from six or seven to forty-five, and the content of these books broadened to include scientific and secular as well as religious topics. Peter's efforts in education, though extensive, were in fact only a tiny beginning. As one of the young Russians he sent abroad to study observed, "How can I learn geography without knowing the alphabet?" Russia needed to establish a much broader base of elementary and secondary schools and a better organized system, tasks that were undertaken later in the 1700s under Catherine the Great.

To a considerable extent Peter's most lasting reforms were cultural and psychological. His symbolic gestures, such as cutting off the beards of boyars or forcing them to wear European dress, seem almost silly, but behind them was his relentless determination that the Russian elite change their outlook and attitudes, giving up the parochial, religious, old-fashioned ways and ideas of Muscovy for the worldly, secular, progressive life-style and thought of Europe. Many resisted or ignored him, but in the long run Peter did succeed in orienting Russian society in a different direction, in forcing it to look to the future instead of the past. This wrenching change of direction had two fateful consequences, however. It alienated the educated elite from the mass of the people, and before long it led to a fundamental questioning of Russian society as a whole, and to ideas of revolution.

RESISTANCE TO PETER

In attempting to transform Russia Peter was determined and ruthless. As early as 1696 he established permanent political police to persecute his opponents. Nevertheless many Russians openly criticized his reforms, and millions more passively resisted, clinging stubbornly to the old ways. For the majority of peasants Peter's reign meant not only new burdens but the introduction of strange and unorthodox customs, both of which they deeply resented. Many believed Peter was the Anti-Christ and feared the end of the world was near.

The most important rebellion against Peter broke out in southeastern Russia, centered on the city of Astrakhan, in 1705. Peter was then heavily engaged in the Great Northern War and could ill afford troops to send against the rebels. Moreover, since the leaders of the uprising espoused a broad range of popular grievances against both central and local government, the insurrection could easily have spread to other parts of southern Russia, the traditional seedbed of rebellion. Peter's opponents in Astrakhan included runaway serfs, Old Believers, and cossacks, but also many conservative Russian citizens who were outraged at the combination of new taxes and iconoclastic policies Peter had imposed on them. In appealing to the Don cossacks for help, the rebels declared:

> We wish to inform you of what has happened in Astrakhan on account of our Christian faith, because of beard-shaving. . . . How we, our wives, and our children were not admitted into churches in our old Russian dress. . . . Moreover, in the last year, 1704, they imposed on us, and collected a [new] tax . . . they also took away all our firearms . . . and our bread allowance [for those serving as frontier guards].[4]

The anger of the rebels soon turned to violence, with the killing of the military governor and several hundred officials and nobles. It required a regular army under one of Peter's leading generals to suppress the uprising. Some of its leaders were publicly executed in Red Square as an example to the population.

Nevertheless in 1707–1708 a new insurrection erupted, this time in the south, led by a disgruntled Don cossack named Kondratii Bulavin, who exhorted his followers against serfdom and the government. With a motley army of over 50,000, Bulavin occupied several key towns and tried to persuade the Dnieper cossacks to join him but was finally defeated by government troops.

At the same time that these revolts were being suppressed Peter had to contend with sporadic uprisings among the Bashkirs, a Turkic people on the eastern frontier of Russia who resented Russian domination and the taxes of Peter's government.

Those in government circles and among the old boyars and conservative churchmen who opposed Peter's policies hoped to use the heir to the throne, Peter's son Alexis, as the spearhead of their discontent. Intelligent but weak-willed and dissolute, Alexis, under pressure from Peter, renounced his right to the throne. Soon afterward he went into self-imposed exile abroad. He was finally persuaded to return to Russia, but before long his name was linked to plotting against Peter. Relations between father and son had never been good, and now Peter acted willfully against Alexis. In 1718 a broadly composed, extraordinary tribunal sentenced Alexis to death, but shortly thereafter he died or was murdered in prison. Five years later Peter promulgated a new succession law, declaring that the tsar had the right to name the heir to the throne, but he died in 1725 without doing so.

SIGNIFICANCE OF PETER THE GREAT

Within fifty years of Peter's death some writers were arguing that his reign had greatly benefited Russia, and others claimed that it had ruined the country. This controversy became a major issue in the intellectual history of modern Russia, reaching a high point in the 1840s in the polemics between the westernizers, who approved Peter's policies, and the Slavophiles, who denounced them (see Chapter 9). In the 1860s the conservative Russian publicist, Michael Katkov, concluded that Peter's rule was "a catastrophe that . . . disrupted the organism of national life and . . . deprived [us] of the instinct and feeling of personal life . . . remaking us into senseless imitators doing everything on order of the government." Soviet historians generally approved of Peter's reforms (and lavishly so in the period of Stalin's dictatorship) although concluding that they reinforced an absolutist system controlled by the aristocracy and a few rich merchants.

Perhaps Peter's reign can best be summed up as a series of paradoxes (which incidentally help explain why it is so controversial):

- Peter coerced Russia into modernization, but it was coming anyway.
- Peter had a vision of a more efficient, modernized Russia, but his reforms were often haphazard, forced upon him by military necessity and the pressure of events.
- Peter wanted to drive barbarism out of Russia but relied on barbaric methods to achieve that goal.
- Peter wanted to change and improve Russian society but left it with serfdom, an entrenched privileged nobility, and a cumbersome and often corrupt bureaucracy.
- Peter cared about the welfare of his people, but his wars and fiscal demands left them burdened, exhausted, and resentful.
- Peter sought good government and encouraged individual merit, but his reign heightened the arbitrary power of the state.
- Peter saw Russia's distant future but failed to convince most Russians of that destiny.
- Peter set a fast pace and employed coercion to make progress, but this practice alienated most Russians and undercut the changes he was trying to make.
- Peter made Russia a great power in Europe, but he achieved this through aggression against Russia's neighbors and at great cost to Russia.

However one assesses these contradictions in Peter's record, three major conclusions concerning his reign emerge. Peter was clearly one of the most influential personalities in modern history, like Napoleon, Lenin, and Gandhi. Russia undoubtedly would have meandered into modern times at some point, but Peter greatly accelerated the process and in so doing changed Russian society fundamentally.

Second, Peter propelled Russia onto the European stage and made her a great power. Since 1700, Russia has been a major actor in European and world affairs.

Finally, Peter put on the agenda for all Russians fundamental questions with which they are still struggling. How can Russian society react to new ideas and technology and still be true to its own traditions and unique culture? Must the West be imitated, or can Western attitudes and methods be modified and adapted to serve Russian needs and interests? Is it possible to fuse Russian beliefs and Western thought? What is the true essence of Russian civilization?

FURTHER READING

Anisimov, Evgennii V. *The Reforms of Peter the Great: Progress Through Coercion in Russia.* Armonk, N.Y.: 1993.

Black, C. E. "The Reforms of Peter the Great." In C. E. Black, ed., *Rewriting Russian History.* New York: 1962.

Cracraft, James. *The Church Reform of Peter the Great.* Stanford, Calif.: 1971.

_____. "Peter the Great." In *Modern Encyclopedia of Russian and Soviet History.* Vol. 27, pp. 224–235. Gulf Breeze, Fla.: 1981.

Hughes, Lindsey. *Sophia: Regent of Russia, 1657–1704.* New Haven: 1990.

_____. *Russia in the Age of Peter the Great.* New Haven: 1998.

LeDonne, John P. *Absolutism and Ruling Class: The Formation of the Russian Political Order, 1700–1825.* New York: 1991.

_____. *The Russian Empire and the World, 1700–1917: The Geopolitics of Expansion and Containment.* New York: 1997.

Marsden, C. *Palmyra of the North.* London: 1942 (a description of St. Petersburg).

Meehan-Waters, B. *Autocracy and Aristocracy.* New Brunswick: 1982.

Peterson, C. *Peter the Great's Administrative and Judicial Reforms.* Stockholm: 1979.

Tolstoi, Alexei. *Peter the First.* New York: 1959 (a novel).

7

Change and Continuity, 1725–1801

A large party, in carriages and on horseback, was approaching the lovely summer estate of the Russian tsars, Peterhof. Since it was early summer, the gardens were at their most colorful, and the elaborate system of fountains was playing beautifully. Tsar Peter III, at the head of the group, looked forward pleasurably to the expected festivities that evening in honor of his name day, July 9, 1762. His wife, Catherine, who was staying at Peterhof while he was at another palace, was a renowned hostess, and he could anticipate a fine time even though he and Catherine were not on good terms. Recently at a state dinner, he had publicly called her a fool, angering her partisans. Lately, there had even been rumors that she was plotting against him, taking advantage of his unpopularity with many prominent officers, nobles, and clerics who resented his often boorish behavior, his open hostility to the Russian Orthodox Church, and his decision to ally with Frederick the Great of Prussia, Russia's archenemy for the last seven years. As Peter and his companions rode into the courtyard of Peterhof, they were surprised to find no one about to greet and assist them. But when they entered the palace, they were dumbfounded and dismayed. Neither Catherine nor a single person from her retinue was there. All Peter found was her ball gown ready for the party.

What Peter did not know and only found out several hours later was that early that morning Alexei Orlov, one of five brothers, guards officers who were Catherine's closest supporters, had roused the tsarina and hustled her into a waiting carriage for an emergency trip to St. Petersburg, the capital. The conspirators against Peter's rule had planned to wait several more weeks to depose him, but the arrest of one of their number had forced their hand. They were determined to win over key elements in the army before Peter even learned what was afoot. Later on the morning of July 9,

a travelling carriage drew up outside the barracks of the Izmailov regiment on the outskirts of St. Petersburg. A guards officer descended and disappeared hastily inside. A few moments later, as a drummer alerted the soldiers, a woman of about thirty, dressed in dusty black, with her hair unpowdered, was handed down from the carriage and almost engulfed by a crowd of shoutings

huzzaing soldiers. Shortly afterwards the crowd parted, and an elderly Orthodox priest advanced bearing aloft the cross. In loud tones officers and men . . .
swore allegiance to the newly proclaimed Empress Catherine, Autocrat of all
the Russias.[1]

The new empress then proceeded to the barracks of the other guards regiments, all of whom enthusiastically declared their backing for Catherine.
By noon she was at the Kazan Cathedral, where the highest Church prelates
confirmed her title, and that afternoon the archbishop of Novgorod administered the oath of allegiance to troops drawn up in front of the Winter
Palace. All but a few officers, who protested and were promptly arrested,
ignored the point that only six months previously they had sworn loyalty to
Peter.

The deposed tsar, after learning of the *coup d'état*, awaited his fate.
Catherine herself rode out to arrest him, and a few days later, while in cus-
tody, he was strangled by Alexei Orlov and others, allegedly in a fight.
Catherine, determined to keep the throne, overlooked the murder, declaring
Peter had died of "a hemorrhoidal" colic and rewarding the conspirators
lavishly.

Catherine the Great knew where she was headed: to sit on the Russian
throne and to make her mark in modern European history. But where was
Russia headed? Catherine herself, in my view, was not quite sure. If Russia
were moving in the direction of becoming an "enlightened" society, then
something would have to be done about serfdom, a reform that might un-
ravel the whole social system and would certainly arouse the bitter opposition of the serf-owning nobility, the state's chief supporters. If Russia were
to evolve toward a society based on law and institutions, or even on classes,
then the arbitrary authority of the autocracy would have to be curbed and
alternate centers of power created almost from scratch. Although Catherine
nodded a few times in this direction, she had no intention of surrendering
her autocratic prerogative. If Russia were to proceed down the path toward
industrialization, as England was just starting to do, the role of the state in
economic life would have to be greatly reduced, private entrepreneurs encouraged, markets found, and techniques learned. This course was beyond
the resources available to Catherine. In all cases she had to work with what
Peter and his successors had left her.

In two important ways Peter's efforts survived him and shaped the future
course of his country: Russia remained a major European power, and Euro-
peanization continued to develop and take root in Russia. Nevertheless in
other significant ways the eighteenth century saw fundamental divergences
from Peter's program of service to the state and of modernization. First,
during the 1700s obligatory service for the nobility was abolished, though
many nobles continued to serve. But because the nobles did not succeed in
establishing an institutional basis for themselves as a class, they were unable to turn their freedom into a regularized device for limiting the autoc-

racy. Moreover, since the nobles no longer owed service to the state, the political and moral justification for their role as serf owners was weakened. Criticism and self-criticism of their position mounted.

Second, the 1700s saw little progress toward Peter's goal of establishing a "regulated" state that rested on efficient institutions and fixed laws. Instead, the political system remained, despite a burgeoning bureaucracy, largely dependent on the personal authority and quasi-religious image of the tsar and on the privileged status and role of the topmost nobility who filled the chief military and administrative positions in the Russian government. No competing sources of power emerged to challenge the autocracy and to push it toward modernity. By the end of the eighteenth century a few intellectuals and conscience-stricken nobles had begun to question the morality of serfdom and the political validity of the tsarist system, both of which, however, persisted largely unchanged.

Third, Russia continued to develop economically, largely under state encouragement, intervention, and control, but it did not possess the requisites to participate in the Industrial Revolution that began at the end of the century in Europe. Thus, by 1800 Russia's rate of economic growth had begun to fall markedly behind that of the west European nations, and its agricultural productivity remained low.

Fourth, Russia's continuing expansion brought new non-Russian peoples under tsarist rule. Their mistreatment by the government sowed the seeds of later conflicts between a Russian majority and non-Russian minorities in the Russian empire.

Fifth, by the end of the 1700s Russia had begun to develop a national consciousness and literature, which laid the foundation for the remarkable flowering of Russian culture in the nineteenth century.

In this chapter we will examine these five themes, beginning with a concise sketch of political developments from the death of Peter in 1725 through the end of Catherine's reign in 1796, then analyzing throughout the eighteenth century Russia's expansion and colonization, its economic and social development, the changing role of the nobility, and the spread of education and culture. We will conclude with a brief description of the rule of Paul I (1796–1801), Catherine's successor.

PETER'S SUCCESSORS, 1725–1762

For one hundred years, beginning with Peter's death and ending with the Decembrist Revolt of 1825, the question of who was to sit on the tsarist throne created political turmoil in Russia. This seems puzzling, when one considers the dominant position that Peter, the tsar-emperor, occupied, but several factors help explain the uncertainties that followed his reign. Peter himself muddied the succession issue by treating the tsardom as private property. In 1722 he declared that he alone would name his successor, but he then failed to do so. Moreover, the nobles, who wanted to exert more political influence, could achieve their goals only through control of the tsar, whom Peter had made the embodiment of the supremacy of the state in Russian society. The locus of power was in the tsar; there was no other way to affect the government. There were no well-defined estates, no autonomous church, no municipalities, no middle class, and not even an independent bureaucracy. Control of the throne itself was the key to political success.

Yet in the thirty-seven years after Peter's death, his successors were neither capable individuals nor strong rulers. Three women reigned in this period. Each possessed a strong personality and had her own ideas, but lovers, courtiers, and advisers largely set and executed policy. The sequence of rulers in the eighteenth century was as follows:

Catherine I	1725–1727
Peter II (a boy)	1727–1730
Anna	1730–1740
Ivan VI (an infant)	1740–1741
Elizabeth	1741–1762
Peter III	1762
Catherine II (the Great)	1762–1796
Paul I	1796–1801

Catherine I, the second wife of Peter the Great, was of humble Latvian origins but had the backing of Peter's colleagues and friends, although Peter's grandson, another Peter, was the logical heir. Pressure from the guards regiments, set up originally by Peter and manned in all ranks mainly by nobles, finally settled the issue in Catherine's favor. On four more occasions in the 1700s the guards, who directly represented noble interests, intervened to determine who should be tsar. In this way the nobility played a significant political role, but they never found a way to institutionalize this influence.

Moreover, the nobles were not a unified and coherent group, and the one attempt they made to formalize their participation in the government foundered on divisions among them. On Catherine's death, Peter II, Peter the Great's young grandson, succeeded her, but he died of smallpox in 1730, leaving no male Romanov in line of succession. A small clique of upper-crust nobility, including members of the Supreme Privy Council, a kind of executive body on which Catherine had relied, decided to offer the throne to Anna, a daughter of Peter's step-brother, Ivan V. In so doing they asked Anna to accept a number of conditions sharply limiting her autocratic power: she was in effect to rule jointly with the council. Anna, eager to ascend the throne, agreed. However, less privileged members of the nobility, jealous of the ploy effected by the council, demanded their share of the political pie, and when Anna arrived to be crowned, the guards demonstrated in her favor. Taking advantage of this turmoil, Anna tore up the conditions and dissolved the Supreme Privy Council.

She ruled for the next ten years as an empress-autocrat but relied heavily on a group of advisers who were predominantly Germans from the Baltic region. One of them, her favorite, Count Biron, was particularly corrupt and cruel, and his persecutions of Old Believers and others aroused bitter enmity among Russians of all classes.

Before dying in 1740 Anna appointed her grand-nephew, Ivan VI, as tsar, but he was only an infant when he ascended the throne, and the so-called German party continued to rule Russia. Again the guards staged a *coup d'état*, putting Peter the Great's daughter, Elizabeth, in power in 1741. Though quite capable and well-meaning, Empress Elizabeth was also vain, lazy, and extravagant. She, too, ruled through favorites, though now they were Ukrainians and Russians. During her reign the influence of French culture spread in Russia, but almost nothing was done to tackle the basic social, economic, and administrative backwardness of Russia.

In 1762, when Elizabeth died, Peter III, Peter the Great's grandson by his oldest daughter and a German princeling, succeeded to the throne. Brought up in a German household, Peter moved to Russia when he was a teenager to prepare himself to become tsar, but he never lost his suspicion of his new surroundings and his admiration for things German, including the leading German sovereign, Frederick the Great of Prussia. In several areas Peter's policies as tsar were quite forward-looking, but his attacks on the Orthodox Church, his attempt to prussianize the army, and his radical volte-face in the Seven Years' War, making peace with Russia's traditional enemy Prussia on the verge of the latter's defeat, alienated broad circles in Russian society. Moreover, his crude, adolescent, and unpredictable behavior gave people little hope for improvement in his rule. The result was yet another palace revolution, as we saw at the start of the chapter, carried out by elements of the guards regiments, with Catherine's connivance. The unfortunate Peter was soon killed, perhaps accidentally, probably deliberately.

CATHERINE THE GREAT, 1762–1796

Although Catherine the Great did not have so abrupt and marked an impact on Russian and European history as Peter the Great, she was a powerful and effective ruler for over three decades. She was both extremely able and a charmer, as the British ambassador to Russia made clear in a 1762 dispatch to London:

> Her Imperial Majesty is neither short nor tall.... Her features were far from being so delicately and exactly formed as to compose what might pretend to regular beauty, but a fine complexion, an animated and intelligent eye, a mouth agreeably turned, and a profusion of glossy chestnut hair produce that sort of countenance which, a very few years ago, a man must have been either prejudiced or insensible to have beheld with indifference.... Her eyes are blue, their vivacity tempered by a languor in which there is much sensibility

and no insipidity. . . . She expresses herself with elegance in French, and I am assured that she speaks Russian with as much precision as German, which is her native language. . . . She speaks and reasons with fluency and precision. . . .[2]

Outgoing, intelligent, hardworking, ambitious, and self-confident, Catherine poured all her considerable energy and skill into the task first of ascending the throne and then of advancing the cause of Russia, her adopted land, and of herself as its "enlightened" ruler. Her love life has often been sensationalized, but there is no evidence that it ever interfered with her judgment or effectiveness as empress or that any of her acknowledged twenty-one lovers exerted influence on state policy solely on the basis of a liaison with her, rather than on their own merits.

In almost every respect Catherine was a self-made woman. Born Sophie of Anhalt-Zerbst, a small German principality, she lived as a child in modest circumstances and without great expectations. It was assumed that at best she might be married to some minor German princeling or nobleman, and it was only a stroke of great good fortune that, through complicated family connections, at age fifteen Sophie was selected by Empress Elizabeth as the fiancee of the heir to the Russian throne, the future Peter III. She and her mother were commanded to go to St. Petersburg to live at Elizabeth's court. Before long her mother was evicted as an agent of the Prussian king, and Sophie realized that her betrothed was no bargain, being coarse, poorly educated, and emotionally underdeveloped.

With spunk and determination, she nevertheless set about preparing herself for her future role as a tsar's wife. She converted to the Orthodox faith, was rebaptized Catherine, learned Russian, and plunged assiduously into finding out all she could about her new country and about the larger world. She read widely, particularly in the works of the French writers of the Enlightenment, and studied politics and human nature close up, first observing the maneuvering and intrigues at Elizabeth's court and then taking part in them. Caught out on one occasion, Catherine shrewdly threw herself on the mercy of Empress Elizabeth, protesting her devotion to Russia and the monarch. Elizabeth forgave her, and by the time Peter III ascended the throne Catherine, in sharp contrast to her husband, had thoroughly russianized herself and had developed a wide circle of powerful friends among the elite of Russian society.

Through self-education and by character and inclination Catherine the Great was indeed an "enlightened despot," comparable to other European monarchs accorded that designation in the eighteenth century. She believed in natural law, the rule of reason, religious toleration, and the orderly functioning of government for the good of society (see Figure 10). Although Catherine was happy to use her acquaintance and correspondence with Voltaire and other leaders of the European Enlightenment to boost her own ego, to build support for her regime, and to spread her

Figure 10. *A portrait of Empress Catherine the Great that suggests her forceful personality. (Courtesy of Sovfoto/Eastfoto)*

fame abroad, she was also genuinely stimulated and inspired by their ideas and advice.

Regarding Russia her intentions were good, but her hell was that, having usurped the throne, she never felt entirely secure on it and thus hesitated to undertake basic social reforms, such as the abolition or amelioration of serfdom. She feared destabilizing the system and alienating her chief political supporters, the nobility. Moreover, she was dealing with a vast country that had huge problems, and on some practical matters she simply felt she could make little headway. She remained dedicated to the ideals of the Enlightenment and to improving Russian society, but as she wrote Diderot, the French philosopher: "You only write on paper, but I have to write on human skin, which is incomparably more irritable and ticklish."

Though adhering to principles of the Enlightenment, Catherine strengthened rather than curtailed the autocracy and opposed the French Revolution. This was not hypocritical as some have charged. In both the concept of enlightened despotism and the Russian political tradition, beneficial change was to be directed from above, and the monarch was not to give up authority but to use it wisely. Moreover, Catherine never espoused radical eighteenth-century ideas such as representative government and liberty. She wanted a more efficient, more humane autocracy but nevertheless an autocracy.

She was particularly sensitive about her authority because despite her repeated proclamations after the deposition of her husband that she was acting in the interests of all the people and for the good of the whole country, she was in fact an outsider, a German upstart, who had seized the throne by force and who had no legal claim to it. To make her even more jittery, two legitimate heirs to the throne existed and several pretenders arose. Ivan VI, deposed in 1741, was now a young man though still imprisoned. In 1764, however, he was killed by his guards during a failed attempt to rescue him and use him against Catherine. A second threat was her son Paul, born in 1754. Although recognized as Peter's son and therefore heir to the throne, Paul was almost certainly sired by a lover of Catherine, Sergei Saltykov. As Paul grew to adulthood, he posed the continuing danger that he might become a rallying point for opposition to Catherine.

Among the pretenders, the most important was Emelian Pugachov, a Don cossack, who in 1773–1774 led the last major peasant revolt, or *jacquerie*, in a series that dated back at least to Bolotnikov in 1607. Although this widespread uprising was directed more against the system than against Catherine personally, it was a frightening affair since it dramatically revealed to Catherine deep-seated weaknesses in Russia's central and provincial administration, as well as the extent of the country's social inequities. The spectrum of those who joined Pugachov reflected the diversity of groups with major grievances against the regime: cossacks whose privileges and autonomy were being undercut, Bashkirs and Tatars whose culture and ethnic rights were being trampled upon, Old Believers persecuted by the Orthodox Church and the government, factory serfs condemned to work in the mines and manufacturing enterprises of the Ural region in inhuman conditions, agricultural serfs ground down by increased taxes and recurring army conscription, and fugitives of every kind from army deserters to runaway serfs and criminals.

Claiming to be Peter III, Pugachov declared an end to serfdom, taxes, and the draft and a war on landlords and the government. Molding his motley supporters into a surprisingly effective force, Pugachov ranged along the Ural and Volga rivers and briefly captured a number of important towns. Because Russia was then engaged in a major war with Turkey, the government nearly panicked, fearing at one time that Pugachov might march on Moscow. Repeatedly defeated by regular troops, he was finally captured and as one account put it, "drawn and quartered but not tortured"! The Pugachov revolt strengthened Catherine's political alliance with the nobility, virtually the only group that supported the government in the disaffected regions. It also bolstered her resolve to undertake fundamental reforms of Russia's administration.

Aware when she came to power in 1762 that governance in Russia was chaotic, Catherine, with her usual determination and acumen, set about putting state affairs into better order. She reformed the Senate to make it more efficient as an administrative overseer, she improved tax collection, and she revamped the budget and fiscal policy. At the same time she was interested in a broader and more deep-rooted approach to Russian problems and decided to convene a representative body of leading officials and citizens to initiate a codification of the laws (the last had been in 1649) and to study what basic reforms should be undertaken. Known as the Legislative or Grand Commission, it included delegates from the nobles, townspeople, the government, state peasants, and non-Russian groups but no serfs and only one cleric. Opening its sessions in 1767, Catherine presented the commission with a long set of "instructions" that she had labored over for many preceding months. Drawing heavily on thinkers of the Enlightenment, Catherine had personally written many sections of her charge to the commission, which was quickly translated into all the main European languages.

After almost two years of deliberations the commission adjourned. It had served quite effectively as a broadly constituted consultative body. It did not reach definite conclusions partly because of its unwieldy size (almost six hundred members) and because few delegates had the education, experience, and judgment to turn Catherine's theoretical considerations into practical law or policy. But it also gave no specific policy direction because it mirrored differences within Russian society, particularly between nobles and merchants, as well as the general reluctance of any group to attack the root institution of serfdom. The Grand Commission, however, did have several positive results: it educated Catherine concerning the basic problems of the society she presided over and the limits of what she could alter; it provided concrete information and opinion that were later incorporated in her administrative reforms; and its subcommittees, which met for several more years, drew up a number of useful proposals.

Partly spurred by the Pugachov revolt, Catherine in 1775 instituted a major reorganization of the countrywide administration of Russia, changes that lasted in some cases until the 1860s and in others until 1917. The most important reform was to divide the nation into provinces *(guberniia)* equal in population—fifty by the end of Catherine's reign—with equal districts within each province. The provincial governors were responsible for coordinating government policy and for overseeing the operations of functionally separate judicial, legislative, and administrative departments in each province. Although not ideal, this was a marked improvement over previous patterns of governance.

In 1785 Catherine undertook two other major reforms, granting a charter of rights and obligations to both the nobility and the towns. The former was more important because it confirmed the liberation of the nobility from compulsory service, first decreed under Peter III in 1762, and because it established noble organizations in the provinces and districts of the reorganized empire. A few historians have argued that the Charter of the Nobility was the first step toward formation of independent interest groups in Russian politics and that it might have opened the door to eventual representative government. But this interpretation is off the mark. Indeed Catherine wanted to establish the nobility as a separate and privileged order in Russian society, but mainly so that they could serve the government more effectively. She certainly did not intend for them to develop into an alternate center of power. The nobles themselves, for reasons to be discussed, did not attempt to turn their charter into a weapon against the autocracy. The complicated and limited system of governance set up for the towns in 1785 did not entirely work, and municipal administration remained a problem for Catherine's successors.

Catherine was of course active in many other areas—social policy, education and culture, economic development, minority affairs, and foreign policy—and her role in these matters will be discussed as part of our review of long-term trends in Russia during the whole period from Peter's death to the end of the eighteenth century.

RUSSIAN EXPANSION AND COLONIZATION

Throughout the 1700s but particularly during Catherine's reign Russia continued to expand its frontiers in all directions and to settle new areas. In many respects this trend marked a continuation of earlier policies and movement, but in the eighteenth century much of the new territory acquired had never been under Kievan or Russian rule, and most of the peoples absorbed were not Great Russians. By 1800 the Russian state was an enormous, multinational empire, prominent in both Europe and Asia, as it has been ever since.

After Peter's death Russia maintained the influential position in European politics he had claimed for it, and the government also continued his interest in exploring and colonizing in Asia. Russian foreign policy in Europe was directed in large part toward weakening Russia's two major western neighbors, Poland and the Ottoman Empire. Since Austria was also concerned about the same countries, Russia and Austria were allied for much of the century. Russia also tried to stay on good terms with Britain, its largest trading partner.

As we saw in the previous chapter, it is hard to evaluate Russia's foreign policies from the sixteenth to the twentieth centuries. Were Russia's leaders motivated primarily by considerations of defense and national security? Were they trying to protect Russia's borders and forestall possible attacks by enemies? Or were they mainly interested in extending Russia's rule and influence over other countries? Were they imperialistic, seeking widened power and profit in Europe and Asia (and perhaps the world)? Unfortunately, the record of the 1700s provides no clear answers to these questions.

On the one hand it can be argued that the Turks, and particularly their protégés the Crimean Tatars, posed a constant threat to the southwestern flank of European Russia. Similarly, the Poles, historically inhabiting a larger and more developed kingdom, could be viewed as a danger. But in fact the Tatars were more of a nuisance than a threat, and the Ottoman Empire was already in that period of decline that was to lead to its collapse in World War I. Moreover, Poland, economically weak and wracked by internal problems, was in no position to menace the Russians. And in Asia no power posed any possible danger to the Russian empire. On balance, then, Russian foreign policy in the 1700s appears more aggressive than defensive, even though Russia's expansion to the Black Sea under Catherine fulfilled a long-cherished goal dating back to Kievan times and extended Russia's southern border to a natural geographic limit.

The chief loser in the game of eighteenth-century European politics was Poland, which was swallowed up by its neighbors before the end of the century (see Map 5). Details of the diplomatic maneuvering that resulted in three partitions and the eventual disappearance of the Polish state are beyond our scope. At the same time the general circumstances of Poland's annexation are important, not least because they shed light on the strong antipathy most Poles have today for the Russians. To be sure, the Poles were to some extent their own worst enemies, but essentially Poland was victimized by stronger neighbors coveting its land.

Although Poland recovered from its defeat by Charles XII of Sweden during the Great Northern War, increasingly in the 1700s it was weakened, partly because it could command fewer resources than most of its neighbors and partly because it was being torn apart by social, religious, and political conflict. Polish peasants struggled against their landlords, Catholics persecuted those of other faiths, and the Polish nobility steadily undermined the power of the king. Finally, by the 1760s civil war erupted in Poland, an irresistible temptation for the major countries surrounding Poland to interfere in its affairs. This led in 1772 to the first partition, under which Russia, Austria, and Prussia each took Polish territory adjoining their states, the whole totaling about one third of Poland. Although most of the land annexed by Catherine was inhabited by Russians, Belarusans, and Ukrainians, the predominance of these nationalities hardly justifies the action. The humiliation of the first partition led to a national revival in Poland, which greatly strengthened the country but also alarmed its neighbors.

After some maneuvering the powers joined in two more partitions, in 1793 and 1795, that eliminated Poland from the map of Europe. In these Russia, Prussia, and Austria annexed lands inhabited primarily by Poles, who became an important and hostile minority within each empire. Although reasons of prestige, economic benefit, and security were advanced for this bare-faced dismemberment of an independent state, greed, opportunism, and a determination to share in the spoils seem to have been the basic motivations. As one contemporary noted about Maria Theresa, the empress of Austria: "She wept but she kept on taking." The Poles of course were bitterly resentful, rebelling against their Russian masters three times in the 1800s before resurrecting their country in 1918, as an outcome of World War I.

Russia's other major territorial gains were in the southwest as the result of several wars against the Ottoman Empire, the most important of which occurred under Catherine in 1768–1774. By the end of the century Russia had acquired all the territory north of the Black Sea from the Dniester River eastward, including the mouths of the Don and Dnieper rivers; had annexed the Crimea, the home of the Crimean Tatars; had obtained commercial rights in the Black Sea and through the Straits at Constantinople; and was vaguely authorized to act as protector of Orthodox Christians under Turkish rule. Strategically, economically, and politically Russia gained a great deal, securing her southern border, opening up profitable trade through the Black Sea, obtaining rich agricultural lands, and weakening one of Russia's main enemies. Nevertheless, the Turkish problem remained a major issue in Russian foreign policy throughout the next century.

Russian colonization of Siberia and the fringes of Central Asia had begun in the 1600s but was stepped up in the 1700s. In addition to encouraging Russians to move out to the frontier regions, the government induced a large group of Catholic and, later, Mennonite Germans to settle along the Volga River. And after acquisition of territory north of the Black Sea, Russians and Ukrainians were settled there in large numbers. Although in earlier times Jews had been prohibited from living in the Muscovite state, Catherine surreptitiously encouraged the immigration of Jews, both into western Russia and into the new lands in the south. Incorporation of the Polish territories also added numbers of Jews to the empire's population. At first they were granted equal rights as citizens, but in the 1790s, for reasons that are unclear, an imperial decree assessed double taxation on Jews of all classes.

As the empire expanded by conquest and colonization, administration of this vast state became more and more difficult. Catherine, although making the reforms noted earlier, essentially followed the policies of her predecessors; that is, she treated the new territories and peoples as integral parts of Russia. This meant that with a few exceptions, centralized rule was established, local rights were ignored, and efforts were made to russify the non-Russian population. For example, Ukrainians lost the last vestiges of their autonomy and were fully absorbed into the empire. Serfdom was also permitted in western Ukraine and selectively in the new lands north of the Black Sea, although not in Siberia and the Asian borderlands.

ECONOMIC AND SOCIAL DEVELOPMENT

Russia, like much of Europe, experienced a remarkable population boom in the eighteenth century. The reasons for this growth are not clear, but improved public order and public health, a feeling of greater security and stability, and an increase in the acreage farmed may all have contributed. In any case the population more than doubled in about four generations, from roughly thirteen million in 1722 to twenty-nine million in 1796. To the latter figure were added another ten million people living in the recently acquired Polish and southwestern lands. The result was a much larger work force and potential market, but it also produced more mouths to feed while agricultural productivity had increased little. The overwhelming majority of the population remained serfs and state peasants living at a bare subsistence level.

Although towns grew with the increasing population, the urban-rural ratio changed slowly: In the early 1700s about 97 percent of the people lived in the countryside and 3 percent in towns, and by 1800 the figures were 92 to 94 percent and 6 to 8 percent. The upper nobility remained a tiny fraction of the population, numbering in the tens of thousands, and the whole noble class reached only the hundreds of thousands, barely 1 percent of the population at most. Over 90 percent of the population were peasants, and the proportion of those who were privately owned serfs grew slowly in the 1700s, reaching an estimated 55 percent by the end of the century, when serfdom was at its height. This meant that by 1800 between fifteen and twenty million Russians were virtual slaves. Another ten to fifteen million were state peasants of various categories who owed heavy obligations in money or kind but were slightly better off than the private serfs.

During the 1700s while the percentage and total number of serfs increased, their situation deteriorated. Not only did the eighteenth-century tsars give to favorites, military heroes, high nobles, and other worthies land containing hundreds of thousands of peasants (often from non-Russian areas in Ukraine and eastern Poland), thereby making the inhabitants serfs, but they also gave all serf owners greatly increased power over their serfs. For example, owners could now interfere in serf marriages, could send recalcitrant serfs into the army, and could administer judicial and physical punishment to serfs, including banishment to Siberia.

Advertisements offering serfs for purchase are reminiscent of the American South: "For Sale: two plump coachmen, two barbers, one knows how to play musical instruments. . . ." But unlike slavery in the United States, serfdom in Russia was not limited to one region of the country but existed almost everywhere, except in the far north, Siberia, and parts of Russian Asia. Finally, data are insufficient to determine how much state taxes on the peasants increased in the eighteenth century, but a reasonable estimate is that they doubled. In short, the 1700s marked the apogee of the institution of serfdom in every respect: numbers, extent, conditions, and oppressiveness. Catherine, though concerned in principle, apparently believed, particularly after the Pugachov revolt, that tampering with serfdom would threaten the whole social system. Consequently, she attempted only minor reforms, encouraging voluntary emancipation of serfs and limiting the use of serf labor in industry.

The inefficiencies and lack of incentives to produce associated with serfdom help explain why the Russian economy in the eighteenth century advanced only slowly. Serfdom held back development of a national market, slowed capital accumulation, and hindered technological innovation and entrepreneurship. But the economic policies of the state were also at fault. Catherine, for example, offered inducements for nobles to found industries and enter trade, but this policy also discouraged merchants and townsmen. Serf artisans and producers, though making a substantial contribution to the economy, were not encouraged. As a result, although Russian nonagricultural output grew in the course of the century, the ground was not prepared for a major takeoff into industrialization, like that occurring in western Europe. At the end of the century Russia was a leading producer of iron and copper, her output of pig iron in 1790 equaling that of England, but in the first decades of the nineteenth century Russia fell far behind.

THE CHANGING ROLE OF THE NOBILITY

As we saw in the last chapter, the nobility began the century tightly harnessed to the service of the state by Peter. Their sons were expected to be ready for education or duty in their teens and were to serve for life. By the end of the century nobles owed no service in peacetime, though they could be summoned in time of need. The nobles had become a dominant and privileged elite in Russian society, far and away the best educated and wealthiest element in the state. The steps along their path to liberation were many, and we need note only a few major ones here. In 1731 the first school for military cadets was opened. Nobles' sons could enroll there and graduate with an officer's commission, thus avoiding the Petrine system of being required to enter the guards regiments as enlisted men and work their way up to officer rank. In 1736 the term of service for nobles was reduced to twenty-five years. In the 1740s one son in each noble family was exempted from service so he could stay home to manage the family's land and affairs. Another decree stipulated that only nobles had the right to own serfs. Finally, in 1762 under Peter III nobles were exempted from state service in peacetime altogether, a privilege confirmed in Catherine's Charter of the Nobility issued in 1785.

Although service was no longer obligatory, the crown of course strongly encouraged it, and in fact most nobles continued to serve in some military or bureaucratic capacity. It was expected that those who did not would be running their estates in the countryside and would be active in local affairs, including the provincial and district assemblies of nobles established in the 1785 charter. But few had any altruistic interest in improving production of their lands, and there was little incentive to do so as long as they did not go too far into debt. From boredom or a sense of responsibility some did participate in local administration, but many frittered away their time or simply vegetated.

In any case, the nobility were not a homogeneous group, as we saw when they split over the conditions the Supreme Privy Council tried to impose on Anna. In addition to differences along lines of rank, wealth, and political influence, the nobility was divided by location and education. At the top of the social pyramid stood the nobles of the two capitals, St. Petersburg and Moscow. These individuals either held important state posts or were wealthy enough to keep a town house in one of the two major cities. They would spend part of the year on their rural estates and part in urban social life. Beneath this elite were the provincial nobility, that is, nobles who either resided or kept town houses in the other major cities of the Russian empire. At the bottom of the scale were the rural nobility, probably half of all nobles, who lived on small estates, owned few or no serfs, and seldom if ever went to the towns. They were generally poor, some little better off than their peasants, and usually poorly educated. There were also "personal" nobles who owned neither land nor serfs.

In fact, education became in the eighteenth century a major dividing line among the nobility and in Russian society generally. Before 1700 only high clergy and a few of the elite were educated at all; even parish priests were generally illiterate or had the most rudimentary education. During the eighteenth century the nobility, as part of their dominance, became much better educated, either through schools or through private tutors. Nobles who lacked the money or the opportunity for education soon found that the top jobs in the tsarist administration were out of their reach and that they were slipping into an inferior social status.

At the same time education affected the outlook of the elite nobles in two ways. Since their education was primarily Western in orientation, they found themselves increasingly isolated from their fellow citizens, whether they were poorer, uneducated nobles or humble serfs. The sophisticated elite increasingly adopted European manners, customs, dress, and even language, thereby opening a huge and unbridgeable chasm between them and their fellow Russians. For example, many educated Russians knew French or German well and read mostly foreign literature. The noted Russian publicist of the nineteenth century, Alexander Herzen, characterized the alienation that resulted as follows: "Foreigners at home and foreigners abroad, idle onlookers—spoiled for Russia by their Western prejudices and spoiled for the West by their Russian habits—they constituted a strange kind of intelligent superfluity, and lost themselves in their artificial life, in sensual pleasures and in an intolerable egoism."

A small minority who found themselves adrift between two cultures but who were determined to do something about it became radical critics of the situation in Russia. They concluded that Russian society as a whole, and particularly the institution of serfdom, needed fundamental change if it were to measure up to the standards that Enlightenment thinkers had postulated as the natural and inalienable rights of all peoples. These critics became the forerunners of the Russian revolutionary intelligentsia of the nineteenth century.

Whatever the differences in education, rank, and wealth among the nobility, the question remains: Why didn't they become an independent political force in Russian society, once they were liberated from obligatory state service? Two related factors were decisive, in my view. First, by the 1700s the tsar largely determined entry into and placement within the noble group. Peter's Table of Ranks institutionalized the dependence of the nobility on state service, appointment to which was controlled by the tsar and his close advisers. To be sure, there were hereditary nobles, and old families persisted in positions of influence and wealth. But status and power mostly depended on service, and the tsar decided who would serve and therefore who would be important. This was true whether service was obligatory or voluntary.

Second, and a natural corollary, the nobility had no separate or autonomous institutional base outside the government. They were not organized as a class; they had no corporate rights except petitioning the tsar, but only rights as individual nobles; and they had no mechanism, since the end of the *boyar duma* and the *zemskii sobor,* to be represented as a group before the tsar. Although Catherine's provincial and district assemblies of nobles could be viewed as the embryo of an independent organization, they were in fact creations of the state, serving mainly state administrative purposes. Only on a few rare occasions in the nineteenth century were they turned to the purpose of representing the independent interests and views of the nobility.

EDUCATION AND CULTURE

As an enlightened despot, Catherine worked hard to broaden and improve education in Russia. Theoretically, a well-run state required an educated populace; practically, Catherine desperately needed trained individuals to staff her administration and help her govern an immense country. More sensibly than Peter, who tried to build an educational system from the top down, Catherine strove to develop an integrated system at all levels. She had some previous developments to work with, but not many.

Some of the state schools Peter had founded failed for lack of funds, teachers, or students, but a few survived and during the middle of the eighteenth century were complemented by the opening of a number of private schools. Moscow University was founded in 1755, although it enrolled barely one hundred students in its first few decades. Catherine began with an idealistic plan for a network of state boarding schools that would produce an enlightened elite. This plan proved impractical, although it did encourage the founding of the first school for women, the Smolny Institute in

St. Petersburg (which in the Revolution of 1917 became the headquarters of Lenin's Bolshevik party). Finally in the 1780s a system of general public and free education was instituted; schools were opened in provincial cities and district towns but not in the countryside. At the same time the first teachers' training institute was founded. By 1796 over twenty thousand pupils were enrolled in the recently created elementary and secondary schools, a paltry number in a country Russia's size, but a start and an authentic triumph for Catherine, who had to overcome lack of interest and funds to create the system.

For most Russians, despite the growing Westernization of elite society, cultural life continued to revolve around Orthodox religion and folk beliefs and tales. The village church remained the center of worship and edification, and communal celebrations focused on religious festivals and holidays. Faith in God and the saints and the rites of baptism, marriage, and death ordered and undergirded existence even for those backsliders who infrequently attended mass. Sickness and nature's vagaries were coped with through folk wisdom and traditional remedies dispensed by influential women healers in the village. Most of Russian culture remained Orthodox, Slavic, and fatalistic.

In sharp contrast, Catherine, as one would expect, vigorously promoted Western-oriented cultural activities, beginning with her own court, where plays, readings, and musical soirées intermingled with games, balls, and other light entertainment. The number of books published in Russia more than tripled in Catherine's reign as compared with the total output up to that time. The empress also encouraged periodicals and newspapers, and as education spread among the nobility and townspeople, an informed and interested, if tiny, reading public developed. Catherine also encouraged the arts, and the Russian theater flourished, producing mainly European plays but also the first plays by Russian authors.

As with much of the cultural development of the 1700s, painting, architecture, and music largely imitated Western models. But to a considerable extent this schooling in European styles and values was the indispensable preparation for the astounding outburst of independent artistic creativity in nineteenth-century Russia that has so enriched world culture. Literature of the 1700s already foreshadowed the cultural efflorescence to come, with development of the first modern Russian poets, playwrights, and authors, including Antiokh Kantemir, Michael Lomonosov, Denis Fonvizin, and Nicholas Karamzin. Lomonosov was also a gifted scientist and a leader of the Russian Academy of Sciences founded just after Peter's death. By the end of the century Russian writers had developed a distinct style and an independent identity, characterized by one historian as the beginnings of a definite national consciousness.

Intellectual debate and social criticism, both important aspects of the European Enlightenment, developed in Russia as well. In Catherine's time a leading critic was Nicholas Novikov, who was also a freemason and publisher of several of the country's most widely read journals. But the boldest commentator on Russian society was Alexander Radishchev (1749–1802). He was an outstanding example of a type of Russian intellectual that became prominent and troublesome to the government in the next century. Radishchev, of noble birth and well educated in Germany and Russia, entered state service and performed creditably as a middle-level administrator in Catherine's regime. At the same time under the influence of Enlightenment thought, particularly the writings of Rousseau, he became increasingly disturbed over what he observed about him in Russian society. He was particularly appalled by the moral and social implications of the serf system; employing a typical eighteenth-century literary device, the travelogue, Radishchev poured out devastating criticism of serfdom in his *Journey from Petersburg to Moscow*, published privately in 1790. Catherine, already alarmed at what she considered the excesses of the French Revolution, which had begun the year before, banned Radishchev's book and had him arrested and imprisoned in Siberia. Thus at the end of Catherine's reign, the state, which had fostered the spread of culture and of "enlightened" ideas, turned to censorship and repression against theories and individuals considered harmful to state interests, a policy followed, with rare respites, by later Russian governments.

THE REIGN OF PAUL I, 1796–1801

The brief rule of Catherine's son, Paul, supplied a disturbing coda to eighteenth-century Russian history. Bubbling to the surface in Paul's reign appeared harsh manifestations of Russian civilization that had been suppressed or minimized under Catherine. Paul was a militarist above all; his mother emphasized civil administration and civic development. The son was irrational and quixotic; Catherine emphasized reason and considered policies and behavior. Paul gave orders without explanation; his mother tried to encourage and lead her people, or at least her officials and the educated public, into accomplishing what had to be done in their and the state's interest.

In Paul's defense, his background may partly account for his instability and failure as a ruler. As noted earlier, he was undoubtedly a bastard son, though accepted by all as the legitimate heir. Catherine, a strong-willed mother, found it difficult to mold Paul as she would have liked. In addition, as we saw, she continually feared him since he had a stronger claim to the throne than she and could always serve as a rallying point for opposition, should it develop. Consequently, fairly early in her reign, when Paul was still a young man, she shunted him aside. He was kept out of state affairs and encouraged to busy himself with military training, which he loved, on his own estates near St. Petersburg (today one of them is a lovely public park, Pavlovsk).

Moreover, because Catherine lived well into her sixties and reigned for over thirty years, Paul had to wait a long time for the throne and had plenty of opportunity to build up resentment against his mother, her advisers, and their policies. Finally, near the end of her reign Catherine indicated fairly clearly that she would probably name her grandson, Alexander, as her successor; he was a handsome and intelligent young man, who with his brother Constantine had been taken away from Paul and his wife at an early age and reared by grandmother Catherine with suffocating tenderness and in accord with "enlightened" principles. In short, Paul had a good deal to be disgruntled about when his mother died unexpectedly in late 1796. Since she had not yet named a successor, Paul ascended to the throne at the age of forty-two.

Not unlike his father, Peter III, Paul instituted some progressive measures in his short reign, encouraging religious toleration and education and attempting to have the obligations of serfs defined and limited. He also finally settled the succession issue that had created such political turmoil throughout the century, decreeing that the throne was to pass to the eldest male heir. But both his policies and his style upset the nobility and the bureaucracy, on whom after all the administration and welfare of the state mainly depended. He was high-handed, which was bad enough, but also inconsistent and unpredictable. As one critic put it, his reign could be characterized as "Order, Counter-order, Disorder." Paul tried to enforce Prussian-style discipline on the army and conducted endless parades and drills, all of which antagonized both officers and enlisted men. Moreover, he seemed completely insensitive to the feelings of either individuals or the citizenry as a whole. This was perhaps because he was wholly self-centered and made a bit giddy by the assumption of despotic power after waiting so long. He reportedly told a senior official on one occasion: "The only person in Russia who is important is the person I am speaking to, and only as long as I am speaking to him."

Paul was thoroughly conservative, probably little understanding the ideas of the Enlightenment or the aspirations of his mother. He tightened censorship, relied on political repression, and joined the European coalition against revolutionary France. But as in other matters his foreign policy was contradictory and unpredictable. In 1800, disgusted with his allies, Paul switched sides, joined Napoleon, and ordered some Don cossacks to set off to oust the British from India.

The alliance with France may have been the final straw in the developing resistance to Paul's rule, and in early 1801 he was deposed and killed in yet another *coup d'état*, which we will discuss at the start of the next chapter.

CONCLUSION

By the end of the eighteenth century Russia was largely what Peter and Catherine had made of it. In many respects Catherine completed what Peter had begun, adding, however, a more reasoned and humane touch to the changes affecting Russian society. The result was an almost schizophrenic country: Europeanized in elite culture and thought, military affairs, and even technology, but deeply Russian and traditional in popular culture, religion, social system, and agriculture; a leading power of Europe politically and economically but with an arbitrary and repressive autocracy and a relatively backward economy; a modern educational system and an ordered and even "enlightened" administration that supervised a degrading and inefficient social system and relied heavily on censorship and coercion.

Russia's historical experience differed from that of western Europe, and she obviously could not be like the West. But neither could she turn her back on Europe and the onrush of new ideas and inventive technology. Russia had to live in a European-dominated world and had to adjust. Neither Peter nor Catherine had found a magic formula to blend the best of Europe with the best of Russia, but probably one did not exist, and none of their successors fared any better.

To Catherine's great credit she demilitarized the society, tried to improve governance, promoted education, helped found a national culture, and confirmed the nobility in their rights while trying to inspire them to higher ideals of rationality and service. On the other side of the ledger, however, she was unable to cope with the problem of serfdom, she enhanced autocratic power without removing its inherent arbitrariness, and she expanded Russian rule over Poles and other non-Russians with little moral or other justification. On balance, one has to conclude about the fascinating Catherine that she did what she could, which may not have been enough for Russia's needs but was far more than her immediate predecessors and most of her successors accomplished.

FURTHER READING

Alexander, John T. *Catherine the Great: Life and Legend.* New York: 1989.

Catherine II. *The Memoirs of Catherine the Great.* New York: 1957.

Garrard, John, ed. *The Eighteenth Century in Russia.* Oxford: 1973.

Kamenskii, Aleksandr. *The Russian Empire in the Eighteenth Century.* Armonk, N.Y.: 1997.

Kelly, Catriona. *A History of Russian Women's Writing.* Oxford: 1994.

Leonard, Carol S. *Reform and Regicide: The Reign of Peter III of Russia.* Bloomington, Ind.: 1992.

Madariaga, Isabel de. *Russia in the Age of Catherine the Great.* New Haven, Conn.: 1982.

McGrew, Roderick E. *Paul I of Russia, 1754–1801.* New York: 1988.

Raeff, Marc. *Origins of the Russian Intelligentsia: The Eighteenth Century Nobility.* New York: 1966.

_____. *Understanding Imperial Russia.* New York: 1984.

Ragsdale, Hugh, ed. *Paul I: A Reassessment of His Life and Reign.* Pittsburgh: 1979.

Raleigh, Donald J., ed. *The Emperors and Empresses of Russia*. Armonk, N.Y.: 1966

Ransel, David. *The Politics of Catherinian Russia*. New Haven, Conn.: 1975.

Rogger, Hans. *National Consciousness in Eighteenth Century Russia*. Cambridge, Mass.: 1960.

Wirtschafter, Elise Kimerling. *Social Identity in Imperial Russia*. DeKalb, Ill.: 1992.

8

Power, Backwardness, and Creativity, 1801–1855

An icy gust of wind from the Neva River swept across St. Petersburg's Senate Square, causing the soldiers drawn up in ragged ranks to hunch down into their tunics. Eyes watering from the cold, they looked about vainly for a sign from their officers. Some units had been there since early that wintry morning, December 26, 1825. For two weeks there had been confusion over who would succeed the deceased tsar, Alexander I. His oldest brother, Constantine, had renounced the throne in favor of a younger brother, Nicholas, in accord with a secret memorandum approved by Alexander several years earlier. But when Alexander died, Nicholas, reluctant to appear a usurper, had hesitated, providing an opportunity for a group of revolutionary army officers to attempt to seize power. They called out elements of four regiments, some three thousand troops in all, to demand that Constantine be made tsar. The Decembrists, as the dissident officers came to be called, wanted a number of liberal reforms in Russia, but the soldiers understood little of this, as is illustrated by the apocryphal story that they clamored for "Constantine and Constitution," believing the latter (a feminine noun in Russian) to be Constantine's wife.

Earlier that morning the soldiers had shot and fatally wounded their commanding general when he had appeared to persuade them to surrender. A high Church official, the Metropolitan Seraphim, had fared better when he appeared in full vestments and bearing a cross to appeal to them to give up: the soldiers had merely shouted at him to retire to the cathedral and pray for their souls. The tsar-to-be Nicholas had himself barely escaped when he met a company of disheveled and disgruntled soldiers in the nearby Palace Square in midmorning. Intending to put the men in formation, Nicholas, without identifying himself, called, "Halt!" to which the troops replied, "We're for Constantine." To avoid a confrontation, Nicholas simply told the unit it should go to the Senate Square to join their comrades already there.

By afternoon the impasse between the rebels ranged in front of the Senate Building, and some twelve thousand loyal troops confronting them across the square remained unbroken. The two top leaders of the Decembrists were nowhere to be found at this crucial moment, and junior conspirators were uncertain what to do. A sullen group of laborers who had been constructing St. Isaac's Cathedral at the end of the square expressed sympathy for the soldiers by tossing stones and pieces of lumber at the government forces.

Because of St. Petersburg's northern latitude, in mid-December dusk comes to the city as early as three in the afternoon. Fearing that the rebellion might spread under cover of darkness, Nicholas finally ordered his artillery to fire grapeshot at the mutineers. Some sixty or seventy were killed, more wounded, and the rest fled. One hundred and twenty-one leaders of the Decembrist movement were arrested, of whom five were put to death after an ₌cial investigation and trial. Decisive action might have carried the day tor the revolutionaries, but since their goals and motives were vague and unpublicized, it seems unlikely they could have succeeded in the long run.[1]

What sort of society were the Decembrists rebelling against? By the early 1800s Russia was a huge but economically underdeveloped country, profoundly conservative yet with the first stirrings of revolutionary ferment, powerful militarily but inherently weaker than its Western rivals, and socially repressive despite spreading education and bursting cultural creativity. In this chapter we will explore these paradoxes, focusing in turn on Russia's serf economy, political stagnation punctuated by efforts at reform under tsars Alexander I (1801–1825) and Nicholas I (1825–1855), the flowering of literature and the arts, the development of revolutionary ideas, and Russia's dominant role in Europe and Asia. We will sketch the picture of what was in many respects a faltering giant: a great empire with endemic structural weaknesses, a socially divided citizenry, and uncertain and conflicting values. In spite of the foundations laid by Peter the Great and built upon by Catherine, Russia in the 1800s was unable to keep pace with the rapid economic modernization and political transformation that the West was experiencing in the nineteenth century.

By the early 1800s the Russian empire included forty-one million people, as compared with twenty-six million in France, only eighteen million in Great Britain, and eight million in the United States. In extent it stretched from central Europe to the Pacific Ocean, and from the Arctic to the Black Sea. Although Slavs were the dominant nationality, many other ethnic groups lived in Russia, including Germans, Finns, Jews, Tatars, Baltic peoples, and Asians of various nationalities. The people were overwhelmingly Orthodox in religion, but there were also Catholics, Lutherans, Jews, and Muslims. Official policy increasingly advanced russification, that is, the imposition on all citizens of Russian language, culture, and administration. The government also encouraged Orthodoxy as the preferred faith. Fewer than two million people lived permanently in towns and cities. St. Petersburg had the largest population, 308,000 inhabitants, with Moscow next at 270,000.

An authoritarian government headed by the autocratic tsar and run by an extensive bureaucracy managed this huge and diverse empire. Administration was cumbersome, inefficient, and often venal. Civil liberties were limited, and censorship, arbitrary actions, and repression were common. Some 450,000 people were nobles, but the largest landholders and serf owners totaled less than 30,000 individuals. Two million people served in the military, and another two million were clergy, merchants, artisans, and urban laborers. All the rest, almost thirty-seven million Russians, were privately owned serfs and state peasants. State and society were richer than they had been in the eighteenth century but were rapidly falling behind the wealth and progress of western Europe.

Most Russians were formalistically religious, little educated, vaguely loyal to the tsar, and increasingly resentful of the harsh life they endured and of the privileged elite who appeared to reap the benefits of their sacrifices. Within Russian culture as a whole and particularly among the educated elite, a deep-seated and divisive clash of values was developing. On the one side were ranged secular, rational, worldly ideas and attitudes associated with the European Enlightenment. Opposed to them were religious, emotional, traditional views and feelings derived from old Russian culture. Eloquent spokesmen for both positions and philosophies arose, and a lively debate ensued throughout the 1800s.

THE SERF ECONOMY

Since so much of the social and economic life of the country was built upon the peasantry and the system of serfdom, we need to take a closer look at rural Russia and its institutions. The primary social unit was the extended peasant family. It customarily included grandparents, parents, and children, with a son's wife moving into the household of her husband's family. The dominant authority in the family was normally the senior male, but in the absence or incapacitation of such an individual, a grandmother or mother could fill the role. The family unit shared work and property, as well as being jointly responsible for taxes and other obligations.

Marriage, usually arranged, took place early in life. Women bore children almost annually since the household needed workers and 45 percent of children died before their fifth birthday. Peasant huts were small, crowded, dirty, smelly, and, in cold weather, smoky, as the one stove was poorly ventilated. Except in times of famine peasants had enough to eat, probably faring as well, or even better, than European farmers of the same era. Disease and the chance that young males might be taken for twenty-five years' service in the tsarist army were constant threats. Peasants looked to God, spirits of nature, or a "good tsar" to protect them in adversity.

American farms are single homesteads with surrounding land. But Russian villages, like European villages, are (and were) clusters of dwellings, usually laid out side by side along one or two muddy streets, averaging forty to fifty houses and several hundred to a thousand in population. Each small dwelling had space within it for animals, such as a few cows, pigs, geese, or chickens, as well as a tiny orchard and vegetable garden in the back. In most villages the surrounding lands were divided into grazing, timber cutting, and tillable fields (and similarly for the lord's acreage). Each household had the right to farm strips of land in the crop fields.

A collective village institution, the *obshchina* or commune, whose forerunner arose in Kievan times, allocated these farming strips among households, usually every ten years, on the basis of the size and needs of the household. The *obshchina*, composed of heads of all the households in the village, made general agricultural decisions, such as what and when to plant, but each household worked its strips individually. The *obshchina* was also responsible as a whole for the general obligations of the village: work or payments to the lord, taxes and conscripts for the tsarist government.

In central southwestern Russia the serfs worked the lord's land as well as their own; in other parts of the country the serfs and state peasants owed payments in produce or money, in lieu of labor on the lord's fields. Depending on the size of his landholdings, his financial situation, and his inclinations, a noble landowner might closely supervise farming on his estate or show little or no interest in it, leaving agricultural decisions almost entirely to overseers and managers. During the nineteenth century the financial position of most noble landholders declined markedly, and by mid-century well over half of them were in debt.

From even this cursory description of the agricultural system its inefficiency and low productivity emerge. Serfs and state peasants had little incentive to produce since a good part of the fruits of their labor went to the lord or to the state in the form of taxes. Moreover, even an ambitious peasant was restrained by having to tailor his farming to the pattern set by common *obshchina* decisions on sowing, tilling, and harvesting. Nobles had little incentive to invest in agriculture or to introduce new farming techniques. As long as their estates produced enough for them to live comfortably, they were content to follow traditional practices. As a result the Russian land as a whole produced only a modest surplus, enough to feed the cities and to export a bit to western Europe, but not enough to accumulate rapidly the capital needed for large-scale industrialization.

Nevertheless, even if there had been general recognition that the serf economy was not very efficient or productive, it would have been difficult to change it. For, as an institution serfdom was still a useful administrative and social mechanism. It permitted the nobles and the government to control the bulk of the population, maintaining the peasants at a subsistence level. The nexus of lord, commune, and household helped keep order, collect taxes, and man the army. Moreover, because the system was so widespread and because so much of privileged Russia appeared to depend on serfdom, most officials feared the social disruption its abolition would cause; in particular they were afraid that the nobility would turn against the government. Only a major military defeat and rapidly changing attitudes finally permitted, in 1861, dismantling of this antiquated socioeconomic system.

The rest of the Russian economy in the first half of the nineteenth century suffered from the same drawbacks that it had in the 1700s, in particular a limited internal market, insufficient capital for investment, state restrictions and interference in the economy, and a small and timid entrepreneurial class. At the same time it did begin to grow, laying the foundations for its remarkable development in the latter part of the century. The number of manufacturing enterprises doubled while the number of workers increased fourfold. Particularly significant was the increasing use of free hired labor, which led some to conclude that Russia would be better off without serfdom. New branches of production were established, and a major cotton textile industry was developed. Transport and communications were greatly expanded, with the building of canals and railroads and the use of steamships on Russian rivers and seas. Trade and a money economy grew, and Russia became an exporter of grain and other raw materials to western Europe. The number and size of towns increased, and the urban population had almost doubled by mid-century.

Despite nascent industrialization and slowly improving productivity, Russia remained essentially an underdeveloped country, with an economy linked too heavily to an inefficient agricultural system. In terms of both economic growth and economic strength Russia began to fall markedly behind western and even central Europe. This trend had two significant results: Russia became increasingly dependent economically on Europe and, though still playing the role of a great power, was relatively weak politically and militarily.

RUSSIA UNCHANGED

At the time few people were aware of this erosion of Russia's position. Reforms were discussed in the reigns of both Alexander I and Nicholas I, but no fundamental changes in the political and social system were made, despite an abundance of new ideas and the first emergence of a revolutionary movement. In part this stagnation can be explained by the fact that Russia continued to enjoy great success as a participant, often even an arbiter, in European affairs. Defeat was needed to force change, as we shall see in the next chapter. But in part the "frozenness" of Russian life in this era stemmed from the fact that under the autocracy only the tsar could initiate peaceful change, and neither Alexander I nor Nicholas I was prepared to undertake radical reform, though they were quite willing to tinker with the system.

Alexander in particular was a disappointment to those who looked for new directions for Russian society. A favorite grandson of Catherine, he had enjoyed a privileged childhood and an exemplary education supervised by a private tutor committed to the ideals of the Enlightenment. He seemed both born and trained to rule brilliantly. Moreover, he was a striking and charming individual. Tall, blond, gracious, and having a lively imagination, Alexander commanded admiration and respect from friends and enemies alike. But he also had an enigmatic personality and character, restless, vague, inconsistent, and in the end quite mystical. He had difficulty putting his ideas into practice, he vacillated on important issues of state policy, and he finally came down much more clearly on the side of absolutism than on that of enlightened change.

Some historians have suggested that the uncertainties and vagaries in Alexander's behavior resulted from his rather tortured upbringing, torn as he was between his father Paul and his grandmother Catherine while trying to please both, and from guilt over his father's murder during the *coup d'é-tat* that brought Alexander to the throne. Although these are plausible suppositions, it is important to note that flights of mysticism and erratic action occurred more often in Alexander's later years and that as a young tsar—twenty-three years old at the time of his accession in 1801—he was quite decisive and seemingly well balanced.

In fact Alexander's reign had a promising start. He annulled some of Paul's most unpopular measures and amnestied people Paul had disgraced, exiled, or imprisoned. Alexander then began regular meetings with a small group of young and liberally minded advisers to plan improvements in Russian society. This coterie, which came to be known as the Intimate or Unofficial Committee, discussed frankly what changes should be made in the autocratic system and whether serfdom should be abolished. All the participants, including Alexander, soon confronted the great complexity and delicacy necessarily involved in reforming the two major institutions of Russian society. No comprehensive plan was propounded, but out of the discussions of the Unofficial Committee did come useful administrative changes, including strengthening the Senate established at the time of Peter the Great and establishing ministries to run various departments of government. Regulations for the personal manumission of serfs were decreed, and serfs in the Baltic provinces were emancipated, though without land. A number of new universities and schools were founded, and the educational system was both extended and improved.

Alexander's concern with domestic issues was interrupted in 1805 by Russia's joining in a European war against Napoleonic France, but Alexander returned to a consideration of reform between 1807 and 1812. The most radical proposal came from Michael Speransky (1772–1839), a remarkably able and far-sighted official, who on the basis of his talent, education, and effectiveness rose from humble origins to become a close adviser of both Alexander and Nicholas. In 1809 Speransky drew up an elaborate system of governance for Russia, which in fact amounted to a constitution. It provided for separation of the administrative and judicial functions of the state, as well as for legislative bodies at four levels and the specification and protection of certain rights for citizens. It was a bold plan, and if it had been adopted, it would have moved Russia much closer to the patterns of political development then unfolding in western Europe. But Alexander put into effect only a small part of Speransky's project, and later, in 1820, he also failed to implement a constitutional proposal submitted by another adviser. At the same time Alexander strongly supported constitutions for France after Napoleon's defeat and for the kingdom of Poland set up under Russian control after the Napoleonic wars. This anomaly in Alexander's political policies is one of the enigmas about him that have never been fully explained. In my view, Alexander retained the basic attributes of the autocratic system in Russia proper in part because he enjoyed the power and authority he wielded and in part because his exploration of radical reform in the deliberations of the Unofficial Committee had convinced him that giving the average Russian a say in government might undermine the whole system and lead to revolution.

In the latter part of his reign Alexander continued to approve some minor reforms but also adopted strongly conservative policies in education and social affairs, including a scheme proposed by the reactionary General Alexis Arakcheyev for military settlements: estates and villages inhabited by enlisted soldiers who between military assignments farmed the land under strict discipline and harsh conditions. Moreover, as we shall see shortly, Alexander pursued antiliberal policies abroad and spearheaded efforts to suppress revolutionary movements in Europe. The tsar also maintained a large army and navy, with over 40 percent of the state budget in 1825 allotted to military expenditures.

Alexander's unwillingness to introduce basic reforms in Russia's social system and political order evoked disillusionment, frustration, and despair among those of the educated elite who opposed serfdom and autocracy and who favored institution in Russia of civil rights and some form of representative government. Particularly disaffected were numbers of younger military officers, most of whom had served in the campaigns in Europe against Napoleon and had been exposed there, and in their education and reading, to the liberal ideas of the Enlightenment. Largely of noble background, these young men, after their return to Russia, formed secret societies to discuss their hopes and ideas for reform and to plot a course of action. Proud of their country's victory over Napoleon and its role in European affairs, they found themselves ashamed and distressed at Russia's economic backwardness, social oppression, and political obscurantism, and as men of action, they determined to do something about the situation. By the early 1820s these idealists had coalesced into two main groups, the Northern Society, whose moderate leaders espoused a limited constitutional monarchy for Russia, and the Southern Society, whose more radical thinkers urged overthrow of the tsar, establishment of a republic, and possibly the abolition of serfdom.

Reports of these dissident activities reached Tsar Alexander, but he seemed little concerned, probably because he was aware that only a small group was involved and that they had no following among the people as a whole. As we saw at the start of the chapter, when Alexander's unexpected death (he was only forty-eight years old) was followed by confusion over the succession, the conspirators seized this opportunity to move against the government. Their plans were not well laid, there was muddle and timidity in executing them, and the Decembrist rebellion was a fiasco.

Although many of the Decembrists were noble officers in guards regiments like their forebears who had participated in seizures of power in the eighteenth century, the Decembrist revolt was not a palace revolution of the traditional type: the Decembrists did not simply want to change tsars but to change government and society. In that sense and even though they acted in splendid isolation from the masses, the Decembrists were the first modern Russian revolutionaries. Perhaps their goals were idealistic and their methods hopelessly impractical, but the Decembrists had a vision of a better Russia and a determination to realize that dream. Consequently, they were soon idolized as revolutionary pioneers, and their tradition inspired the Russian revolutionary movement throughout the nineteenth century. Even Lenin and the Bolsheviks acknowledged the Decembrists as their progenitors.

Alexander's youngest brother, Nicholas, who at age twenty-nine came to the throne in late 1825 during the tumult of the Decembrist rising and reigned for almost thirty years, was militaristic in outlook and deportment. Half-Prussian through his mother and tutored by a general, he had felt most comfortable as a youth in military drill and routine. He wanted Russia to be well ordered, efficient, and strong, and he applied his considerable determination and capacity for hard work to that end. Meticulous about detail, he personally supervised the investigation and trial of the Decembrists, clearly convinced that such dangerous and harebrained activities as theirs should never be allowed in a properly run autocracy.

Although reserved, suspicious, and characterized by an almost fanatical sense of duty, Nicholas was by no means stupid, and he was well aware that Russia faced serious problems. In 1842 Nicholas stated candidly:

> There is no question that serfdom in its present state in our country is an evil palpable and obvious to everyone. However, to attack it now would be, of course, an even more disastrous evil.[2]

He nevertheless took several steps to mitigate the harshness of serfdom, including decrees that serf families could not be broken up and that serfs could not be sold apart from the land. He also implemented the recommendations of one of the many bureaucratic commissions he established, regularizing and ameliorating the obligations of state peasants. At the same time Nicholas carried out a number of administrative and bureaucratic reforms designed to make the existing system work better. Among the most significant were a massive codification of Russian laws in 1838 overseen by Speransky and a series of financial improvements supervised by his minister of finance, Egor Kankrin.

The government's slogan of "Autocracy, Orthodoxy, and Nationality" summed up the ideology of Nicholas's conservative regime. He reinforced the tradition of the authoritarian state and is reputed to have said, "I regard the whole of human life as service." Defending the prerogatives of the autocracy, Nicholas did not hesitate to resort to arbitrary action, censorship, and police surveillance and harassment to hector the government's critics and suppress dissent. Although the notorious Third Section of His Majesty's Own Chancery, established by Nicholas, was a forerunner of the political police set up by twentieth-century dictatorships, it was quite inefficient and unwieldy and achieved rather minuscule results despite enormous efforts.

Nicholas strongly supported the Orthodox faith and espoused Russian nationality as a supreme good. He applied russification measures to the western provinces of the empire, and after the Poles revolted against Russian rule in 1830, Nicholas suppressed the rebellion bloodily and abolished the Polish constitution, replacing it with new regulations that greatly restricted Polish autonomy and repressed Polish culture.

There is no doubt that despite minor improvements under his rule Nicholas essentially preserved and defended the old system and the traditional outlook of Russia. The ideal of service to the state, together with the authority of the government, was maintained and extended. The autocracy and serfdom remained basically unchanged, while the bureaucratic civil service grew to oversee almost every aspect of life. Russian society was still divided into classes, or *estates,* with the upper nobility retaining extensive privileges of status, wealth, and influence. Although there were merchants, artisans, and other free townspeople, almost no middle class or bourgeoisie comparable to that in western Europe developed. This was because Russia had a predominantly agrarian economy and because the government dominated all activity: its bureaucrats outnumbered all other nonlaboring and nonagricultural workers, it controlled education and the professions, and it played a leading role in finance, production, and trade. Even the towns were, or had until recently been, predominantly administrative centers. In such a centralized, hierarchical structure there was no place for independent interest groups or for pluralistic inputs to policy and operations. Finally, except among those who espoused the ideals of the French Enlightenment, the rights and aspirations of the individual were largely ignored in Russian society. State, church, army, and village commune all stressed the good of the whole community over that of the individual person.

CREATIVITY AND DISSENT

What causes sudden surges of human creativity, such as the Renaissance? How can one explain a flurry of brilliant artistic activity, as occurred in mid-nineteenth-century Russia? In the space of not more than thirty or forty years, a dozen Russians produced some of the greatest works in world literature and Western music. It was an astounding, and largely inexplicable, performance. It was also paradoxical that these creative heights were reached at the very moment when Russian society, under Nicholas I, was culturally repressed. The government was trying to block new ideas with censorship and persecution, and the atmosphere was one of stagnation and disillusionment. Moreover, the official and widely held values were mystical and religious, related to the traditional tenets of Orthodox Christianity and the conservative principles of autocracy and privilege. Under such circumstances how could magnificent secular works of literature and music be written and composed?

It is tempting to answer that the coincident movement of dissent and criticism stimulated this creative flowering, but it is almost impossible to support such a causal connection. Most of the literature was about life not revolution, and the writers represented a broad spectrum of political and social views. All one can say is that artists and revolutionaries existed side by side and that to some extent both combined what Russia had learned from Western culture with Russian traditions and ideals to create brilliant new art and thought. It is also true that both writers and critics of the system moved in the same circles, a special group in Russian society known as "the intelligentsia."

This subclass was composed of individuals well educated in both Russian and Western culture whose main focus was intellectual life and discussion and who were deeply concerned about the nature of their own society and the future of Russia. The intelligentsia, although predominately from the upper classes, included sons and daughters of the poorer clergy, of lower-ranked civil servants, and of service and professional townspeople. They worked at all sorts of jobs, from tutoring and teaching to serving in the tsarist army and bureaucracy. Most felt alienated from the government and "official" society; on the other side, though they did not always acknowledge it, the intelligentsia were almost completely cut off from the mass of the Russian people: the peasants and the small but growing number of workers. They had varying criticisms of the existing situation and system, while propounding a wide range of solutions, from conservative to revolutionary. A common mistake of American students is to equate the intelligentsia with revolutionaries, whereas in fact a majority of intelligentsia preferred peaceful change in Russian society.

The remarkable outpouring of outstanding literature from writers among the intelligentsia began in the 1820s and 1830s with the poetry and prose of Alexander Pushkin, perhaps the most versatile and lyrical of all Russian writers. His long poem *Eugene Onegin* describes "the superfluous man," the individual who, restlessly but in vain, seeks a place and purpose in life and society, a story that became the basis of a magnificent opera by Tchaikovsky. Unfortunately Pushkin's brilliant career was cut short at the age of thirty-eight, when he was killed in a duel. His place as the premier Russian poet was taken by Michael Lermontov, who composed moving romantic poems and also wrote a superb realistic novel, *A Hero of Our Times*. He, too, died in a duel, when only twenty-six years old.

Nicholas Gogol, often considered the founder of Russian romantic realism, wrote about everyday life. His rollicking comedy, *The Inspector General*, and highly enjoyable novel, *Dead Souls*, satirized rural Russian society and its petty landlords and officials. In such short stories as "The Overcoat" and "The Nose," Gogol, with macabre humor but considerable empathy for his protagonists, depicted the dreary life and outlook of the "common man," the downtrodden bureaucrat or citizen struggling to exist in a society filled with pomposity and privilege. Although Gogol was politically conservative, his work was hailed by the radical critics among the intelligentsia who urged that literature be used as a weapon against the evils of government and society.

From the 1850s to the 1870s three giants dominated Russian literature. Ivan Turgenev's most influential book, *Fathers and Sons,* incisively portrayed the conflict between a more moderate older generation and a new breed of radicals personified by Bazarov, a "nihilist" who rejects all old values and mores in the name of materialistic science. Fyodor Dostoyevsky, perhaps the greatest of psychological novelists, depicted Russian life realistically, in such works as *Crime and Punishment* and *The Brothers Karamazov*. Yet the essence of his books was the conflict of emotions and ideas. He was thoroughly critical of Western materialism and values while seeing true salvation in a refinement of selfless love attained only through suffering.

Dostoyevsky's contemporary, Leo Tolstoy, remains a favorite epic novelist, best known for the broad sweep and riveting detail exemplified in his lengthy depiction of Russia's struggle against Napoleon, *War and Peace*. Tolstoy had the knack of making scenes and characters seem more vital and absorbing than reality itself. In the late 1870s Tolstoy underwent a religious "rebirth" and became an influential advocate of nonviolence and a devastating critic of the artificiality and immorality of modern life.

Russian artists of the mid-nineteenth century excelled in music as well as in literature. The first great Russian composer was Michael Glinka, who lived from 1804 to 1857. His operas, and those of other composers later in the century, effectively joined classical musical forms from Europe with Russian folk melodies, songs, and stories. This tradition was followed in the 1860s through 1880s in the works of a group of outstanding composers known as the "Mighty Bunch" or "The Five": Modest Mussorgsky,

Nicholay Rimsky-Korsakov, Milii Balakirev, Cesar Cui, and Aleksandr Borodin. Working separately at about the same time was Pyotr Ilich Tchaikovsky. Together, these six composers produced romantic ballets, operas, symphonies, and other pieces that have enchanted lovers of classical music in Russia and abroad ever since.

While Russian writers and musicians were producing impressive masterpieces, essayists and social critics such as Vissarion Belinsky were engaged in a lively debate over philosophical and political issues. Much of the discussion focused on the nature of Russian society and the direction it ought to follow. Although almost all the debaters were schooled in a common body of European philosophy, especially German idealism, they reached diverse and often conflicting conclusions. Most were optimistic about Russia's future, rejecting the gloomy assessment of Peter Chaadayev in 1836 that because "we are not Western or Eastern and have the traditions of neither," Russia had contributed nothing to world culture.

The two main schools of thought that developed were the westernizers and the Slavophiles, small informal groups of noblemen intellectuals in Moscow. The former, as the name indicates, believed that Russia should adapt essential values and institutions developed in the West to the needs of Russian society. The westernizers stressed secular and rational thought and were voluntarists; that is, they believed that individuals and groups could act to change and improve society. Looking with favor on Peter the Great, they urged the expansion of education and the reform of Russian institutions. Although some later became revolutionaries, most westernizers urged the introduction into Russia of civil freedom and constitutional government through peaceful, evolutionary change. Two prominent westernizers, Alexander Herzen and Michael Bakunin, became increasingly critical of the government and went into exile in Europe in the mid-1840s. Herzen became a prominent journalist and mild revolutionary, while Bakunin moved in a sharply radical direction to become a leading anarchist.

The Slavophiles were romantic nationalists who idealized the Russian past, rejected Western civilization as a model for Russian development, and espoused a future good society in Russia based on the spiritual values of Orthodoxy and the social values of the people, especially as expressed in the peasant commune. At the same time they were critical of the government and the tsar, arguing that the mystical bond between ruler and people that had existed in old Russia had been broken by the interference of the bureaucracy and by the changes introduced by Peter. It was therefore necessary to restore a simpler, purer form of rule that would both protect the rights of Russians and give the tsar freedom to rule. The Slavophiles also criticized the established Church and urged its purification and the widespread propagation of basic Orthodox ideals. With these changes, the Slavophiles concluded, Russia could build a unique civilization that would be far superior to Western societies and that would contribute constructively to world culture. This visionary future would be based on brotherly love, peace, and harmony.

These contrasting attitudes toward the West and differing views of Russia's mission and future remained important issues of intellectual discourse in Russia in the nineteenth and early twentieth centuries and are still current in Russia today.

RUSSIA—ARBITER OF EUROPE, COLONIZER OF ASIA AND AMERICA

For several decades in the first half of the 1800s Russia was considered the most powerful country in Europe and played a prominent, if not dominant, role in European affairs. This position was a result of Russia's major contribution to the defeat of Napoleon and to the peace settlement that followed. At the same time Russia was busy extending its borders, primarily in Asia, where tsars Alexander and Nicholas annexed most of the Caucasus and expanded Russian colonies in North America. Finally, throughout this period the Russian government was deeply involved with Turkey, an imbroglio that culminated in the Crimean War, 1854–1856.

Tsar Alexander had come to the throne determined to keep his country at peace, but in the first ten years of his rule he waged war with Persia, Turkey, Sweden, and France. The struggle with Persia grew out of a request for protection from the small Christian state of Georgia in the Caucasus. The Russians assisted the Georgians against both Persian and Turkish incursions and pressures, and by 1810 Alexander had incorporated Georgia and several small neighboring areas into the Russian empire (see Map 6, Chapter 9). Conflict with Turkey that lasted from 1806 to 1812 and with Sweden in 1808–1809 resulted in Russia's acquiring two strategically important territories on its western border, Bessarabia and Finland.

But the main foe during Alexander's reign was revolutionary France led by Napoleon. Alexander opposed France because of Russia's political ties to Austria, Prussia, and Great Britain; its close economic relations with Great Britain; and Alexander's personal opposition to Napoleon's plans for dominating and transforming Europe. Alexander considered Napoleon a parvenu and usurper. Armed conflict broke out first in 1805–1807 but Napoleon soundly defeated the Russians at the battles of Austerlitz, Eylau, and Friedland. In July 1807 a famous peace between Napoleon and Alexander was signed at Tilsit, and for the next four years the two major powers on the continent of Europe were uneasy allies eyeing each other warily.

The Tilsit agreement finally broke down over several issues. First, Napoleon wanted the Russians to adhere strictly to his "continental system," which was essentially a Europe-wide economic blockade against Great Britain, France's major remaining foe. Not only did many Russians ignore the restrictions and continue to trade with Britain, but to the extent the blockade was observed, this harmed the Russian export economy, the English having been the Russians' major trading partner over the preceding decades. Moreover, the Russians resented their defeat at the hands of the French and the growing French domination of Europe. The French in turn considered the Russians an unreliable ally and the only important obstacle to complete French hegemony on the continent. Finally, the two governments differed over policy in the Near East, in the Balkans, and in Poland and northern Europe, and there were other minor irritants in the relationship.

At last in June 1812, without declaring war, Napoleon invaded Russia, with the largest military force ever assembled in Europe, the so-called Grand Army, which at its height included six hundred thousand troops. However, less than half were French, with the rest supplied reluctantly by Napoleon's allies. The Russians were outnumbered more than two to one and were forced to fall back steadily before Napoleon's advance. Eventually, in September 1812 the Russians, under a newly appointed and popular commander, Prince Michael Kutuzov, made a stand at Borodino, a village just west of Moscow. In one of the bloodiest battles in history the Russians lost over a third of their force, some forty thousand men, while Napoleon's army suffered proportionate losses, over fifty thousand casualties, all in one day's fighting. Though forced to retreat, the Russians lost few prisoners and Napoleon could not destroy the remnant of the Russian army. He entered Moscow unopposed a few days later, believing the capture of Russia's traditional mother city would compel Alexander to surrender. But to Napoleon's indirect overtures for peace the tsar responded "at this moment no proposition of the enemy can induce me to terminate the war, and by that to weaken the sacred duty that I have to perform in avenging my injured country."[3]

Russians of all classes rallied patriotically around Alexander and the army, and Napoleon soon found himself in an untenable position. Harassed by Kutuzov's forces; with greatly extended lines of communication and supply; unable to draw much support from Moscow itself, which had been first evacuated and then partially destroyed by mysterious fires; and with the harsh Russian winter approaching, Napoleon withdrew in mid-October. In one of the great disasters of military history Napoleon's forces, weakened by disease, dwindling military and food supplies, and the raids of guerrilla bands and half-frozen to death by the bitter cold, staggered out of Russia. Only fifty thousand men out of the original six hundred thousand escaped death or capture. In the succeeding months the victorious Russian armies carried the war to Europe and played a major role in the ultimate defeat of Napoleon. The campaign concluded with Alexander's marching into Paris at the head of his victorious troops.

The triumph of 1812–1813 had several important consequences. It was then, and has always been since, both a source of national pride and a reminder of Russia's vulnerability to attack from the West. It greatly increased Russian prestige in Europe and ensured major Russian influence in European affairs for several decades to come. At the same time it may have led Russian leaders to consider their country more powerful than it in fact was, and it may thus have reduced the pressure for basic reforms.

Alexander was a leader at the Congress of Vienna, which worked out a peace settlement for post-Napoleonic Europe. Under pressure from the other powers Russia had to settle for a smaller kingdom of Poland under Russian rule than Alexander had sought, but the tsar did obtain approval for his formulation of the Holy Alliance: a high-flown proclamation by the leading monarchs that they would band together to promote peace and Christian brotherhood in the world. Its practical manifestation was the Quadruple Alliance (Russia, Austria, Prussia, and Great Britain, with France joining in 1818), a powerful political coalition that acted to regulate the affairs of Europe for over a decade. In particular, the alliance, under Russian and Austrian prodding, moved firmly to suppress revolutionary movements in various parts of the continent. Although an internationalist in outlook, Alexander saw collective action primarily as a means of safeguarding the restored order in Europe and forestalling revolution.

Nicholas I pursued the same goals, but with such added vigor that he earned the unfortunate sobriquet of "the gendarme of Europe." In 1830, when revolutions broke out in France and Belgium, Nicholas would gladly have intervened against them, but the Poles also rose in revolt against their Russian masters, and the Russian army had to be employed to restore order there. However, in 1848, when revolution again swept across Europe, Nicholas sent Russian troops to help quell the uprising in Hungary, an intervention that was repeated a little over one hundred years later when the Soviet army put down the popular revolution of 1956 in Hungary.

Nicholas also extended the gains his predecessor had made in the Caucasus, acquiring part of Armenia in 1818 and waging a long war against Caucasian mountaineers led by the brilliant and tenacious Muslim warrior Shamil. In the Pacific Nicholas encouraged the development of Russian Alaska, but in 1867 under his successor, Alexander II, it was sold to the United States.

Although Russia had been in conflict with the Muslim Turks of the Ottoman Empire since the sixteenth century, only in the first half of the nineteenth century did relations with Turkey, the so-called Eastern Question, become a major issue in tsarist foreign policy. The Russians and the Turks were at loggerheads in the 1800s—four major wars—for several reasons. Religious differences created one set of problems. The Orthodox Russians asserted the right to protect Christian minorities in the Ottoman Empire, particularly Christian groups in Turkish-ruled lands in the Balkans who were closest to Russia, some of whom were fellow Slavs. The Russians also claimed they should be allowed to manage and safeguard Christian holy places in the Near East, preserving them not only against Muslim but also Catholic interference.

A second set of issues centered on economic and strategic control of the Black Sea and of the Straits, the passage between the Black Sea and the Mediterranean. In the 1800s the tsars struggled to obtain the right of free passage through the Straits first for merchantmen and later for warships.

Finally, relations between Russia and Turkey were strained because the Ottoman Empire was rapidly weakening; in fact it became known as "the sick man of Europe." As Turkish power declined, Russia expanded in the Caucasus on the eastern border of the Ottoman Empire. Even more important was what would happen to territories under Turkish rule in Europe itself—in the Balkans and therefore on Russia's southwestern border. The Balkan peoples themselves rebelled against the Turks in a series of nationalist uprisings, but in addition the great powers, and particularly Austria, strove to exert influence in the Balkans. Consequently, while the Russians tried to reduce or eliminate Turkish control over the Balkans, they had also to contend with the intrusion of Austrian and later German power there. At the same time France and Great Britain were eager to prevent a Turkish collapse, from which the Russians would reap enormous gains, and as Ottoman power eroded, they strove to block any excessive accretion of influence to the tsars.

Beginning in the 1820s when the Greeks rebelled successfully against their Turkish overlords, recurring crises developed in the Near East and the Balkans over these issues. On almost every occasion the Russians and most of the other European great powers were drawn in, yet for three decades a major war among them was somehow averted. In the late 1840s and early 1850s, however, Tsar Nicholas I, who had until then managed Russian policy quite skillfully, made two major miscalculations. After extended conversations in England in 1844 Nicholas believed that he had reached an understanding with Great Britain to consult in advance and to act together on all issues relating to Turkey. In retrospect it appears that he assumed this gave Russia more scope in the Balkans than in fact the British leaders intended. In addition, Nicholas—or at least his emissary in Constantinople, the capital of the Ottoman Empire—underestimated the resistance of the Turks to Russian pressure and demands.

Although the details of the negotiations and the particular issues at hand need not concern us, the result was that the Turkish sultan appealed for support to the European powers, and when war broke out between Russia and Turkey in 1853, France and Great Britain soon sided with the Turks. Austria, although not participating, kept a threatening pressure on the Russian flank, and Nicholas found himself isolated and outnumbered. In September 1854 an Anglo-French expeditionary force landed on the Crimean peninsula and after a grueling campaign, marred by gross incompetence of the generals on both sides (which prompted Tennyson's famous poem "The Charge of the Light Brigade") and heavy sacrifices and casualties all around, the Russians were defeated and in 1856 had to sign the humiliating Treaty of Paris.

The Crimean War burst the bubble of Russia's superpower status in Europe, revealing to the West its military weakness and social and political backwardness. Although Russia, as we shall see in Chapter 10, continued for the next sixty years to play a significant role in European affairs, her position was now that of a junior player struggling to keep up with the varsity. Even more importantly the war displayed in glaring fashion to the new tsar, Alexander II (Nicholas had died near the end of the war), and to the Russian educated elite the serious internal problems of Russia and the urgent need to reform its archaic socioeconomic system and its cumbersome and inefficient government.

CONCLUSION

In several respects the history of Russia in the first half of the nineteenth century represents a golden opportunity missed. With a burgeoning population and a slowly rising level of education, the Russian government, drawing on the experience of neighboring Europe, might have bent every effort to accelerate the country's economic growth and to initiate processes of industrialization and modernization. Instead Russia, although developing slowly, fell markedly behind the booming European economy, which left the empire considerably weaker than its great power rivals for the rest of the 1800s and into the 1900s.

To be sure, to be able to surge ahead economically the tsars would have had to abolish serfdom and greatly reduce the overweening and stultifying intervention of the government in all aspects of social, economic, and political life. To contemporaries it seemed that Alexander, favorite of Catherine, child of the Enlightenment, and a man of imagination and ability, might be the perfect tsar to undertake these necessary changes. Yet his complex personality and his enjoyment of power prevented him from grasping the nettle of reform, even after his glorious triumph over Napoleon. Constitutional projects languished and serfdom continued. Out of frustration with the lack of progress came the Decembrist uprising in 1825 and in the 1840s the beginning of a revolutionary movement among the intelligentsia.

Under Nicholas hopes for reform dimmed, given his character and outlook, with the result that Russia marked time, its social problems festering and its political climate frozen. Nicholas could wield a "big stick" in Europe and Russia's international prestige was high, but even this bubble was burst by Russia's humiliating defeat in the Crimean War.

By 1856 Russian society was in a fairly desperate situation. Much of its educated elite, although creative participants in European culture and bringing renown to their country in such fields as literature and music, were alienated from the government and out of touch with 90 percent of the population, who remained uneducated, burdened, and a potential "dark force." Under-developed economically, repressed politically, divided socially, Russia nevertheless continued to absorb European values and modernizing influences and tried valiantly to compete with Western societies that were already stronger and were moving rapidly in quite a different direction. It was urgent that Russia seek its own salvation, find its own path, and move into the modern world on its own terms. The task facing the new tsar, Alexander II, was monumental, to say the least.

FURTHER READING

Blackwell, W. *The Beginnings of Russian Industrialization, 1800–1860*. Princeton, N.J.: 1967.

Dziewanoski, V. K. *Alexander I: Russia's Mysterious Tsar*. New York: 1990.

Hartley, Janet M. *Alexander I*. London: 1994.

Lincoln, W. B. *Nicholas I*. Bloomington, Ind.: 1978.

Malia, Martin. *Alexander Herzen and the Birth of Russian Socialism*. Cambridge, Mass.: 1961.

Monas, Sidney. *The Third Section*. Cambridge, Mass.: 1961.

Moon, David. *The Russian Peasantry, 1600–1930: The World the Peasants Made*. London: 1999.

Raeff, Marc. *Michael Speransky*. The Hague: 1957.

Riasanovsky, N. *Nicholas I and Official Nationality*. Berkeley: 1959.

Roosevelt, Priscilla. *Life on the Russian Country Estate: A Social and Cultural History*. New Haven: 1995.

9

Reform, Reaction, and Modernization, 1855–1904

In nineteenth-century Russia the people, proud of the country's armed might, loved to watch parades and other military ceremonies. The tsar, the first soldier of the Russian empire, often presided at these occasions. In that respect Sunday, March 13, 1881, was like many other holidays. Tsar Alexander II, known to many as the "tsar-liberator" for his freeing of the serfs, planned to review a parade around noon, and then visit a royal cousin on his way back to the Winter Palace in the heart of St. Petersburg. But unknown to Alexander, twenty-seven determined revolutionary terrorists, members of a radical fringe group called the "People's Will," had fixed that Sunday as his date of execution.

After four unsuccessful attempts to assassinate the tsar, the terrorists had recently rented a small basement shop on one of St. Petersburg's main streets, from which they halfheartedly sold cheese to disguise their main activity: burrowing a tunnel under the street with the aim of blowing up the emperor's carriage should it pass that way. On March 13, just before Alexander left for the parade, his mistress had persuaded him not to return by his usual route, which would indeed have taken him along the street in front of the cheese shop. But the terrorists, aware that as a precaution the tsar often took alternate ways home, not only had a large cache of dynamite in their tunnel under the street but had posted five of their number along other streets and squares of the capital. Four of them were armed with a primitive, near-suicidal bomb of nitroglycerin that had to be tossed at extremely close range; the fifth, Sophia Perovskaia, a young woman of twenty-six from a noble family, was the lookout and supervisor.

As soon as Sophia saw that Alexander intended to take a different route back to the palace, she signaled by hand for the bomb throwers to take up new positions. A short while later when the imperial entourage started down a street called the Catherine Canal Embankment, Nicholas Rysakov stepped close to the carriage and hurled his weapon (see Figure 11). The explosion wrecked the wheels of Alexander's carriage and wounded several onlookers, but the tsar himself was unhurt. Foolhardily but overcome by

Figure 11. *A painting showing a bomb exploding under Alexander II's carriage during his assassination by terrorists, March 1881.*

curiosity and by concern for the wounded, Alexander dismounted from the carriage and approached Rysakov, whom the police had instantly seized.

At that moment a second assassin moved out of the crowd to within a few yards of Alexander and threw his bomb at the tsar's feet. Both Alexander and his assailant were mortally wounded, dying several hours later. Twenty others were also wounded, and blood was spattered across the snow banked on both sides of the street. Later the Church of the Savior's Blood was built on the spot where Alexander was killed.

Five terrorists were executed, but one of their leaders declared triumphantly: "An overwhelming weight has fallen from our shoulders. Reaction must end in order to make way for the rebirth of Russia." That did not happen, making the terrible events of that gray late winter afternoon in St. Petersburg only an episode in a continuing pattern of violence, reform, and reaction that marked the last half of the 1800s in the tsarist empire.[1]

In the two decades before his assassination Alexander II had presided over an impressive burst of reforms that considerably altered the old order. With these changes and under the impact of the rapid economic development and social transformation of the country, Russia moved belatedly down the path of modernization. At the same time, however, retrograde forces—from individual tsars and officials through most of the landed nobility down to proto-fascist elements in the cities—strongly opposed reform and tried to bind Russia in a traditional framework. They insisted on long-established values and fought bitterly to preserve privilege and autocratic rule. This reactionary attitude and its reflection in state policy, together with the dislocation and discontent caused by the massive socioeconomic changes taking place, led to conflict and finally to the Revolution of 1905.

THE ERA OF THE GREAT REFORMS, 1855–1881

In three important respects Russia at the time of the accession of Alexander II in 1855 differed markedly from the country his uncle, Alexander I, had inherited half a century earlier. First, Russia was a good deal bigger, both in territory and in population. Finland, Bessarabia, and the Caucasus had been added, but even within its old boundaries, the number of inhabitants of the Russian empire had increased dramatically, from about forty-one million to fifty-nine million people. This meant that the agricultural economy, with little or no increase in productivity, had more people to support and less land per person. The result was widespread peasant unrest.

Second, the Russian economy as a whole was changing but was falling farther behind that of western Europe. The first signs of nascent industrialization appeared, the number of free workers grew, and trade and a money economy expanded, while the position of the nobility deteriorated. In these circumstances continuing the system of serfdom made less and less sense to a number of contemporary observers.

Finally, after its defeat in the Crimean War, Russia was considerably weaker vis-à-vis its rivals in Europe than it had been in 1801.

Alexander II, the eldest son of Nicholas I, ascended the throne at the age of thirty-seven, having been prepared for his responsibilities both through tutorial education and through occasional participation in state affairs. Conservative in outlook and upbringing, he seemed an unlikely candidate for the role of "tsar-liberator." Yet several factors worked to turn Alexander into an effective reformer. Since he was realistic and hard-headed, he concluded early in his reign that serfdom would have to be eliminated and other changes made if more serious difficulties were to be avoided. He was also patriotic, deciding that if Russia were to be powerful again, its government and social system would have to be brought up to date. Moreover, Alexander, respecting the ability of the senior civil servants charged with implementing change, steadfastly supported them, even in the face of strong noble opposition. Like his predecessors, Alexander had no intention of destroying the autocracy, but, unlike them, he became convinced of the need for basic reform if it were to be saved.

This last point is well illustrated by his famous remark to the Moscow nobility in 1856: "It is better to begin to abolish serfdom from above than to wait until it begins to abolish itself from below. I ask you, gentlemen, to think over how all this can be carried out." Thus, starting with the elimination of serfdom, Alexander launched a series of "Great Reforms" that transformed Russian society but by no means solved all its problems. Affecting some fifty-two million people, over 85 percent of the entire population, ending serfdom was at the time the most extensive and influential government-directed social change undertaken in human history. Extremely difficult and complex, the reform was carried out remarkably smoothly and quite effectively.

There was of course opposition, particularly among the nobility and some bureaucrats. But the majority of articulate society strongly favored the emancipation, for three main reasons, in my view. In the first place, the serf system was increasingly indefensible on moral grounds; hardly anyone could support the practice of Russians' owning other Russians. As education spread in the 1800s, serfdom became increasingly repugnant to the Russian elite, including many nobles. Second, defeat in the Crimean War convinced Russia's military and bureaucratic leadership that a thorough overhaul of the country's antiquated economic and social system was needed. Armaments were outdated; transport and supply had failed in the Crimean War; and Russia's serf army had no trained reserves. Finally, many Russians were beginning to realize that for Russia to move ahead, free labor and an expanding industry were needed.

Soviet historians argued that fear of revolution, or at least of massive peasant *jacqueries* like that of Pugachov eighty years earlier, also motivated the reformers, both inside and outside the government. Yet most contemporary comment about emancipation does not allude to the danger of peasant rebellion. It may, however, have affected many people subconsciously as Tsar Alexander's remark to the Moscow gentry suggests.

Much oversimplified, the main issue in the reform was who would get how much land. The more conservative nobles suggested freeing the serfs without land but having the nobles compensated for the loss of serf labor or dues. The most radical position was to provide the peasants with all the land, not only the fields they worked for themselves but also the lord's tillable acres, with compensation to the lord for the land but not for the lost services. The peasants apparently expected to get most of the land, as their proverb suggests: "O lord, we are yours but the land is ours."

For four years beginning in 1857 the terms of the emancipation were discussed in provincial committees of the nobility and in the Main Committee, the government's supervising body for the reform. Details were worked out in editing commissions, and on March 15, 1861, the emancipation manifesto was proclaimed, shortly before Lincoln freed the American slaves. The compromise reached was quite reasonable under the circumstances. It favored the nobility but not so greatly as one might have expected, given their long role as a privileged elite and the tremendous pressure they exerted on the tsar and the government during discussion of the reform. The peasantry did not get as much land as they wanted, but their situation might have been tolerable had they not undergone a population explosion that doubled their numbers in the next fifty years and created a desperate need for land. The provisions of the reform let the lord keep most of his land and in principle gave the liberated peasants what they had traditionally farmed. In practice, and particularly in central Russia, where land was most valuable, the peasants finally received some 10 to 25 percent less land than they had previously tilled. Moreover, the government compensated the lord for the lost services of his serfs and collected this amount from the peasants in so-called redemption dues spread over forty-nine years. This was a heavy burden, which in the long run the peasants could not pay.

Because it was a useful social and administrative device, the reformers retained the *obshchina* (peasant commune), with two unfortunate effects. It meant the peasant was still bound to the village and its collective assembly, which determined when and how he would farm, as well as his share of taxes to the government. As some cynics observed, the peasant, far from being emancipated, exchanged one master (the lord) for another (the *obshchina*). However, he had always been part of the commune so this undoubtedly rankled less than his failure to obtain all the land. But keeping the *obshchina* also meant the peasant remained a second-class citizen, with special status and institutions and without the same standing as other subjects of the tsar. In fact, the government, concurrent with the emancipation, introduced new peasant courts and local organs of government (the *volost* system).

However much the terms of the emancipation favored the interests of the nobles, this arrangement did them little good since few were able to manage their estates profitably, and noble indebtedness steadily climbed in succeeding decades. As noted, the situation of the peasants also deteriorated because of a population explosion among them and the scarcity of land. In addition, having to stay in the commune dampened individual incentive, and the productivity of peasant farmers, even as freemen, remained low.

Nevertheless, the emancipation had two important positive results: it removed a moral and economic millstone from around Russian society's neck, and it provided a supply of free labor for the development of capitalist agriculture and industry. Available for hire were household serfs who were freed without land and serfs who took "beggars' allotments," quarter shares of land in exchange for no redemption dues, which proved too small to support them. In addition, some landed peasants left the village temporarily for off-season work in factories.

Most of the other "Great Reforms" followed the pattern of changes that had occurred earlier in Western society, but they stopped short of providing Russians with full civil liberties or a national representative government. Instead the reforms in Russia made the governance of the country more orderly, efficient, and just, but within the framework of autocracy. The judicial reform of 1864 was a good case in point: it provided for trained and independent judges, open and sensible judicial procedures, and equality before the law. It gave Russia one of the most advanced and fair judicial systems in Europe. At the same time, because there was no political or constitutional reform accompanying it, the tsarist government was later able to carry out a number of extralegal actions, through imperial decrees, administrative regulations, and so-called extraordinary measures (which amounted to a form of martial law).

Other important reforms established partial self-government at two local levels. A series of municipal institutions were created in 1870, and new district and provincial organs called *zemstvos* were set up in 1864. The latter were assemblies whose members were elected separately by all classes: nobles, townsmen, and peasants. Although the nobles predominated and although the *zemstvos* had limited budgets and were restricted to managing only such local issues as education, public works, health, and welfare, they provided excellent training in politics and governance for future liberal opponents of the autocracy and served local needs quite well, certainly far better than the centralized bureaucratic government had in the past. The central ministries in St. Petersburg continued to control and administer most fiscal, police, and economic activity at the local level, and governors and other bureaucrats did not hesitate to pressure or interfere with *zemstvos*. Nevertheless, the success of these unusual institutions belies the common adage that Russians have no experience with representative government and prefer authoritarian rule.

Another reform of Alexander's reign was an extensive reorganization of military affairs that helped modernize the army by introducing universal conscription, reducing the term of military service to six years, and creating a reserve. Also, education was expanded and improved, journalism and book printing were encouraged, censorship was eased, and Orthodox parishes and church administration were reorganized.

Taken together, the "Great Reforms" produced a significant transformation of Russian society, though the core of the political system, the autocracy, remained largely untouched. The reforms served as a significant safety valve, releasing long pent-up resentments and offering many the promise of a better future. At the same time the reform era aroused false hopes, leading some to believe that more had changed than in fact had and encouraging others to dream of a constitutional system and the establishment of full civil freedoms.

For the long run the most influential impact of the reforms was to open the door to rapid social and economic change and to permit the accelerated industrialization and modernization of the country. This was an important step in restoring Russia's strength, but it may have been too little, too late, as its rivals in the West—and even Japan to the East—accelerated at about the same time the pace of their social and economic development, making it even harder for Russia to catch up to them.

TERROR AND REACTION

Although in 1880 and 1881 Alexander had not turned his back on reform, considering at that time a semi-constitutional project prepared by a liberal adviser, Count Michael Loris-Melikov, he had disappointed many in the intelligentsia who believed his reforms had not gone far enough and who were appalled at his appointment on occasion of avowedly conservative ministers and his lapses into reactionary policy. Moreover, a series of unto-ward events in the 1860s strengthened the hand of those who were urging the tsar to hold back. There were outbreaks of student rioting; a revolution in Poland in 1863, which aroused nationalist and conservative feeling in Russia; and an attempt to assassinate the tsar in 1866. Moreover, in some areas such as religion and education (after the appointment of a reactionary minister of education in 1866) the conservatives were given virtually a free hand. Religions other than Orthodoxy were repressed, and measures to squelch national movements in Poland and Ukraine were taken. Romantic supporters of the government also began to develop an idealized kind of Slavic nationalism that came to be known as Pan-Slavism. Vague and ab-stract, it argued that all Slavs in Russia and eastern Europe were true broth-ers and should be united in common purpose and in interacting cultures un-der the general and benevolent leadership of the Russian state, the largest Slavic country.

A combination of dismay at apparent slips into reactionary policy under Alexander and of disillusionment with the limited nature of his reforms produced in the 1860s a new, more radical opposition among the intelli-gentsia. The "generation of the sixties" voiced more fundamental criticisms of Russian society and espoused more revolutionary solutions than their forerunners of the 1840s. Many were nihilists, who on principle rejected old values, institutions, and policies and who, according to their detractors, stood for nothing (hence their name). In fact, they did believe in science and rationality, and some, like Nicholas Chernyshevsky, went on to propound utopian societies of socialist harmony and plenty. In rejecting traditional authority and conventions they sought a freer, simpler life for all, as well as personal liberation. Among their ranks were a number of able and coura-geous women who brought to the revolutionary movement a special emo-tional intensity and moral fervor.

The majority of the revolutionaries of the 1860s favored radical change but urged peaceful means and popular education to bring it about. Their views, broadly categorized as populism, motivated several thousand of them to "go to the people" in the early 1870s. Young radicals went to the coun-try-side to work among the peasantry, whom they idealized as a fount of moral purity and untainted simplicity. The peasants, bewildered and suspi-cious, did not know what to make of these well-meaning city folk who wanted to help them. In the end the "people" either ignored the populists or in a few cases turned them over to the police as dangerous troublemakers.

When it was clear that this and other efforts to promote radical change by education, example, and propaganda were having no effect, a small group of revolutionaries, the People's Will, broke off from the mainstream of populism and turned to terrorism. Although numbering probably fewer than one hundred persons, these intelligent and zealous revolutionaries suc-ceeded in killing more than a dozen prominent officials and frightening much of society. Their rationale was explained by Andrew Zhelyabov, speaking in his own defense at his trial for complicity in the 1881 assassination of Alexander II:

> This temporary movement to the people showed our ideas to be impracticable and doctrinaire. . . . From dreamers we became workers. We took to deeds, not words. Action meant some use of force. . . . Circumstances were forcing me, among others, to declare war against the existing political structure.[2]

The program of the People's Will adopted a year earlier had defended violence:

> The purpose of terroristic activities . . . is to break the spell of governmental power, to give constant proof of the possibility of fighting against the government, to strengthen in this way the revolutionary spirit of the people and its faith in the success of its cause, and, finally, to create cadres suited and accustomed to combat.[3]

But in practice terrorism and assassination only repelled much of educated society, puzzled the peasants, and strengthened the position and determination of conservatives. The result was that the era of the Great Reforms ended not only in the murder of the tsar-liberator but in a period of reaction and counter reform that immobilized political life in Russia for twenty-five years.

Since Alexander III (1881–1894), who succeeded to the throne at the age of thirty-six, greatly admired his grandfather, Nicholas I, it is perhaps no accident that there were striking parallels between the two reigns. Both tsars came to the throne after periods of change and reform that had ended in tragedy: a revolt and an assassination. Both were determined to restore law and order; both wanted a well-regulated and efficient state; both believed in the sanctity and power of the autocracy; and both were ardent Russian nationalists. To some extent both also reacted against their predecessors' policies. Alexander III had never been close to his father, and in the last years of Alexander II's reign the son had deeply resented the father's open flaunting of a mistress, who in 1880 was even moved into the imperial palace with her bastard children by Alexander II.

Whatever personal and psychological reasons might have influenced Alexander III to reject the reform policy of his father, it is also clear that he did not believe further change would be good for Russia. From the late 1860s, long before he came to power, he had increasingly adopted a traditional and religious outlook consonant with the philosophy of his former tutor, Constantine Pobedonostsev, a conservative intellectual who served after 1880 as head of the Holy Synod, the council that managed the affairs of the Orthodox Church. Pobedonostsev was highly critical of the Great Reforms and believed wholeheartedly in defending and buttressing the autocratic power of the tsar. He stressed moral values while sharply criticizing science, materialism, and the growing industrialization of Russia.

Austere, not especially bright, and somewhat self-righteous, Alexander III did his best to turn back the clock in Russia. Such an effort was singularly inappropriate because Russia's society and economy were at that very moment changing rapidly and fundamentally. Consequently, political retrenchment resulted in substantial incongruencies and asymmetries in the system and made subsequent efforts to readjust that much more difficult. The only areas in which Alexander III's administration acted to take account of the new realities were fiscal policy and labor legislation designed to ameliorate slightly the dreadful conditions under which Russia's new working class toiled.

Otherwise a stern repression and systematic reaction ruled. For example, in the countryside, although they could not undo the emancipation of the serfs, Alexander and his conservative advisers created a new instrument of control that bypassed both the existing administrative framework and the reform-era institutions of *volosts* and *zemstvos*: the post of *land captain,* an official charged with supervision of all rural affairs, who combined both judicial and administrative authority, in direct violation of the separation of functions sought by the reformers of the 1860s. Alexander III and his counter reformers also limited the jurisdiction and effectiveness of the self-governing *zemstvos* and the municipal institutions set up under Alexander II.

At the level of the central government nothing was done to modify autocracy in any way, but in fact the complexity of governing a slowly modernizing society meant that Alexander III had to rely, more than any of his predecessors, on the state bureaucracy, which on occasion blocked some of his reactionary measures. But most were passed, including tight restrictions on the press and universities, and Alexander III did not hesitate to resort to extralegal steps, such as sending opponents into exile in Siberia and decreeing areas of the empire subject to stringent "temporary regulations."

Alexander III was a dedicated nationalist, favoring, as one observer put it, "Russian principles, Russian strength, Russian people." He disliked Germans and detested Poles and Jews. In his reign anti-Semitism flourished. Admission quotas for Jews in secondary schools and universities were established, and restrictions were enforced to limit Jewish habitation to the so-called Pale of Settlement, an arc of territory in western Russia where Jews had traditionally lived. The first pogroms, or riots, directed against Jewish property and Jewish individuals occurred, if not with government encouragement at least with government indifference. In the non-Russian territories of the empire russification policies begun earlier in the century were greatly intensified, provoking nationalistic resistance among the minorities.

In 1894 Alexander III died unexpectedly of a stroke, and his son Nicholas II ascended the throne at the age of twenty-six. More intelligent than his father but not broadly educated, Nicholas was weak-willed and ir-resolute, perhaps because his father had tyrannized him. Although a de-voted family man and quite charming when he wished to be, Nicholas was also suspicious and narrow-minded. He had few qualities necessary to lead a complex society in turbulent times. He did not really understand the swift changes taking place in Russia and remained committed to preserving the autocracy and traditional values. Early in his reign he labeled as "senseless dreams" the aspirations of a group of liberal aristocrats for limited repre-sentative government, and during the first decade of his rule he continued his father's reactionary policies. He also supported russification, extending it even to Finland, which had enjoyed some autonomy since it had come under Russian rule in 1809.

Nicholas, however, could be influenced by powerful personalities, and he supported for a time the program of economic modernization advanced by his minister of finance, Sergei Witte. Witte was typical of the new bureau-crats emerging in the latter half of the nineteenth century, an individual from non-noble origins who worked his way up in government service by talent, hard work, and imagination. Witte believed fervently that if Russia were to remain competitive with European nations, it would have to mod-ernize, particularly by exploiting its natural resources and building up its economy. He supervised what has been called "the Witte system": this in-cluded subsidies and tariffs to promote heavy industry and Russian ex-ports; extensive borrowing from abroad to accelerate Russian industrializa-tion; stabilization of the fiscal system, including adoption of the gold standard; building of railroads; and accumulation of capital for these pur-poses by taxing the peasantry and by selling Russian grain in European markets. Witte was astonishingly successful, but the cost to the peasantry was heavy, contributing to widespread agricultural disorders that began in 1902 and lasted off and on through 1907.

ECONOMIC AND SOCIAL MODERNIZATION, 1861–1905

Witte's efforts were part of a larger process of economic and social develop-ment that swept over Russia in the forty-odd years from the emancipation of the serfs in 1861 to the Revolution of 1905. The newly freed peasants were perhaps least affected by these sweeping changes in Russian society, but even they felt the impact of Russia's rapid modernization. In the first place new factories and workshops drew heavily on peasant labor. At first peasants worked in industry primarily on a seasonal basis, returning to their villages for key agricultural tasks such as sowing and harvesting. But later they resided permanently in the cities, perhaps leaving their families in the countryside until they could earn enough to support them in town. Un-der either arrangement part of their wages went to pay their share of village and communal taxes. Second, improved transportation and communica-tion meant that new ideas, including appeals for revolution, spread across much of Russia. If not fully aware politically, peasants at least began to think about joint action against the landowners and the government.

At the same time the economic position of the majority of peasants, particularly those in the densely populated "black-earth" provinces in south Russia, deteriorated. The peasant population grew in this period on an average of eight hundred thousand persons a year, reaching almost one hundred million by 1905. Although some peasants emigrated to Siberia and to Russian Asia, their numbers were far fewer than the natural increase of people. This population boom resulted in part from improved conditions of health and public order in the villages. Peasants also ate better, and in some areas a new and reliable crop, potatoes, was widely adopted to add variety and carbohydrates to the customary rural diet of coarse rye bread and cabbage. Peasants may also have had a more positive attitude about the future as a result of emancipation and so risked ever larger families.

A significant consequence of this population explosion was a shortage of land. From 1861 to 1905 the average size of a peasant's share of the communal land decreased by 46 percent and his livestock holdings dropped by one-third. The price of land doubled. By 1900 the peasants' redemption dues were 119 percent in arrears. A serious famine occurred in 1891, and extensive peasant disorders broke out in 1902–1903. A substantial increase in agricultural productivity might have compensated for the population explosion, but in fact the yield per acre increased only slightly in this period, primarily because the *obshchina* system of collective ownership and farming provided little incentive to improve farming methods or to work harder (see Figure 12). To make matters worse, world grain prices declined markedly in the last quarter of the nineteenth century, which hurt both peasant and noble agriculture.

To the difficulties created for the peasants by growing numbers, insufficient land, and low productivity must be added the heavy exactions imposed on them by the government. Quite deliberately, successive tsarist administrations from the 1870s on squeezed the peasantry to support the state budget and to help finance industrialization. Three methods were used: direct taxes levied through the commune, indirect taxes on such widely used items as vodka, salt and kerosene, and buying of grain relatively cheaply and then exporting it abroad at higher prices. At times in the 1800s vodka revenues alone made up one-third of all state income, making the government a chief contributor to public drunkenness and burgeoning alcoholism among Russian males. Given the peasants' overall situation it is hardly surprising to find them playing a major role in the Revolution of 1905.

The nobility, both as an economic force and a social class, declined in the post-emancipation era. Noble landholding fell by almost 30 percent, and much of the land the nobles retained was mortgaged. Only a small minority ran their farms well or developed large capitalist-style agricultural enterprises. Another small group went into industry, banking, or professional

Figure 12. *A meeting of village elders, 1910. (Courtesy of the Board of Trustees of the Victoria and Albert Museum)*

work, but the majority remained civil servants or barely subsisted on their estates. Still influential at court and in the bureaucracy, they were nevertheless increasingly challenged by upstarts from lower echelons in society, like Witte.

While agriculture lagged, with the peasantry struggling to survive and the aristocracy slipping, Russian industry was growing by leaps and bounds. To some extent its expansion was made possible by extraction of capital from the agricultural sector, but several other factors promoted an industrial boom. To begin with, Russia, like the United States and Japan, was able to benefit from the earlier European experience with industrialization by installing the latest technology and machinery and by drawing heavily on European capital for investment. Second, the Great Reforms not only furnished a pool of peasant labor for the new factories but created an atmosphere of legality and stability that encouraged both Russian entrepreneurs and foreign investors. Finally, the tsarist government actively supported industrialization through subsidies, tariffs, large government orders, and outright ownership of key sectors, such as railroads.

Between 1861 and the 1880s Russian industry grew at a moderate pace, the number of factories increasing from about ten thousand to twenty thousand and the value of their output from about 200 million rubles to I billion rubles. By 1905 the number of factories passed forty thousand, and total output soared to over 4 billion rubles. Railroad trackage grew from about one thousand to over twenty-five thousand miles between 1860 and 1905. Russia became a major producer of coal, iron, and petroleum and began to export manufactured goods to Asia and parts of Europe. Russia's rate of industrial growth in the two decades before the Revolution of 1905 was 8 percent a year, equaling that of the United States at a comparable period in its development.

This first surge of Russian industrialization had certain distinguishing characteristics. Production was highly concentrated, both in a few major cities and regions—such as Moscow, the Urals, Ukraine, St. Petersburg— and in large factories, such as the Putilov works, which gathered thousands of workers in one place. This concentration resulted in some economies of scale but also produced large clusters of workers, giving them greater solidarity and later facilitating the spread of revolutionary ideas among them.

Another special feature of the growth of Russian industry was the dominant role played by the state, both directly by state investment, management, and purchases, and indirectly through favorable economic and fiscal policies. The other major bloc of capital for Russian industrialization came from abroad, from European and American investors. Foreign investment in Russia grew from 100 million rubles in 1880 to 900 million rubles in 1900, and by 1914 one-third of all Russian industry was foreign-owned.

The dominance of state and foreign capital in the Russian economy had several important effects. It meant that revolutionaries could charge that the country and especially its working class were being exploited by a privileged few around the tsar and by foreigners. In addition, Russian loans from France helped tie Russia to France diplomatically and militarily. Moreover, because the government and foreign investors played such a prominent role, the development of a Russian capitalist class was stunted. Russian businessmen never had the economic strength and political clout of their counter-parts in Europe and the United States. They were never powerful enough to force needed political changes, and even when they worked together with Russia's professional classes, as during World War I, they succeeded only in harassing the autocracy rather than reforming it.

The social impact of industrialization on Russia was much like its effects in western Europe a half century earlier. Cities expanded in size and number, and the urban population of Russia doubled. The number of workers shot up, reaching over 2.25 million by 1905. Most of the proletariat worked and lived under deplorable conditions, as these excerpts from reports of government factory inspectors in the 1880s show:

Sanitary conditions in the workers' settlement of Yuzovka are highly conducive to the contraction and spread of disease. The market place and streets are full of filth. The air is rotten with the stench from factory smoke, coal and lime dust, and the filth in gutters and organic wastes on streets and squares.... The majority of workers lived in so-called "cabins" built in the outskirts of the settlement.... These cabins are simply low, ugly mud huts.

The roofs are made of earth and rubbish. Some of them are so close to the ground that at first sight they are nearly unnoticeable. The walls are covered with wood planks or overlaid with stones which easily let in the dampness. The floors are made of earth. These huts are entered by going deep down into the ground along earthen stairs. The interiors are dark and close, and the air is damp, still, and foul-smelling. . . . The furnishings are completely unhygienic, although frequently the workers live here with their families and infant children. . . .

The very worst, most unhealthy conditions I saw were in tobacco factories. . . . The shops where tobacco is chopped and dried are so filled with caustic dust and nicotine fumes that each time I entered one of these rooms I had spasms in my throat and my eyes watered. If I stayed there very long I even became dizzy, though I am a smoker myself. Yet even women sometimes work in this atmosphere. . . . Children work in these tobacco factories as wrappers, baggers and packers. There were even children under twelve working there. . . .[4]

In addition, wages were low, hours long, and the workers were at the mercy of arbitrary regulations and fines imposed by management. Forming unions and striking were prohibited, although as early as the 1870s the first illegal strikes occurred.

Almost as important as their physical situation in creating a revolutionary frame of mind was that most workers found adjusting to factory discipline and city life difficult. Away from the traditional routine and values of family, village, and church, they sought some new purpose and anchor for their lives. Some fell into drunkenness and petty crime; others readily joined social or discussion groups. Open to new ideas, such workers' circles debated Marxism and other revolutionary creeds, under leaders who were usually intellectuals, not workers.

COMPETING IDEOLOGIES

As the pace of economic and social change in Russia quickened in the last quarter of the nineteenth century, intellectual ferment accelerated as well. Most educated Russians sought solutions to Russia's problems in two schools of political philosophy that had developed earlier in Europe: socialism and liberalism. Among the Russian intelligentsia two main categories of socialism emerged in the 1880s and 1890s: Marxism and peasant socialism. A bit later, just after the start of the twentieth century, an organized liberal movement developed. Since all three ideologies played important roles in the revolutionary events of the 1900s, we need briefly to examine each of them.

Karl Marx developed his theories in the midst of the Industrial Revolution in Europe. He was outraged at the misery and exploitation he saw all about him, concluding that the promise of freedom and equality trumpeted by the leaders of the French Revolution had not been fulfilled. Marx explained the injustice of contemporary life by arguing that the material world—and in society this meant the economic factor—was the basic reality; under industrialization therefore the productive forces (the factories) and the relations of production (who owned the factories) determined social, political, and intellectual life. Applying this *materialist,* or economic, interpretation to history, Marx argued that, powered by conflict between positive and negative forces (the *dialectic method*), human development would pass, according to immutable laws, through five stages: primitive communal or clan society, slave-holding society, feudalism, capitalism, and socialism. When society reached the final phase of the socialist stage of history, known as communism, the dialectic contradictions within it would cease and a future good society for all mankind would be established.

From this set of ideas, known as *dialectical* and *historical materialism,* Marx drew certain conclusions about the society around him. Europe, he believed, had passed from feudalism to capitalism in the upheaval of the French Revolution, and another great revolution would be needed to complete the passage from capitalism to socialism. This revolution, Marx was convinced, was inevitable and in fact was being prepared by the capitalists themselves. Driven by economic necessity, they were exploiting the workers so unmercifully that the capitalist system would be forced into a crisis of diminishing profits and overproduction and would collapse. Confronted with their imminent demise, the capitalists would resist, only to be overthrown by an organized and class-conscious proletariat. By this time workers would be the overwhelming majority of the population, and they would establish a dictatorship of the majority as a transition to a one-class society in which the state as a coercive mechanism would wither away. In the new socialist society all its citizens would own the productive forces, thereby liberating them from the artificial constraints on production imposed by the capitalists. This would produce a superabundance of goods, and each individual could then receive under socialism enough to meet basic needs. At the same time each new-type socialist citizen, eager to help the whole society, would work and contribute to the full extent of his or her talents. According to Marx, the socialist or proletarian revolution needed to bring all this about had not yet occurred anywhere in Europe, but the crisis of capitalism was deepening all the time.

At this point you may well be wondering how on earth could these theories of Marx, so closely tied to European experience and to the advanced industrialization of the West, have any relevance for underdeveloped, predominantly agricultural Russia. Marx himself never satisfactorily answered this question, although on several occasions he talked optimistically about the possibility that Russia might be able to develop a unique brand of socialism, building on the collective tradition of the peasant commune. But even before his death in 1883, Marx's writings had been translated into

Russian (the censor thought they were too ponderous to be dangerous), and a few Russian revolutionaries, eyeing the rapid industrialization of their country, had begun to speculate that Marxism might be a useful political program, if it could be adapted to Russian conditions. Before long, wretchedness and desperation made Russian workers quite willing to listen to any theory that promised to improve their lot and put them in charge, no matter whether its fine points really applied to Russia or not.

In the 1880s a few Russian populists, in exile in Europe, converted to Marxism, and by the 1890s several dozen Marxist revolutionaries were active within Russia, leading workers' discussion circles. One of those early Marxists was Vladimir Ilich Ulianov, who later adopted the revolutionary pseudonym Lenin. Lenin's father was a provincial civil servant at the middle level, his mother the daughter of a doctor. Lenin grew up in moderate circumstances and excelled at school. Not unhappy or deprived, he turned to revolution mainly from idealism but partly also because his older brother was executed for complicity in a plot to assassinate the tsar. Expelled from university for participation in student agitation, Lenin read widely in European political philosophy and in the history of the Russian revolutionary movement and became a dedicated Marxist. In the 1890s Lenin was exiled to Siberia for his propagandizing and organizing efforts among the workers of St. Petersburg. He used his time there to study and write, and he soon became an acknowledged leader of the Russian Marxists. They had founded an embryo party, known as the Russian Social Democratic Labor party, in 1898, but most of its members were almost immediately arrested by the police.

In this period Lenin and his colleagues engaged in extensive polemics against two competing sets of ideas, which they were convinced would undercut the development of a strong Marxist revolutionary movement in Russia. One was *economism,* the view of some workers and intellectuals that the main goal was to improve the economic and social conditions of the Russian proletariat. They sought shorter hours, higher wages, improved factory safety, and decent housing. The Marxists argued that such a program only deceived the workers. As long as the capitalists owned the factories and used their economic power to control the government (although in Russia they in fact did not), concessions wrung from the capitalists would be only temporary and inadequate. The only correct course of action was political: organizing the workers for the eventual socialist revolution. The Marxists made some headway in their arguments, though in practice they often had to lump the workers' economic demands with the Marxist political platform.

The other ideology against which the Marxists struggled was *peasant socialism.* It grew directly out of the earlier populist movement, but its proponents argued that instead of education or "going to the people," organization and revolutionary activity were the correct weapons for effecting radical change in Russia. The leaders of peasant socialism believed that Russia could avoid some of the worst evils of capitalism as it had developed in Europe by moving directly from its present agricultural, semifeudal system to socialism, drawing heavily on the peasantry and their socialist experience with the peasant commune. In the 1890s and the first decade of the 1900s the peasant socialist movement spread rapidly, and its followers were soon organized as the Socialist Revolutionary (SR) party, a main rival of the Marxists from then on. The SRs, though counting heavily on the peasants, also courted workers, establishing cells at factories and workers' settlements and enjoying considerable success.

Although both Marxists and peasant socialists favored revolution to bring about the changes they desired, large numbers of Russians in the professions, among the nobility, and in the civil service opposed using violence and espoused peaceful, evolutionary reform. They were just as strongly hostile to the tsarist government, but their vision of the future was not socialism but *liberalism.* This was a rather loose set of social and political principles that had evolved in Europe in the nineteenth century, building on the ideas of the Enlightenment and the experiences of the French and American revolutions. Unlike socialists, liberals had no strict doctrine, but they generally believed in full civil freedoms in Russia; equality for all citizens, including the peasantry; benevolent social and economic reforms, with no infringement of private property; free trade and laissez-faire economic policies; and some form of representative government, through a constitution or some other mechanism. A few believed in a *republic,* that is, in abolishing the tsardom, but most would have been content to see Russia reformed under a constitutional monarchy over which the tsar could still preside. The liberals also began to organize in the early years of the twentieth century, forming the Constitutional Democratic party in 1905 (known as the Kadets from its Russian initials, K. D.).

At about the same time that the socialist and liberal movements were getting established in Russia, nationalism increasingly affected some of the non-Russian groups within the empire. Polish demands for reestablishment of an independent Poland, or at the very least for greater Polish autonomy, had recurred throughout the nineteenth century, culminating in the rebellions of 1830 and 1863 and reviving again in the 1890s. The Finns, particularly after the repression practiced under Nicholas II at the turn of the century, clamored for a separate or an autonomous Finland. To a lesser degree they were joined by the Baltic peoples—Estonians, Latvians, and Lithuanians—and by Armenians and Georgians in the Caucasus. Even more threatening to the centralized structure and policies of the Russian empire was the emergence of a nationalist movement among Ukrainians. Growing out of a literary renaissance and an interest in Ukrainian history, Ukrainian nationalism was beginning by 1900 to press social and political demands against the dominance in the empire of Great Russians.

These threads of disaffection within the Russian state—socialism, liberalism, and nationalism—began to come together in the first years of the twentieth century to threaten the tsardom. Their impact was greatly intensified when Russian society suffered, in short order, an economic and then a foreign policy crisis. The economic emergency was created by a severe depression in the first years of the twentieth century and by sporadic peasant disorders across a number of provinces in 1902 and 1903. How serious these economic disruptions would have become is unclear because in 1904 they were overshadowed by Russia's involvement in a losing war with Japan that helped spark the Revolution of 1905.

Before looking at that dramatic revolution, we need to review quickly the way in which developments in Russian foreign policy ended in Russia's going to war. As you recall, the Crimean War reduced Russian influence in Europe and checked Russian expansion into the Balkans. But this was only a temporary setback. Before long Russia joined Germany and Austria-Hungary in an informal alliance system, called the Three Emperors' League, that lasted for most of the period between 1873 and 1887. This meant the Russian empire was once again an active participant in European politics and in the European balance of power.

Moreover, Russia was soon embroiled with the Ottoman Empire again. New crises arose when subject peoples of the Turks in the Balkans tried to fulfill their nationalist aspirations by rebelling, and when the European powers, who had lent the Turkish sultan large amounts of money, were dissatisfied with his fiscal policies and plans for repayment. The Russians would probably have been dragged in anyway, but the sudden upsurge among educated Russian opinion of vociferous feelings of Pan-Slavism brought great pressure on the government to assist Russia's Slavic and Orthodox brethren in the Balkans.

Between 1875 and 1877 occurred a string of events, any one of which might have been resolved peaceably, but the cumulative effect of which was to bring Russia and Turkey to the brink of war. The Turks, rejected by Western public opinion after their bloody suppression of a Bulgarian revolt, were prepared to make substantial concessions, but Alexander II, pushed by inflamed nationalist feeling in Russia, took his country into war against the Ottoman Empire. After an early defeat the Russians' superior numbers brought them a considerable victory, which was reflected in a preliminary peace treaty signed in March 1878 that gave the Russians substantial gains in the Balkans. At the Congress of Berlin, a subsequent conclave of all the European powers, Russia's spoils were somewhat reduced; after 1885, when the Bulgarians repudiated Russian tutelage, Russian influence in the Balkans was minimal for the next twenty years. But this issue was only dormant, and when new crises erupted in that region after 1908, great power entanglement there led eventually to World War I, as we shall see in Chapter 10.

After the Congress of Berlin European statesmen encouraged Russia to look in other directions. Otto von Bismarck, the architect of the unification of Germany, who had claimed for himself the role of "honest broker" at the Congress of Berlin, declared: "Russia has nothing to do in the West. She only contracts nihilism and other diseases. Her mission is in Asia. There she . . . stands for civilization." Whatever Russia really stood for in Asia, the empire did expand notably in that direction from the 1840s on (see Map 6). At first the push was into Central Asia, an area of steppe, desert, and high plateaus inhabited by warlike, nomadic Muslim tribes. To forestall their constant raids the Russians established control over much of the region in the 1860s and 1870s. The British were alarmed, fearing a Russian threat to Afghanistan and even to British India, but by the end of the century the main focus of Russian interest in Asia had shifted to the Far East.

Under aggressive administrators in that region the Russians moved into the basin of the Amur River in the 1850s, occupied the southern half of Sakhalin Island, and in 1860 founded the important Pacific port of Vladivostok, meaning "ruler of the east." In the 1890s the Trans-Siberian Railroad was built, linking European Russia and the Far East, and in the early twentieth century the Russians were extending their influence into Manchuria and Korea. Here, however, they confronted not the enfeebled resistance of a declining Chinese empire but the vigorous expansionism of a newly modernized and ascendant Japan. The clash of interests led to war in 1904, and to a major crisis in Russian society.

CONCLUSION

Not since the days of Peter the Great had Russian society been in such ferment as it was in the second half of the nineteenth century. The decision to emancipate the serfs transformed a socioeconomic system that had predominated for almost 250 years. Together with the other Great Reforms and growing economic ties with Europe, the abolition of serfdom helped launch an accelerating modernization of Russia's society and economy. By 1900 Russia was partly industrialized and, with its rich natural resources, had the basis to become a powerful modern nation.

Yet substantial problems remained unsolved. Backward and inefficient agriculture acted as a brake on the economy. Overpopulation and government taxation created a land-desperate and impoverished peasantry ripe for revolution. In the cities an uprooted and exploited proletariat listened attentively to calls for action from a spectrum of revolutionary agitators. In the border-lands of the empire non-Russian minorities, resentful of the government's russification policies and fired by nationalist enthusiasm, struggled for autonomy or independence.

These issues, however, might have been worked out if only Russia had changed as much politically as it had socially and economically. But spo-

EXPANSION OF RUSSIAN EMPIRE, 1801-1904

Corinne Abbazia Hekker Graphics

Boundary of Russia, 1801

Expansion in Europe and
the Caucasus, 1801 - 28

Expansion in Central Asia,
1801 - 95

Expansion in the Far East,
1858 - 60

Ceded to Japan in 1905 after
Russia's defeat, Russo-
Japanese War, 1904 - 05

JAPAN

Sea of
Okhotsk

Sakhalin
Island

Vladivostok

Sea of
Japan

KOREA

Liaotung
Peninsula

MANCHURIA

R U S S I A N   E M P I R E

S I B E R I A

MONGOLIA

C H I N A

SINKIANG

TURKESTAN

Volga River

Ural River

Astrakhan

Caspian Sea

FINLAND, 1809

St. Petersburg

Moscow

Battle of
Borodino,
1812

Kiev

CRIMEA

CAUCASUS

Black Sea

The
Straits

OTTOMAN   EMPIRE

POLAND,
1815

Warsaw

BESSARABIA
1812

0   600

MILES

MAP 6

radically under Alexander II and blatantly and forcefully under Alexander III and Nicholas II, the government acted to preserve the autocratic system virtually unaltered. The tsar was still an absolute sovereign, and no national policies could be carried out without his sanction. Nor were the people as a whole, not even interest groups among them, to have any say in national governance, whatever small measure of self-government existed at the local level. The tsar needed the bureaucracy to rule, to be sure, but the bureaucracy could do nothing without the tsar's approval.

As a result, the ruling elite became increasingly isolated from the rest of society, and both sides girded for a decisive struggle over what Russia's future should be. As the country changed and as the political crisis matured, Russia continued to play a major role in European and world policies. But if it could not resolve its domestic schism, it was hardly strong enough to survive a major showdown on the international stage.

FURTHER READING

Black, C. E., ed. *The Transformation of Russian Society: Aspects of Social Change Since 1861*. Cambridge, Mass.: 1960.

Blackwell, William. *The Industrialization of Russia*. 2d ed. Arlington Heights. Ill.: 1982.

Brooks, Jeffrey. *When Russia Learned to Read: Literacy and Popular Literature, 1861–1912*. Princeton, N.J.: 1988.

Brower, Daniel. *The Russian City Between Tradition and Modernity, 1850–1900*. Berkeley, Calif.: 1990.

Carew Hunt, R. N. *The Theory and Practice of Communism*. New York: 1957.

Emmons, Terence, ed. *The Emancipation of the Russian Serfs*. New York: 1970.

Engel, Barbara Alpern. *Between the Fields and the City: Women, Work, and Family in Russia, 1861–1914*. Cambridge, England: 1994.

Figner, Vera. *Memoirs of a Revolutionist*. New York: 1927.

Fischer, George. *Russian Liberalism*. Cambridge, Mass.: 1958.

Freeze, Gregory. *The Parish Clergy in Nineteenth Century Russia*. Princeton, N.J.: 1983.

Gatrell, P. *The Tsarist Economy, 1850–1917*. New York: 1986.

Gregory, Paul. *Before Command: An Economic History of Russia from Emancipation to the First Five-Year Plan*. Princeton, N.J.: 1994.

Keep, John. *The Rise of Social Democracy in Russia*. Oxford: 1963.

Lincoln, W. Bruce. *The Great Reforms*. De Kalb, Ill.: 1990.

Maynard, Sir John. *The Russian Peasant and Other Studies*. London: 1942.

Menning, Bruce W. *Bayonets Before Bullets: The Imperial Russian Army, 1861–1914*. Bloomington, Ind.: 1992.

Miller, Forrest. *Dmitrii Miliutin and the Reform Era*. Nashville, Tenn.: 1968.

Mosse, W. E. *Alexander II and the Modernization of Russia*. New York: 1958.

Pierce, Richard. *Russian Central Asia, 1867–1917*. Berkeley: 1960.

Robinson, Geroid T. *Rural Russia Under the Old Regime*. New York: 1932, 1949.

Rogger, Hans J. *Russia in the Age of Modernization and Revolution, 1881–1917*. New York: 1983.

Stites, Richard. *The Women's Liberation Movement in Russia*. Princeton, N.J.: 1978.

Treadgold, Donald. *The Great Siberian Migration*. Princeton, N.J.: 1957.

Venturi, Franco. *Roots of Revolution*. New York: 1960.

Von Laue, T. *Sergei Witte and the Industrialization of Russia*. New York: 1963.

Worobec, Christine D. *Peasant Russia: Family and City in the Post-Emancipation Period*. Princeton, N.J.: 1991.

10

Revolution, Reform, and War, 1904–1917

The small steamer rolled from side to side, but the three men inside the cabin seemed oblivious to this motion as they bent their heads over several sheets of paper on the table in front of them. There was animated discussion, and from time to time one of them corrected the Russian script of the document. In less than an hour they arrived at their destination, disembarking at Peterhof, the country palace of the Emperor of all the Russias, Nicholas II. While two of the men waited in an anteroom, the third, Sergei Witte, met with Nicholas and his advisers, including the tsar's uncle, Grand Duke Nikolai Nikolaevich. A sense of urgency marked the discussions, for a general strike was paralyzing St. Petersburg, the capital, and riots and disorders were spreading throughout Russia. It was clear to everyone that decisive action would have to be taken promptly.

Witte, who had returned to Russia only a few weeks previously to public acclaim because of his successful negotiation of a peace treaty with Japan at Portsmouth, New Hampshire, had submitted a report to Nicholas II the day before urging reform as the best means of choking off the growing revolution. He now summarized that report and concluded by iterating his view that the tsar had only two alternatives. Either the Russian ruler could move along a path of reform, or he must choose a dictator to suppress the civil unrest by force. The meeting adjourned without a decision but was reconvened after lunch, when Witte presented a draft imperial manifesto promising reform, the document that he and his colleagues had been working on during the boat trip to Peterhof that morning. No one raised objections during the meeting, but the next day the tsar asked other senior officials to make recommendations. Witte, learning this, sent word to Nicholas that he would be willing to head a government committed to restoring order and initiating reform but only on the basis of the report they had just discussed, without modifications.

The following morning, October 30, 1905, Baron Vladimir B. Fredericks, the secretary of the imperial court, explained to Grand Duke Nikolai Nikolaevich that since Witte would be available only on his own terms, the tsar would have to establish a dictatorship after all and that the grand duke was the logical person to be appointed dictator. Hearing this, the grand duke pulled a revolver from his pocket and exclaimed, "Do you see this revolver? I am now going to the tsar and will ask him to sign Count Witte's program and manifesto. Either he will do this or I shall shoot myself in the head!" Whether Nikolai Nikolaevich repeated his dramatic threat to the tsar is unknown, but returning a short while later after seeing Nicholas, the grand duke reported that the tsar would accept Witte's program and manifesto.

After meeting with Witte again that afternoon, Nicholas II signed the document, which was immediately promulgated and became known as the October Manifesto. It only partially succeeded in quelling the revolutionary movement, but it did establish civil freedoms and a limited form of constitutional government in Russia, a system that lasted, with some modifications, until the collapse of the tsardom in the Revolution of 1917. That Nicholas was not entirely happy with his decision is shown by what he confided to his diary that night: "After such a day my head began to hurt and my thoughts were confused. God help us and comfort Russia."[1]

Nicholas's "headache" over granting extensive reforms is understandable. He had come to the throne determined to preserve the autocratic legacy of his predecessors. Yet Russian society was changing rapidly, and when the tide of unrest and revolution threatened to sweep away the traditional system, Nicholas decided his only course was to give ground a little. But he remained committed to the absolutist principle and resented the concessions he was being forced to make. As a result, the period between the Revolution of 1905 and the outbreak of war in 1914 saw a changing society, but one whose top leadership still clung to an outmoded past. As economic development and social transformation altered Russian life irrevocably, the tsar and his conservative supporters were able to block evolution of the political system, preserving many old ways of governance. Russia on the eve of World War I was markedly asymmetrical: an antiquated state structure ruled a modernizing society. Whether the former would eventually have changed enough to synchronize with the latter remains a fascinating but unanswerable question, since the war cut off whatever line of development Russia was embarked on.

THE REVOLUTION OF 1905

The early twentieth-century popular uprising against the tsarist government is known as the Revolution of 1905 because the peak of revolutionary activity occurred in that year. In fact, however, its first manifestations date to 1904, and the revolutionary movement in the countryside and in the army continued into 1907. During these years the tsarist regime faced a major challenge to its authority, the breadth and intensity of the opposition reflecting in part the enormous socioeconomic changes that had taken place in Russian society in recent decades. Comparing the Revolution of 1905 to the Decembrist Revolt only eighty years earlier, one is struck by how isolated from and unrepresentative of the whole society the Decembrists were and how by contrast almost every social group participated in the 1905 revolution.

Some of the participants came from totally new classes: industrial workers and people from the professions and business. Others, such as the national minorities, were newly aroused, whereas the peasants had a long tradition of rebellion but had never acted countrywide and en masse before. Finally, mutinies in the army and navy marked the first time that military rank and file had risen against authority. The very breadth of the revolutionary forces in 1905 was also an element of weakness. Each group had somewhat different aims and favored different methods of struggle. Yet the wide range of revolutionary cadres—middle-class liberals, workers, peasants, non-Russian minorities, soldiers, and sailors—and the spontaneous nature of much of their antigovernment activity clearly foreshadowed the Revolution of 1917, and for these and other reasons Lenin called 1905 a "dress-rehearsal" for the more decisive uprising twelve years later.

Russia's war with Japan in 1904–1905 triggered the Revolution of 1905 but did not cause it. The revolution grew out of long-standing grievances, social injustices, and political frustrations in Russian society. The strain and sacrifice of war, coupled with humiliating Russian losses and the country's final defeat by Japan, provided the immediate pretext to attack the government.

During Russia's expansion into the Far East and well into the war itself members of the tsarist administration consistently underestimated the strength and skill of the Japanese government. The minister of the interior even went so far as to observe that "a short victorious war" might not be a bad thing since it would dampen the growing popular unrest. Yet the Russian army suffered a series of defeats on land in the Far East, as well as a naval disaster at the Straits of Tsushima between Korea and Japan, where Japanese warships almost totally destroyed a major Russian fleet that had sailed halfway around the world from the Baltic Sea. Only because Japan was feeling the war's financial burden and thanks to the diplomatic skill of Witte was Russia able to salvage a reasonable peace, the Treaty of Portsmouth signed in August 1905. The Russo-Japanese War was significant in two major respects: it marked the first defeat in modern times of a European power by an Asian nation, and it added fuel to the burgeoning revolutionary movement in Russia.

In the first years of the twentieth century, grain prices in Russia dropped and agricultural wages declined, making the plight of the already desperate peasantry worse and seeming to confirm the peasant saying, "The shortage will be divided among the peasants." As the following description shows, most peasants lived at the margin of existence:

[In] a village eighty miles from Moscow, . . . the people lived in wooden huts
. . . thatched with straw. . . . The stoves were great erections of clay, upon
which some of the family slept. Many had no chimney. There was a little opening over the door near the roof, which let out the smoke after it had warmed,
and blackened both walls and people. . . . Clay was the material for cooking
vessels, and clay or wood for plates and dishes. China was a rarity for holidays. Splinters of wood supplied the function of forks. The general sleeping
place was the floor, on straw, which was brought in each night and taken out
in the morning. All clothes were home spun. . . . The usual footgear was birch-
bark sandals; leather boots only on holidays, and to church, and a pair lasted
more than ten years. . . . For a long time there was only one cloth coat in the
village: it was borrowed by friends for festive occasions. . . . Meat was a rarity.
The rye-bread was supplemented by cabbage-soup and barley-porridge. . . .[2]

Under such conditions it is hardly surprising that beginning in 1902 the
peasants began to protest, particularly in the areas of greatest land hunger
in south central Russia. A wave of peasant disorders started in 1904 and
expanded considerably in 1905.

At about the same time strikes were spreading through a number of industrial centers, and by 1905 hundreds of thousands of workers were on
strike. A number of these strikes included demands for political reform, as
well as insistence on higher wages and shorter hours. Terrorist activity, dormant for a number of years, resurfaced, and several tsarist officials were assassinated.

But it was the liberals who took the political initiative in challenging the
tsarist government. In November 1904 a meeting of representatives of *zem-
stvo* organizations called for equal status for the peasantry, civil freedoms,
and a representative legislative assembly. In March 1905 the Union of
Unions was formed to bring together over twenty professional associations
of lawyers, doctors, engineers, and other occupations, and it sought similar
reforms.

In early 1905 the first dramatic clash between the government and the
people took place in an incident on January 22, 1905, a day subsequently
known as "Bloody Sunday." In hopes of diverting radical workers from
direct antigovernment activity, the ministry of interior had begun in 1904
to support associations of workers organized and supervised by the police. In St. Petersburg an ambitious, idealistic, and slightly muddled priest,
Father George Gapon, headed such a group. On Bloody Sunday he led a
crowd of peaceful working-class petitioners, men, women, and children
carrying icons and pictures of the tsar, to the imperial palace. Unaware
that Nicholas II was away, they intended to present him with an address
that was couched in the high-flown rhetoric customary in such petitions
to the throne but that also proved to be ominously prophetic. It said in
part:

Lord, we workers, our children, our wives and our old helpless parents have come to seek justice and protection from you. We are impoverished and oppressed, unbearable work is imposed on us, we are despised and not recognized as human beings. . . . We are pressed ever deeper into the abyss of poverty, ignorance and lack of rights. . . . We have no strength left, O Lord. . . . If thou wilt not respond to our plea, we shall die here on the square before thy palace.[3]

And die they did. In a tragic display of incompetence, security officials in St. Petersburg, without the knowledge of the tsar or higher authorities, chose to disperse the unarmed crowd by force, firing into several columns of protesters. More than a hundred people were killed and many more wounded. Public opinion reacted strongly against the government, and Bloody Sunday marked an important turning point in the development of the Russian revolutionary movement generally, destroying the myth of a mystical bond between the people and a gentle and caring father-tsar.

From January 1905 on the government found itself increasingly powerless as a series of parallel protest activities by liberals, workers, peasants, national minorities, and soldiers and sailors engulfed Russia. It was an impressively broad national movement for change, manifesting itself in speeches, meetings, proclamations, mutinies, strikes, riots, assassinations, land seizures, and demonstrations. A popular rejection of the tsarist administration, the revolution was largely leaderless and spontaneous.

The government could do little. In August the unpopular war with Japan was finally ended. That month the tsar issued a decree establishing a consultative legislative assembly to be elected by a restricted franchise. But this was clearly too little too late. By October the strike movement culminated in a general strike that shut down almost all activity in St. Petersburg and produced the urgent conference between Nicholas II and Witte described at the opening of the chapter.

The October Manifesto that Witte proposed and the tsar signed, albeit reluctantly, promised the people a broadly representative legislative assembly to be called the Duma, as well as full civil liberties, that is, freedom of press, assembly, and speech. A short time later the tsar made further concessions, legalizing trade unions, canceling the remaining redemption dues owed by the peasants, and relaxing restrictions against minority nationalities. Although disorders continued, these reforms divided the opposition and thus marked the first step in the government's regaining control of the situation. To be sure, the extreme parties, the Marxist Social Democrats and the peasant Socialist Revolutionaries, together with most workers rejected Nicholas's package of concessions as totally inadequate and continued to clamor for a constituent assembly and radical economic changes. The peasants, who wanted land, were hardly mollified. But much of the educated public, especially the middle and professional classes, was satisfied. The Kadets, the leading liberal party, which had only recently been formed, decided that the reforms did not go far enough but that they would press for further change within the system granted, and they condemned continuing violence. The Octobrists, a newly established party of businessmen and moderately conservative landowners, concluded, as their name indicates, that the October concessions were sufficient and no further reforms were needed. By December 1905, although underneath, Russian society was still seething, at the top, articulate elements had opted for peaceful evolution and had begun to rally around the government in its efforts to restore order.

Two developments in the fall of 1905 had particularly frightened educated and propertied circles in Russian society: the continuing violence and illegal land seizures perpetrated by the peasantry and the political radicalization of the workers, especially in St. Petersburg and Moscow. During the October strikes the workers of the capital had spontaneously formed a coordinating committee of elected representatives from many of the main factories to supervise and direct the strike movement. Modeled on similar committees formed that summer in several small industrial towns, which in turn may have been adaptations to the city and the workers' situation of the traditional communal assembly in the village, the St. Petersburg committee took the name *Soviet,* or *Council, of Workers' Deputies.* This body soon began to exercise a number of welfare, administrative, economic, and political functions and was the forerunner of the soviets that, after being reestablished in the Revolution of 1917, became the basic institutions of the new revolutionary state.

Although the St. Petersburg Soviet and the soviets that soon sprang up in a number of other cities were formed by and for the workers and most remained worker-dominated, the radical parties did their best to use the soviets as platforms for revolutionary agitation and as political weapons against the factory owners and the government. They had some success, and in particular Leon Trotsky, a talented speaker and writer for the Social Democrats and a leader of the Bolsheviks in 1917, gained considerable renown as chairman of the St. Petersburg Soviet and a forthright champion of the rights of the masses. But the continuous upheavals and constant strikes began to take their toll among the tired and poverty-stricken workers, and in mid-December 1905, when the Soviet tried to organize a massive strike to win the eight-hour day for workers, the movement collapsed and the government arrested the leaders of the St. Petersburg Soviet. In protest the Moscow Soviet took to the barricades, and for eleven days workers in Moscow battled government troops and artillery in a heroic but futile struggle.

Emboldened by its success against the soviets, the government, with support of much of public opinion, enlarged its efforts to restore order. It attacked the peasant revolution directly by sending punitive military expeditions into the most disaffected provinces to put down peasant unrest by force. It dispatched similar repressive units to the Baltic provinces to quell nationalist disorders there and along several main railway lines to restore lines of communication throughout the country.

Several factors worked in the government's favor, in addition to the shift of public attitudes against further violence and the exhaustion of the workers. With the war over in the Far East the government was able to bring back to European Russia reliable units to be used in suppressing civil disorder (though mutinies and unrest in the armed forces continued sporadically through 1906). In addition, the government's financial position, badly weakened by the war with Japan and the revolutionary disruption of the Russian economy, was salvaged when Witte managed to secure a major loan from France. Finally, conservative forces began to organize and soon were actively supporting the government's repressive policies. A proto-fascist organization, the Union of the Russian People, was formed, with a reactionary political, religious, and Russian nationalist platform. Furthermore, conservative gangs, the Black Hundreds, were tolerated by the police. Spurred by primitive anti-Semitism, they were involved in pogroms against the Jews that broke out all too often in 1905 and 1906. On a few occasions honest government officials or military officers intervened to protect the Jews and Jewish property, but more frequently the authorities stood by and let the mobs wreak havoc on the Jewish community.

By spring of 1906, when the first Duma convened, the government had clearly mastered the revolution, although peasant and military disorders continued throughout the year and into 1907. The Revolution of 1905 had succeeded in forcing the tsarist regime to make significant changes, but it had failed in its larger purpose of toppling the old structure entirely.

THE DUMA PERIOD, 1906–1914

Between the Revolution of 1905 and the outbreak of World War I in 1914 Russia had a brief interlude of "normal" development, marked by a limited constitutionalism, renewed economic growth, rapid social evolution, basic changes in agriculture, and a remarkable spurt of cultural creativity. Some historians see this period as the beginning of the peaceful emergence in Russia of a modernized, democratic society, quite similar to Western societies. Others, however, see these few years as a desperate, last-ditch effort by reactionary forces to paper over some of Russia's most fundamental flaws, a ploy that was doomed to fail, whether the war had come or not. In their view the changes of the Duma era succeeded only in temporarily staving off an inevitable and sweeping social revolution, the first portents of which appeared in 1913 and early 1914.

In December 1905, when the government was still feeling threatened, the tsar had approved a broad franchise for elections to the Duma, the legislative body promised in the October Manifesto. Virtually all adult Russian males could vote, although voters did not elect representatives directly but through assemblies of electors. By April 1906, when Nicholas II issued the Fundamental Laws, the constitution that set forth the specifics of the new system, the government felt strong enough to water down in several ways the power of the Duma. A reorganized State Council (an advisory body set up by Alexander I) was designated a coequal legislative chamber, alongside the Duma, with its members chosen to ensure that it would be very conservative: half were appointed by the tsar, and half were chosen by several elite groups and institutions. In addition, the Fundamental Laws contained a provision that allowed the tsar to issue legislation when the Duma was not in session, although such laws were to be approved or rejected by the Duma when it reconvened. Finally, the first section of Article I of the Fundamental Laws reaffirmed the theoretical basis of autocracy in the following terms:

> The All-Russian Emperor possesses Supreme and Autocratic Power. To obey His authority not only from fear but also from conscience is ordered by God Himself.[4]

Other sections reserved to the tsar and his ministers authority over foreign and military affairs and over certain parts of the state budget.

The elections to the First Duma evoked some lively campaigning. Although most members of the radical parties boycotted the election, opponents of the government still won a comfortable majority of the seats. This was no small shock to the government, which had expected the peasants to be a conservative political force. Some of the electors chosen by peasant voters supported nonparty Duma deputies, but a large number backed Kadet or other antigovernment candidates.

The scene when Tsar Nicholas II convened the Duma reflected some of the basic divisions of Russian society, with the Orthodox clergy on his right hand, and higher nobility on his left, and the rest of the population (the Duma deputies) in front of him. In the Duma sessions the opposition, emboldened by its electoral success, pressed vigorously for additional concessions. They wanted to exert greater control over the state budget and to make the tsar's ministers responsible to the Duma, and they particularly urged sweeping land reform. When the government resisted staunchly on these issues, an impasse resulted. Only three months after the Duma was convened, the tsar dissolved it. Some two hundred Duma deputies challenged the government by calling on Russian citizens not to pay taxes or serve in the army until the government made further concessions, but the public did not respond, and the deputies were arrested. At the same time the government continued its policy of forcibly restoring order, not hesitating to use such extralegal measures as military courts-martial, which condemned several thousand people to death in 1906–1907, and administrative banishment, which sent over twenty thousand individuals into exile in Siberia.

The extreme left parties decided to participate in the voting for the Second Duma, and peasant electors, angered over the government's recalcitrance on the land issue, supported radical candidates, with the result that the Kadets lost ground to the leftists while government and conservative parties gained seats but remained in a minority. The Second Duma therefore proved even less tractable than the first, from the government's point of view, and after three months of wrangling it too was dissolved.

The government, now led by a resolute prime minister, Peter Stolypin, acted illegally to change the electoral law, issuing in July 1907 new regulations that greatly reduced representation of peasants and of national minorities and provided that the gentry would choose one half of the electors. Or, put another way, under the revised franchise one elector represented each 250 landowners, 1,000 large urban property holders, 15,000 small property holders, 60,000 peasants, and 125,000 workers. This weighting of the elections had the desired result, as the Third Duma consisted of 270 conservative deputies, 114 Kadets, 30 leftists, and 17 nonparty deputies, giving the government a comfortable working majority.

The Third Duma deputies served their full terms of five years, and the Fourth Duma, elected in 1912, lasted almost to its prescribed end, before the 1917 Revolution interrupted its work. Although the tsarist government controlled both the Third and Fourth Dumas, the evolutionary impact of these two bodies is important in two ways. First, the Dumas provided useful political experience, not just for the deputies and party members themselves but for the articulate public as a whole, who followed Duma debates closely and who, in newspapers and journals, expressed opinions on a wide range of issues that the Dumas considered. In other words, educated Russians not only had a little taste of political democracy but obviously savored it. Second, the Dumas did accomplish a good deal in noncontroversial areas. For example, they pushed the government to begin improving and modernizing the Russian armed forces. Duma committees helped work out important legislation related to public education, labor safety, and social insurance. The Dumas also encouraged more effective economic and fiscal policies by the government.

Finally, the Dumas played some role in the most significant legislation of the prewar period, the *Stolypin reforms* in agriculture. The general features of these changes in Russian rural life had been developed during Witte's premiership in 1905–1906. A major goal was to make agriculture more productive so that it would be less of a brake on the economy as a whole. Another objective was to give peasants a sense of proprietorship, thereby encouraging them not to seize land illegally as they had in 1905 and not to follow the enticements of revolutionary parties that promised to expropriate land in the peasants' behalf. Witte believed that to accomplish these aims it would be necessary to break up the village commune, making each peasant an individual owner, and to eliminate the old strip system of farming, giving each peasant instead a consolidated plot of land. Since the individual peasant would then control his own land, crops, and profits (after government taxes), he would have an incentive to work harder and to use newer farming techniques, thereby notably raising yield per acre throughout the country.

Stolypin took over this program, and between 1906 and 1911 it was initiated in a series of laws and administrative regulations. Since the war cut short its implementation, it is difficult to assess how successful the Stolypin land reform might have been, but one has to respect Lenin's judgment that if completed, it would have significantly reduced the potential for revolution among the peasantry. Like the emancipation of the serfs, it was a major social revolution, and it would have turned some hundred million Russian peasants into small landowners. By 1915, it is estimated, only a little over a million peasant families, having withdrawn from the commune, had both acquired ownership of their land and consolidated their strips into a single plot. On the other hand, almost a quarter of all peasant families had left the commune and owned their own land, though it was still scattered among the various communal fields. The remaining peasants were only in the preliminary stages of the reform process.

How did the peasants feel about the Stolypin program? No one is entirely sure because most of our evidence is filtered through the government agencies responsible for administering the reform at the grassroots level. It is significant, however, that although the commune continued to exist until its replacement by the collective farm in 1928–1929, many peasants during the Revolution of 1917 seized land and used it as if they owned it individually. On the other hand, since the Stolypin policies provided only limited opportunities for the peasants to acquire *more* land and since the peasant population continued to multiply, one wonders whether even the most successful promotion of private ownership and land consolidation could have blunted the peasants' desperate hunger for additional land or could have solved the problem of the growing numbers of landless and nearly destitute peasants.

In the Duma years the Russian economy resumed the rapid industrial growth that had characterized it in the 1890s. Between 1906 and 1914, industry increased at about 6 percent a year, and enough miles of railroads were added to make the Russian empire second only to the United States in total trackage. New manufacturing sectors developed, banking and service enterprises expanded, and mining and other extractive industries grew rapidly as the richness of Russia's natural resources began to be tapped. The pre-1900 pattern of heavy concentration in large factories and a few places continued, and foreign capital retained its major role in many sectors of the Russian economy. The labor force increased to about 3.5 million workers. Just before the outbreak of World War I, labor unrest revived notably, and in the spring and summer of 1914, on the eve of the war, the strike movement reached its highest peak since 1906. Clearly this restiveness reflected basic divisions and unresolved tensions in Russian society.

Moreover, despite its impressive economic growth, Russia remained substantially less developed and modernized than the European nations with which it was competing in foreign affairs.

Were Russians better off in 1914 than before the Revolution of 1905? Unfortunately data to permit a clear answer to that question are not available. Probably the average real income of both peasants and workers was slightly higher, although some of the poorest individuals were in desperate straits. Yet even if the standard of living was rising in prewar Russia, so were the expectations of the people. Many certainly wanted far more than they were getting. And the masses' resentment of privileged Russia, a hostility that had simmered just below the surface for centuries with only occasional eruptions like the Pugachov Revolt, was perhaps nearing the boiling point. After the Revolution of 1905 the people felt less powerless, and for the first time they began consciously to heed the appeals of the revolutionary intelligentsia. Convinced they were being deprived of basic equity and increasingly desperate over the conditions in which they lived, the bulk of Russia's workers and peasants were attuned to revolution.

Another factor helping to create a revolutionary situation on the eve of the war was the rigid and unyielding nature of the tsarist regime. The tsar, his closest advisers, and the conservative elite in Russian society were determined to resist change, and the bureaucracy was so structured that major reform of the political system could come only from the top. Since there was no established mechanism for innovation, only occasional powerful personalities, such as Witte and Stolypin, could develop new approaches. And though both were politically conservative, their fate was hardly encouraging to potential reformers: Nicholas II, pressed by reactionary circles, dismissed Witte as premier in April 1906, and Stolypin was assassinated in 1911. After that no strong, reform-minded individual appeared inside the government. There was no further opportunity for the system to modify itself before it was blown away by the revolutionary storm of 1917.

Does all this mean that Russia was moving steadily and inexorably toward revolution? Not necessarily, argue many historians, pointing to several signs of peaceful progress during the Duma era. Not only were peasants being encouraged to become stable individual proprietors, but the economy was booming, and the benefits of that boom were just beginning to reach the workers. Higher education was spreading, and the government and the Duma, working together, initiated a broad educational program designed to put all Russian children into elementary school within fifteen to twenty years. There were a dramatic increase in cooperatives, continuing improvement in communications and transportation, slow but steady progress in public health, beginnings of an intellectual and social renaissance among a few Orthodox religious thinkers, and rapidly growing advanced science and technology. But these evolutionary trends needed time to make their impact felt, and that time was not vouchsafed them. In any case, the changes of the Duma years may have been too late, after centuries of social oppression, political absolutism, religious obscurantism, and personal exploitation. Perhaps too many grievances and too much resentment had accumulated for Russian society to avert the violent explosion that the country's disastrous involvement in World War I made almost certain.

THE SILVER AGE: RUSSIAN CULTURE, 1890–1917

In the years immediately preceding the war Russia experienced not only economic and social change but also a surge of artistic and intellectual creativity. Perhaps not so dazzling as the cultural outpouring in literature and music that marked the mid-1800s, this new outburst nevertheless made major contributions to world culture in such fields as poetry, theater, ballet, music, design, and painting. Russians participated significantly in the twentieth-century modernist movement, and today we are still enjoying and benefiting from the pioneering works of Russian artists active in the period from the 1890s to the Revolution of 1917.

Russian culture in this era could draw on its own rich past, as well as being stimulated by the ferment and excitement of such European artistic movements as realism and impressionism. Moreover, after 1905 the intellectual climate in Russia was freer, with little censorship and a growing appreciative public. On the other hand, the achievements of the outstanding artists of this Silver Age are all the more remarkable when set against the relatively low cultural level of the country as a whole. Although the number of graduates of schools and universities was shooting up, on the eve of the war 50 percent of Russia's population was illiterate, and the overwhelming majority of the population was acquainted only with folk culture and the emotional religious experience of the village church.

Russian theater developed remarkably in the last part of the nineteenth century and the first years of the twentieth. Particularly prominent were a famous director, Konstantin Stanislavsky, whose "Stanislavsky method" has influenced actors ever since; an outstanding theater company, the Moscow Art Theater; and a subtly powerful playwright, Anton Chekhov. Chekhov also wrote wonderful short stories, but beginning in 1895 until his death in 1904 he produced a string of successful plays that, though set in Russia of his times, deal with such modern and timeless themes as loneliness, boredom, alienation, and frustrated dreams. Among the classics Chekhov bequeathed to playgoers the best known are *Three Sisters* and *The Cherry Orchard.*

Emerging early in the 1900s, Russia's first major revolutionary author, Maxim Gorky, drew on his experiences drifting about Russia as a youth for such realistic works as the play *The Lower Depths,* and the novel, *Mother.* Gorky was bitterly critical of Russian society and eloquently argued the need for radical change. Embracing the Revolution of 1917, he remained the dean of Soviet writers, despite disagreements with Lenin and Stalin, until his death in the 1930s.

In sharp contrast to the psychological probing of Chekhov or the revolutionary realism of Gorky were the symbolist writers, primarily poets, who came to the fore after 1905. They espoused aestheticism, beauty, "art for art's sake," and individual lyricism, exploring and expanding language in new and dramatic ways. The most talented was Alexander Blok, famed for his mystical poem about the revolution, *The Twelve,* but the most active politically was Vladimir Mayakovsky. He threw himself into propaganda work after 1917 and in the 1920s helped develop an avant-garde revolutionary theater, but, disillusioned and depressed, committed suicide in 1930. A few lines from his poem "The Cloud in Trousers" suggest the imagination and brashness of Mayakovsky, even though they are less powerful in translation:

> *But it seems,*
> *before they can launch a song,*
> *poets must tramp for days with callused feet,*
> *and the sluggish fish of the imagination*
> *flounders softly in the slush of the heart.*
> *And while, with twittering rhymes, they boil a broth*
> *of loves and nightingales,*
> *the tongueless street merely writhes*
> *for lack of something to shout or say.*[5]

In the early 1900s Russian artists excelled in bringing together various art forms in a single presentation that was markedly more than the sum of its parts, what today we might call a "multimedia" work. This approach was pioneered by a group of young artists who published a daring journal, *The World of Art,* which combined content (prose, poetry, criticism) with beautiful typography, layout, and illustration. The *World of Art* movement soon spread to the ballet and theater, where the artist Alexander Benois and the impresario Serge Diaghilev brought together the best dancers, such as Anna Pavlova and Vaslav Nijinsky, with the music of the most daring new composers, such as Igor Stravinsky, and mounted the performance against sets, costumes, and lighting designed by outstanding modern artists. The result was integrated and stunning presentations that were the sensation first of Russia, and then, when Diaghilev took his Ballet Russes company abroad, of all Europe.

At about the same time a brilliant group of avant-garde artists was developing in Russia, who were influenced by postimpressionism in Europe and contributed importantly to modern art in the West after World War I. For example, Vladimir Tatlin was an important leader in the constructivist movement, N. J. Goncharova and M. F. Larionov developed rayonism, Kazimir Malevich initiated suprematism and was a forerunner of minimal art, and Marc Chagall and Vasily Kandinsky, both of whom emigrated to the West after the 1917 revolution, were important abstract artists.

Finally, Russian intellectuals contributed significantly to modern science and scholarship in this period. Russians built on earlier achievements in such fields as mathematics, chemistry, and engineering. At the same time they made new contributions in physics, biology, physiology, psychology, and history. Russian scholars and scientists were supported by an expanding system of higher education, including new universities and research institutes, additional specialized technical and professional institutions, and a growing array of scholarly and scientific libraries and journals.

Put briefly, the quality and output of Russian intellectual and cultural life on the eve of the war were remarkably high, especially in relation to the general level of education and culture in the country. Whatever its deficiencies in social and political terms, Russian society could be proud of its artistic and creative contributions, an area in which Russia was not only not "backward" but was instead a leader of world culture.

RUSSIAN INVOLVEMENT IN WORLD WAR I, 1914–1917

As the American scholar and statesman George Kennan pointed out in his book on prewar diplomacy, the origins of Russia's involvement in World War I are to be found in the fateful decision, taken in the early 1890s, to ally with France. This flew in the face of Russia's recent diplomatic tradition, which had stressed the ideological and power advantages of Russia's remaining closely linked with the German and Austro-Hungarian empires, since they dominated both central Europe and Russia's western borders. The tie with France also seemed to defy common sense, for France was not only far away, anti-autocratic in ideology, and a potential rival in the Near East, but also isolated, vengeful, and therefore a potential troublemaker on the European scene. Nevertheless, a number of factors worked to bring Russia and France together. The Russians wanted support against their chief rival in the Balkans, Austria-Hungary, and they also feared the increasingly aggressive and militaristic German empire. Russia, like France, seemed to be alone and vulnerable in the lions' pit of European power struggles, once the Three Emperors' League with Germany and the Austrian empire had dissolved in the 1880s. Finally, the French were Russia's chief creditor, and they suggested that a political-military alliance could only strengthen the economic connection.

After the first formal ties were established in 1893–1894, the French over the years cleverly drew the Russians into their military embrace, ensuring that the vast numbers of Russia's peasant army would be thrown against the Germans, should the French ever have the chance they had sought for so long to avenge their defeat at the hands of the Germans in 1871 and to recover the lost territories of Alsace and Lorraine. Following Russia's defeat by Japan, the French alliance seemed even more important to Russia's leaders. When it was supplemented in 1907 by an understanding with Great Britain, they felt secure in a powerful system, soon known as the

Triple Entente. The difficulty, however, was that the opposing system, the Triple Alliance of Germany, Austria-Hungary, and Italy, emboldened the Russians' archenemy in the Balkans, the Austrians, to be more aggressive in that region.

Beyond our scope are the details of the militarism, diplomatic maneuvering, and imperialistic rivalry that marked international relations in Europe in the decade before 1914. The most important point for Russia was that in 1908 during the crisis over Bosnia and, to a lesser extent, in 1912–1913 during the Balkan Wars the Russians believed they had been forced to back down diplomatically under pressure from the Austrians, supported by Germany. Therefore, when in 1914, as restitution for the assassination of the Austrian heir to the throne by a Serbian nationalist, the Austrian government tried to force humiliating concessions from Serbia, Russia's ally in the Balkans, the Russian leaders were in no mood to compromise, believing their status as a great power was at stake.

The crisis was exacerbated in all countries by intense nationalist feeling, and Russia was no exception. Although some government officials knew that Russia was no match for German economic and military power and one predicted that Russia's defeat would result in "hopeless anarchy, the outcome of which cannot be foreseen," others feared that a Russian concession might mean the eventual domination of the country by its central European rivals, and publicists and orators beat the drums for Russian patriotism and Slavic unity. Consequently, when the crisis turned into war between the Entente nations, Russia, France, and England, and the Central Powers, Germany and Austria-Hungary, Russian public opinion welcomed the conflict, and all parties and groups except the Social Democrats rallied around the throne and vowed enthusiastically to support the war effort.

In the beginning Russia's war aims were simply to check German and Austrian ambitions, to fulfill its treaty obligations to France, and to defend Russian territory. After Turkey entered the war at the end of 1914, Russia's principal goal became obtaining the Turkish Straits and Constantinople. In a secret treaty signed in 1915 France and England agreed to support Russia in this imperialistic acquisition after the war.

On the fighting front against Germany the Russians fared poorly. Their opponents had a fivefold advantage in artillery, and three times as many rifles and machine guns as the Russian soldiers. The latter fought bravely but were poorly led and supplied. Mismanagement and inefficiency plagued the government's conduct of the war. As the French had hoped, the masses of Russian troops managed to tie up many German divisions in 1914 and helped to save France from being overrun, but by 1915 the Central Powers had crossed Poland and advanced into Russia proper. Refugees from the occupied western regions poured into the central cities, adding to the already existing problems of food, housing, and fuel supply.

The Russian army remained intact, but its defeats and losses mounted. By the end of the fighting in late 1917 the Russians had mobilized over fifteen million men and had lost six to eight million killed, wounded, and taken prisoner, with perhaps another two million deserters. The mobilization of such large numbers of men both weakened the domestic economy and changed the character of the army. Its largely untrained peasant recruits, uprooted from their traditional routines and circumstances, became radicalized under conditions of defeat and harsh discipline into a potentially revolutionary force.

On the home front the strain of the war led, by 1916, to a gradual breakdown of the economy and a sharp decline in civilian morale. A number of Russia's educated elite had thrown themselves into the war effort, attempting in several public and voluntary organizations to make up the deficiencies of the government in medical and hospital services, war production, food distribution, and other areas. But the transport system could not meet the enormous demands placed on it, and supplies to the cities began to dwindle. Resulting shortages worsened the plight of urban workers who were already suffering as the cost of living rose faster than their wages. In the countryside the peasants, short of labor because of the army mobilization and facing low prices for grain and high prices for the few manufactured products that were available, began to produce less, mainly feeding themselves, a course that naturally intensified the food supply problems in the cities.

Even the economic hardships, coupled with the military defeats and sacrifices, might have been bearable if the Russian masses had some sense of what they were fighting for and if they had had inspired leadership at the top. Instead, the tsar and his advisers refused to promise reforms after the war while furnishing only incompetent and aimless direction of the war effort. The disintegration of the Russian government at its highest levels was symbolized by the notorious influence of Gregory Rasputin, a self-proclaimed holy man who was able to affect government appointments, if not policies, because Nicholas's wife, Alexandra, believed "Our Friend," as she called Rasputin, was able to stop the bleeding of their hemophilic son, the heir to the throne (see Figure 13). Realizing that his presence in court circles was only discrediting the monarchy, a group of conservative conspirators murdered Rasputin, who to their horror seemed impervious at first to the poison they had given him, but finally succumbed when shot and pushed into the river.

The government refused to accept proposals for reform and cooperation made by a large majority of deputies to the Fourth Duma, and the tsar continued to endorse the appointment to ministerial posts of second-raters and incompetents. Even the tsar's cousin commented, "The Government itself is the organ that is preparing the revolution." In 1916 and early 1917, as economic and living conditions worsened and the military situation deteriorated, talk that a change was needed grew, and rumors of a *coup d'état* circulated in the capital, now called Petrograd because St. Petersburg had too Germanic a sound in Russian. Many predicted revolu-

Figure 13. *Nicholas II and his family, with members of the court. Uniforms and military ceremonials played an important role in court life. (Courtesy of the Library of Congress)*

tion, yet when it actually occurred, it happened suddenly and with no immediate forewarning.

CONCLUSION

It is hard to see how Russia, once involved in massive, draining war, could have avoided some sort of violent upheaval. In four important ways World War I brought on a revolutionary crisis. First, the war accelerated the disorientation of Russian society that the processes of modernization, industrialization, and urbanization had launched in the preceding decades. Tens of millions of Russians were physically displaced, some by mobilization into the army, others as refugees from the war zone, and many more who moved voluntarily to undertake war work in factories and in various war-related organizations. This great migration of individuals within the country meant that old ties, habits, and attitudes were disrupted and people were exposed to new ideas and experiences. The result was to weaken the fabric of the old society, leaving many people and groups searching for new roots and increasing the potential for radical social and political change.

Second, the war intensified the sense of injustice and resentment that had been building among the Russian masses in the previous decades. Although at first there was a surge of patriotic support for the war, people became both exhausted and bitter as the war dragged on. Russian losses in people and territory were enormous; many families suffered personally and directly, and almost everyone was affected indirectly. The harsh conditions under which the workers and peasants labored and lived seemed increasingly intolerable, and the sacrifices of the soldiers at the front, pointless. As a historian of the Russian army has recently concluded, "The soldiers felt they were being used and recklessly expended by the rich and powerful, of whom their officers were the most visible, immediate representatives."[6] War-weariness, despair, and hatred of the old system became dominant at all levels of Russian society. The people's only hope seemed to lie in victory, which seemed increasingly distant and illusory, or in radical change, some sudden liberation from their bonds and burdens.

A third immediate effect of the war was to bring about a partial collapse of the Russian economy, with a resultant deterioration of conditions in the major cities. As the real income of both workers and peasants declined, as the transportation and distribution systems ceased to function effectively for civilian needs, and as food and fuel shortages in the cities worsened, people's attitudes toward the government and the war hardened until finally they simply refused to tolerate the situation any longer.

Finally, Russia's participation in the war completely discredited Nicholas II and his already weak regime. People were therefore able to discard the tsar and his government entirely, with almost no one coming forward to defend them. For centuries the Russian masses had retained faith in the divinely inspired tutelage of the benevolent "father-tsar." But in the twentieth century this faith dissipated, as workers and peasants wondered why the tsar did nothing to ameliorate their lot. During the war many held Nicholas responsible for the grief, suffering, and fear the war brought: "If the tsar were a good tsar, why couldn't he save Russia and its people?"

Nicholas's own actions did not help matters. He associated himself personally with the war effort, finally making himself commander-in-chief of the Russian army and moving to general headquarters at the front to oversee operations. In this way he became linked to the continuing defeat, loss of life, and sacrifices. He did nothing to correct the incompetence and moral corruption of the government. People despised the tsarist ministers and bitterly criticized their mismanagement of the war effort. It was bad enough to suffer and to lose, but to do so in part because the country was being run by a clique of misfits and sycophants, some of them selected by Rasputin, was intolerable.

By 1917 Russia was a society twice changed, first by the economic, social, and political developments of the late nineteenth and early twentieth century and then by the devastating impact of World War I with its disruptions, sacrifices, and despair. That the old government and system could not go on was clear to all—except perhaps the tsarist leaders themselves— but what was to replace it? The answer lay both in Russia' past and in the circumstances of Russia's dramatic revolution.

FURTHER READING

Ascher, Abraham. *The Revolution of 1905* (2 vols.). Stanford, Calif.: 1988, 1993.

Charques, Richard. *The Twilight of Imperial Russia*. London: 1974.

Gray, Camilla. *The Great Experiment: Russian Art, 1863–1922*. London: 1962.

Haimson, Leopold. "The Problem of Social Stability in Urban Russia, 1905–17." *Slavic Review* 23, 4 (1964), 620–642; 24, 1 (1965), 1–22.

_____. "The Problem of Political and Social Stability in Urban Russia on the Eve of War and Revolution Revisited. *Slavic Review* 59, 4 (2000), 848–875.

Hosking, Geoffrey. *The Russian Constitutional Experiment . . . 1907–1914*. New York: 1973.

Keep, John H.L. *Last of the Empires*. Oxford: 1995.

Kennan, George F. *The Fateful Alliance: France, Russia and the Coming of the First World War*. New York: 1984.

Lieven, Dominic. *Nicholas II: Twilight of the Empire*. New York: 1994.

Lincoln, W. B. *In War's Dark Shadow: The Russians Before the Great War*. New York: 1983.

Massie, Robert K. *Nicholas and Alexandra*. New York: 1967.

Mehlinger, H., and Thompson, J. *Count Witte and the Tsarist Government in the 1905 Revolution*. Bloomington, Ind.: 1972.

Oberlander, E., et al. *Russia Enters the Twentieth Century*. New York: 1971.

Smith, C. Jay. *The Russian Struggle for Power, 1914–17*. New York: 1956.

Stavrou, T. G., ed. *Russia Under the Last Tsar*. Minneapolis: 1969.

Waldron, Peter. *Between Two Revolutions: Stolypin and the Politics of Renewal in Russia*. DeKalb, Ill.: 1996

Wallace, D. M. *Russia on the Eve of War and Revolution*. New York: 1962.

Revolution, Civil War, and the Founding of Soviet Society, 1917–1928

Everyone was glad it was warmer. During the street demonstrations the past two days people had shivered and nearly frozen, but despite the bitter cold they had continued their protests against the shortage of bread and against the war. Now by midmorning, Saturday, March 10, 1917, the thermometer had climbed to twenty degrees Fahrenheit and crowds of strikers, unemployed workers, students, and housewives were again on the streets, heading for the center of Petrograd, the Russian capital. The mood of the demonstrators on the previous two days had been amiable, almost jolly, as if they were on holiday. On Saturday, however, more clashes with the police occurred, as more and more workers left work to join the protest marches. By noon three hundred thousand people, or about one-fifth of the city's total population, were milling about. Some, besides demanding bread, shouted "Down with the tsar," and a few even called out a truly revolutionary slogan, "Down with tsarism!" Nevertheless, Tsarina Alexandra, who despite her involvement in government affairs during the war understood almost nothing about popular attitudes, wrote to Nicholas about the throngs on the streets of Petrograd: "If the weather were very cold, they would all probably stay at home."

In Znamenskaia Square, at the end of Nevsky Prospect, the main street of the city, a revolutionary orator was haranguing a large crowd when mounted police arrived to break up the demonstration. The speaker urged the throng not to move on, as ordered. The detachment commander then raised his pistol and took aim. Before he could fire, a cossack, a member of the capital's security forces, rode forward and cut the commander down with his saber. Although cossacks and army troops had been tolerant toward the demonstrators previously, this was the first time that anybody from the government's side actively supported the protesters. The next day soldiers from the Pavlovskii guards regiment attacked a police unit, and that night members of the Volynskii regiment, who, under orders, had fired on unarmed demonstrators in the morning, vowed not to do so again. The next morning when their commanding officer again ordered them out against the crowds, the soldiers mutinied and killed him.[1]

These incidents marked the turning point of the revolution that overthrew the tsardom. Once the cossacks and the troops stationed in Petrograd sided with the revolutionaries, the government was helpless. The police were too few to restore order if military force could no longer be relied on. The subsequent arrest of the tsarist ministers and the abdication of Nicholas II were anticlimactic.

THE FEBRUARY REVOLUTION:
THE COLLAPSE OF THE TSARIST SYSTEM

The popular uprising that led to the disappearance of tsarist rule after three hundred years of the Romanov dynasty took place February 24–28, 1917, according to the old-style (Julian) calendar then in use in Russia and is known in Russian and most Western historiography as the February Revolution. According to the new-style (Gregorian) calendar used in the West and adopted in Russia in 1918, the tsar's downfall occurred March 8–12, and so it is sometimes referred to as the March Revolution. Under either name this revolution was the first of two that took place in 1917 and that together are usually designated the Russian Revolution. Since the second upheaval, which brought Lenin and the Bolsheviks to power, happened October 24–26, 1917, old style, or November 6–8 new style, it is called the October Revolution (or the Great October Socialist Revolution in Soviet historiography). Yet during the Soviet era its anniversary was celebrated on November 7 with a huge parade reviewed by Soviet bigwigs in Moscow's Red Square.

The February Revolution and the October Revolution were two separate events, but many writers argue they were simply stages in one continuous radical transformation of Russian society in 1917: a people's rebellion sparked by the oppression and injustice of tsarist rule that culminated in the founding of an entirely new social and political system, Soviet socialism. Others, minimizing the shifts of political power reflected in the two revolutions, stress the more fundamental and long-range modernization of Russian society in its economic, social, and intellectual aspects, a process that began in modern times with the emancipation of the serfs in 1861, that was accelerated in the massive Soviet industrialization drive after 1928, and that is only now being completed in the post-Soviet era. In our account we will try to include both perspectives on the Russian Revolution: its specific features and its long-run impact on both Russia and the rest of the world.

The protests over bread shortages, the strikes, and the street demonstrations in Petrograd that led to the collapse of the tsardom occurred spontaneously, without particular leaders or heroes. Although radical socialists egged on the crowds, the demonstrations constituted a genuinely popular revolution in which the bulk of the citizens expressed their refusal to tolerate the existing situation and government any longer. Casualties numbered about 1,500 individuals, mostly insurgents. Once the soldiers joined the crowds, the old regime simply disappeared, and this deliquescence of authority was repeated throughout the country. Nicholas II soon abdicated, without protest, and no one came forward to defend the autocratic system.

The nature of the February Revolution raises an important question about Russian society: How could the old order be discarded so easily? The answer lies in part in the discrediting of the tsarist regime at the top and in the terrible burdens and discouragement of the war, for which people blamed the tsarist government, as we saw in the last chapter. But the tsardom vanished in a moment because of longer-range weaknesses as well. In the latter part of the nineteenth and the beginning of the twentieth centuries the traditional belief system and norms that had bolstered the autocracy for so long began to erode rapidly. The tsar had counted on ingrained obedience and on gratitude for his benign rule, on the rituals and divine support of the Orthodox Church, on a system of classes in which each group knew its place and acknowledged its obligation to serve the state, and on a mystical sense of the rightness and goodness of Slavic tradition. By the 1900s these values had become vitiated or outmoded, and no new conservative tenets had emerged to replace them. The old order rested on custom and inertia; once these weakened it was easily toppled.

Tsar Nicholas abdicated in favor of his brother, but the latter refused the throne. It soon became clear in any case that almost no one supported continuation of the monarchy, even if it were reformed. Nicholas and his family met a tragic fate. After spending some fairly pleasant months under mild "house arrest" in Siberia, the deposed tsar, his wife, and their five children were brutally murdered in July 1918 by local authorities to prevent their possible capture by anti-Bolshevik forces involved in the Russian civil war then raging. The Bolshevik leaders in Moscow callously approved this execution.

Even before the tsar abdicated, a group of liberal leaders had formed a committee of Duma members, which soon appointed a provisional government. Its ministers were mainly members of the Octobrist and Kadet parties, plus a few other moderates. From the start the Provisional government labored under several handicaps. Its own members as well as the populace at large considered it temporary and transitional until a constituent assembly democratically elected by all the Russian people could convene and decide on Russia's permanent future government. In addition, the Provisional government represented a considerable range of political views, particularly after May 1917, when moderate socialists joined the cabinet. As a result, it could not agree on even temporary solutions for some of Russia's most urgent problems. Finally, the Provisional government tried to govern in an atmosphere of unrealistic popular expectations, revolutionary euphoria, and widespread feelings of liberation that impelled people to reject all authority.

In practical terms, moreover, the Provisional government almost immediately found itself sharing power in the country with a grassroots organization, the Soviet. On March 12, in the same Petrograd building in which Duma members were meeting to form the Provisional government, assembled a group of revolutionary activists: representatives of the workers, a few socialist and radical politicians, and some soldiers. They soon decided to reconstitute the soviet that had played such a dramatic role in the Revolution of 1905. In recognition of the contribution troops of the Petrograd garrison had made in the recent revolution, the resurrected organization was called the Soviet of Workers' *and* Soldiers' Deputies. It chose an executive committee dominated by moderate socialist politicians.

The Petrograd Soviet soon exercised considerable authority because workers in such key sectors as transport, communications, and supply looked to it for guidance and because it had influence over troops stationed in Petrograd and other major cities, particularly after March 14, when the Soviet issued Order Number 1, a call for sweeping reforms in the army and the election of soldiers' committees in each unit. As it became established, the Soviet acted as a check, or watchdog, on the formal administration of the country, the Provisional government, creating a situation of "dual power" that lasted until the October Revolution seven months later.

The February Revolution spread quickly throughout the Russian empire. As in Petrograd, tsarist authorities were replaced, usually without bloodshed, by public committees, and soviets soon formed, first in the cities and then more slowly in district towns and villages. Outside Russia, the Central Powers welcomed the revolution because they thought it might lead to an unraveling of Russian society and a collapse of Russia's fighting capacity. The Allies and the United States were also delighted, first on ideological grounds since they could now fight side by side with another democracy instead of an autocracy, and second, because they hoped the new government would invigorate the Russian war effort and strengthen Russia's contribution to the Western cause.

But what did the Russian people think about the downfall of the tsar? Most of them were overjoyed, embracing the revolution as a panacea for all of the country's and their own problems. Exhilarated and optimistic, they exercised their new freedom to the fullest, attending meetings, founding parties, sending petitions and telegrams to Petrograd, and talking, always talking. At the same time, except for a common belief in the glory and value of "the Revolution," all had their own ideas about the future: workers expected higher wages, the eight-hour day, and better working conditions; peasants counted on more land and higher grain prices; the national minorities dreamed of autonomy, local rights, and, in a few cases, independence; soldiers and sailors wanted fairer treatment, civil and political rights, and their own committees. Moreover, most individuals believed their dreams would come true, if not right away, at least in the near future.

The reality of course was far different. The Provisional government had to struggle with the same problems that the tsarist regime had confronted, most prominently the war and its effects. In retrospect we can see that the war was destroying orderly society in Russia and that at heart people were sick of the war. But at the same time inertia, the lingering effects of patriotism, fear of the Germans, and, among educated classes, a sense of duty to Russia's allies, all combined to make it unthinkable that Russia should pull out of the war. The Provisional government announced it would continue to fight and to support the Allied cause. The Petrograd Soviet also endorsed the war, although at the same time calling for a redefinition of Allied war aims to eliminate annexations of others' territory and indemnities against the losers.

The Provisional government promised independence to the Poles and full autonomy to the Finns but could not agree on policy toward the other national minorities. Both the Provisional government and the Soviet backed expanded civil liberties, immediate elections to the Constituent Assembly, and lifting of restrictions against religious minorities and Jews. But they were far apart on what social and economic policies should be followed. Nevertheless the Soviet decided to tolerate the Provisional government as long as "it fulfills its promise and effectively combats the old regime."

A month after the February Revolution a new element was introduced into the situation, when on April 16, V. I. Lenin (see Figure 14), who had been in exile in Europe for ten years, arrived back in Petrograd. Although the German government helped Lenin return by letting him pass across German territory and although the Bolsheviks later secretly accepted money from the Germans, neither Lenin nor his party were German agents, as has sometimes been charged. They took money from whatever source was available and used it for their own purposes. In this case, Lenin intended to stir up a radical revolution in Russia, for which the Germans assisted him, but he counted on that revolution's spreading to Europe and to Germany itself.

Lenin was now leader of the Bolsheviks, an important faction of the Russian Social Democratic Party. Lenin and his followers had established a separate identity within the party beginning in 1903 at the party's Second Congress, where they had argued that the party should be a small, elite, highly disciplined band of professional revolutionaries. His opponents, soon known as Mensheviks, favored a larger, broadly based, more open party. After 1914 the two factions also disagreed over World War I. Lenin interpreted the war as the result of struggles among the capitalists over colonial empires and over trade, and he concluded that capitalism was in a final phase of decline, which Lenin dubbed "imperialism." Most Bolsheviks followed Lenin in denouncing all sides to the struggle and urging the workers to turn the imperialist war into a civil war against the capitalists; most Mensheviks approved defensive military action to protect Russia while calling for a peace of justice and brotherhood.

The Mensheviks welcomed the February Revolution and accepted the Provisional government in part because they clung to orthodox Marxist theory, which taught that all societies, including Russia, had to pass

Figure 14. V. I. Lenin, 1870–1924. (Courtesy of the Library of Congress)

through a capitalist phase of development, however brief, before they could undergo a proletarian revolution and enter the final stage of history, socialism. For the Mensheviks the February Revolution represented the overthrow of the old feudal order in Russia's equivalent of the French Revolution, and Russian society was now in its capitalist, or "bourgeois-democratic," phase. They considered it doctrinally correct to support the bourgeois-democratic Provisional government and to use the freedoms it granted to proselytize the workers for the forthcoming proletarian or socialist revolution. In a set of statements known as the April Theses, Lenin attacked this view. He called on the Russian people to struggle against, rather than support, the Provisional government; to begin at once to prepare the transfer of all power to the Soviet; and to end the war immediately. This radical program shocked even his fellow Bolsheviks and was ignored by moderate socialist and liberal politicians as extremist nonsense.

Undaunted, Lenin continued to espouse his ideas, reflecting two of his most dominant traits as a revolutionary leader: his tenacious will that often wore down and overpowered the resistance of doubting comrades and his devout conviction of both the necessity and the possibility of a socialist revolution in Russia. As the spring wore on, the tide of events began to move in a direction that favored Lenin's view of the situation. The war dragged on, and the Provisional government was weakened by a crisis over its alleged retention of the imperialist war aim of acquiring Constantinople and the Straits. Social and economic conditions worsened instead of improving after the February Revolution. The government made no progress on two key issues, land reform and rights for minorities, partly because its liberal leaders stuck resolutely to democratic principles. They insisted that such fundamental questions as redistribution of land, which the peasants were vociferously demanding, and whether the future Russian state should be a federal system, as the non-Russian nationalities insisted, could only be settled by the free vote of all Russian citizens through their representatives in the soon-to-be elected Constituent Assembly. Yet they did not do enough to speed up preparations for the elections, and they could not agree on how to meet the most immediate social and economic problems.

More important than the government's ineffectiveness, however, was the growing disillusionment of the masses with the results of the February Revolution. Not only had it not solved everyone's problems, but most individuals were worse off. When it seemed they were no nearer achieving their cherished goals, many people grew frustrated and bitter, blaming privileged Russia—the educated leaders of the Provisional government—for the dashing of their hopes. War-weariness was spreading rapidly, and even front-line troops became restive. The government nevertheless pushed forward with its plans to mount a major military offensive designed to relieve pressure on the Allies on the Western Front. Workers became embroiled in sharp disputes with factory owners, and peasants began to seize private and state land illegally. As mass attitudes and actions became increasingly radical, authority and order began to dissipate in the country and tensions mounted. Clearly a new crisis was imminent.

THE BOLSHEVIKS COME TO POWER

Two climactic events in summer 1917 paved the way for the Bolsheviks to take power with relative ease in the fall. The first was the July Days, a spontaneous mass uprising in Petrograd on July 16 and 17. People poured into the streets of the capital with no specific purpose in mind except to show their dislike of the Provisional government and their disgust with the existing situation. Some may have also vaguely wanted the Soviet to replace the government. During the demonstrations Victor Chernov, a Socialist Revolutionary leader and a member of the Soviet, was trying to persuade a crowd to disperse when an outraged worker interrupted, shaking his fist at

Chernov and bawling, "Take power, you son-of-a-bitch, when they give it to you." But Chernov and other moderate socialists in the Soviet did not believe they should assume power at a time not yet ripe for a socialist revolution. The riots in Petrograd died down, and the Provisional government regained control of the situation for a time, but the July Days had shown how revolutionary the masses were and how shaky the government's position was.

The second event was a bungled attempt by General Lavr Kornilov to seize power and establish a military dictatorship in the country. After the major offensive planned by the Provisional government had failed, in part because some military units proved unreliable, the prime minister, a socialist liberal named Alexander Kerensky, had supported a movement within the top command to restore discipline in the army and to put down unrest on the home front. Kerensky thought he was using General Kornilov to strengthen the government, but Kornilov believed Kerensky was giving him a free hand. The result of this tragicomic misunderstanding was that Kornilov, encouraged by conservative elements in Petrograd, rashly ordered troops to move against the capital. Kerensky, fearing that Kornilov intended to take over the government, appealed to the Soviet and the masses for support, thereby alienating himself from conservative circles and making him dependent on radical elements. Railway and communications workers prevented the movement of Kornilov's troops, while revolutionary agitators persuaded many of his soldiers to give up. As a result, the attempted coup was a fiasco, and the position of the radicals was strengthened. Even more importantly, most Russians were now frightened of the possibility that reactionary forces, however vaguely defined, might attempt a counterrevolution, threatening whatever gains "the Revolution" had provided. Throughout the fall of 1917 the Bolsheviks effectively used the bogey of counterrevolution in their bid for power.

By September 1917 the Bolsheviks' slogan "Peace, Land, and Bread" was winning over large numbers of workers, soldiers, and peasants. The Bolsheviks also promised non-Russian minorities the right of self-determination. Their program fitted well the goals of many Russian citizens, and the Bolsheviks soon obtained a majority in the Petrograd and Moscow soviets. In the meantime the war continued to go badly, and the Provisional government under Kerensky seemed paralyzed, despite several attempts to rally democratic elements around it.

The vulnerability of the liberal-moderate socialist coalition that was trying to govern Russia arose from several factors. It lacked strong leadership, Kerensky in particular being a vain, mercurial, often impractical person who between bouts of apathy and despair rushed around giving speeches and exhorting his fellow countrymen without accomplishing much. Moreover, as noted earlier, the moderate socialists were reluctant partners in the coalition cabinet since according to Marxist theory the government should have been a capitalist one. They were not willing to assume power themselves because it was the wrong historical moment for a socialist government, yet they were stalemated by the liberals from taking immediate steps to alleviate the socioeconomic ills of Russia. Finally, the circumstances were such that even a united government with strong leadership could not have survived so long as it continued an unpopular war and refused to grant the people's most urgent demands. On the very eve of the Bolsheviks' assumption of power, several moderate socialists proposed a program of peace and land reform to Kerensky, but by then it was too late.

As the Mensheviks and the Socialist Revolutionaries, tainted by their association with the war and with the Provisional government, lost influence with the masses, the Bolsheviks gained strength. In an amazing turnabout the Bolsheviks had grown from a tiny fringe group of around twenty thousand at the time of the February Revolution to a huge party of about two hundred sixty thousand with substantial influence in the army and among the urban masses. Within the party a sharp debate erupted in September–October 1917 over whether to attempt an armed revolution. Lenin, with his brilliant political acumen, argued vigorously that now was the moment to strike while the Provisional government was weak and while a majority of articulate opinion favored the Bolsheviks. Others urged caution and a longer period of preparing the masses for action. Lenin finally forced through a decision to move toward revolution.

The Bolsheviks' success in the October Revolution, during which they took power as it slipped from the hands of the Provisional government, was facilitated by two events occurring on the eve of the revolution. One was formation of the Military Revolutionary Committee (MRC) of the Petrograd Soviet in the third week of October. Although it was charged with preparing defensive measures in the event of a German attack on Petrograd and with coordinating the movement of troops in the capital, it soon became, under the forceful leadership of Leon Trotsky, a planning committee for the Bolshevik uprising. Several days before the revolution the MRC posted its own commissars with most military units in the capital and announced that no military orders were valid unless countersigned by the MRC. This meant that the government had lost control of the troops in Petrograd, and although only a few of them joined in the Bolshevik uprising, the rest declined to defend the Provisional government.

Second, Trotsky, who did an excellent job organizing and directing the revolution, cleverly managed affairs so that Kerensky was provoked to move against the Bolsheviks on November 5. This permitted them to appear not as illegal subverters of a democratic government but as righteous defenders of freedom and "the Revolution" against the dark forces of reaction.

On November 6–7 the Bolsheviks took control of key locations in the capital—banks, post offices, railroad stations, and government buildings—most often without a struggle. On the night of November 7 they also captured the Winter Palace, former seat of the tsars (see Figure 15), arresting

Figure 15. *A popular demonstration in front of the Winter Palace, former residence of the tsars in Petrograd, during the early days of the Russian Revolution of 1917.*

the ministers of the Provisional government, who had retreated there. Only a few military units tried half-heartedly to defend the palace, and Kerensky, after slipping out of the city, could not rally a sufficient military force from the regular army to recapture Petrograd from the Bolsheviks. Casualties during the October Revolution in the capital were only a few hundred, and most of the citizenry passively accepted the new order with a wait-and-see attitude.

On November 8 Lenin formed a Soviet government called the Council of People's Commissars, and presented to the Second Congress of Soviets, made up of deputies from soviets throughout Russia, decrees calling for immediate peace and for nationalization of all land and its transfer to the peasantry for their use. He also decided to proceed with elections to the Constituent Assembly late in November.

Outside Petrograd the October Revolution proceeded unevenly. In some cities power passed quickly to Bolshevik-dominated Soviets, but in others fighting erupted, and it was days or even weeks before the Bolsheviks established their authority. The peasants, happy with the decree on land, generally acquiesced in the Bolshevik takeover, and most of the army, except a number of officers, supported the new Soviet government after Lenin pushed through an armistice with the Germans pending peace negotiations.

During his first weeks in power Lenin had to deal with a serious political crisis. Most delegates to the Second Congress of Soviets, including many of the Bolsheviks, had been sent to the congress with instructions from local soviets to support formation of a new government that included all the socialist parties, including the Mensheviks and Socialist Revolutionaries (SRs). But since the moderate socialists opposed the Bolshevik assumption of power and their delegates had walked out of the Second Congress on that issue, Lenin had formed an all-Bolshevik government. Not wishing to share power, Lenin would have preferred to continue that arrangement, but pressure not only from Soviet representatives but from within the Bolshevik party and from key trade unions, including the railway workers, forced him to enter negotiations with the Mensheviks and SRs for creation of an all-socialist cabinet. By the end of November the talks collapsed, the pressure dissipated, and Lenin reorganized the Council of People's Commissars to include a few individuals from the Left Socialist Revolutionaries, a radical faction of that party. In this way Lenin established what was essentially a one-party government, a practice that became a central feature of the Soviet system from then on.

A couple of months later Lenin made it clear that the Bolsheviks intended to dominate not only the government but also the general political life of the country. Lenin had permitted elections to the Constituent Assembly, as promised in the Bolshevik platform, but since the majority of voters were peasants and the Socialist Revolutionary party was closest to the peasants, the SRs won a majority of seats in the new assembly. When it convened in January 1918 and it became evident the Bolshevik minority could not control the assembly, Lenin forcibly dissolved it. Although the moderate socialist parties occasionally contested local Soviet elections during the next few years, for all practical purposes the Bolsheviks, by that act, created a one-party dictatorship over the country, which existed until 1991.

The October Revolution meant that in a few days, or weeks at most, power in the largest country in Europe had been transferred into the hands of a radical socialist minority bent on entirely restructuring Russian society and on carrying their "proletarian revolution" to the advanced countries of the West and eventually to the whole world. Lenin justified the socialist revolution in less industrialized Russia by saying that special circumstances, such as the war and the revolutionary actions of the Russian peasantry, had permitted it and that the October Revolution would fulfill the capitalist stage of history in Russia as it proceeded. It was a rather vague formulation, but Lenin counted on the socialist revolution's spreading to highly industrialized Western Europe; once the proletariat had come to power there, they could give Russia the assistance it needed to develop an advanced economy and support true socialism. As Lenin often put it, the Bolsheviks needed to hold on to power in Russia until their ally, the workers of the West, came to their aid.

We know that the October Revolution had fateful consequences for modern world history, but what sort of a revolution was it? It was certainly not an evil conspiracy designed to fasten a new form of human bondage on the Russian people, as some extreme anti-Communists have argued. On the other hand it was not a great libertarian revolution opening the way to freedom and plenty for all of Russia, as Soviet historians claimed. Neither vilifying the Bolsheviks nor glorifying the masses is a convincing way to interpret the revolution. Rather the Bolsheviks were able to build upon deep popular feelings—resentment of the injustice and oppression associated with old privileged Russia, fear of counterrevolution, revulsion against the war and the sacrifices it entailed, and dreams of a better, securer, more just future—to come to power and have the chance to construct a new order. That many of the aspirations of the masses were unfulfilled and that the Bolsheviks built a revolutionary society quite unlike that which their early members envisaged are key elements of the story that will unfold in the remaining pages of this book. But it is important to remember that the vision, the dream, the yearning for a future good society that animated so many Russians in 1917—not the reality of what actually happened afterward—had a powerful impact on the rest of the world.

CIVIL WAR AND FOREIGN INTERVENTION, 1918–1921

Within six months of their coming to power the Bolsheviks had to confront major internal and external challenges to their authority that led to a bitter, no-holds-barred conflict lasting almost three years. An intriguing question is to what extent this desperate struggle for survival determined the contours of Soviet society. How much of the harshness, intolerance, and authoritarianism of the Soviet system can be traced to its birth pangs in civil strife and economic stringency? Or, put another way, if the Bolsheviks had been allowed—nay, even assisted—to put their ideas into effect without outside interference and without the necessity of improvising to stay alive, what sort of socialist society might have emerged? There are no precise answers to these questions, but several factors need to be borne in mind when considering them. Russia was not an advanced country in 1914, and regardless of the further devastation caused by the civil war, Russia's three-year involvement in World War I had nearly wrecked the economy. So the Bolsheviks would not have had extensive resources to work with, in any case.

Second, as we have seen, Lenin and his party made clear, well before major armed attacks against them began, that they would brook no interference with their rule and that they would not share authority with other parties or interest groups, nor with the people. This was partly because Lenin and the Bolsheviks believed the party should not only lead, but act on behalf of, the people and partly because Lenin was convinced that the Bolsheviks must hold power in Russia until the Russian Revolution could spark a revolution in Europe and the advanced proletariat of the West could come to the Bolsheviks' assistance. Consequently, Bolshevik Russia, even at peace, was not likely to be a democratic, participatory society. At the same time it seems fair to conclude that the rigors and exigencies of the civil war and foreign invasion intensified authoritarian trends within Bolshevism and reinforced attitudes and policies that emphasized control, centralization, and suppression of dissent.

The issue that touched off the civil war and intervention was not dissolution of the Constituent Assembly or the Bolsheviks' radical economic measures, such as repudiation of Russia's foreign debt and nationalization of property—though these acts hardly pleased many people at home and abroad—but rather Lenin's policy toward the war. By making peace with the Central Powers, as he eventually did in March 1918, Lenin alienated millions of patriotic Russians, who concluded that the Bolsheviks had sold the country down the river, as well as the Allied powers, whose leaders believed the Russians had betrayed their cause and were forcing the Western democracies to make even greater sacrifices to defeat Germany and Austria-Hungary. To be sure, neither the anti-Bolsheviks nor the Allied statesmen were delighted with the Bolsheviks' revolutionary policies and with their appeals to workers throughout the world to revolt, but the primary reason they took up arms against the new Soviet regime was because it had made peace with the German enemy.

Ironically Lenin was faced with a no-win situation. He had promised the Russian people peace; if he didn't deliver, his government would not last long. Yet he also knew that peace meant not only humiliating concessions to the Germans but probably stirring up widespread opposition against the Bolsheviks. Faced with this dilemma, Lenin risked the potential of attacks from foes within and without against the certainty of German occupation and popular rebellion if he tried to continue the war. Yet even within his own party he had a major struggle before convincing a slim majority of Bolsheviks to accept the Peace of Brest-Litovsk, under which Russia lost a quarter of its territory and population, a third of its industry, and three quarters of its coal mines to Germany and Austria-Hungary. Lenin believed that the peace treaty was a temporary surrender, a scrap of paper to be torn up when the proletarian revolution broke out in Germany, as he was convinced it would. In fact, the treaty lapsed eight months after it was ratified in March 1918, not because of a revolution in Germany but because the Allies won the war despite Russia's defection.

In December 1917, at the time armistice negotiations with the Germans began, the first anti-Bolshevik forces were formed in south Russia, primarily from high officers in the army and cossack soldiers. Major hostilities did not begin, however, until May-June 1918, when a military front against the Bolsheviks was set up in Siberia, supported by Czechoslovak troops who had formed part of the Russian army and were being evacuated to the Western Front when they clashed with the Bolsheviks. Other fronts were established in north Russia, supported by British and American troops, and before long in northwest Russia, with assistance from the British. Later, anti-Bolshevik, or White, armies were also active in southwestern Russia, supported by the French, and in the trans-Caspian area, supported by the

British. The military history of the civil war is both extremely complex and beyond our scope, but as a glance at Map 7 shows, at one time Soviet Russia, the Bolshevik state, was surrounded on all sides by anti-Bolshevik forces and was compressed into a relatively small area in central Russia.

The civil war was greatly complicated by the participation of non-Russian minorities, who often were at odds with the Russian Whites, since the latter favored a centralized Russia and were generally unwilling to make concessions to the nationalities. At various times in the period 1918–1921 a majority of the Finns, the Baltic peoples, the Poles, the Armenians, the Georgians, the Ukrainians, and the Muslim peoples of Central Asia were fighting the Bolsheviks. To confuse the picture even further, some members of these national groups were Bolsheviks and supported Lenin and the Soviet government in their efforts to incorporate the minority areas into Soviet Russia. When the struggle finally ended in the early 1920s, the Poles, the Finns, and the Baltic peoples had established their independence, and the others had been absorbed in the Soviet state.

The third important element in this drawn-out and fierce struggle were the foreign powers who intervened in the Russian civil war. In the summer of 1918 the Central Powers, worried that the Bolsheviks were not completing the economic payments required under the Treaty of Brest-Litovsk, occupied western territory of the Soviet state. At about the same time Britain, France, the United States, and Japan decided to intervene in Russia, mainly in hopes of restoring a military front against the Germans and partly for anti-Bolshevik or imperialistic reasons. Although the American president, Woodrow Wilson, disapproved of this action, he went along with his allies as a gesture of wartime unity. Allied troops, mainly Japanese but including seven thousand Americans, were landed in the Russian Far East, British and American troops in north Russia, and, later in 1919, French troops at Odessa in south Russia. The greatest Western contribution to the anti-Bolshevik cause, however, was not direct military support, most of which was withdrawn in 1919 after the victory over Germany, but military equipment and financial assistance for the White forces. This aid unquestionably helped the anti-Bolshevik armies fight on considerably longer than they otherwise could have and was therefore a source of much Soviet resentment against the Western powers.

After the defeat of Germany, the Western intervention took on a definitely anti-Bolshevik character, but public opinion in the democracies was unwilling to support a major effort to bring down the Bolshevik regime, and the whole enterprise petered out by 1920 (although Japan did not remove its troops until 1922). The legacy of intervention was suspicion and mistrust between the Soviet government and the West, which hampered their relations over the next seven decades.

At the same time that the Bolsheviks were desperately defending the Soviet state against White armies and foreign interventionists, they were also on the offensive, trying to stir up revolution in the West. When the German

BRITISH & U.S.

Murmansk

MILLER

Archangel

FINNS

Helsinki

YUDENICH

Petrograd   Vologda

Reval

Riga

Moscow

Vilnius

Minsk   Orel   Saratov   Samara

Warsaw

Kiev

Lvov   Kharkov   Tsaritsyn

WRANGEL   Rostov

Odessa   DENIKIN   KRASNOV   Astrakhan

Bucharest   Novorossiisk

Sofia

FRENCH   Krasnovodsk

Constantinople   Baku   BRITISH

Perm   Ekaterinburg   Omsk

Kazan   Cheliabinsk   KOLCHAK

Ufa   CZECHOSLOVAKS

Bukhara

Teheran

0   400
MILES

THE CIVIL WAR, 1918-1921

	Area controlled by the Bolsheviks		Red Partisans
Attacks by Whites and Intervention troops		Partisans opposed to both Reds and Whites
Area occupied by Entente		Railroads

MAP 7

radical leader Karl Liebknecht was let out of jail in the fall of 1918, Lenin announced in a burst of optimism: "The release from prison of the representative of the revolutionary workers of Germany is a sign of new epoch, the epoch of victorious socialism which is now beginning for Germany and for the whole world."[2] For a time Lenin convinced himself that the proletarian revolution predicted in Marxist theory was about to erupt in Europe, partly because of the Russian example and partly because of disillusionment and economic hardship in Germany and Austria following their defeat. To distinguish his movement of revolutionary socialism from the moderate or evolutionary socialists in Russia and Europe, Lenin had his party renamed the Russian Communist party (Bolshevik). He sent propaganda, agents, and a little money to spur the revolutionary cause in Europe, and short-lived Communist uprisings in Hungary and in southern Germany momentarily raised Lenin's hopes. In March 1919 Lenin founded the Communist International (Comintern), a league of revolutionary socialist parties dominated by the Bolsheviks that was dedicated to promoting world revolution.

Although revolution did not spread to the West, neither were the Western powers able to snuff out the revolution in Russia. Consequently, some observers have viewed relations between Soviet Russia and the West in these years as a stand-off, with neither side able to achieve its maximum goals. And although many in Europe and the United States were terrified of "the Red menace" and the potential spread of communism, many others were swayed by Soviet appeals for peace and an end to intervention and by Soviet calls for a new postwar order based on social justice and economic equality.

In the all-out struggle to survive, the Russian Communists adopted stringent policies at home. As early as December 1917 they established the Cheka (from its Russian initials), the forerunner of the Soviet secret police, and by the summer of 1918, when a political opponent shot and wounded Lenin, both the Bolsheviks and the Whites were resorting to terror and extensive political coercion. Lenin and Trotsky defended such repressive policies as necessary to make sure the revolution and the Soviet state survived, but a leading European Communist, Rosa Luxemburg, sharply criticized these actions.

The social and economic policies the Bolsheviks adopted between 1918 and 1921 are sometimes called war communism, and indeed demands of the war effort dictated many of these measures. But they might also be called militant communism because some policies were ideologically motivated and were designed to introduce socialist concepts in Russia. Industry was nationalized and tightly controlled; private enterprise and trade were reduced to a minimum; the state provided all public and social services, including education and culture; and the Orthodox Church and other faiths were persecuted.

Soviet policy toward the peasants was ambiguous. They were allowed to keep the land they had seized in 1917, and additional public land was given them. At the same time, since the Soviet government needed grain to feed workers in the cities and troops of the growing Red Army, it resorted to requisitioning of peasant surpluses. This policy greatly angered the more prosperous peasants and one reason the civil war lasted so long was that peasants kept switching back and forth between the Reds and the Whites. At last, when they realized that the anti-Bolshevik forces were determined to take the land back and to restore many aspects of the old order, the majority of peasants passively sided with the Bolsheviks.

The Soviet government survived as much because of the deficiencies of its opponents as its own strengths. To be sure, the Soviet forces had interior lines of communication, and the Red Army, built up to a force of several million men and effectively organized and led by Trotsky, often with assistance from former tsarist officers, fought bravely for the most part. Yet the disorganization, disunity, and reactionary attitudes and policies that characterized the Whites made them far less formidable opponents than they might have been. Moreover, as we saw earlier, they failed to reach an agreement with the national minorities, thereby losing valuable support. The Allied powers, in the face of a public opinion weary of war and partially sympathetic to the Bolsheviks, could not provide decisive assistance.

The last episode of the civil war and intervention was an attack on Soviet Russia by Poland that led to a bloody summer of fighting in 1920. With the military situation stalemated in the fall, peace was agreed to on the basis of a compromise boundary line between the two countries.

THE NEW ECONOMIC POLICY AND COEXISTENCE, 1921–1928

By the winter of 1920–1921, when it was clear that Soviet Russia had survived, the major question for the Bolsheviks became, What next? Lenin's hoped-for revolution in Europe had not materialized and did not seem imminent. Little help could be expected from that quarter, although Lenin hastened to restore diplomatic and commercial relations with the Western capitalist countries (except the United States, which refused to recognize the Soviet state until 1933), and he was quite happy to grant economic concessions to capitalists willing to invest in Russia. But few were interested, and it was soon apparent that Soviet Russia would basically have to go it alone.

At the same time the Bolsheviks faced a disastrous situation at home. The civil war and intervention had completed the wrecking of the Russian economy begun in 1914. By 1920 industrial production was at only 20 percent of its 1913 level, and even agricultural production was only two thirds of what it had been. The country was virtually a wasteland, with some regions facing famine and spreading epidemics of typhus and smallpox. Some fifteen to twenty million people had been killed or had died of disease and starvation between 1914 and 1921. Moscow and Petrograd had shrunk to less than half their prerevolutionary size. Workers in the cities were dissatisfied, and several million Red Army veterans needed to be employed and resettled. The peasants were violently resisting further requisitioning of their grain and were demanding nonexistent manufactured goods before they would sell their produce. Peasant uprisings reminiscent of 1905 and 1917 broke out in a number of regions, and in March 1921 a major revolt erupted in Kronstadt, an industrial town and naval base not far from Petrograd. The Kronstadt rebellion was particularly alarming because all through 1917 and much of the civil war, the Kronstadters had been among the most loyal and spirited supporters of the Soviet government. Significantly, what they now demanded went to the heart of the political dilemma the Bolsheviks faced:

> immediate re-election of the soviets by secret ballot and upon the basis of free political agitation, "in view of the fact that the existing soviets do not express the will of the workers and peasants," freedom of speech and press for "workers, peasants, and for the Anarchists and the left socialist parties"; freedom of meeting, and free trade unions and the formation of peasants' unions; liberation of all socialist political prisoners, . . . abolition of all special political departments (in the army, navy, and transport) "since no one party can enjoy privileges for the propaganda of its ideas and receive money from the state for this purpose"; equal rations for all, except those engaged in work detrimental to health; . . . full rights for the peasants to "do as they please with all the land" and to keep their own cattle, "provided that they use no hired labour"; and the right of individual small-scale manufacture, again without the employment of hired labour.[3]

Lenin had no intention of meeting the democratic political demands of the Kronstadt rebels and ordered the uprising suppressed by force. But he fully recognized that economic concessions would have to be made to save the revolution and Bolshevik rule. At the Tenth Party Congress in March 1921 he set forth his reform program, the New Economic Policy (NEP). It was not a retreat to capitalism, as some anti-Bolsheviks believed, but rather an example of Lenin's tactical flexibility as expressed in his dictum "one step backward, two steps forward." Lenin knew that changes were needed to restore the economy of Russia before a forward movement toward socialism could be contemplated.

NEP had three main features, all designed to stimulate economic recovery. Peasants were allowed to pay the government a fixed tax in money or in kind and could sell anything they produced beyond that in the open market; this was an effective incentive for them to grow and distribute more. Second, much of industry was denationalized, with the government retaining ownership of only "the commanding heights," that is, the largest factories, transportation, and the banks, with the rest reverting to private ownership. Finally, most retail trade and much of the labor market were freed from government control and allowed to operate privately and for profit.

NEP worked exceedingly well, despite the famine of 1921–1922, which private relief assistance from the United States did much to alleviate. Industry surpassed its prewar output levels by 1926–1927, and agriculture nearly reached its 1913 production total the following year. Moreover, with peace at hand life settled into a normal routine, and many older Soviet citizens later viewed the NEP years as a happy and relatively prosperous time. Some outside observers have argued that the seminationalized, semiprivate structure of the Soviet economy under NEP could have provided a continuing mechanism of economic and social development for Russia, even though it was not fully socialist. It is clear though that Lenin never envisaged NEP as anything but a temporary measure. Before Lenin was able to work out how Soviet Russia, still an underindustrialized country, could advance toward socialism in the absence of revolution in the West, he suffered a stroke in May 1922 and died twenty months later in January 1924.

The March 1921 Party Congress was important not only because it launched NEP but also because key decisions concerning the party and concerning the state structure were taken there. Throughout its history the Bolshevik (Communist) Party had been regulated internally according to the rules of democratic centralism. Under those rules ideas and policies could be freely debated at various levels of the party before a decision was made. Once the decision was taken, however, it was binding on all party members and units. In practice, however, party members had been free to continue discussion of controversial questions and had on occasion even formed groups within the party to oppose various policies. At the Tenth Congress, Lenin insisted on adoption of a rule against "factionalism," which stated that once a decision had been made, no organized group could continue to agitate against it. Although Lenin did not enforce this new provision rigidly, it gave Joseph Stalin, Lenin's successor, a powerful weapon against internal opposition and helped him establish a dictatorship within the party.

The March 1921 party conclave also encouraged the movement already developing to make Soviet Russia a federal state, giving the national minorities some cultural and structural autonomy as long as the Communist party retained power in each region and ensured political subjugation to the national government. The result was the emergence between 1922 and 1924 of the Union of Soviet Socialist Republics (USSR), a constitutional structure that lasted until 1991. Each of the union's fifteen republics was run by governments controlled by the Communist party, and although each republic had the theoretical right to secede from the Union, it was understood that such a step would never be taken since it would be inimical to the welfare of the larger state, the Soviet Union, the first socialist nation in the world.

During the NEP period the Soviet government continued the ambiguous foreign policy it had initiated in 1918 when it was struggling to survive. On the one hand, the government called for peace, for normal relations between itself and all other nations regardless of their ideology, and for active trade and commercial intercourse between socialist Russia and the capitalist West; on the other, the Communist party, which ran the Soviet government, agitated vigorously for immediate world revolution, the overthrow of capitalist governments in the West, and destruction of the traditional international order. Moreover, through the Comintern and its ties with Communist parties abroad the Russian Communists sought actively to promote these revolutionary objectives. No wonder Western politicians and diplomats were perplexed.

Nevertheless, with the exception of the United States, the Western nations, because they too wanted trade, peace, and normal relations, established ties with the Soviet state and even invited the Soviet leaders to such Europe-wide meetings as the Genoa Conference of 1922. This respectability reflected nicely Lenin's doctrine of peaceful coexistence: his view that socialist states and capitalist states could live quietly side by side interacting on matters of mutual interest. What Lenin did not stress in the 1920s was another aspect of the theory of coexistence, that the socialist society should try to gain all the advantage it could from such a relationship, and that eventually—after a period of time that Lenin did not specify—coexistence would disappear in a "frightful collision" between the socialist and capitalist systems, from which socialism would emerge triumphant on a worldwide scale. As we shall see in Chapter 13, the "frightful collisions" idea had to be revised in the 1950s after the advent of nuclear weapons.

THE STRUGGLE FOR POWER

While Lenin lived he dominated the Communist party and the Soviet state by virtue of his experience, his intellect, and his strong will. Although other comrades did not hesitate to disagree with him, he was widely admired and respected, and his views generally carried the day. In the early 1920s Lenin, even before his first stroke in May 1922, began to lose his grip on the party and state. In the first place he was unsure, as we have seen, about how socialism could best be built in Russia, and so he could not provide clear direction and ideological guidance. Moreover, since the party and the state were larger and more complex than they had been in the immediate aftermath of the October Revolution, it was much harder for Lenin to be on top of everything. One of the younger party members on whom Lenin came to rely for administrative and organizational detail was Joseph V. Stalin, who became general secretary, or chief administrator, of the party in 1922 (see Figure 16).

Stalin, meaning "steel," was a revolutionary pseudonym. His real name was Dzhugashvili, and he was born in the Caucasus in Georgia in 1879,

Figure 16. *Joseph V. Stalin, 1879–1953.*
(Courtesy of Sovfoto/Eastfoto)

the son of a poor shoemaker. Rebellious as a youth, Stalin was expelled from the theological seminary to which his devoted mother had sent him for a pious education and was soon involved in daring revolutionary activity, probably including robberies to raise money for the cause. Stalin rose in the ranks of the Bolshevik party by determination, hard work, thoroughness, and, perhaps most important, by being self-effacing. How much the later abnormality of his personality can be traced to resentment over his humble origins and over the subsidiary role in which his better educated and more brilliant comrades cast him is unclear, but at the time Stalin swallowed his pride and reliably and uncomplainingly did what he was told. Extremely ambitious, he realized the importance of ingratiating himself with Lenin and before World War I had become the latter's assistant on issues affecting national minorities and the right of socialist self-determination.

Returning from exile in Siberia right after the February Revolution, Stalin was an industrious and loyal comrade in the years of the revolution and civil war, although he had his first disagreement with Trotsky at that time. Stalin was always willing to take on boring tasks that had to be done, yet as early as 1921 when he helped arrange the forcible incorporation of his native Georgia into the new Union of Soviet Socialist Republics, he showed he could be ruthless and decisive. Partly because of Stalin's methods and attitudes in that case, Lenin became increasingly critical of Stalin in 1922 and 1923. After his first stroke Lenin returned to work and planned to present to the Twelfth Party Congress in the spring of 1923 a major criticism of Stalin, recommending his demotion. Luckily for Stalin, just before the congress convened, Lenin had a further paralyzing stroke, which incapacitated him until his death in January 1924.

He had earlier written down, however, some of his growing doubts about Stalin, a document that came to be known as Lenin's Testament: "Comrade Stalin, having become *gensek* [general secretary of the party], has concentrated boundless power in his hands, and I am not sure that he will always manage to use this power with sufficient caution. . . . Stalin is too rude, and this fault . . . becomes intolerable in the office of general secretary. Therefore I propose to the comrades that they devise a way of shifting Stalin from this position. . . ."[4]

After Lenin's incapacitation Stalin allied with two other party leaders, Lev Kamenev and Gregory Zinoviev, in an effort to isolate Trotsky and reduce his power. When Lenin died, Stalin delivered the funeral oration; for reasons that are still unclear, Trotsky failed to attend the funeral and did not publish Lenin's Testament (which also contained some milder criticism of Trotsky), even though Trotsky was the best-known Bolshevik after Lenin, and was Lenin's logical successor. By early 1925 Trotsky had been replaced as Commissar for War; in 1926 he was removed from the Politburo, the party's ruling executive committee, and then expelled from the party; in 1928 he was exiled; and finally, in 1940, an agent of Stalin's police murdered him while he was in exile in Mexico.

Beginning in 1925 Stalin turned against Zinoviev and what was known as the Left Opposition, allying himself with more moderate leaders in the party, such as Nicholas Bukharin. In 1928, however, following his triumph over Trotsky and the Left Opposition, Stalin reversed himself again. Now he attacked his erstwhile supporters, dubbing them the Right Deviation and reducing their role in the party to insignificance. As a result, Stalin emerged from the power struggle to succeed Lenin as undisputed leader of the party and dictator of the Soviet Union. He triumphed in part because his opponents consistently underrated him, in part through skill and ruthless ambition, in part because he cleverly controlled and manipulated the party from his position as general secretary, and in part because he espoused a persuasive ideological platform. The last point we will examine at the start of the next chapter, but Stalin's methods and his mastery of the party boded ill for the future of the Soviet people.

CONCLUSION

Indeed their recent past had been difficult enough, full of stress and high drama. During the decade from 1917 to 1927 a centuries-old social and political system was jettisoned, a disastrous and brutal war was ended only to be followed by three more years of bitter fratricidal struggle, a new society struggling to find its identity and to set fresh goals was born, and an unheralded yet powerful leader emerged to dominate the country and extend the revolution. It was little wonder that some Russians thought of it as a new "Time of Troubles."

In retrospect we can see that those years had several distinguishing characteristics. In the first place, the Russian Revolution saved Marxian socialism, which had been nearly destroyed as an influential movement by nationalist feelings aroused at the outbreak of World War I. Lenin and the Bolsheviks, even though they came to power in a backward country, rescued the socialist ideal and ensured that it would survive for most of the twentieth century as an alternative way of organizing modern society.

Second, the Russian Revolution fulfilled some aspirations of the people and dashed others. From it the Bolshevik or Communist party emerged as the strongest force in the new society, yet the events of 1917 intensified the Leninists' distrust of mass organizations and other parties. The course of the revolution reinforced their belief that they knew what was best for the people and that their way was the correct way. The Bolshevik leaders had no intention of letting the masses decide important issues, and the result was that even though the people wanted an all-socialist government responsive to the popularly elected soviets, what they were given was a one-party dictatorship over the government and country with the Bolsheviks dominating and using the soviets for the party's own purposes.

On the other hand, the Bolsheviks did meet popular demands in a number of areas: they gave the peasants land; they brought peace, at least temporarily; they tried to provide greater equity; and they gave many Russians a sense of dignity and self-worth that they had never had before. In short, the people had gained and they had lost, as so often happens at major turning points in human history.

Finally, the revolutionary years provided remarkable evidence that a single individual can affect the course of history. It is hard to conceive of the Russian Revolution without Lenin. He returned to Russia to galvanize his party, he insisted stubbornly on bidding for power at the only moment when the Bolsheviks could probably have succeeded, and he forced through the peace with Germany, without which the revolution could not have survived.

FURTHER READING

Avrich, Paul. *Kronstadt 1921*. Princeton, N.J.: 1991.

Chamberlin, W. H. *The Russian Revolution, 1917–21* (2 vols.). New York: 1965.

Cohen, Stephen. *Bukharin: A Political Biography*. New York: 1974.

Daniels, Robert V. *The Conscience of the Revolution: Communist Opposition in Soviet Russia*. Cambridge, Mass.: 1960.

Figes, Orlando. *A People's Tragedy: The Russian Revolution, 1891–1924*. New York: 1995.

Fitzpatrick, Sheila; Rabinowitch, Alexander and Stites, Richard, eds. *Russia in the Era of the NEP*. Bloomington, Ind.: 1991.

Graham, Loren R. *Science in Russia and the Soviet Union: A Short History*. Cambridge, Mass.: 1993.

Hasegawa, T. *The February Revolution: Petrograd 1917*. Seattle: 1981.

Howe, Irving. *Leon Trotsky*. New York: 1978.

Keep, John H. L. *The Russian Revolution: A Study in Mass Mobilization*. New York: 1976.

Kennan, George F. *Soviet-American Relations, 1917–20* (2 vols.). New York: 1967.

Koenker, Diane P.; Rosenberg, William G. and Suny, Ronald G., eds. *Party, State, and Society in the Russian Civil War*. Bloomington, Ind.: 1989.

Lewin, Moshe. *Lenin's Last Struggle*. New York: 1968.

Mawdsley, Evan. *The Russian Civil War*. Boston: 1987.

Pethybridge, Roger. *One Step forward, Two Steps Backward*. New York: 1990.

Pipes, Richard. *The Formation of the Soviet Union*. Cambridge, Mass: 1954.

Rabinowitch, A. *The Bolsheviks Come to Power*. New York: 1976.

Raleigh, Donald J. *Revolution on the Volga: 1917 in Saratov*. Ithaca, N.Y.: 1986.

_____. *Experiencing Russia's Civil War: Politics, Society, and Revolutionary Culture in Saratov, 1917–1922*. Princeton, N.J.: 2002.

Read, Christopher. *From Tsar to Soviets: The Russian People and Their Revolution, 1917–1921*. New York: 1996.

Reed, John. *Ten Days That Shook the World*. New York: 1935 (eyewitness account of the October Revolution).

Schapiro, Leonard. *The Origin of the Communist Autocracy, 1917–22*. Cambridge, Mass.: 1955.

Service, Robert. *Lenin: A Political Life* (3 vols.). London: 1985–1995.

Sholokhov, M. *And Quiet Flows the Don*. New York: 1966 [novel about the Russian civil war].

Stites, Richard. *Russian Popular Culture: Entertainment and Society Since 1900*. New York: 1992.

Thompson, John M. *Revolutionary Russia, 1917*. New York: 1988.

Tucker, Robert C. *Stalin as a Revolutionary, 1879–1929*. New York: 1973.

Von Laue, T. *Why Lenin? Why Stalin? A Reappraisal of the Russian Revolution, 1900–1930*. Philadelphia: 1964.

Wade, Rex. *The Russian Revolution, 1917*. Cambridge: 2000.

Wildman, Allan K. *The End of the Russian Imperial Army* (2 vols.). Princeton, N.J.: 1979, 1987.

Wood, Elizabeth A. *The Baba and the Comrade: Gender and Politics in the Russian Revolution*. Bloomington, Ind.: 1997.

The Second Revolution, the Stalinist System, and World War II, 1928–1946

Who broke the chains that bound our feet, now dancing,
Who opened lips that sing a joyous song,
Who made the mourners change their tears for laughter,
Brought back the dead to life's rejoicing throng.
Who is in heart, in every thought and action,
Most loving, true and wise of Lenin's sons—
Such is the great Stalin.[1]

This excerpt from "The Song of Stalin" illustrates the extent of the official adulation of Stalin at the height of his power. Yet this individual was responsible for launching a virtual civil war against the peasants in which millions died and for instituting purges and repression against the general population in which millions more perished. At the same time he oversaw the industrialization of Russia, the survival of the Soviet Union in World War II, and the establishment of Soviet dominance in Eastern Europe. Because he was a suspicious, secretive person presiding over a xenophobic, terror-ridden system, we know little about Stalin's motives and purposes, and he remains in many respects an enigma. Clearly, however, his tyrannical rule and the later reaction against it shaped Soviet society for much of the twentieth century and traces of the Stalinist legacy persist in post-Soviet Russia.

THE REVOLUTION FROM ABOVE:
INDUSTRIALIZATION AND COLLECTIVIZATION

In 1917 the Bolsheviks seized political power in Russia but, despite sporadic experiments under war communism, they did not radically transform Russia's socioeconomic system in their first decade of rule. Beginning in 1928–1929, however, Stalin and the Communist party carried out a second major revolution, one that completely changed the configuration of Soviet society. Until the Chinese Communist revolution some twenty years later, it was the most sudden and thoroughgoing alteration in a people's way of life in history, even surpassing in its sweep and in the numbers of people affected the French Revolution of 1789.

Stalin and a few party leaders, not the people as a whole, decided on this revolution and then drove it through in the 1930s. The dislocation, suffering and outright loss of life were enormous, but the achievements were also considerable. As a Soviet citizen once shouted at me, when I questioned the costs of this second revolution, "Yes, yes, it was a frightful price to pay, but it was all worth it—it made us strong and respected!" Indeed, the goal of making the Soviet Union powerful enough to withstand any external threat strongly motivated Stalin and his comrades to force through rapid industrialization. In a 1931 speech Stalin, in his usual blunt, didactic fashion, summed up this line of argument, dismissing complaints that the pace of industrialization was too fast:

> To slacken the tempo would mean falling behind. And those who fall behind will get beaten. But we do not want to be beaten. No, we refuse to be beaten! One feature of the history of old Russia was the continual beating she suffered because of her backwardness. She was beaten by the Mongol Khans. She was beaten by the Turkish beys. She was beaten by the Swedish feudal lords. She was beaten by the Polish and Lithuanian gentry. She was beaten by the British and French capitalists. She was beaten by the Japanese barons. All beat her— because of her backwardness, because of her military backwardness, cultural backwardness, industrial backwardness, agricultural backwardness. They beat her because to do so was profitable and could be done with impunity. . . . That is why we must no longer lag behind. . . .
>
> We are fifty or a hundred years behind the advanced countries. We must make good this distance in ten years. Either we do it, or we shall go under.[2]

Just ten years and three months later Hitler's Nazi armies invaded Russia!

Other reasons sparked the industrialization decision. Ideologically, Marxist theory ordained that a socialist society must be highly industrialized, must have an overwhelming preponderance of workers. Yet the Soviet Union under NEP was only partly industrialized, with fewer workers than peasants. Politically, Communist rule was to be on behalf of the proletariat. How long could the party continue to govern confronted by increasingly prosperous peasants, small businessmen, and private traders, whose class interest and actions were distinctly petty bourgeois? Economically, something had to be done. The post-1921 NEP recovery was faltering, and a different path to growth and prosperity had to be found.

All in the party agreed on the necessity to industrialize; the difficult question was how to do this, in the absence of revolutions in the highly industrialized countries of the West. At the very end of his life Lenin talked vaguely about using cooperatives or about the importance of stimulating revolutions in Asia, but he patently had no answer. How to industrialize, because it was such an urgent question for the Communist party, became an important issue in the debates that accompanied the struggle for power after Lenin died. The position of the Right Deviation, led by Nicholas Bukharin, was to industrialize through intensified NEP, very much as the western European countries had originally done it. This would mean encouraging a productive agriculture, the surplus of which could be accumulated to invest in industry and to trade abroad in exchange for advanced technology. In other words the Soviet Union would benefit from the normal exchange between city and countryside, the former making larger numbers of manufactured goods to trade for the latter's increasing crop yields, with government taxation of this process providing capital with which to build new factories.

Opponents criticized the Right's plan on three main grounds: it was a slow process, as the Right leaders readily admitted, whereas the Soviet Union needed to build its strength and its socialist base quickly for both national security and ideological reasons. Second, it permitted politically unreliable peasants and traders to play a dangerously key role in the process. Finally, and most damningly, the urban-rural economic nexus, instead of improving, began to break down in 1927–1928, when peasants reacted to higher government-set prices on manufactured articles they desired by withholding grain from the market. Faced with unfavorable terms of trade, peasants ate more, stored grain, fed it to their livestock, and made it into illicit vodka. Supplies to the towns, to the army, and for export dwindled.

The Left Opposition, headed first by Trotsky and later by Zinoviev, argued that only high-tempo industrialization could produce the rapid economic growth socialist Russia required. Consequently, the peasantry must be taxed and squeezed in order to provide "primitive socialist accumulation" of capital, which could then be quickly infused into the rapidly expanding industrial sector. The Right denigrated this scheme as visionary, concluding "You can't build today's factories with tomorrow's bricks."

But another aspect of Trotsky's views, part of his theory of permanent or uninterrupted revolution, was that the Bolsheviks must carry the proletarian revolution into Europe and Asia as quickly as possible because the building of socialism in Russia depended on the triumph of the world revolution abroad. Or, put another way, the Soviet Union could and should launch the process of rapid development but could complete it only with the help of outside revolution, which the Communist party should work vigorously to promote.

Between 1924 and 1928 Stalin occupied a middle position, not accepting high-tempo industrialization but criticizing the proposal of the Right as too slow and dangerous. Most importantly, Stalin vigorously attacked Trotsky's view that Russia had to depend on revolutions abroad, propounding instead a doctrine that came to be known as "socialism in one country." He based his case on a single quotation from Lenin, taken out of context. In a 1916 article Lenin had speculated that in exceptional circumstances it might be possible for a country that experienced a proletarian revolution to build socialism alone, in its own borders, without help from the international socialist revolution that both Marx and Lenin had previously considered integral to the process. Lenin, however, made it clear that this could happen *only* in an advanced industrialized country. Stalin nevertheless applied the idea to Russia, and it was naturally immensely popular. In essence what Stalin told his fellow citizens was that we Soviet comrades, by our own effort, sweat, and ingenuity, can build the glorious socialist future in our homeland without having to rely on help from outside. It was an appealing nationalistic vision and helped him to secure support from within the Communist party in his struggle against Trotsky and his other rivals.

After he had defeated the Left Opposition and as he was emerging in 1928 as the undisputed head of the party and leader of the country, Stalin adopted the Left's high-tempo plan as his own and determined to carry through a radical transformation of Soviet society. According to Robert C. Tucker, one of Stalin's best biographers, Stalin may have wanted to emulate his hero, Lenin: to make his own revolution to match the one Lenin had led in 1917, and to make his mark in Soviet and Communist history as Lenin had. The program Stalin espoused initially had three major components: complete nationalization and socialization of all nonfarming activity, from large industry to small service establishments; central state planning, under which economic decisions were made at the top and transmitted down to all enterprises; and extensive expansion of mechanization and new technology in every branch of economic activity. The State Planning Commission, known as Gosplan, drew up the First Five-Year Plan for the Soviet Union in August 1928, with the substantial but not unthinkable goal of increasing industrial output by 120 percent by 1934. In the following year Stalin decided to up the pace of industrialization and doubled the goal. This required herculean efforts and seemed an unattainable objective.

Another aspect of Stalin's economic revolution was *collectivization:* transferring all peasant land, whether managed by the commune or by individuals, into new agricultural units called collective farms, which all peasants had to join. They were also required to contribute most of their livestock and tools to the collective farm. As you might expect, this pooling of assets delighted poor peasants with little to contribute and outraged better-off peasants with considerable assets to surrender. The party labeled the latter *kulaks* and during collectivization directed its main attacks against them.

Collective farms operated throughout the Soviet era. Members of the farm shared the work and the profits, according to the number of workday units an individual had contributed. But before profits the farm had to provide a certain share of its produce to the state: in 1929 a fixed amount to be delivered, and later, most commonly, a certain percentage of the output to be sold to state agencies. From the party's point of view an obvious advantage of the collective farm system was that it gave party planners and state administrators greater control over agricultural production and particularly made more predictable how much the state-run economy would obtain from agriculture. When peasants were individual proprietors and could trade on the open market, it was difficult for the government to know what was going to be produced and how much of it would enter the marketplace.

In my view this degree of control was the main reason Stalin and his advisers finally opted for collectivization and pushed it so hard. Stalin in particular seems to have been influenced to adopt compulsory collectivization by the success of a forcible grain collection campaign that he carried out in the Urals and Siberia in 1928. Nevertheless, according to some economic historians, Bolshevik planners never intended collectivization to be the main method of organizing agriculture, but when peasants started to withhold grain from the market and thus threatened the industrialization drive, overzealous party officials at the national and local levels began to push collectivization as a way of intimidating the peasants, and it soon acquired a momentum of its own. In any case, at the end of 1929 and the beginning of 1930 collectivization was pursued so vigorously that Stalin had to make a speech, "Dizzy with Success," urging restraint on party cadres and offering peasants a chance to withdraw from the collective farms. Many did so, but in subsequent months pressure to form such farms was slowly but steadily increased until by 1936, 90 percent of all farming in the Soviet Union was collectivized, with most of the rest organized in farms run directly by the state.

Many collective farms were organized by pressure and, if required, by force. Young Communist activists were recruited to go door to door in villages trying to persuade peasants to join. If they were not won over, the army would be called in, the village surrounded, and the most recalcitrant peasants loaded on trucks to be taken to railheads for transportation to farms in Central Asia or to forced labor camps in Siberia. This campaign went hand-in-hand with an intensified Communist attack on organized religion. Many priests were arrested, and most Orthodox churches, synagogues, and mosques were closed. Schools and the media trumpeted atheism, and believers were harassed and persecuted

Many peasants, rather than turn their livestock over to the collective farm, slaughtered them. As a result, Soviet livestock herds were reduced by as much as one half and had not recovered their pre-1929 numbers when they were decimated again by World War II. In 1933 a major famine struck Ukraine and southwestern Russia, areas where resistance to collectivization had been strong. Stalin insisted that grain exports and government grain procurement be maintained, covered up the disaster, and made little effort to stop the famine. Some four to five million people perished.

Whatever the debates on the origins of collectivization, almost all Western analysts agree that the program was an economic disaster. Peasant disruption and resistance meant that under the First Five-Year Plan agricultural output increased only 65 percent of its planned target, creating the necessity to ration food in the Soviet Union. Moreover, in the long run, collective farm agriculture did not prove to be efficient, and it remained a major problem for subsequent Soviet leaders, as we will see in Chapters 13 and 14.

Industrialization under the First Five-Year Plan enjoyed greater success. The plan was declared completed at the end of 1932, after four years and three months. Although there were many difficulties and its goals were not fully met, considerable progress had been made. The planners had counted on good weather, large crop yields, and substantial increases in agricultural productivity; in fact, there were two years of bad weather and crop failures, plus the disastrous collectivization already discussed. The planners had also assumed reduced defense costs and growing trade with the outside world. Instead, because of Japanese expansion in Manchuria, the Soviet Union spent more on defense, and the great world depression that began in 1929 meant that Soviet foreign trade fell off, with the Soviet Union therefore unable to buy as much Western technology as it needed.

The Second Five-Year Plan was completed in 1933–1937, and the Third Plan was two-thirds over when Hitler attacked the Soviet Union in June 1941. During the twelve years of intensive industrialization, from 1928 to 1940, Soviet industry grew fitfully but at an average pace of 12 to 14 percent a year, an impressive performance surpassed only by the Japanese in the 1950s and 1960s. The urban population doubled, as did the number of workers. The plans emphasized heavy industry, which showed the greatest gains. For example, steel production increased fourfold, coal production fivefold, and generation of electric power ninefold. Plan goals were set in terms of quantity output, so that generally quality was slighted. Improving the quality of goods in the Soviet economy persisted as a major objective of Soviet planners.

Outside heavy industry the Five-Year Plans achieved much less success. Production goals for light industry and for consumer goods and services were consistently underfulfilled, and agriculture lagged even farther behind. As with raising quality, increasing agricultural output and production of consumer goods was a continuing concern of the Soviet regime.

No one can doubt that the massive effort to industrialize the Soviet Union in the 1930s produced a substantial economic base for the society and paved the way for the nation to become the second largest industrial power in the world (after the United States) after World War II. The more difficult questions are, How was it done and what did it cost? In the 1960s and 1970s, Soviet leaders encouraged developing nations in the Third World to follow the Soviet pattern of industrialization and with it the Soviet ideology of Marxism-Leninism. For some ruling elites in Asia, Africa, and Latin America, this was a tempting idea, in the light of apparent Soviet successes. Only a few countries chose to take this route, however, and the economic collapse of Soviet socialism in the late 1980s greatly diminished the appeal of this model of industrialization.

In analyzing the Soviet performance one feature stands out. Soviet industrialization required total mobilization of all resources, material and human, of the country. In turn, this demanded prescriptive centralized planning of the economy and maximum control over every institution and individual member of the society. High-tempo growth under Soviet conditions left no room for the operation of autonomous interest groups or the iniatative and wishes of private individuals. Party and state set the goals, chose the methods, managed the effort, and ensured that each Soviet citizen made the contribution that the plan required. In this way industrialization greatly reinforced the authoritarian trends already present in Bolshevism, with which Stalin was enamored. As a result, the Stalinist system can best be summed up as a blend of Bolshevism (one-party rule), industrialization (mobilization and total control), and Stalinism (paranoia and the use of terror).

Stalin and the party used three basic instruments to ensure all-out participation by the Soviet people in industrialization and in the Stalinist system: persuasion, incentives, and coercion. All three played a continuing role in Soviet society. Western critics sometimes overlook the genuine enthusiasm with which many Soviet citizens supported the industrialization effort, despite the heavy sacrifices it required. Several appeals the party stressed were particularly enticing. First, the vision of the future encompassed good times and material comfort. The hard work, low pay, and wretched conditions of the present were simply a down payment on the better life for all socialism promised. "Perhaps you, but certainly your children, will enjoy prosperity and happiness in the decades ahead," exhorted party members and government propaganda.

Second came appeals to patriotism, both the ideological variety calling for diligence and devotion to defend the socialist revolution and the first workers' state and the nationalistic sort that urged people to sacrifice so that Mother Russia could become strong enough to repulse external enemies. Chauvinism became increasingly prominent as the threat from Nazi Germany grew.

Finally, there was the subtle call to commit oneself to this great crusade, to find personal satisfaction in working shoulder to shoulder with one's fellow comrades for the good of all. Some of these themes can be identified in the following passage from a Soviet novel about the heroic construction of a new factory:

> On the landing of the steel-trellised tower stood Gleb, Shidky, and Badin, the members of the Factory Committee.... Right and Left in long rows red flags blazoned like beacon-fires....
>
> In the distance a band was playing a march, and from the depths came the thunderous clamor of the people mingled with the roar of the Diesel engines and the clanging of metal. It was impossible to distinguish the roar of the crowd from the roar of machinery. Brynza was right: machines and people are one....

The factory! What strength had been put into it, and what struggle! But here it was—a giant, a beauty! Not long ago it had been a corpse, a devil's mud-heap, a ruin, a warren. And now the Diesels roared. The cables vibrated with electricity, and the pulleys of the ropeway sang. Tomorrow the first giant cylinder of the rotary furnaces would begin to revolve, and from this huge smokestack grey clouds of steam and dust would roll. . . .

And he, Gleb, no longer existed; there was only an unbearable rapture in his heart which was almost bursting from the flooding blood. The working class, the Soviet, the great life they were constructing! God damn it, we understand how to suffer, but we also know the grandeur of our strength. . . .[3]

As a second mode of mobilizing the citizenry for industrialization, Stalin and the party provided two kinds of incentives. The first was material, primarily higher pay for producing more or for working in dangerous conditions or in a remote area. Under war communism some ideologues had wanted to move toward equal pay for all, but Stalin made clear in the early 1930s that in building socialism the motto would be "to each according to his work" and that the slogan "to each according to his needs" would come into effect only when socialism had triumphed completely, on a worldwide scale. Engineers, technicians, and skilled workers were paid more than laborers and unskilled workers, and almost everyone was paid on a piecework basis. Norms or goals of output were set for different categories of work, and those who overfulfilled their norms were rewarded financially, as well as being lionized. In fact, the Soviet government encouraged a whole movement to stimulate record-breaking output, called Stakhanovism after Alexis Stakhanov, a Soviet coal miner who consistently produced amounts of coal way beyond his production quotas. Another, more subtle incentive was the chance to move ahead in society, to achieve quickly higher status and more prestige. Those who were loyal to the party and worked hard could expect to be promoted rapidly, and Stalin created a whole new generation of upwardly mobile administrators and technicians to staff the party and the government.

Finally, persuasion and incentives were backed up by coercion. Labor discipline in the factories was tightened, and those who worked poorly faced not just peer pressure, ridicule, and ostracization but loss of their job, cancellation of their work card (needed for employment anywhere), and even sentencing to a correctional labor camp as a "wrecker" or "saboteur" of the industrial effort. We now know that many of those sent to the camps were put to hard labor, undertaking especially dangerous or heavy construction tasks or carrying out routine jobs, such as timbering or mining, but in unbearable climatic conditions. Millions died in the forced labor camps. Moreover, coercion was used against the peasants and religious believers, and anyone who resisted party policy, or just tried to stand aside, was subject to harassment, intimidation, and eventually arbitrary arrest, imprisonment, and dispatch to the camps.

These methods of ensuring total immersion of the whole population in the industrialization drive were applied in all areas of Soviet life. No area could escape being harnessed to the overall effort. The arts, science, education, sports, what was left of the Orthodox and other churches in Russia, and even the writing and teaching of history—all were expected to orient their goals and activities to promote industrialization. It was a country-wide, across-the-board struggle.

What was the cost? Much of the price the Soviet people paid has already been alluded to: millions dead, millions more in labor camps, and the party and state intruding into every aspect of a person's life. Moreover, in the 1930s Soviet wage earners suffered a decline in their standard of living from its level in the 1920s, and because of the influx of new workers into the cities housing conditions deteriorated and for several years food was rationed. Most peasants were clearly worse off, although many who moved to work in the new factories eventually improved their lot. Was industrialization worth the cost? Some Soviet citizens believed it was, as we saw at the start of the chapter. Others did not, and it is a question that can only be answered in the long run in terms of an individual's own values and principles. Nevertheless, in assessing the outcome of industrialization it is important to consider whether another way, a different plan and set of methods, might have achieved comparable results but at a lower cost.

THE STALINIST SYSTEM

We noted earlier that the Stalinist system grew out of an agglomeration of three elements: the authoritarian traditions of Bolshevism, the total mobilization and control demanded by industrialization, and the suspiciousness and resort to terror of Stalin himself. Before turning to this last point, we need to summarize the formal structure of Soviet society in the 1930s.

The country was a federation of Soviet socialist republics, as Stalin's new constitution of 1936 confirmed. The various republics and smaller national units operated under the slogan "national in form, socialist in content." This policy meant that although the party encouraged some autonomy in cultural matters and local government, it enforced Communist orthodoxy in ideology and exerted tight political control over the minorities. On the one hand, the minorities fared better under this arrangement than they had under tsarist russification. They had a chance to develop their own languages, cultures, and traditions. They benefited from expanded educational opportunities, some economic development, and the exercise of local rights. On the other hand, the non-Russians felt oppressed and exploited, resenting Communist, predominantly Great Russian, domination; the strict centralized control of the party; and Moscow's siphoning local natural resources and economic profits to fuel the Five-Year Plans. In addition, local environmental degradation, migration of Russians into non-Russian republics, and limited openings at the apex of political power embittered the minorities. Paradoxically, cultural autonomy and resentment of economic and political control fused to produce a virulent, subterranean nationalism that erupted in 1988–1991 to bring down the federated Soviet system.

Federal, republic, and local governments were all based on soviets, councils of deputies at various levels elected directly by all Soviet citizens. The population was expected, exhorted, and pressured to vote, and turnouts of 99 percent of the electorate were regularly achieved. Elections were not a political contest since only a single slate of candidates was presented to the voter (a few defiant voters crossed out the list or otherwise marred their ballots, but they were exceptional). The Communist party arranged the nomination of candidates (not all were party members) and controlled the soviets' decisions. The highest representative body was the Supreme Soviet, which confirmed the official government, the USSR Council of Ministers.

Only about 7 percent of the population were party members, but the party set and revised ideology and policy, managed and oversaw the government, and directed and controlled judicial, social, economic, and cultural life. It exerted its power through party units in every institution and at every level of the system. For example, each university (or whatever organization a citizen was associated with) had a party committee that advised the administration, organized meetings of students and employees to explain national policy and to encourage everyone to work harder, and kept a weather eye on the general conduct and progress of the institution and its members. Each party unit elected representatives to the next highest party body, and the topmost group was the Central Committee, several hundred leading party officials who elected the Politburo, or executive committee, usually consisting of ten to fifteen members, which in effect ran the country. Party members were expected to be exemplars of rectitude and diligence, and their conduct and activity were constantly scrutinized by party officials and by the secret police. Consequently, some individuals chose not to enter the party, although it was the chief avenue for advancement to the highest positions in almost all fields of endeavor.

A huge bureaucracy and managerial class ran day-to-day life in the Soviet Union. When the 1936 Constitution was adopted, the USSR officially became a one-class proletarian society, although subgroups of workers, collective and state farmers, and the toiling intelligentsia were recognized. In principle the whole society owned the means of production: all significant economic enterprise. In fact, the state, directed by the party, ran the economy, and the average citizen had no say in its operation. Collective farmers were permitted a small plot of private land and a few animals, and all citizens owned personal property, including, for the few who could afford it, an automobile. Public housing provided cramped quarters for a very low rent; education and medical care were free. By 1940 almost all Soviet citizens under age fifty were literate, and by 1990 there was universal seven-year education and almost no illiteracy.

These basic features of Soviet life were established or consolidated under the Stalinist system. Because of the system of incentive pay and the superior economic and political position of high state and party officials, the 1930s saw increasing social differentiation. The Yugoslav Marxist critic Milovan Djilas even argued that the elite of the government and the party formed a "new class" of rulers determined to defend their privileges against the mass of the population.

A puzzling aspect of the Stalinist system was its increasing reliance on terror. Historians have advanced various explanations of this phenomenon, but none seems entirely satisfactory. Lenin and the early Bolsheviks had resorted to terror in the desperate days of the civil war and had not hesitated to use force to suppress bloodily the peasant uprisings and the Kronstadt rebellion in 1921. Yet it was never a regularized part of the early Soviet system. Political opponents were encouraged to emigrate or to drop out of politics; the secret police existed but had limited jurisdiction and authority; and only a few forced labor camps existed. Even Stalin in the late 1920s did not eliminate the rivals he defeated, sending a few such as Trotsky into exile and demoting others, such as Bukharin and Zinoviev. Between 1934 and 1938, however, all this changed in an escalating series of purges, arrests, banishments to labor camps, and finally mass terror against a large part of the population.

Attempts to explain this nightmarish period as the consolidation and reshaping of power by Stalin, as an evolving component of the Stalinist system—the cleansing of the party—that somehow ran amok, or as a coldly calculating effort by Stalin to ready the country for war and to ensure that he would have a free hand in foreign policy are, singly, or even taken together, simply not convincing. Since Stalin destroyed both the records and most of the high officials involved, we will probably never know precisely what led to the purges and terror. Rational and policy considerations there undoubtedly were, but any persuasive explanation of this era must take account of Stalin's personality and outlook. Much of what occurred only makes sense if it stemmed in part from the disturbed mentality, pathological cruelty, and extreme paranoia of Stalin himself. Insecure despite having established a dictatorship over the party and the country, hostile and defensive when confronted by criticism of the excesses of collectivization and of the sacrifices required by high-tempo industrialization, and deeply suspicious that past, present, and even yet unknown future opponents were plotting against him, Stalin began in 1934 to act as a person beleaguered. He soon struck back wildly at enemies, real or imaginary. The atmosphere of uncertainty, fear, and denunciation spread rapidly through the Soviet system and soon began to feed on itself. Petty tyrants sprang up at all levels of the party and the bureaucracy, and soon almost the whole society was engulfed by recriminations, irrational punishments, and paralyzing terror.

Our account can only touch on what happened at the highest levels of the party and government, but readers are reminded that the terror reached into almost every Soviet family and that its victims suffered terribly in both psychological and physical terms (an unforgettable account is *Journey into the Whirlwind* by Evgeniia Ginzburg). During 1933–1934, shortly after the Second Five-Year Plan started, considerable grumbling spread countrywide about the continuing rapid pace and intense pressure of the industrialization drive. This was reflected within the party, and just before and during the Seventeenth Party Congress criticism of Stalin surfaced, which undoubtedly irked him. Sergei Kirov, head of the party organization in Leningrad (formerly Petrograd, renamed after Lenin's death), proved to be the most popular figure at the congress, and Stalin may have seen Kirov as a rival. Some months later, on December 1, 1934, an assassin, apparently with the complicity of the Leningrad secret police, murdered Kirov. Whether Stalin ordered the killing is unproven, but he clearly benefited by the elimination of a political competitor for power.

In any case the investigation of Kirov's murder touched off a widening offensive aimed at first at such 1920s opponents of Stalin as Kamenev, Zinoviev, and several other "Old Bolsheviks" of Lenin's generation. In January 1935 this group was arrested and imprisoned, and a few months later they were accused of complicity in Kirov's murder. In the summer of 1936 Zinoviev, Kamenev, and fourteen others were publicly tried, the charges now including not only subversion of the party but treason to the Soviet state on the grounds that some of the alleged conspirators had connived with Trotsky, who was still in exile in Europe, and with agents of the Nazis. Further trials took place in 1937 and 1938. In these "show" trials most of the defendants confessed to crimes they had not committed, probably as a consequence of intimidation (perhaps torture), drugs, and psychological brainwashing. The last technique became the basis of Arthur Koestler's famous novel *Darkness at Noon*. Those not prepared to confess were generally shot without trial. Nicholas Bukharin, however, may have outwitted his persecutors as the following excerpt from his initial plea and final statement at his trial reveals:

> I plead guilty to . . . the sum total of crimes committed by this counterrevolutionary organization, irrespective of whether or not I knew of, whether or not I took a direct part in, any particular act [his denial of guilt].. . .
>
> For when you ask yourself: "If you must die, what are you dying for?"—an absolutely black vacuity suddenly arises before you with startling vividness. There was nothing to die for, if one wanted to die unrepented. And, on the contrary, everything positive that glistens in the Soviet Union acquires new dimensions in a man's mind [his rejection of Stalinism].[4]

Stalin had him shot.

The terror reached its climax in 1936–1938. Its dimensions are hard to believe. Post-1991 archival research indicated that 1.6 million people were arrested, and up to 3.6 million individuals were in prisons, labor camps, and internal exile settlements. In 1937–1938 alone, 680,000 people were condemned to death for alleged crimes against the state and the revolution. But others were executed outside the Ministry of Internal Affairs (secret police) system, and several million prisoners died of deprivation in the forced labor camps. Thus, adding estimated purge deaths of 3–4 million to 1932–1933 famine losses of 4–5 million, the victims of Stalinism up to World War II total 8–9 million, far surpassing even the death toll perpetrated by Hitler and the Nazis. Stalin's blunders at the outset of the war in 1941–1942 cost several million more unwarranted deaths, making Stalin history's most terrible executioner.

The purges particularly targeted the Communist Party itself, with 40 percent of its members arrested and its top leadership decimated. Almost 70 percent of the delegates to the Seventeenth Party Congress in 1934 were arrested, most of whom were shot. One hundred ten of the 139 members of the 1934 Central Committee were killed or driven to suicide. The generation that had made the October Revolution and built the Soviet state was eliminated, with few exceptions. Their places were quickly filled by a rough, less educated, ambitious new generation willing to knuckle under to Stalin, among whom were future leaders of the Soviet Union, Nikita Khrushchev and Leonid Brezhnev.

The army was decimated, as well. Only a few years before Hitler's attack on the Soviet Union, the Red Army lost to the purges three of the five highest-ranking officers (called marshals of the Soviet Union), thirteen of fifteen commanders of army groups, 90 percent of all generals, and 80 percent of all colonels. Other elites in Soviet society—the professions, economic managers, and writers and artists—were similarly destroyed. Even the secret police fell victim, several of its chiefs being accused and executed. Finally, in early 1939 the purge wound down, perhaps because Stalin recognized that conflict with Germany was an imminent possibility. Throughout and after the purges the official cult of Stalin continued to grow unabashedly. The monstrous crimes associated with the terror did nothing to temper the fulsome praise and repetitive flattery the Soviet press heaped on Stalin, tributes that he apparently craved and accepted as his due.

SOVIET CULTURE, 1917–1953

An area greatly affected by the conservatism, rigidity, and authoritarianism of the Stalinist system was the arts. For a decade after the October Revolution experimentation and daring marked much of the work in Soviet literature, theater, and the visual arts. Some of this was a continuation of the modernism and avant-garde trends that we saw characterized Russian culture in the first years of the twentieth century. But this artistic boldness was now linked to a sense of responsibility to society and to the glorious new order the revolution was to bring. Mayakovsky, among many others, placed his talents at the service of the new Soviet state, designing posters, writing propaganda poems, and staging pageants and plays with revolutionary themes. A few artists, like Marc Chagall, felt uncomfortable bearing this burden of social commitment and moved to the West. But many others, like Vsevolod Meyerhold, the innovative theater producer, and Sergei Prokofiev, the composer, while keeping in touch with artistic movements in the West, continued to develop bold new forms and themes within Soviet Russia. As a result, the 1920s were years of great artistic ferment and of considerable achievement, with Soviet artists making significant contributions to world culture in such fields as music and the cinema. For example, Sergei Eisenstein, the creative film producer and director, helped to pioneer new techniques, and his major films remain classics today.

Much of this modernist art and experimental creativity was quite incomprehensible to the masses of Soviet society, many of them illiterate or barely educated. Consequently, some critics, within the arts and within the party, began to insist that Soviet culture should strive to achieve greater simplicity and directness, and that it should instruct and uplift the average Soviet citizen. This point of view received a decisive boost when the "second revolution" began in 1928. Every aspect of Soviet life was to be conscripted to help drive the engine of industrialization, and the arts were soon assigned the role of instilling enthusiasm, patriotism, and a dedication to higher production goals among the Soviet public. Artists were called upon to serve as "engineers of the soul." This new trend was officially confirmed in 1934, with promulgation of the doctrine of "socialist realism," which remained the guiding principle of the arts in the Soviet Union.

The doctrine of socialist realism required the artist or writer to portray life not as it really was but as it ought to be. Individuals were to act positively, and events were expected to develop in ways that accorded with the policies and goals of the party. Heroes should be clearly delineated, and villains appropriately characterized. Happy endings were common, and although the charge that too often the farm boy meets girl but marries tractor was exaggerated, many socialist realist stories and plays had a predictability and sameness that made them tedious, if not downright boring. Socialist realist art, for example, did not intend to portray a "real" worker or peasant but rather a romanticized version of what they ought to look like.

Although a few creative artists, like the composer Dmitri Shostakovich and the poets Anna Akhmatova and Boris Pasternak, were able to continue to produce fine pieces, even when criticized for not adhering to the guidelines of socialist realism, most Soviet literary and artistic works of the 1930s and 1940s were banal and uninteresting. How much they served their purpose of inculcating uplifting values and attitudes among the bulk of the population is difficult to tell, but certainly the vitality of Soviet intellectual and cultural life declined in this period. Science and technology, which had been given an influential role to play in industrialization, continued to advance, although even there, in certain fields, party orthodoxy intruded, as for example when Stalin endorsed the erroneous views of the agronomist Trofim Lysenko, mandating that all scientists adhere to them.

STALIN AND THE WORLD, 1928–1946

During the late 1920s the Soviet Union continued the two-track foreign policy it had begun as soon as the Soviet state was established: promotion of proletarian revolutions abroad, and accommodation and trade with other nations. As had happened earlier, pursuit of the former goal made the latter more difficult at various times, and in 1927 there was even a "war scare" in the Soviet Union, a fear that Great Britain, perhaps assisted by France, might attack the USSR, partly as a result of revelations of Soviet-sponsored subversive activity in England.

Stalin and Trotsky had clashed over how much emphasis to give to inciting socialist revolutions in other countries, with Trotsky urging a more aggressive policy in this regard. But whatever line the Soviet Union took seemed to backfire. In China Stalin, after Trotsky's expulsion from the party, pressured the small Chinese Communist movement to ally temporarily with the larger Nationalist forces led by Chiang Kai-shek. In 1927, however, Chiang turned on his Communist collaborators and destroyed all but a remnant of the Chinese Communist party. On the other hand, in Germany Stalin advised the German Communists not to make common cause with the moderate Marxist party, the Social Democrats, against the nascent Hitlerite movement. Again, the result was disaster: the Communists fought the Social Democrats tooth and nail, thus making it easier for Hitler and the Nazis to come to power. Once firmly in control, Hitler crushed both the Communists and the Social Democrats.

With Mussolini's Fascists in power in Italy and Hitler's Nazis gaining strength in Germany in the early 1930s, and since both fascism and Nazism made communism their chief foe, the Russian Communists agitated vigorously in international meetings for general disarmament and for the signing of nonaggression pacts. This effort met a fairly limited response, although the Soviet Union succeeded in completing nonaggression and mutual defense treaties with Poland in 1934 and with France and Czechoslovakia in 1935.

Beginning in 1933–1936 Stalin and his foreign policy advisers took a new tack. On the diplomatic front they urged strengthening the League of Nations, to which the USSR was admitted in 1934, and they espoused the doctrine of collective security. The latter was a call for the nonfascist states, including both the Soviet Union and the Western democracies plus the latter's allies in Eastern Europe, to band together against the menace of Mussolini and Hitler, who were in the process of forming the Rome-Berlin Axis (later joined by militaristic Japan). Meanwhile in the domestic politics of the nonfascist European countries Communist parties were instructed by Moscow to seek political alliances and coalitions with democratic (and occasionally even conservative) parties to ensure that local fascist elements would not seize power. This new policy was called "the united front," or, in the case of France, where such a Communist-democratic coalition came to power temporarily, the Popular Front.

In 1935 and early 1936 the strategy of collective security suffered two serious setbacks. Mussolini conquered Ethiopia, for which the League of Nations administered a slap on the wrist, and Hitler remilitarized the Rhineland area of Germany in defiance of the Versailles peace treaty after World War I, while Britain and France did nothing. In the middle of 1936 General Francisco Franco led a conservative rebellion in Spain against the leftist antifascist government there. The resulting Spanish Civil War provided a major test of the collective security and united front policies, a test failed by both, which revealed fundamental weaknesses in each.

During the Spanish Civil War, Fascist Italy and Nazi Germany supplied financing, weapons, and even some troops to the Franco forces. The Soviet Union eventually aided the existing government, the Loyalists, in the same fashion. But Great Britain and France adopted a stance of neutrality, arguing that it would be illegal to assist the Loyalists. Since collective security depended on the major antifascist powers' acting together, the Anglo-French position undercut the possibility of preventing or punishing Axis intervention in Spain and raised grave doubts in Stalin's mind about the reliability of the Western democracies as partners in the struggle against Hitler. Moreover, within Spain mutual suspicion and mistrust between the democratic parties and the Communists weakened the Loyalist war effort, and in the end the Communists used the situation to destroy some of their political enemies on the left. This outcome naturally alarmed democratic elements in the rest of Europe about the real purposes of the Communists in a united front.

By 1938, after Hitler had swallowed up Austria and German ambitions seemed boundless, it was clear that Europe was moving toward war. It became a three-sided game, almost like a love triangle, as shown in the chart below:

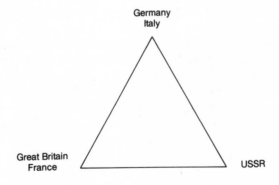

Germany
Italy

Great Britain
France

USSR

The question was which two would ally against the third. At the time the most likely and natural alignment appeared to be the Soviet Union and the Western democracies against the Axis. But since strong conservative and profascist forces existed in France and, to a lesser extent, in Britain, a combination of Germany-Italy with the Western countries against the Communist menace, so detested in fascist and Nazi propaganda, was certainly a possibility, one that Stalin and his advisers greatly feared, given their Marxist distrust of capitalism. Least likely seemed a match between the USSR and the Axis, separated as they were by an immense ideological gulf. Yet that is just what happened.

Two developments in 1938 apparently led Stalin to decide to cast his lot with Hitler, as incredible as this tie seemed. The first was the outbreak in 1937–1938 of substantial armed clashes with Japan along the border between the Soviet Union and Japanese-occupied Manchuria. The Red Army acquitted itself well, but Stalin was concerned that if he became involved in war with Hitler, Japan might seize the opportunity to attack Siberia, catching the USSR in the vise of a two-front war.

Second was a crisis over Czechoslovakia, details of which are still being debated by historians and in any case lie beyond our scope. The essential point for Stalin, however, was that when Hitler brazenly threatened the Czech government, an important ally of both the Soviet Union and the Western powers, the latter reneged on their treaty obligations, backed down, and meekly handed Czechoslovakia on a silver platter to Hitler at the Munich Conference in September 1938. What sort of collective security was this? What did this say about the reliability of the Western powers as allies against Hitler? Did it not suggest that they hoped to get the Soviet Union embroiled with Germany and then stand aside?

The USSR was also pledged to aid Czechoslovakia and undertook some military preparations, but it remains unclear whether the Soviet Union would have made good on its commitment. The Soviet government said that it was prepared to, but since its promise was contingent on French support of the Czechs, which did not materialize, the Soviet Union never had to act.

Regardless of what Soviet intentions were, the lesson Stalin drew from the whole affair was plain. In early 1939 the Soviet foreign minister who had been the architect of the policy of collective security, Maxim Litvinov, resigned, and in a speech of March 10 Stalin subtly suggested the possibility of negotiations to the Germans.

Secret talks got under way a few months later. Although concurrently Soviet diplomats continued to negotiate with the Western democracies about a possible alliance, neither side trusted the other, and those talks languished. On August 23, 1939, the conclusion of a nonaggression treaty between the Soviet Union and Nazi Germany was announced to an astonished world. Hitler achieved his immediate aim, the neutralization of the Red Army, and within ten days he launched an invasion of Poland. This prompted Britain and France to declare war on Germany, and World War II had begun.

Tens of thousands of loyal Communists around the world resigned from their parties because of this bizarre about-face, in which the Soviet Union joined hands with communism's worst enemy. Stalin seems to have been unconcerned; he had achieved his objectives by this diplomatic coup. First, he had avoided getting entangled in a war with Hitler, especially at a time when the Red Army and Soviet industry were not fully prepared for such a major conflict. Second, he apparently hoped that the Germans, once Britain and France came into the war, would be checked by the Western powers and that the two sides would exhaust themselves in a long struggle. Finally, he had made the Soviet Union far more secure; a by-product of the pact with Hitler was Soviet acquisition of eastern Poland under a secret protocol (not published or acknowledged officially in the Soviet Union until 1989) and Soviet domination of the Baltic states and of Bessarabia on the USSR's southwestern border (all of these were annexed to the Soviet Union in the summer of 1940). This meant that Stalin had gained considerable territory as a buffer between the Soviet Union and the West, distance that in fact proved valuable when the Nazis invaded the USSR in 1941. In addition, there is some evidence that Stalin, shrewd as he usually was, genuinely believed he had made a deal with Hitler that might last for some time. In *Mein Kampf* and in numerous speeches Hitler had made clear that eventually he intended to conquer Communist Russia. Perhaps Stalin thought it was just brave talk and that because Hitler must be a realist, as Stalin was, Hitler would be content with the division of territory and influence in Eastern Europe that the Nazi-Soviet pact provided for.

Whatever the reasons, Stalin and his advisers acted as if the new alliance were a long-term arrangement. The Soviet government soon provoked a quarrel with Finland that led to war, but the Finns fought courageously, though far outnumbered, and retained their independence, although they had to cede some territory to the USSR. The Soviet side assumed that they had a free hand in the Balkans and even revived the old question of Russian interest in the Straits, pressing the Turkish government for bases there. Hitler and his advisers resented this Soviet "pushiness," and in December 1940 Hitler decided to invade Russia the following year.

When the Nazi armies rolled into Russia on June 22, 1941, having earlier in 1940 and 1941 defeated Norway, the Low Countries, and France and having occupied much of the Balkans and Greece, no one was surprised, except perhaps Stalin. Suspicious that the capitalist West was trying to push him into war with Germany, misled by disinformation planted by German intelligence, and sure that Hitler would not be so foolish as to invade the Soviet Union when Great Britain on his other flank remained undefeated, Stalin refused to believe warnings of the impending German attack from British intelligence, his own military authorities, and Soviet agents abroad. A Soviet friend of mine who at the time was in an army unit not far behind

Figure 17. *Russian prisoners captured during the German invasion in the summer of 1941.*

the front line told me that only some forty-eight hours before the attack were they put on alert.

Caught unaware, the Red Army fell back, sometimes in good order, sometimes in disarray, with heavy losses and with large numbers of prisoners taken (see Figure 17). For the first few days the party and Soviet government made no response, leading to speculation that Stalin panicked at that moment. He finally made a radio address to the Soviet people exhorting them to a patriotic defense of their socialist homeland, and he soon created a five-man Defense Committee to organize and direct the war effort. The British, who had been standing alone against Hitler for the past year, rallied to the Soviet cause, and an Anglo-Soviet treaty was signed in July 1941. After the United States entered the war in December 1941 following Japan's attack on Pearl Harbor, the so-called Grand Alliance of the Soviet Union, Great Britain, and the United States (later joined by Free France) was formed to fight Hitler and Mussolini.

In July 1941 the Germans made a decisive breakthrough on the center front but decided not to throw all their strength at Moscow, turning instead to the south with its agricultural and mineral riches, as well as the oil fields of the Caucasus. Nevertheless, by November–December 1941 Nazi forces had besieged Leningrad and were only a few miles from Moscow, where winter weather and Soviet resistance finally halted the German advance. Leningrad held out for two and one-half years at a cost of one million dead, and a Soviet counterattack eased the pressure on Moscow. During the summer of 1942 the Germans renewed their advance, making large gains in the south. At the end of 1942 in a brutal and devastating battle at the city of Stalingrad (formerly Tsaritsyn, now Volgograd), the Red Army in house-to-house and sometimes hand-to-hand fighting checked the German advance. Moreover, because Hitler refused to order a retreat, most of the German Seventh Army was captured there. The Soviet forces, however, failed to follow up their advantage, and a second major turning point in the military history of the war occurred at the Battle of Kursk in July 1943. Soviet units led by tanks badly defeated and routed a strong German force, starting a German retreat back across Russia that ended only with the occupation of Berlin by the Red Army in April 1945 (see Map 8).

In addition to military mistakes in Russia the Germans made a major political mistake. When the Nazi forces first entered Russia, many people, particularly Ukrainians, welcomed the Germans because they resented Communist rule and exactions. If the Germans had treated the occupied population decently and had met their most basic demands, such as breaking up the collective farms and reestablishing religion, they would have greatly weakened the Soviet people's will to resist and perhaps have won the war. But in part because Nazi ideology considered Slavic peoples as "subhuman" and in part because the Germans wanted to exploit the occupied territories economically, they instituted a reign of terror. Before long the local population began to resist and partisan bands that formed did much to harass the Germans throughout the war. Moreover, word of what German rule was like spread behind the Soviet lines and stiffened the resistance of the Soviet population.

Relations between the Soviet Union and its Western allies were far from smooth during the war. The latter provided $11 billion in Lend-Lease aid to the USSR, and both sides were committed to the total defeat of Hitler, but prewar suspicions and mistrust lingered. The major bone of contention was how soon the Western powers would open a second front against the Germans, thus relieving pressure on the Russian front. The Allies insisted they needed time to prepare it, that it would be disastrous to launch an invasion of Nazi-occupied Europe prematurely, and that diversionary efforts, such as the campaigns in North Africa and the Allied landing in Italy, did in fact weaken the Nazis and draw forces away from the German-Soviet front. The Soviet leaders kept pressing for an early invasion of Western Europe (it finally took place June 6, 1944); they feared that the Allies were deliberately holding back, hoping the Germans and the Russians would exhaust each other, thereby reducing Western casualties and preserving Allied strength as a way of assuring Western domination of the postwar world.

Specific incidents also fueled the bad feeling among the members of the Grand Alliance. For example, Western leaders allied with those Poles who had escaped from Poland and were still fighting Hitler were appalled at the Soviet attitude toward the discovery in eastern Poland of a mass grave of several thousand Polish officers who had been brutally murdered. Despite strong indications that the perpetrators of this Katyn Forest massacre were

THE EASTERN FRONT
WORLD WAR II
1939-1945

ALLIED SUPPLY LINE
FROM U.S. & BRITAIN

0   400
MILES

Corinne Abbazia Hekker Graphics

(War with Russia
1939 - 1940)
Joined Germans
in attack on
Russia, 1941

Murmansk

White
Sea

Archangel

N. Dvina

FINLAND

NORWAY

SWEDEN

U. S. S. R.

Leningrad
Tikhvin

DENMARK

Baltic Sea

ESTONIA

Riga

LATVIA

LITHUANIA

Kalinin

Volga

Kazan

"Polish
Corridor"

Danzig

Moscow

Gorky

Vilnius

Kuibyshev

EAST
PRUSSIA

Smolensk

Oka

Berlin

Tula

GERMANY

Russia

Oder

Warsaw

Brest-
Litovsk

FARTHEST GERMAN
ADVANCE, 1941 - 1942

Allies,
April 26,
45

Torgau

Elbe

POLAND

June

Kursk

Voronezh

Danube

CZECHOSLOVAKIA

1939

Lvov

Kharkov

Stalingrad

Vienna

1941

AUSTRIA

Budapest

HUNGARY

1940

1941

ROMANIA

Kiev

UKRAINE

Dnieper

Don

Volga

Rostov

Bessarabia

(Taken by
Germans
in 1941)

Belgrade

Bucharest

YUGOSLAVIA

Yalta

Kuban

Mozdok

ITALY

Sofia

1940

Novorossisk

CAUCASUS MTS.

BULGARIA

Black   Sea

Batum

Tbilisi

GREECE

Istanbul

Erevan

ALBANIA
(to Italy, 1939)

Ankara

ALLIED SUPPLY LINE
FROM PERSIAN GULF

Izmir

T   U   R   K   E   Y

Athens

IRAN

CRETE

(Taken by the
Germans, 1941)

| | 1938 Boundaries | Front lines in Russia | ***** Russian boundary, 1941 |
| | Axis and occupied areas June 22, 1941 | 1941 / 1942 / 1943 / 1944 | Russian and Allied drives, 1941 - 1945 |

MAP 8

Soviet forces (which later proved to be the case), the Soviet government refused to permit an independent investigation and blamed the Germans. Difficult diplomatic issues connected with the shape of the postwar world also evoked disagreements among the allies, but we will take those up in Chapter 13.

CONCLUSION

In May 1945 the Nazis surrendered, and three months later, after a belated Soviet entry into the war against Japan and a token invasion of Manchuria, the Japanese gave up as well. The Soviet Union suffered the greatest loss of life, an estimated twenty-seven million military and civilian dead, of any participant in World War II, as well as extensive destruction of almost one third of the country. Yet the Great Fatherland War, as World War II was known in the Soviet Union, acted as a psychological purge, removing the suspicion, tension, and uncertainty of the 1930s. The people and the party gradually banded together in an all-out struggle to defend the country and repulse the German aggressors. By the end of the war Soviet morale and prestige were high, buoyed not only by victory but by the wartime toleration of Orthodox religion and of greater intellectual freedom. Most citizens looked forward to a better life, and Soviet writers were heralding the Soviet people as saviors of Western civilization from Nazism, just as the Russians had saved Europe from the Mongols in the thirteenth century and from Napoleon in 1812. Although again the vastness of Russia, assisted by General Winter and General Mud, had helped the nation survive, Soviet patriotism could justifiably boast of the triumphs of the Red Army and of the total mobilization of the people for the war effort. As a result, the Soviet Union emerged from World War II as one of two superpowers, along with the United States. These two large countries would dominate world affairs in the decades ahead.

At the same time the Soviet Union was a scarred and exhausted society. Within a period of seventeen years the Soviet population had experienced forced industrialization and modernization, the brutal reorganization of rural life in the country, a chilling and inexplicable terror that killed millions of people, and a wearing, savage, and devastating modern war that lasted almost four years. People were shell-shocked and bewildered. What had their sacrifices meant? Where were they headed? Would Stalin, whom, after some doubts, they had loyally followed in the fight for survival, at last turn out to be a benevolent leader, a "good tsar"? For Soviet society in 1945–1946 the future was open, and great hopes could be cherished.

FURTHER READING

Barber, John and Harrison, Mark. *The Soviet Home Front, 1941–45*. New York: 1990.

Brown, Edward J. *Russian Literature Since the Revolution.* Cambridge, Mass.: 1982.

Clark, Alan. *Barbarossa: The Russo-German Conflict, 1941–45.* New York: 1965.

Conquest, Robert. *The Great Terror.* New York: 1968.

Curtiss, John S. *The Russian Church and the Soviet State.* Boston: 1953.

Dallin, Alexander. *German Rule in Russia, 1941–45.* New York: 1957.

Fitzpatrick, Sheila. *Everyday Stalinism: Soviet Russia in the 1930s.* London: 1999.

Getty, J. Arch, and Oleg V. Naumov. *The Road to Terror: Stalin and the Self-Destruction of the Bolsheviks, 1932–39.* New Haven, Conn.: 1999.

Ginzburg, Evgeniia. *Journey into the Whirlwind.* New York: 1975 (unforgettable memoir of a victim of the purges).

Glantz, David M., and Jonathan House. *When Titans Clashed: How the Red Army Stopped Hitler.* Lawrence, Kans.: 1995.

Gorodetsky, Gabriel. *Grand Delusion: Stalin and the German Invasion of Russia.* New Haven, Conn.: 1999.

Kennan, George. *Russia and the West Under Lenin and Stalin.* Boston: 1960.

Koestler, Arthur. *Darkness at Noon.* New York: 1970 (novel about the purges).

Kotkin, Stephen. *Magnetic Mountain: Stalinism as a Civilization.* Berkeley, Calif.: 1995.

Lewin, Moshe. *Russian Peasants and Soviet Power.* London: 1968.

Medvedev, Roy. *Let History Judge: The Origins and Consequences of Stalinism.* New York: 1973.

Pinkus, Benjamin. *The Jews of the Soviet Union.* Cambridge, Mass.: 1988.

Scott, John. *Behind the Urals: An American Worker in Russia's City of Steel.* Bloomington Ind.: 1989.

Tucker, Robert C. *Stalin in Power: The Revolution from Above, 1928–1941.* New York: 1990.

Ulam, Adam. *Expansion and Coexistence . . . 1917–73.* New York: 1973 (a history of Soviet foreign policy).

Volkogonov, Dmitri. *Stalin: Triumph and Tragedy.* New York: 1991.

Ward, Chris. *Stalin's Russia.* New York: 1999.

13

The Soviet Union as a Superpower: Change, Stagnation, and "Cold War," 1946–1984

Despite the harrowing devastation of the struggle against Hitler, Soviet society, under Stalin's relentless discipline, recovered from the war fairly quickly. But the system remained rigid, inefficient, and unproductive, especially when compared to the surging economies of the Western countries. Moreover, the wartime alliance between the Soviet Union and the West soon deteriorated into a mutually suspicious and hostile relationship. When Stalin died in 1953, his successors, led by Nikita Khrushchev, modified Stalinism in an effort to spark the economy and to spur creativity. They also sought to avert the danger of nuclear war by improving relations with the West. For a brief period in the late 1950s, Soviet society appeared to blossom, but Khrushchev's reforms soon foundered.

Senior party leaders critical of Khrushchev's policies ousted him (but did not purge him) in 1964 and set about restoring stability and building up Soviet military power. Although their efforts largely succeeded, economic growth slowed, dissident intellectuals castigated the system, and a better-educated populace became increasingly cynical and bitter about the inflexibility, arbitrariness, and waste that characterized post-Stalin society. In the mid-1980s a young, energetic party chief, Mikhail Gorbachev, introduced sweeping changes that eventually led to the collapse of the Soviet system, a subject treated in Chapter 14.

RECONSTRUCTION AND RENEWED STALINISM

Although triumphant over the Nazis, the Soviet people after the war faced the monumental task of recovering from the staggering losses and devastation suffered in the four-year struggle for survival. In the first two postwar years, they had to cope with minimum rations, a near famine in Ukraine, lack of housing, inadequate fuel and clothing, and wrenching social and psychological adjustments. Nevertheless, many citizens took up the challenge of recovery with considerable hope. They assumed that the relaxation of Stalinist orthodoxy during the war—the slight leeway given artistic and personal expression, the encouragement of the Orthodox religion, the resuscitation of Russian national heroes and traditions—would carry over into the postwar era as a reward for their devotion and courage that had made victory possible. Some even believed that reconstruction would take place at a moderate pace, given the enormous sacrifices that they had made in the war, and that the wartime allies of the USSR, particularly the United States, might help them recover.

The Soviet people did not have to wait long to have these hopes dashed. In a February 1946 speech, Stalin announced his harsh and forbidding program for the postwar Soviet Union. He called for sacrifice, superhuman work, and rigid conformity. He made clear that the Soviet government would rebuild the country by its own exertions, with minimal help from the West, whose capitalist system Stalin plainly distrusted. Soviet citizens were stunned but had no choice but to settle grimly to the task.

In 1946 and 1947 several developments underscored the completeness and the severity of the renewed Stalinism imposed on the country. As soon as the war was over, the Soviet government made strenuous efforts to recover its citizens who had fallen into Western hands. Some of these were prisoners of war (POWs) captured by the Germans and liberated by the Allies; others were civilians whom the Germans had taken to Germany for forced labor or who had retreated from Russia with the German armies rather than fall under Soviet rule again. In a tragic and terrible blunder, the Western governments at first cooperated with Soviet authorities in repatriating both POWs and civilians, many of whom strongly resisted going back. Once they were home, Stalin had many of them shot, imprisoned, or sentenced to forced labor.

At the end of the war Stalin also persecuted several non-Russian nationalities. He snuffed out further expressions of nationalism and autonomy among the Caucasian peoples and the Ukrainians, who had been permitted during the stress of war to revive a sense of self-identity and traditional values as a means of encouraging them to make an all-out effort in the fight against Germany. In addition, the Soviet dictator accused some smaller national minorities of collaborating with the Germans. He abolished the autonomous territorial enclaves of the Volga Germans (who had immigrated to Russia in the late eighteenth century), the Crimean Tatars, and the Chechen-Ingush, a mountain people in the Caucasus, sending their leaders to forced labor camps and deporting the rest of the population to Siberia and Central Asia.

Stalin also became concerned about the attitudes of Soviet citizens who during the war or postwar occupation of Germany and Eastern Europe had come into close contact with Western cultures and values. Perhaps he recalled how in the course of the Napoleonic campaigns liberal ideas had infected young Russian officers, inspiring some of them to lead the Decembrist Revolt. The Soviet ruler recognized that hundreds of thousands of Red Army and government personnel abroad could compare, generally unfavorably, Soviet conditions with the standard of living that they observed in such countries as Romania, Hungary, and even war-torn Germany. To prevent such potential disaffection from spreading, Stalin sharply curtailed relations between the USSR and Europe and the United States. By imposing this "iron curtain," as Winston Churchill dubbed it, Stalin prevented Soviet citizens from traveling in the West and blocked the importation of Western visitors, materials, and ideas.

Stalin also instituted the Fourth Five-Year Plan, with high goals for total output and strong emphasis on heavy industry. Not only did this require substantial exertions by the population, but the slighting of housing and consumer industry meant that living conditions for the average citizen improved only slightly and slowly from the stringent level of wartime. The Soviet people were expected to work hard but to benefit little. Nevertheless, by the early 1950s, with the help of reparations from Germany, Eastern Europe, and Manchuria, the country was largely rebuilt, and production surpassed prewar levels.

THE COLD WAR

During the crusade against Fascist Italy and Nazi Germany, the capitalist West and the Communist USSR were linked in a common struggle for survival. For the moment, leaders of this Grand Alliance shelved, but did not abandon, their differing ideological principles. Stalin even agreed in 1942 to the Atlantic Charter, a vague statement of humanitarian and democratic war aims worked out by Roosevelt and Churchill. At the first major meeting among the allies, the Teheran Conference of November 1943, the Big Three (Stalin, Roosevelt, Churchill) established cordial personal relationships. In 1944 they approved creation after the war of a successor to the League of Nations, the United Nations. They conceived this new international body, however, as a mechanism for extending great power control into the postwar world; the USSR, Britain, and the United States, as well as later allies, France and China, each retained veto power over all important decisions of the UN's chief executive organ, the Security Council. The Soviet government also acknowledged its responsibility to repay Allied Lend-Lease aid, which eventually totaled $11 billion and whose trucks and logistical equipment were critical to the Soviet counteroffensives against Germany in 1943–1944 (in the end it repaid only part of the debt). Moreover, Stalin supported the idea of easing trade restrictions after the war, and he agreed to joint occupation and control of Germany following its defeat.

Beneath this atmosphere of allied cooperation, however, disagreements over political and diplomatic questions cropped up. (Allied quarrels over military issues are discussed in Chapter 12). These differences led to disruption of the alliance and the beginning of a long, hostile relationship be-

tween the Soviet Union and the West known as the "cold war." Since the
1950s historians have vigorously debated the origins of and blame for the
cold war. "Revisionist" scholars attacked the dominant Western view that
Communist expansionist policies and the Soviet government's xenophobic
refusal to cooperate with its former allies caused the break. Instead, they
contended, economic and anti-Communist considerations in U.S. foreign
policy spurred a drive for American dominance in Europe and the rest of
the world designed to surround the socialist bloc and to ensure Western
control of vital resources and trade routes. In the face of this American-led
"imperialism," they argued, the Soviet Union reacted defensively, taking
steps to safeguard its security and its economic independence.

As with so many heated historical issues, elements of truth exist on both
sides. Although we know little about how Stalin viewed the postwar world,
a few clues suggest that initially he wished to continue cooperating with his
wartime partners. He needed peace and stability so that the Soviet government could concentrate on the huge task of rebuilding the country. He also
may have hoped that his wartime allies would aid Soviet reconstruction efforts. Yet at the same time he was suspicious of the Western nations, fearing
that their capitalist ideology and leadership might drive them to constrain
or even attack a weakened Soviet Union. Further, the Soviet dictator was
determined to advance the security of his country. In particular, in the light
of the historic record of attacks on Russia from Europe, he sought to ensure that pro-Soviet governments ruled the nations of Eastern Europe, providing a buffer zone for the USSR's defense. Moreover, he could herald the
establishment of Communist regimes there as part of the inevitable advance
of Marx's world socialist revolution.

Western leaders, for their part, saw Soviet efforts to dominate Eastern
Europe as antidemocratic and expansionist, and they feared the revolutionary potential of strong Communist parties in France, Italy, and several
Asian countries. As a result, they adopted the policy of "containment," designed to check the spread of Soviet power and of Communist revolution
by establishing military bases and building "areas of strength" in countries
surrounding the Soviet Union. Not surprisingly, Stalin and his colleagues
viewed such efforts as a menacing "encirclement" of their nation and
protested vigorously.

Each side was thus to a considerable extent imprisoned by its own per-
ceptions and misconceptions. The breakdown of joint action and policy,
the mutual recriminations, and the growing enmity between the Soviet
Union and the West sprang from deep ideological mistrust, each party believing the other to be intrinsically committed to worldwide dominance.
Marxism-Leninism taught that as the capitalist system neared its death
throes, it would do everything possible to crush socialism and thus stave off
its inevitable defeat. Conversely, Western leaders believed that the Communists were bent on world revolution and could be checked only by vigorous
counteraction.

Two significant postwar issues reflected how these divergent worldviews played out in practice: the treatment of Germany once it was defeated and the political alignment of Eastern Europe. After initial confusion within all the Allied governments, the Soviet Union, Britain, the United States, and France agreed at the February 1945 Yalta Conference and the July 1945 Potsdam Conference to control Germany jointly even though each power had its own zone of occupation. The victorious nations also determined that Germany should pay substantial reparations, half of which would go to the Soviet Union because of its greater wartime losses. Stalin apparently favored a unitary German state under common supervision, recognizing that if Germany were split up, its richest regions would fall under Western influence. His economic planners, however, seem to have convinced him to treat Germany primarily as a resource for the restitution and recovery of the Soviet Union. The Western leaders, in contrast, wanted to permit gradual restoration of the German economy and polity so that the country would not be a drain on the postwar world.

These different approaches led during 1945–1947 to escalating Soviet-Western quarrels over the level and methods of Soviet transfers to the USSR of east German factories, goods, and equipment as part of Germany's reparations payments. Western officials concluded that the Soviet Union was "milking" Germany and expected the West to cover any shortfall that resulted. Soviet officials felt that they were only taking what they rightfully deserved. In addition, disagreements arose over denazification, the reestablishment of German political parties, and economic relations among the four zones of occupation. In frustration the British and U.S. governments began to coordinate activities in their two zones of occupation and invited the French to join them. Alarmed that the Western Allies were creating a reunified west Germany that might later be armed against the USSR, Stalin applied pressure against them in June 1948 by cutting off land access to Berlin, which was under four-power joint control but which lay over 100 miles inside the Soviet zone of occupation. Rejecting the use of force, the Western authorities responded to this blockade of Berlin with an intensive airlift of supplies to their sectors of the city. They also made clear their determination to stay in Berlin. After eleven months Stalin called off the blockade, but by the end of 1948 the de facto division of Germany had occurred. Before long two separate German states emerged, the German Democratic Republic (East Germany) under Soviet domination and the Federal Republic of Germany (West Germany) allied to the West.

Disagreements over Eastern Europe further poisoned Soviet-Western relations at the end of the war. At the February 1945 Yalta Conference (see Figure 18), which American critics have erroneously called a "betrayal" of Eastern Europe, the Western powers in fact obtained from the Soviet Union a promise to hold free elections in Poland and, by implication, in other nations of the region. Churchill and Roosevelt also agreed, albeit reluctantly, to the reimposition of Soviet control over the Baltic states, a part of eastern

Figure 18.   *Prime Minister Churchill of Great Britain, President Roosevelt of the United States, and Soviet leader Stalin during their summit meeting at Yalta in the Soviet Union, Febrary 1945. (Courtesy of UPI/Bettmann Newsphotos)*

Poland, and Bessarabia. Poland was compensated for territory lost in the east with land in the west taken from Germany and from which the German population was forcibly deported.

Nevertheless, in the spring of 1945, Stalinist operatives forced creation of a Communist-dominated government in Romania and postponed elections in Poland. In the next three years Communist politicians, with indirect support from occupying Red Army forces, undercut coalition governments in most of Eastern Europe and set up regimes modeled on and subservient to the Soviet system. The climax of this process occurred in early 1948, when a Communist-dominated government came to power in Czechoslovakia and shortly afterward the respected Czechoslovak foreign minister, Jan Masaryk, committed suicide. The Western powers protested violations of the Yalta agreement, but they could do little. Some historians have suggested that the United States should have offered extensive economic aid to the USSR in exchange for political concessions in Eastern Europe, but it is unlikely that Congress would have supported such a gamble. Military intervention was out of the question since the Western countries rapidly demobilized their forces after the war while the Red Army remained on the ground in much of Eastern Europe. Why Stalin reneged on his Yalta promise is unclear, but zealous Soviet and East European Communists who wanted to spread the socialist revolution westward may have convinced him that he could guarantee the USSR's security only if he established in Eastern Europe not just neutral, but strongly pro-Soviet Communist regimes (see Map 9).

Almost before it had been established, Soviet hegemony over Eastern Europe was broken by the defection of Communist Yugoslavia under its wartime hero-leader, Josip Broz, known as Tito. The Yugoslav Communists had come to power on their own, as a result of a long guerrilla struggle against conservative opponents and the Germans, and Tito and his comrades had no intention of submitting completely to Soviet domination. Angered at Tito's resistance to Soviet orders, Stalin in 1948 expelled Yugoslavia from the *Cominform,* the organization of Communist parties that had replaced the Comintern. Stalin reportedly said that he would wiggle his little finger, and that would be the end of Tito. But Tito opposed Soviet subversion staunchly, and Stalin apparently decided that military occupation of Yugoslavia would be too costly.

The United States took the lead in responding to perceived Soviet revolutionary expansionism. In June 1947, to counter the growing strength of large Communist parties in France and Italy, the U.S. government launched the Marshall Plan, a program of extensive economic aid to Europe to buttress its reconstruction and economic stability. The West European countries participated willingly, and Marshall Plan assistance contributed significantly to their economic rejuvenation in the postwar era and to the decline of Communist influence in the region. Although several coalition governments in Eastern Europe expressed interest in the Marshall Plan, Soviet authorities, after brief hesitation, forbade their enlistment, accusing the United States of trying to insinuate imperialist control over Eastern Europe through the program.

A postwar Communist revolution in Greece alarmed Western statesmen, who were unaware that Tito, not Stalin, was its chief supporter. Stalin's diplomatic pressure on Turkey to cede to the Soviet Union bases on or near the Turkish Straits and abortive Soviet efforts to annex a slice of northern Iran further upset democratic leaders. As a result, American president Harry S. Truman announced in the spring of 1947 that the United States would provide economic and military support to Greece and Turkey and to any other country threatened by communism, a principle soon known as the Truman Doctrine. In practice Western support facilitated the triumph of conservative Greek forces over Communist rebels in a fierce three-year civil war.

The height of the cold war was reached in 1949 and 1950. In the former year the Western powers banded together in a mutual assistance alliance known as the North Atlantic Treaty Organization (NATO). Before long the

SOVIET
TERRITORIAL
GAINS IN
EUROPE,
1939-1949

Atlantic
Ocean

Corinne Abbazia Hekker Graphics

UNION
OF
SOVIET
SOCIALIST
REPUBLICS

NORWAY
SWEDEN
FINLAND
DENMARK
GREAT
BRITAIN
IRELAND
London
NETHERLANDS
BELGIUM
GERMAN
FEDERAL
REPUBLIC
LUXEMBURG
Paris
FRANCE
SWITZER-
LAND
ITALY
PORTUGAL
SPAIN
Madrid

POLISH
ADMIN.
Kalingrad
Danzig
GER.
DEM
REP
Berlin
Warsaw
POLAND
Prague
CZECHOSLOVAKIA
Vistula
Bonn
Danube
Vienna
AUSTRIA
HUNGARY
Budapest
Belgrade
YUGOSLAVIA
Rome
ALBANIA
GREECE

Leningrad
ESTONIA
LATVIA
LITHUANIA
Minsk
Kiev
Dnieper
Odessa
BESSARABIA
ROMANIA
Bucharest
BULGARIA
Istanbul
TURKEY

★ Moscow
Volga

BOUNDARY OF
USSR, 1938

Yalta
Black Sea
Don

Mediterranean Sea

USSR in 1938
Acquired by the USSR, 1939 - 1945
Soviet satellite states
Communist but not Soviet satellite

0   600
MILES

MAP 9

Soviet Union responded by creating an Eastern alliance system, the Warsaw Pact. Also in 1949 the Chinese Communists came to power, winning a civil war waged off and on since 1927 and intensively since 1945. Their opponent, Chiang Kai-shek, was forced to retreat to Taiwan, and the Soviet Union gained a major ally in Asia. In a later section of this chapter we will trace the stormy course of relations between the Soviet Union and the People's Republic of China, the new Chinese state.

Next door to China the Korean peninsula, like Germany, had been divided into two zones of occupation after the defeat of Japan, a northern one under Soviet control and a southern one under American control. As the cold war intensified, these two zones had followed the German pattern, and embryonic separate states had been set up. In June 1950 a Communist army from North Korea invaded South Korea. American forces under UN sponsorship rushed to the defense of the South Koreans. U.S. leaders believed that Moscow had instigated the attack, but Soviet archival evidence indicates that Stalin acquiesced in the invasion and supplied equipment, arms, and high-level military advisers only after persistent North Korean appeals for Soviet assistance. He apparently feared that withholding support would drive the North Koreans into the arms of the Chinese. When the former neared defeat, the Soviet leader sent air-defense forces, including a few Soviet pilots, and encouraged the Chinese Communists to intervene, which they did. He may have hoped to get the Americans and Chinese tangled in a long ground war in Asia, but the latter withdrew after a military stalemate was reached, roughly along the line of division of the country before hostilities began.

Taken as a whole, Stalin's foreign policy after the war achieved some important Soviet objectives. Except Greece, which aligned with the West, and Finland, which remained independent but was careful not to antagonize the Soviet Union, the whole belt of states in Eastern Europe lying between the Soviet Union and Western Europe became Communist, although Yugoslavia (and later tiny Albania) rejected Soviet direction and dominance. Through the Council of Mutual Economic Assistance these countries were closely linked to the Soviet Union economically, usually on terms favorable to the latter. East Germany was incorporated into the Soviet bloc, Communist control was established in North Korea, and a Communist revolution took place in China, albeit with minimal help from the Soviet Union.

On the other hand, Soviet actions in Eastern Europe and Germany and the invasion of South Korea provoked a strong reaction from the Western powers. Moreover, the Soviet Union, with establishment of a pro-American state in West Germany, lost any chance to extend its influence in Germany as a whole, and the position of Communist parties in France and Italy weakened. The Soviet government faced continuing hostility in the West, and its prospects in the rest of the world did not seem bright. Still, the Soviet Union was secure, and in 1949 had developed its own atomic bomb.

IDEOLOGICAL RIGIDITY AND REPRESSION

As the cold war intensified and Soviet citizens struggled to rebuild their nation, Stalin tightened his grip on the Soviet system. Although named generalissimo in the glow of victory, the Soviet dictator remained suspicious and secretive. He continued the loose administrative arrangements employed in the war, which permitted him to play off ambitious subordinates against each other. The Central Committee and the Politburo met irregularly, and he did not convene a Party Congress until seven years after the war. The Soviet dictator reestablished firm control over the armed forces, and he took harsh measures to reimpose communism in the Baltic region and western Ukraine. Overcoming guerrilla resistance in these areas, the government sent to the labor camps or exiled to Siberia tens of thousands of Balts and Ukrainians.

Stalin also launched a virulent ideological attack on capitalism abroad and on deviations from Stalinist orthodoxy at home. During the wartime Grand Alliance, Stalin and the Soviet government had played down the Marxist-Leninist view that the socialist and capitalist systems were inherently antagonistic, but in 1947 Stalin reaffirmed strongly that the world was divided into two camps, a peace-loving socialist one led by the Soviet Union and a war-mongering, aggressive one led by the United States. He called upon the Soviet people to make sacrifices to ready the Soviet Union for defense against threatened attacks by American imperialism, and he appealed to all "progressive" people in the world to rally to the Soviet cause.

The domestic implications of this ideological hardening were a crackdown in Soviet intellectual life and a new emphasis on Stalinist orthodoxy. A number of Soviet writers, composers, and artists were attacked for "bourgeois cosmopolitanism," that is, for not adhering closely enough to socialist realism in their work and to the Stalinist line generally in their attitudes. Since a large proportion of those castigated were Jews, an undertone of anti-Semitism permeated the campaign.

As he grew older, Stalin became increasingly suspicious, isolated, and irrational. He ruled virtually alone, acting through a personal secretariat and through a set of party and government officials who were expected to carry out his orders unquestioningly and who were too frightened to suggest alternative policies. Consequently, we know little about the motivations for Stalin's policies or what was occurring behind the scenes. In 1952, for reasons that are unclear, Stalin convened a Party Congress, the first since 1939. He also made some slight shifts in foreign policy. Whether these moves presaged a major change of direction and the initiation of new programs, as some have speculated, or whether they were simply the groundwork for a violent new purge, as others have concluded, is simply not known. Muddying the situation was the "Doctors' Plot," charges that were published a few weeks before Stalin died accusing a group of physicians, including several who worked in the Kremlin, the seat of the government and the party, of attempting to poison high officials. Many of the doctors were Jews, but whether this story was an omen of a new reign of terror with a strong anti-Semitic tone is not clear. After Stalin's death the doctors were exonerated.

THE SUCCESSION TO STALIN AND THE RISE OF KHRUSHCHEV

On March 5, 1953, Stalin, who was then seventy-four years old, died, apparently from natural causes. Rumors that he was poisoned seem to be pure speculation. With Stalin gone and no arrangements for the succession, the Communist leaders who had surrounded him in his last years appealed, in rather apprehensive tones, for the Soviet public to remain calm and for support for "collective leadership," that is, for rule by the members of the Politburo (at that time called the Presidium). At the same time they began jockeying for position, hoping to capture the supreme power that Stalin had wielded.

First, however, Stalin's successors decided to deal with the danger posed by Lavrenti Beria, the head of the secret police (known as the KGB after its Russian initials). Apparently they feared not only the power that he derived from control over the country's internal security forces but also his ability to use information about each of them that Beria had collected over the years. Moreover, Beria, from motives unknown, was espousing liberal reforms at home and concessions in foreign policy, ideas that frightened his insecure and conservative colleagues. At a dramatic meeting on June 28, 1953, they arrested the secret police chief, charging him with antiparty activities and treason. In December Beria was secretly tried and executed.

The two main candidates to succeed Stalin were Georgi Malenkov, a pudgy, colorless party stalwart who had seemed for a time in the early 1950s to be the heir apparent, and Nikita Khrushchev, an ebullient, dynamic, and versatile diamond-in-the- rough who had apparently lost favor with Stalin in the dictator's last years. After Stalin's death, Malenkov became premier, and the party elite chose Khrushchev first secretary of the party. Although Malenkov sought broad support by urging greater emphasis on consumer-goods production, Khrushchev gained the backing of influential military and economic officials by appearing to favor a continuing focus on heavy industry and by opposing proposed cuts in the defense budget. Effectively using his control of party affairs and key party appointments, Khrushchev gradually eclipsed his rival, and in February 1955 he engineered Malenkov's demotion from premier to minister of electric power stations.

Hardly a commanding presence, the new leader of the Soviet Union was short, plump, and homely (see Figure 19). In the words of one of his personal secretaries, however:

His broad face, his double chins, his enormous bald head, his large turned-up nose, and protruding ears could belong to any peasant from a central Russian village.... And only his eyes, his tiny, shrewd, gray-blue eyes that variously radiated kindness, imperiousness, and anger, only his eyes, I repeat, showed him to be a thoroughly political man who had gone through fire and water and was capable of making the most abrupt changes.[1]

His temperament and curiosity impelled Khrushchev to innovate and to propose significant changes in Soviet domestic and foreign policies. His training and experience kept him within the bounds of socialist orthodoxy and a one-party system. Born the son of a peasant turned coal miner in south central Russia, Khrushchev received only primary schooling before becoming a machinist and fitter in the mines. Radicalized by Marxist literature as a teenager, he joined the Bolshevik party and fought in the civil war. Afterward he rose by grit and ambition through the party, which provided him with two years of education along the way. He directed party affairs in Moscow in the mid-1930s and then served as party boss of Ukraine from 1938 to 1949. Spared from the purges, perhaps because Stalin admired his work in Moscow, Khrushchev had nevertheless acquiesced in the terrible "cleansing" of 1937. The new Soviet leader had also overseen the forcible incorporation of eastern Poland into the USSR in 1939 after the Nazi-Soviet pact and the reintegration of Ukraine into the Stalinist system after World War II, both processes involving suppression of anti-Soviet guerrillas and the shipping of hundreds of thousands of people to the forced labor camps. Later, when he denounced Stalin's crimes, Khrushchev hardly came to the subject with clean hands.

Khrushchev and his colleagues faced the considerable dilemma of how to reduce the rigidity and inefficiency of the Stalinist system without endangering the absolute control of the party over the government and society. The Soviet economy had become increasingly wasteful and unproductive in Stalin's last years. The population as a whole was cowed by the threat of terror and exhausted from the continuing demands that Stalin imposed upon them. Party officials and government bureaucrats had been paralyzed in making decisions or introducing new ideas because they were unsure of Stalin's views and opinions and because he might decree at any time a new orthodoxy or policy that would put them in the wrong—and hence at a minimum demoted and disgraced and at the worst packed off to a forced labor camp. At the end of the Stalinist era, the system was creaking to a halt, with productivity, commitment, and progress all faltering.

The first steps of Stalin's successors were aimed at reducing the arbitrary terror of Stalinism. Thousands of political prisoners were released, and Soviet citizens were assured that random arrests were a thing of the past. The party emphasized "strict Leninist legality," which gave people a clear idea of where they stood and how far they could go in thought and action before running afoul of the regime. Intellectuals were encouraged to be more

Figure 19. *Nikita S. Khrushchev, Soviet leader, 1956–64, talking with Yugoslav leader Tito at the United Nations in 1959. (Courtesy of the United Nations)*

creative and to innovate to some extent. Managers and bureaucrats were instructed to think of new ideas and to participate more actively in economic decision making.

These measures improved the social and political climate of Soviet life, but Khrushchev shrewdly recognized that to spark the Soviet economy and society, to instill widespread initiative and commitment, the party would have to confront the repressive and conformist legacy of the old system more directly. Stalinism was out of date, and new methods were required if the Soviet Union were to function efficiently and to have any hope of competing with the United States. Moreover, much like the situation Lenin faced in 1921, the Soviet Union could not count on revolutionary help from abroad. Europe was recovering rapidly from the war, the Third World was busy achieving independence, and the chances of imminent world revolution were dim. Nor, given the suicidal danger of nuclear weapons, could the spread of communism be forced by the Soviet Union as long as the United States was prepared to counter Soviet expansion. Consequently, the effort to improve Soviet life and to move toward the ultimate goal of full communism would have to come from within.

In these circumstances Khrushchev took a daring gamble. To rejuvenate Soviet society (and perhaps also to tarnish his political opponents who were closely associated with Stalin), Khrushchev decided to attack Stalinism and then to replace it with a reformed system. The risks of such a course were great. The Soviet power structure and foreign Communist parties were filled with longtime Stalinists who would almost certainly resist a frontal assault on their recent hero and patron. Even more dangerous, criticism of Stalinism could logically lead to condemnation of the party itself and of the political monopoly through which it controlled Soviet society.

Of the top party leaders, only Khrushchev had the audacity to spearhead the debunking of Stalin. He hit upon the clever idea of focusing his criticism not on the system as a whole but on Stalin himself. The party could thus be right, even though Stalin had been wrong. After Khrushchev's attack on the former Soviet dictator, some independent-minded Soviet citizens took the next logical step, asking in party meetings, "If the party is right and acts in our interests, how could it have permitted Stalin to misbehave so outrageously?" Party leaders quickly silenced these mavericks, either by demoting or arresting them.

The campaign of "de-Stalinization" was launched in February 1956 at the Twentieth Party Congress, to which Khrushchev delivered a long "secret speech," castigating Stalin for a number of errors and crimes. The speech was secret only in the sense that it was not published and was intended primarily for party officials, but Western governments soon obtained a copy, and Soviet citizens were shortly apprised of its gist by word of mouth. Khrushchev acknowledged Stalin's achievements in the party before 1934 and his success in industrializing the Soviet Union. But he went on to charge Stalin with having nurtured "a cult of personality" for his personal aggrandizement. This course had violated well-established party norms and had led to grievous mistakes, including the murder of guilty and innocent alike in the purges, the failure to prepare the Soviet Union adequately for the German attack in 1941, poor military leadership during World War II, and repression and foreign policy errors in the postwar era.

Khrushchev also gave a chilling description of working with Stalin:

> Stalin was a very distrustful man, sickly suspicious. . . . He could look at a man and say: "Why are your eyes so shifty today?" or "Why are you turning so much today and avoiding to look me directly in the eyes?" The sickly suspicion created in him a general distrust even toward eminent party workers whom he had known for years. Everywhere and in everything he saw "enemies," "two-facers," and "spies." Possessing unlimited power he indulged in great willfulness and choked a person morally and physically. A situation was created where one could not express one's own will.[2]

Some of the individuals Stalin had falsely accused were rehabilitated in the speech itself, when details of their cases were discussed. Others were restored to a place of Bolshevik honor in succeeding months, and in particular almost all the military leaders Stalin purged were subsequently vindicated. Most of the several million political prisoners in jail and in the camps were released in 1956 and 1957. The attack on Stalin was renewed at the Twenty-second Congress in 1961, at which time his body was removed from Lenin's mausoleum on Red Square and places named after him were renamed.

Khrushchev's de-Stalinization campaign scored some successes at home. The party reined in the secret police and reduced arbitrary repression. Some energy and initiative were pumped back into the system. A loosening of rigid party controls over Soviet culture that had begun to develop shortly after Stalin's death and that was known as "the thaw" from the title of a 1954 novel by Ilya Ehrenburg intensified after 1956, despite sporadic attempts to reimpose tight socialist orthodoxy. Vladimir Dudintsev's novel *Not by Bread Alone* scathingly castigated bureaucratic obscurantism in the system, and Yevgenii Yevtushenko's poems, which he read to large and enthusiastic audiences, called for honesty in public and private life and vigilance against a return to Stalinism. In November 1962 Khrushchev even personally approved publication of Alexander Solzhenitsyn's damning indictment of the forced labor camps and of the Stalinist system as a whole, the novel *One Day in the Life of Ivan Denisovich*.

At the same time Khrushchev never fully trusted intellectuals and artists. In the fall of 1963 cultural watchdogs in the party arranged for the Soviet leader to view an exhibition of mildly abstract art. Khrushchev was disgusted and annoyed, commenting on one still life that it was full of "messy yellow lines which looked, if you will excuse me, as though some child had done his business on the canvas when his mother was away and then spread it around with his hands." Moreover, he made sure that party control of cultural and intellectual life was maintained despite a slight easing of restrictions and some encouragement for the intelligentsia to be independently creative.

PEACEFUL COEXISTENCE AND TROUBLES IN EASTERN EUROPE

In addition to his daring de-Stalinization campaign, Khrushchev proved innovative in the foreign-policy arena. Before he died, Stalin had failed to resolve the strategic problem of how the Soviet Union should react to the American monopoly of nuclear weapons. The Soviet dictator had ordered a crash program to develop Soviet nuclear capabilities, but he had not reconsidered the overall international position of the USSR in this light. Khrushchev and his colleagues soon tackled the issue. Given the enormous destructive power of atomic and hydrogen bombs, it was suicidal, the Soviet leaders realized, to predicate Soviet doctrine and external actions on the Leninist premise of a "frightful collision" between the socialist and capitalist systems. Instead Khrushchev propounded an extension of the Leninist principle of peaceful coexistence, arguing that capitalism and socialism could live side by side until the time when socialism, by nonviolent means such as economic example, political competition, and propaganda, would win over the world's peoples, and a global system of socialist states would be established. Or to put it another way, for socialism to triumph, as it was bound to according to the laws of history, war was not inevitable. The victory could come by peaceful means.

Soviet ideologists developed the new theory of the non-inevitability of war during 1954 and 1955, and Khrushchev enunciated this doctrine at the Twentieth Party Congress in February 1956. Even earlier, however, Stalin's successors had begun to ameliorate the confrontational policies of the cold war, and there is some evidence that Stalin himself was beginning to soften his foreign policies on the eve of his death. In 1952 and 1953 Soviet authorities encouraged Chinese and North Korean acceptance of an armistice in the Korean War. In the civil war that had erupted in Vietnam after World War II, Khrushchev and his colleagues endorsed a cease-fire in 1954 and a partition of the country between forces of the Communist revolutionary leader Ho Chi Minh and French-backed conservative elements in southern Vietnam. Also, the Soviet Union and the Western powers agreed in 1955 on a peace treaty with Austria that ended their postwar occupation of that country in exchange for an Austrian pledge of neutrality.

In 1958 Khrushchev reversed the closure of his nation that had existed since World War II and admitted Western tourists, scholars, and business-people to the USSR. He vigorously sought trade with the Western world and promoted cultural exchange agreements with the United States and other countries. Soviet performing arts groups, exhibits, students, and academicians came to the West and vice versa. Finally, the Soviet leader developed closer diplomatic, political, economic, and cultural ties with the countries of Asia, Africa, and Latin America and was delighted when Fidel Castro, the leader of a revolution in Cuba, finally declared in 1961 that he was a Marxist-Leninist and would establish a socialist system in Cuba.

Although the new policies associated with peaceful coexistence (or peaceful competition, as it should more accurately be called) did much to refurbish the Soviet image and to enhance Soviet influence in the world, Soviet foreign policy also ran into marked setbacks in the 1950s and early 1960s, some within the socialist block itself and some in relations with the Western powers. Stalin had encouraged the view that international socialism was a monolithic movement wisely modeled on the Soviet experience and benevolently directed by the Soviet government. Many critics of the Soviet Union and most Western leaders unhesitatingly accepted this picture of socialist unity and Soviet control. Yet as early as 1948 the myth was shattered, when the Yugoslav Communists chose to pursue their own course free of Soviet dictation.

After Stalin's death it became increasingly difficult to maintain unanimity within the bloc and direction by Moscow. As part of his de-Stalinization policies Khrushchev relaxed the Soviet grip on Eastern Europe slightly, and some Eastern European leaders persecuted in Stalinist times were rehabilitated. This was not enough, however, and in 1956 open opposition to Soviet domination erupted in Poland and in Hungary. The Polish assertion of greater independence was spearheaded by Wladyslaw Gomulka, a popular Polish Communist, and other party leaders. In a dramatic showdown in Poland in October 1956 Gomulka and his colleagues reportedly told a visiting Soviet delegation headed by Khrushchev that if Moscow tried to enforce greater conformity on Poland, the Polish people—down to the last man, woman, and child—would fight. The Soviet leaders backed down, and Gomulka was permitted to initiate reforms in state and party affairs in Poland.

Events in Hungary had a less benign outcome. For a number of months in 1956 there had been growing restiveness among Hungarian intellectuals and party members, but no individual or group emerged to focus and direct this discontent, as had occurred in Poland. Instead the mood of disaffection spread to the general populace, and in October-November 1956 a popular rebellion against the existing government and against Soviet dominance in Hungary broke out. Reformers under Imre Nagy struggled to control the situation, but dissatisfied rebels continued to attack Hungarian security and party institutions and personnel. At first Khrushchev and his colleagues seemed willing to negotiate with the new Hungarian leaders.

In early November, however, as public pressure in Hungary for the removal of Soviet troops and the withdrawal of Hungary from the Warsaw Pact mounted, the Soviet leadership decided to act lest Hungary slide into the Western camp. They may also have feared the impact of Hungarian reformism on political and social stability at home. With sixty thousand troops, the Soviet army crushed the rebellion. More than four thousand Hungarians were killed or wounded, and subsequently three hundred rebels were executed and ten thousand imprisoned. Thousands of Hungarians fled to the West. Since almost everyone, including many people within the socialist bloc and the Soviet Union, knew that the rebels were just average citizens—not counterrevolutionaries and hooligans as the Soviet media charged—the suppression of the uprising gravely damaged the image of the Soviet Union as a defender of the rights of the masses, and many Communists in the West left the party at that time.

ORIGINS OF THE SINO-SOVIET SPLIT

In the late 1950s Khrushchev encountered mounting difficulties in his relationship with the Chinese Communist leader Mao Tse-tung and in the Soviet Union's formal ties with China. The roots of the growing Sino-Soviet hostilities were deep and many-branched. After Stalin's advice to the Chinese Communists in 1927 to cooperate with Chiang Kai-shek had resulted in their near destruction by Chiang, the Communist revolutionary movement in China went its own way, fighting mainly on its own against the Nationalists and then, after the Japanese invasion of China in 1936, against the Japanese as well. Until near the end of World War II the Soviet

Union maintained rather distant relations with both Nationalist China and the Communist Chinese in order not to offend Japan, with which it had signed a nonaggression treaty in 1941 designed to prevent the Red Army from being caught in a two-front war. Soviet entry into the war against Japan in the summer of 1945, after the defeat of Germany, made the Soviet government a cobelligerent with Nationalist China, and it reached an agreement with Chiang Kai-shek in August 1945. Because Stalin wanted to maintain this relationship and because he was not eager to see an independent Communist movement come to power, the Soviet Union provided little direct support to Mao Tse-tung and his comrades as they battled to victory in China. Instead Soviet authorities helped indirectly by turning over to the Chinese Communists Manchuria, which the Red Army had occupied in August 1945, as well as the Japanese war material captured there. They also provided some logistical support to the Chinese Communist armies.

Nevertheless, the Chinese Communists could feel justifiably that they had made their own revolution and were not beholden to anyone, least of all to Stalin and the Soviet comrades. Mao apparently resented the niggardly Soviet assistance to his revolution, and these feelings were intensified when Soviet aid to the new Communist Chinese government in 1950 was limited and required repayment with interest. In addition, the Soviet government drove a hard bargain in the diplomatic and territorial arrangements that accompanied signing of a formal alliance between the two largest socialist countries. Finally, in what was clearly a personal affront, Stalin refused to treat Mao as an equal when the latter visited Moscow in December 1949.

Despite these inauspicious portents, relations between the USSR and the People's Republic of China were ostensibly close in the 1950s. From the Soviet point of view it was important to keep the Chinese as allies during the Korean War, for which the Chinese supplied "volunteers," and while Moscow was having difficulties elsewhere in the socialist camp, notably in Yugoslavia, Poland, and Hungary. For their part the Chinese modeled their system and pattern of rapid development on the Stalinist experience. Moreover, the new government needed Soviet economic and military assistance, no matter how limited, and it wanted Soviet diplomatic backing in its efforts to oust the Nationalists from Taiwan and to win admission to the United Nations.

As the 1950s progressed, however, frictions increased. Mao was displeased with Khrushchev's de-Stalinization campaign, both because he had not been consulted about its advisability and because he thought it implied too "soft" a line in international affairs. After Stalin's death Mao considered himself the senior Communist leader and the chief Marxist theoretician in the world. Yet, Khrushchev treated him as a junior ally, and Mao was further offended by Khrushchev's brash and informal style. Quarrels developed over the amount and quality of Soviet aid, and the Chinese bitterly resented the high-handed manner and methods of Soviet advisers and technical assistance personnel in China.

Lying behind these surface irritants, however, were divisive territorial and political-ideological issues. Ever since the seventeenth century, when Russian expansion eastward reached the border of the Chinese empire, the regions lying between these two great countries and the exact boundaries between them had been in dispute. The Chinese believed that in the late nineteenth century and in the first half of the twentieth century, when China was weak, the Russians, whether tsarist diplomats or Soviet comrades, took advantage of its relative decline in power to extract unfair territorial concessions from China. The Soviet authorities, on the other hand, argued that their position in the Far East was historically justified and that since 1949 they had been more than generous in trying to make boundary adjustments that would satisfy the Chinese.

The political-ideological questions centered in part on sibling rivalry within the international socialist movement. The Soviet leaders assumed they should head the movement, given their revolutionary seniority and greater power. The Chinese, historically sensitive on issues of precedence and ruling the largest Communist country in the world, resented the Russians' self-proclaimed role and in any case believed that the Soviet leaders often erred in their direction of the socialist bloc. Moreover, in Southeast Asia and in South Asia, the Soviet Union and the People's Republic of China competed for influence directly, the Soviet Union supporting the North Vietnamese against China and the Chinese backing Pakistan against the Soviet Union's friend, India, for example.

The ideological dispute arose in part over Khrushchev's new doctrine of the noninevitability of war and his policy of peaceful coexistence. The Chinese insisted that these ideas were violations of true Leninism, making the Soviet leaders guilty of the serious ideological crime of "revisionism" (changing Marxist orthodoxy). The Chinese ideologists took a "hard" line, maintaining that the world Communist movement should actively foment revolutions in the Third World and should aggressively undermine world imperialism at every opportunity. They insisted that it was wishful thinking to believe socialism could be achieved peacefully, by parliamentary or other nonviolent means, and that coexistence was only a trap designed by the imperialists to lull the socialist states into passivity while the capitalist armies prepared to encircle and destroy them. In retort, the Soviet leaders accused the Chinese of being adventurists and warmongers and of endangering the security of the socialist system in the nuclear age. By 1960 the differences between the Soviet Union and China had erupted into public denunciations and direct action. The Soviet side cut off aid to China and withdrew its advisers and technicians, including those who had been assisting the Chinese to develop nuclear technology.

UPS AND DOWNS IN SOVIET-WESTERN RELATIONS

Flare-ups of the cold war broke through the calmer atmosphere of peaceful coexistence on occasion during the late 1950s and early 1960s. Germany continued to be a touchy issue between Moscow and Washington, with Soviet leaders charging that the West was rearming West Germany as a future aggressor against the USSR. In November 1958 Khrushchev suddenly announced that the Soviet Union would sign a unilateral peace treaty with the German Democratic Republic and give the East Germans control of the access routes to the Western sectors of Berlin unless the Western powers agreed within six months to withdraw their occupation forces from Berlin and recognize the city as an independent entity. The Soviet leader thought that he could pressure the West to recognize the German Democratic Republic as a Soviet satellite and to relinquish Berlin. He apparently also hoped that a success over Berlin would quiet domestic critics of recent cuts that he had made in Soviet ground forces and would show the Chinese and their sympathizers in the world socialist movement that he could be tough on the imperialists. His calculations failed, however, when the Western powers rejected the ultimatum and reaffirmed their determination to stay in Berlin.

Khrushchev then sought broadened accommodation with the West, making a successful visit to the United States in September 1959 and unilaterally cutting Soviet troop strength in 1960. But the Soviet shooting down of an American U-2 spy plane torpedoed plans for a summit meeting in May 1960. Moreover, the nuclear buildup undertaken by the new U.S. administration of John F. Kennedy in 1961 and the continued flight of talented East Germans to the West alarmed Khrushchev and his advisers. Once again, they stepped up pressure on Berlin. American president Kennedy stood firm, and in angry response Khrushchev agreed in August 1961 to East German leaders' plans to cut off the German Democratic Republic from West Germany by erecting a barrier between the two states. In Berlin this barrier took the form of a 12-foot-high concrete wall (which stood until 1989). In a dramatic highlight of the Soviet-Western confrontation over Berlin, Kennedy then flew to the divided city and proclaimed publicly in accented but crowd-pleasing German, "Ich bin ein Berliner" (I am a Berliner). Finally, in the fall of 1961 Khrushchev quietly eased the pressure on Berlin and agreed to negotiations on the issue, which dragged on until 1972. The Berlin Wall harmed the image of socialism and the Soviet Union, and his backdown over Berlin weakened Khrushchev's position at home.

The gravest crisis of this period, and indeed of the entire postwar era, occurred in October 1962. In the late 1950s the Soviet Union had begun to reorient its military capability and its strategic doctrine around "rocket forces," that is, long-range ballistic missiles equipped with nuclear warheads. The United States, however, had substantial superiority over the Soviet Union both in missiles and in total numbers of nuclear weapons, including those delivered by planes and those launched from submarines. In what was apparently a daring but foolhardy effort to overcome this inferiority before the United States knew what had happened, Khrushchev undertook to place medium-range Soviet missiles in Cuba, whence they could threaten the southeastern United States. American intelligence soon discovered this Soviet gambit, and President Kennedy after several days' somber discussions with his advisers ordered a blockade of Cuba to prevent further Soviet missile shipments to the island and asked the Soviet government to withdraw the missiles already in place.

It was a tense confrontation. If the Soviet Union refused to back down, the United States would have to invade Cuba, and a Soviet-American war, with the likelihood of devastating nuclear exchanges, could hardly be averted. At first, Soviet ships continued steaming toward the American naval forces stationed off Cuba, but at the last minute they either turned back or, if they had no military cargo, submitted peacefully to being stopped and searched. Khrushchev communicated his willingness to withdraw the missiles in exchange for an American pledge not to invade the island and a secret U.S. commitment to remove its missiles (largely obsolete) from Turkey. Kennedy agreed, and the American face-saving promises permitted Khrushchev to claim that he had thwarted the aggressive designs of American "imperialism." He failed, however, to convince his critics in the Politburo, and two years later, they used Khrushchev's backdown over Cuba as one of the reasons for ousting him from power.

The Cuban missile crisis sobered both sides in the East-West struggle, and in the following year the Soviet Union and the Western powers signed a treaty banning all but underground tests of nuclear devices. The Soviet and American governments also agreed to establish a "hot line" of direct communications between Moscow and Washington, permitting the top leaders of each country to talk promptly and without intermediaries in the event of another major crisis.

KHRUSHCHEV: REFORMER OR REPAIRMAN?

Although his setbacks in foreign affairs provided ammunition for Khrushchev's opponents, failures on the domestic front led more directly to his downfall in 1964. Yet he accomplished a good deal, and the Soviet population clearly benefited from his efforts. Was Khrushchev a far-seeing reformer determined to recast Soviet socialism? Because he acted primarily as an energetic repairman, rushing here and there to apply patches to breakdowns in the system, the answer has to be no. Nevertheless, his domestic changes pushed Soviet society in new directions, and some of his policies foreshadowed the reforms Gorbachev would institute three decades later.

Neither doctrinaire ideologue nor innovative theorist, Khrushchev approached the problems of Soviet life pragmatically. Yet he sincerely sought improvement. He believed deeply in socialism's promise to provide a better life. He was convinced that citizens could be enlisted in the struggle to achieve that goal if they were properly exhorted and rewarded. Although Khrushchev never doubted the validity of the one-party system, the party, he believed, should guide and direct the people toward socialism, without resorting to random terror. In optimistic moments he even concluded that the Soviet citizenry could build a fully Communist society "in the main" within twenty years.

Many of his policies reflected these convictions. He strove to establish "socialist legality," that is, to ensure the rule of law and justice in people's civic and daily lives. As a result, individuals felt a much greater sense of personal security, for they knew that if they eschewed antiparty and anti-Soviet activities, the regime would not resort to arbitrary and illicit actions against them.

On coming to power Khrushchev recognized that the Soviet economy was near crisis. He turned his attention first to the faltering agricultural sector, reducing taxes on the collective farmers' private plots and assisting collective farms with higher prices for their products and increased investment funds. In February 1954 he launched a daring crash program to bring under cultivation for the first time millions of acres of virgin lands in Kazakhstan and southwestern Siberia. This effort initially increased the Soviet annual grain yield from 82.5 million to 125 million tons, but uncertain rainfall and overcultivation led to falling output in later years. The Soviet leader also urged many farms to switch to corn production in order to provide more fodder for Soviet livestock, thereby increasing meat production.

Nikita Sergeevich, as his admirers called him, strove to improve industrial efficiency, increase housing, and strengthen planning. Reversing the position that he had adopted during his power struggle with Malenkov, Khrushchev now encouraged the production of consumer goods and tried to curtail military expenditures. Moreover, he radically reorganized economic administration, dividing the nation into 107 regional economic councils called *sovnarkhozy.* He hoped to break the central bureaucracy's stranglehold on economic policy and to increase local participation in and supervision over decision making and production. This reform had some economic advantages as well as many drawbacks. Politically, however, it antagonized vested interests in the party who had been running the economy from Moscow. Their disgruntlement, plus growing doubts about the impact of de-Stalinization in Eastern Europe and the effectiveness of the policy of peaceful coexistence, led before long to a revolt of the party elite against Khrushchev's leadership.

In the early summer of 1957 his opponents combined against him, although, unfortunately for them, they failed to develop a common or coherent platform. While the Soviet leader was away in Finland, the Presidium (Politburo) voted to remove him. Khrushchev, however, outmaneuvered his foes, calling a meeting of the Central Committee of the party, in which he controlled a majority, to overrule the Presidium and to denounce what he called the "antiparty group" of his enemies. Unlike the days of the purges or even the recent fate of Beria, Khrushchev's opponents were not shot but merely demoted to minor positions or allowed to retire on pensions.

In the late 1950s and early 1960s Khrushchev continued to seek ways to bolster the Soviet economy and had some early successes. On his visit to the United States in 1959 Khrushchev declared jubilantly to his capitalist hosts, "We will bury you." He did not mean that literally socialism would conquer capitalism, but rather that with the gains he believed the Soviet Union was making, the day was not far off when the Soviet Union would outproduce the United States and would thus win over the rest of the world to its socialist way of organizing modern industrial life.

For the Soviet people Khrushchev improved housing and provided modest annual increases in their standard of living while promising much more within twenty years. He markedly improved the lot of Soviet farmers and pensioners. The Soviet leader also accelerated the Soviet space program, which resulted in the launching of the first space satellite, *Sputnik,* in 1957. In ideology he argued that the Soviet Union had now completed the phase of building socialism and was in "the transition to communism." Moreover, in a new party program adopted in 1961, Nikita Sergeevich abandoned earlier Soviet rhetoric about class struggle and the dictatorship of the proletariat and called for collaborative efforts to create a "state of all the people." He espoused greater involvement of citizens in public life and a concomitant reduction of the state's role. He harangued individuals throughout the country to work harder and to participate in grassroots efforts to improve the economy and social life. In addition, Khrushchev sought to broaden citizen participation in local and district Soviets, and he established "comradely courts," in which fellow citizens judged minor offenders against public propriety and social order. At the same time he strengthened the party's role in running the country and suppressed criticism of the party and of himself.

Juxtaposed to the record of improving the conditions of Soviet citizens' lives, however, Khrushchev increased Russian domination over non-Russian groups in the Soviet Union. He also cracked down on organized religions, forcing the closure of many churches and harassing clergy, bishops, and ordinary believers. Finally, Nikita Sergeevich did nothing to halt the continuing environmental degradation of the USSR that had begun in Stalinist times.

What had seemed in the late 1950s like a positive prognosis of socioeconomic development and an improving quality of life had considerably dimmed four or five years later. Moreover, in the early 1960s Khrushchev introduced a major revamping of the Communist Party structure, including term limits for holders of most party posts. The organizational changes in the party and earlier in the economy ruptured longstanding patron-client relationships and threatened the careers of many top bureaucrats and party leaders. Unaware of the increasing resentment of his associates and laboring under the burden of continuing economic problems at home and clear defeats abroad, Khrushchev found himself in October 1964 ousted from power in much the same fashion he had won it. A colleague, Leonid Brezhnev, rallied a majority of top party leaders against Khrushchev and then blocked his efforts to appeal to the party's Central Committee. Khrushchev was retired to a comfortable apartment in Moscow and a villa just outside the city, while his erstwhile comrades denounced him for reckless experimentation, attempting to establish a new "cult of personality," and "harebrained scheming."

In his almost ten years as dominant leader of the USSR Khrushchev implemented de-Stalinization, largely successfully; experimented brashly, with limited results; and created for the outside world a new image of the Soviet Union as a dynamic society. Yet, much like the nineteenth-century tsars, Khrushchev had tinkered with the system rather than changing fundamentally its structure or principles. The Soviet Union was still a bureaucratic, authoritarian state dominated by one party that was in turn run by a handful of top leaders. Probably Khrushchev could not have gone further without endangering the party's monopoly of power. He had made unlikely a return to Stalinism, but he had not launched a more creative and responsive system. Yet his efforts helped inspire Gorbachev and the reformers of the 1980s.

BUREAUCRATIC STABILITY
UNDER BREZHNEV AND HIS SUCCESSORS

The succession to Khrushchev proceeded smoothly, despite the predictions of some outside social scientists that in a system that concentrated authority at the very top a change of leaders was bound to result in intense political struggle and perhaps violence. Leonid Brezhnev (see Figure 20), who dominated Soviet politics for almost twenty years, from 1964 to 1982, was a workers' son who had become an engineer. He rose through the ranks of the party as a protégé of Khrushchev, serving in supervisory positions in industry, in agriculture, and, during the war, in the army. Stolid and cautious, he used his bureaucratic experience and his ties in the party to bolster his position. He pursued moderate, low-key policies and was careful not to rock the boat. For the first decade after Khrushchev's ouster Brezhnev had to maneuver among potential rivals, emphasizing the collective nature of the party's rule and playing the role of first among equals. After 1975, he openly became the sole leader and even permitted a minicult of personality to grow up around him.

At first Brezhnev and his colleagues largely continued Khrushchev's policies, although they dismantled some of his organizational experiments and ended his antireligious campaign. Under pressure from the armed forces, they soon began a major buildup of Soviet military capabilities, both in conventional weapons and in nuclear missiles and submarines. This pro-

Figure 20.   *Leonid Brezhnev, Soviet leader, 1966–82, with then Soviet foreign minister, Andrei Gromyko. (Courtesy of United Nations/Tass)*

gram created a further strain on the Soviet economy, and Brezhnev wrestled unsuccessfully with the problems of increasing Soviet productivity and arresting the decline in the rate of Soviet economic growth, which dropped from 8 to 10 percent in the 1950s to 3 to 4 percent in the 1970s. Brezhnev struggled, also in vain, with the deficiencies of Soviet agriculture.

Early gains in the populace's standard of living leveled off by the mid-1970s, and Soviet citizens grew increasingly disillusioned about the party's promises of a glorious socialist future. Goods shortages and inadequate consumer services were the rule. In an effort to make daily life more tolerable, almost everyone had to participate in the so-called second economy, semilegal activities that the regime winked at: moonlighting in private jobs, pinching state equipment and supplies, buying and selling on the black market, and bribing storekeepers and headwaiters to obtain scarce items and restaurant seats. Having to resort to these measures irked Soviet citizens and made them cynical about the regime and party. Nevertheless, the majority of the populace tacitly assented to an unwritten "social contract" with the regime: the government would guarantee them an orderly, stable society; lifetime employment at which they did not have to work too hard; and a reasonable standard of living. In return, the people would accept authoritarian, oligarchic rule and not press for social, economic, or political freedom.

Brezhnev abandoned his predecessor's promises about the transition to communism, arguing instead that the Soviet Union had reached a stage of "developed socialism." Never entirely clear about what this entailed, the new Soviet leader seemed to have in mind a more efficient, technologically advanced, productive society. In 1977 Brezhnev proudly superintended ratification of a new Soviet constitution. The document made only minor changes in Stalin's 1936 Constitution, updating and clarifying some legal provisions and reaffirming the leading role of the party in the Soviet state.

Brezhnev and his colleagues managed to calm the political waters roiled up by Khrushchev's slapdash reorganizations and twists of policy. They slowed the pace of de-Stalinization while vetoing efforts to rehabilitate the tarnished dictator. They also proclaimed a new approach in party life, dubbed "trust in cadres," that is, reliance on the ability and wisdom of party leaders and stalwarts. The change produced political stability but also encouraged dealmaking among party, government, and economic officials at the local level. In addition, some regional party leaders became petty despots and slid into favoritism and corruption. Party officials' privileges in pay, housing, special stores, vacation retreats, and elite schools evoked widespread resentment among the population. Citizens also bridled under the regime's bureaucratic, almost arrogant indifference to popular needs and aspirations.

DÉTENTE AND ITS EROSION

Brezhnev and his colleagues generally supported Khrushchev's inclination after the Cuban missile crisis to seek closer relations with the West. Surprisingly, U.S. intervention against the Communist revolution in Vietnam did not block closer U.S.-Soviet relations, though it certainly strained the ties between the two countries at times. After World War II an indigenous revolutionary movement led by the Communist Ho Chi Minh had sprung up in Indochina, which the French had colonized in the nineteenth century and which the Japanese had occupied in 1941. Both nationalists and Communists fought against reestablishment of French rule, in a broadly based movement that the Soviet government encouraged but aided directly only slightly. In 1954 the Soviet Union and the Western powers agreed to establish the independent states of Laos and Cambodia in part of Indochina and to partition the remainder, called Vietnam, into a northern Communist-dominated zone and a southern anti-Communist zone. At the end of the 1950s the United States gradually assumed the responsibility of assisting South Vietnam in the civil war that it was waging against Communist insurgents who received extensive assistance from North Vietnam. This commitment led finally to massive American armed intervention in Vietnam. Since North Vietnam was an ally of the Soviet Union and South Vietnam was an ally of the United States, there was. always the risk that Soviet support of Ho Chi Minh and his forces would severely damage Soviet-American relations. During the course of the war, however, both the Soviet and American governments, although highly critical of each other's stance in the Vietnam struggle, tried to minimize the deleterious impact of the war on their political relationship. Washington played down Soviet aid to the North Vietnamese, and Moscow conveniently overlooked the American military assault on its Indochinese ally.

In the summer of 1968, however, peaceful coexistence and Soviet foreign policy in general suffered a serious setback when a new crisis erupted inside the socialist camp. A group of Communist reformers in Czechoslovakia led by Alexander Dubcek had begun during the preceding six months to introduce changes designed to "humanize" Czechoslovak socialism. The reforms were almost entirely related to internal party affairs and domestic policies, and Dubcek and his followers were careful to stress that they had no intention of altering Czechoslovakia's adherence to the Warsaw Pact or its close alliance with the Soviet Union. Why these assurances failed to satisfy the Soviet leaders is not entirely clear. The most likely explanation is that they feared not only how far the Czechoslovak reformers might go and what impact this might have within the Soviet Union but also the possibility of growing pro-West German sentiment in the Czechoslovak party.

In any case the Red Army, supported by other Eastern European forces (but not Romania), invaded and occupied Czechoslovakia in August 1968. Unable to resist, the Czechoslovaks soon found themselves back under a Communist government run by pro-Soviet hard-liners. Yugoslavian and Italian Communist leaders protested the brutal repression of independent socialism in Czechoslovakia, as did Western statesmen, but Soviet leader Brezhnev was unfazed, announcing instead that the Soviet Union had the obligation to interfere in the affairs of Communist societies that appeared to be "damaging either socialism in their own countries or the fundamental interests of the other socialist countries," a precept subsequently known as the Brezhnev doctrine. The armed intervention in Czechoslovakia seriously harmed Soviet prestige worldwide and set back the evolving cooperation between the Soviet Union and the West after 1963. Brezhnev's repression of the Czechoslovak reformers also ignited protests among Soviet students and intellectuals and strengthened the growing dissident movement in the USSR.

In the early 1970s the Soviet Union embarked on a new phase of coexistence, usually called détente. In international parlance the word means relaxation of tensions, but the Soviet leaders pushed it further in a consistent effort to reach agreements with the United States and the Western European nations on several important issues. The most significant by far was arms control. In the late 1950s and through the 1960s both the United States and the Soviet Union had tacitly agreed to a nuclear stalemate, called by its critics a "balance of terror." Each side made sure that it had enough nuclear weapons that could survive an attack by the other side to permit it to launch a devastating retaliatory strike. The certainty that retaliation would occur prevented, or deterred, the other side from attacking. This strategy of deterrence seemed to work, but it depended on neither side's getting too far ahead of the other in the arms race.

Consequently, in the late 1960s Soviet-American negotiations on arms control had been initiated, but these had been frozen during the frigid Western reaction to the Soviet invasion of Czechoslovakia. In the early 1970s progress was made, and in 1972 Brezhnev and President Richard Nixon signed an agreement banning antiballistic missile systems and a treaty limiting strategic weapons on both sides, the Strategic Arms Limitation Treaty, known as SALT I. To be sure, the treaty mainly structured rather than curbed the arms race, as both the Soviet Union and the United States sought to improve the quality and survivability of their nuclear arsenals. A second agreement, SALT II, was signed in 1979, but it was not ratified, although both countries informally abided by its provisions. From the Soviet point of view pursuit of arms limitation accords had two important advantages. It helped reduce tension between the superpowers and presented the Soviet government as essentially peace-loving and accommodating. Second, it helped retard the Western military buildup and extension of the West's superiority in advanced technology and sophisticated military hardware.

Besides progress on arms control, détente helped produce a provisional settlement of the German question. Finally recognizing the reality of the division of Germany and the determination of the Western powers to remain in Berlin, Soviet leaders agreed in 1970–1971 to a peace treaty with West Germany and to revised arrangements safeguarding the status of West Berlin. These accords paved the way for convocation of a European security conference in Helsinki, Finland, in the summer of 1975. After World War II the Soviet Union and the Western powers had been unable to agree on peace treaties for Germany, Poland, and Czechoslovakia. Therefore, there was no formal recognition or international sanction of the new boundaries that had resulted from the war and the Soviet reorganization of Central Europe afterward (see Map 9). At the Helsinki meeting the Western powers agreed to recognize the sensitive borders between Poland and East Germany and between Poland and the Soviet Union, as well as other boundaries in the region, in exchange for a Soviet promise to increase trade, cultural contacts, and the protection of human rights across all Europe. The Helsinki Accords and the earlier admission to the UN of both

East and West Germany completed the process of legitimizing the postwar order and finally achieved a long-desired Soviet goal of gaining international recognition for the socialist regime in East Germany and for the Soviet position in Eastern Europe.

Although Brezhnev could point by the mid-1970s to a substantial buildup of Soviet military might and to some successes in the USSR's relationship with the West, he ran into difficulties in other parts of the world. Efforts to patch up the Sino-Soviet quarrel ran afoul of the internal radicalization of Chinese politics during Mao's Great Proletarian Cultural Revolution of the late 1960s. In March 1969 armed skirmishes broke out on the Soviet-Chinese border along the Amur River, and both sides threatened sterner action. But by 1970 the crisis cooled, and Brezhnev initiated negotiations with the Chinese. These talks made little progress, however.

In the Middle East Soviet policy encountered a major setback in 1967, when the Soviet Union's client Arab states suffered a humiliating defeat in a renewed war with Israel. The USSR had to bear the heavy cost of replacing the Arabs' huge losses of arms and equipment. Moreover, in 1972 the Egyptian government, anti-Communist in outlook and annoyed by Soviet meddling and dictation, rebuffed Soviet aid and expelled Soviet advisers. Finally, the Soviet Union was excluded from the peace process in the Middle East that resulted in the Egyptian-Israeli peace signed at Camp David in 1979.

From its apogee in the mid-1970s détente rapidly eroded over the next decade. Three major trends drove this deterioration of Soviet-Western relations. Neither side liked the weapons policy of the other despite progress in negotiating SALT II. American strategists, on the one hand, feared growing Soviet preponderance in heavy missiles with large warheads that might be used in a preemptive strike on the United States and objected to Soviet deployment of intermediate-range missiles that could reach targets in both Asia and Europe. Soviet leaders, on the other hand, condemned the placement of American cruise missiles in Europe and the proliferation of warheads on the United States' more accurate missiles. By the early 1980s, although both sides were abiding by the unratified SALT II agreement, the nuclear stalemate was tense and each country was racing to develop more sophisticated weapons.

Second, human rights proved to be a thorny issue in Soviet-Western relations. Efforts by Brezhnev and Nixon in the early 1970s greatly to expand trade between the superpowers foundered on public and congressional criticism of Soviet restrictions on the emigration of dissatisfied Soviet Jews, who wished to leave the USSR for Israel or the West. After the 1976 elections, new president Jimmy Carter pressed the Soviet leaders to end repression of intellectual and religious dissidents and to expand Jewish emigration. Brezhnev sharply rejected these American protests and clearly resented what he considered as U.S. interference in the domestic affairs of the Soviet Union.

Finally, Brezhnev's continuing campaign to extend Soviet influence in the Third World alarmed anti-Communists in Washington and other Western capitals. Although Soviet gains were in fact small, the Red presence in Somalia, Ethiopia, Angola, and Nicaragua sparked calls for stern measures to stem the flood of Communist expansion. In December 1979 the Soviet invasion of Afghanistan crystallized these apprehensions and ruptured détente for the next half decade.

The Soviet leaders blundered into Afghanistan partly because they misperceived the political situation there and partly because they greatly underestimated the grit and will to resist of the Afghan people. Without Soviet assistance, a weak Marxist government had come to power in Afghanistan in 1978. Because of popular opposition to its radical policies, this regime was on the verge of collapse in December 1979. Apparently the Soviet leaders believed—quite erroneously, according to all available evidence—that the Marxist government would be replaced by an anti-Soviet, Islamic regime linked to the United States and China. To preserve "socialism" in Afghanistan and to enhance Soviet security by ensuring a pro-Soviet government on the USSR's southern border, Moscow ordered in the Red Army. The Soviet leaders obviously expected to overcome Afghan resistance and to set up a puppet government in a matter of weeks.

The Afghan people, with a long history of opposition to British and Russian interference in their country and with a fervent dedication to their land and to Islam, fought a bitter, wasting guerrilla struggle for nine years, substantially assisted with arms, supplies, and money from the American and Chinese governments. The Soviet Union finally had more than one hundred thousands troops in Afghanistan, suffered substantial casualties, and bore most of the fiscal costs of the war. The country of Afghanistan was devastated, hundreds of thousands of Afghan citizens were killed, and three to four million Afghans fled to Pakistan and Iran.

The war in Afghanistan tied up a considerable number of Soviet troops and equipment, drained the budget, and was unpopular at home. Although there were some analogies to the futile American effort a decade earlier in Vietnam, there were important differences, among them that Afghanistan lay along the Soviet border, thereby posing a different sort of security problem, and that religion as well as nationalism played a key role in sparking the Afghans' struggle against foreign invaders whom they considered infidels.

Undercut by the Soviet invasion of Afghanistan, détente suffered another blow in 1980 with the accession to office of a new American president, Ronald Reagan, who was committed to an expansive military buildup and to global opposition to what he later called the Soviet "evil empire." Moreover, the crushing in 1981 of an independent Polish worker's movement, Solidarity, further strained Soviet-Western relations. Solidarity, which numbered ten million members, had arisen spontaneously in the summer of 1980 to protest economic inequities and government mismanagement and corruption in Poland. But when Solidarity pressed for political control and threatened one-party socialist rule, Polish General Wojciech Jaruzelski, under pressure from Moscow, declared martial law in December 1981 and banned Solidarity. Western leaders protested vigorously but could do nothing.

Détente collapsed in part because each side conceived the process differently. U.S. leaders and the public believed that it meant not only a relaxation of tensions but positive and trusting cooperation. For their part, Brezhnev and his colleagues never assumed that détente signified a cessation of superpower competition in the world arena. They wanted to reduce tensions where possible and to strike deals of mutual self-interest, but not to abandon their revolutionary prerogative of stirring up trouble for the imperialists wherever they could.

By the time of his death in 1982, Brezhnev's foreign policy lay in shambles. He had achieved nuclear parity with the United States and had used military strength to expand Soviet influence in the Third World, but the breakdown of détente and the war in Afghanistan placed heavy burdens on the Soviet Union. His successors faced a spiraling arms race, a continuing dispute with China, and expensive commitments abroad.

THE CHANGING SOVIET SOCIETY

Brezhnev's continuation of earlier efforts to assert the Soviet Union's rightful place in Europe and the world and his emphasis on political stability masked deep-seated changes in Soviet society during the 1960s, 1970s, and early 1980s. Soviet citizens became increasingly urbanized and more highly educated in that period. Two out of three people now lived in cities, ending the dominance of rural culture and outlooks in Russian and Soviet life. In 1981 over 10 percent of the Soviet population had completed higher education, compared to 1.5 percent in 1959; more than 70 percent had completed secondary school, against 12 percent in 1959. Most people were also more knowledgeable about the outside world and more skeptical about the regime's claims and record.

A generation gap had developed as well. By 1980 those under the age of fifty had only the dimmest memory of World War II, and those under forty-five had no adult experience with Stalinism. An aging leadership shaped by the Stalin era thus ruled a predominantly post-Stalin population. Younger people were increasingly critical of the deceptions, inefficiencies, restrictions, and failed promises of Soviet socialism. They came to believe that the system could do better, that basic changes were needed.

A handful of brave citizens turned their doubts into active opposition to the regime. A few fighters for religious freedom demanded autonomy for churches and congregations and an end to government interference in religion. A small group of intellectuals espoused basic human rights, including freedom of expression and adherence to the law. Writers and artists resorted to *samizdat*, that is, the creation of works that would never receive official approval for publication but that were circulated privately among the intelligentsia. Dissidents published an underground journal, *The Chronicle of Current Events,* and formed committees for the defense of human rights. Prominent scientists like the renowned physicist Andrei Sakharov and authors like Alexander Solzhenitsyn joined the campaign. The dissidents among the intelligentsia, most of whom were atheists, nevertheless supported the religious dissenters. They also came to the defense of Jews who were being denied permission to emigrate (called "refuseniks") and non-Russians who were protesting Moscow's suppression of the autonomy and cultural integrity of ethnic minorities in the USSR.

Brezhnev and his colleagues treated the dissidents harshly, expelling them from their jobs and housing, imprisoning them, forcing them into exile abroad, and, horribly, confining them in mental hospitals. Solzhenitsyn was only one of many talented writers, musicians, ballet stars, and other artists who were forced out of the country. Sakharov was confined to the provincial city of Gorky (now called by its traditional name, Nizhnii-Novgorod) to cut off his contacts with Western scientists and journalists.

The dissidents, who never numbered more than a few thousand people, had little influence on the mass of their fellow citizens and irritated rather than threatened the regime. Yet they sparked worldwide concern over human rights abuses in the USSR, served as a conscience for educated Soviet citizens, and kept alive the hope that alternatives to Soviet socialism might one day emerge among the Soviet peoples.

Apart from the dissident movement, a growing number of Soviet citizens rallied around the cause of environmentalism during the Brezhnev era. Russian and Soviet industrialization from the 1880s into the 1960s had polluted the country's air and water, exploited and wasted natural resources, and seriously degraded the environment in the Soviet Union. The regime suppressed information about environmental problems and covered up two major accidents resulting from production of nuclear and biological weapons in the 1950s and 1960s. The government was unable, however, to stop the growth of a spontaneous citizens' movement formed in the 1960s to end the pollution of Lake Baikal in Siberia, the deepest lake in the world and the habitat of unique plants and fish. Other groups took up different environmental issues, sometimes with success, as when strong opposition forced the government to drop a plan to divert Siberian rivers to Central Asia. Citizens' associations also formed in pursuit of other interests such as historical preservation and the revival of non-Russian traditional cultures. Moreover, the government itself relied from time to time on studies prepared by technical and other specialists in the intellectual community. Individuals involved in informal associations or specialized task forces frequently turned into strong supporters of reform in the Gorbachev era.

During the Brezhnev era more citizens became aware that Soviet society suffered from major social problems, which the regime ignored or swept under the rug. Alcoholism pervaded Soviet life. Those under the influence of alcohol committed a majority of crimes, including rape, assault, and robbery, and the crime rate was rising. Heavy drinking also fostered wife and child abuse and became the single most-cited reason for divorce. Drunkenness led to substantial absenteeism and to poor performance and accidents on the job. Although alcoholism had been a problem in tsarist times as well, Soviet authorities refused to recognize it as a disease. Moreover, because state revenues depended in part on the sale of vodka, the regime made no effort to curtail supplies. Although the Soviet government concealed most of the relevant data, such crimes as theft of state property and juvenile delinquency rose sharply. Poverty existed, with perhaps as much as 20 percent of the population having inadequate housing, food, and clothing.

Under Brezhnev public health declined, and the health care system, which the regime consistently under funded, fell behind its Western counterparts. Life expectancy for men dropped, and the infant mortality rate climbed. Except in a few specialized fields. Soviet medical techniques and facilities became increasingly outdated.

Rising divorce rates in these years had a direct connection to the shifting status of women, who shared in the social and attitudinal changes under Brezhnev. Making up 54 percent of the population at the end of the 1970s, many women benefited from the higher levels of education and the somewhat improved standard of living since Stalin's death. In addition, women increasingly made independent choices about marriage, divorce, family size, and career path. Yet because of inadequate sex education and the shortage and poor quality of birth-control devices, many Soviet women had four to six abortions, and some as many as a dozen.

In the 1980s almost 100 percent of non-Asian Soviet women of working age were either studying or held jobs, compared to about 75 percent in 1939. Women predominated in education, retailing, agriculture, and health care, but these careers paid little and had low status. Moreover, women seldom held the top posts, and overall they earned only 73 percent of the average male wage. Women were also poorly represented at the highest levels of the party and government, with only 4 percent of Central Committee members women and no female ministers in the Soviet cabinet.

Finally, women continued to carry a heavy double burden, that is, combining full-time employment with up to thirty hours a week of domestic responsibilities, including shopping, cooking, cleaning, washing, and caring for children. Although women made some progress, Soviet society remained largely patriarchal in many ways, and the full equality promised by the socialist vision of 1917 remained out of reach.

The Brezhnev years saw a marked shift in the composition of the Soviet population as the proportion of Slavs declined while the percentage of Central Asians climbed from 6 to 10 percent between 1959 and 1979. Moreover, projections showed that by the twenty-first century one-third of youngsters entering the work force and the army would be non-Russians, many of whom would speak Russian poorly. Party leaders' fears that such a shift would erode the Russians' domination of political and economic life prompted the Brezhnev regime to adopt pro-natalist policies, encouraging the Slavs to have large families.

Although Brezhnev promised ethnic groups a continuation of Leninist policies that respected minority cultures, nationalism flourished among non-Russians as they became better educated and more urbanized along with the rest of the population. Study of indigenous language and literature expanded, and groups to advance local culture were established. Non-Russian intellectuals and elites increasingly resented Russian domination of the central institutions of the party and government and protested what they viewed as Moscow's economic exploitation of the local regions.

When Brezhnev died in 1982, Yuri Andropov, reputedly the ablest member of the ruling Politburo, succeeded him. Although Andropov espoused greater efficiency and labor discipline and tentatively put forth some economic reforms, his poor health and early death in 1984 prevented him from making any substantial impact. Andropov's successor, Konstantin Chernenko, a nonentity in his mid-seventies, was clearly a transitional figure. He was in power only a little over a year, dying in early 1985. Chernenko cautiously continued the policies of the Brezhnev years, introducing no innovations or reforms.

Mikhail Gorbachev, who succeeded Chernenko, represented a different generation and soon began to develop a sweeping set of radical reforms for the Soviet system.

CONCLUSION

Brezhnev and his immediate successors did little to build upon the modest changes in the Soviet system initiated by Khrushchev or to renew Nikita Sergeevich's failed efforts to rejuvenate the economy and society. Instead, they opted for political continuity and for the expansion of Soviet military power. But by the early 1980s, the Soviet Union faced a series of crises abroad and a stagnant economy and a cynical, apathetic citizenry at home. Yet long-term subsurface changes in society and the patent inability of the aging leadership to keep up with the rapidly advancing nations of Europe and Asia prepared the ground for a major upheaval in what deceivingly appeared to be a placid and stable society. The stage was set for Mikhail Gorbachev.

FURTHER READING

Bialer, Seweryn, ed. *Stalin's Successors: Leadership, Stability, and Change in the Soviet Union.* New York: 1981.

Boym, Svetlana. *Common Places: Mythologies of Everday Life in Russia.* Cambridge, Mass.: 1994.

Breslauer, George. *Khrushchev and Brezhnev as Leaders*. Boston: 1982.

Brzezinski, Z. *The Soviet Bloc: Unity and Conflict*. New York: 1960.

Cohen, Stephen, Alexander Rabinowitch, and Robert Sharlet, eds. *The Soviet Union Since Stalin*. Bloomington, Ind.: 1980.

Edmonds, Robin. *Soviet Foreign Policy: The Brezhnev Years*. New York: 1984.

Ellis, Jane. *The Russian Orthodox Church: A Contemporary History*. Bloomington, Ind.: 1986.

Fursenko, Aleksandr, and Timothy Naftali. *One Hell of a Gamble: The Secret History of the Cuban Missile Crisis*. New York: 1997.

Garthoff, Raymond. *Détente and Confrontation: American-Soviet Relations from Nixon to Reagan*. Washington, D.C.: 1985.

Holloway, David. *The Soviet Union and the Arms Race*. New Haven, Conn.: 1983.

Kagarlitsky, Boris. *The Thinking Reed: Intellectuals and the Soviet State, 1917 to the Present*. New York: 1990.

Khrushchev, Nikita. *Khrushchev Remembers* (2 vols.). Boston: 1970, 1974.

Lapidus, Gail. *State and Society in the Soviet Union*. Boulder, Colo.: 1990.

Mastny, Vojtech. *The Cold War and Soviet Insecurity: The Stalin Years*. New York: 1996.

McCauley, Martin, ed. *Khrushchev and Khrushchevism*. Bloomington, Ind.: 1987.

Rubinstein, A. *Soviet Foreign Policy Since World War II*. Boston: 1981.

Shulman, Marshal. *Stalin's Foreign Policy Reappraised*. New York: 1965.

Smith, Hedrick. *The Russians*. New York: 1983.

Tompson, William J. *Khrushchev: A Political Life*. New York: 1996.

Valenta, Jiri. *Soviet Intervention in Czechoslovakia, 1968*. Baltimore: 1979.

Zinner, Paul. *Revolution in Hungary*. Cambridge, Mass.: 1961.

14

The Gorbachev "Revolution" and the Collapse of the Soviet Union, 1983–1991

During most of the day and evening of January 12, 1991, arguments, scuffles, and demonstrations had swirled around the parliament building in Vilnius, the capital of Lithuania. Lithuanian nationalists confronted supporters of a newly formed "national salvation committee," who were calling for dismissal of the Lithuanian parliament and institution of emergency rule by Soviet president Mikhail Gorbachev. Lithuanian radio and television stations broadcast news and commentary backing the defenders of Lithuanian rights. At about 2 A.M. on January 13, reporters heard shots from the area around the main television transmission tower. Units from the local Red Army garrison were storming the tower. To overcome the token resistance of local guards and a handful of Lithuanian nationalists, the Soviet forces used tanks and machine-gun fire. Fourteen people were killed—shot, beaten, or crushed under tank treads.

Only ten months earlier the Lithuanians had asserted their right to independence and proclaimed their intention to withdraw from the Soviet Union. Conservative opponents of Mikhail Gorbachev viewed this Lithuanian act of defiance as symbolic of the political and moral disintegration of the nation caused by the reforms that the new Soviet leader had introduced upon coming to power in 1985. They determined to stop the Lithuanians at any cost. In the months preceding the January violence, elements from the army, the secret police, and the former Lithuanian Communist party had harassed Lithuanian draft evaders, seized various public buildings and presses, and sent tanks rumbling by the Lithuanian parliament building as part of military "exercises." None of these activities had deterred the Lithuanians, and the killings at the TV tower only intensified their struggle for freedom from Soviet domination.

On January 13 and for days after, thousands of pro-independence Lithuanians rallied around the parliament building, erecting makeshift barricades. Others created a shrine near the television tower, to which hundreds brought flowers daily. Moscow authorities, including Gorbachev, insisted that the local Red Army commander had acted on his own and that they had known nothing about the attack until afterward. Reformers doubted this account and protested the violence. Although an uneasy calm prevailed in Lithuania the rest of the winter and Lithuanian and Soviet authorities renewed negotiations on the Baltic state's transition to independence, many observers concluded that the bloody January night in Vilnius symbolized the basic dilemma of the Gorbachev era: how to transform Soviet socialism without breaking up the USSR and without precipitating civil conflict between reformers and conservatives. This chapter recounts Gorbachev's unsuccessful efforts to solve that dilemma.

THE ORIGINS OF THE GORBACHEV REFORMS

Mikhail Sergeevich Gorbachev seemed an unlikely politician to shake up the Soviet system. A party worker his entire life, he had ascended into the circle of the Communist elite by the late 1970s and faithfully served Brezhnev, Andropov, and Chernenko in turn. His colleagues on the Politburo chose him party leader in March 1985 partly for his dynamism and partly because his rivals for the post were mediocrities. Yet his supporters also believed Gorbachev to be a loyal and dedicated Communist, which indeed he was. Several circumstances, however, set Gorbachev apart and soon spurred him on the road to reform. He was younger than the other top leaders. Born in 1930, he had been too young for service in World War II and had missed most of the Stalin era. As a university student, he had shared in the enthusiastic hopes for betterment generated by Khrushchev's halting reform efforts. Thus, Gorbachev represented a new generation tied neither to the patriotic myth of the Great Fatherland War nor to the tired jargon and primitive standards of Stalinism. He and his cohorts wanted to rejuvenate socialism and improve Soviet life.

In addition, Gorbachev, unlike his predecessors, who were engineers and technocrats, had studied law and approached Soviet problems from a broad social and humanitarian perspective. Finally, both Gorbachev and his talented, university-educated wife, Raisa, had become well acquainted with Western ideas and writings as students. In the 1960s they had traveled in Western Europe, observing firsthand the growing disparity between Soviet and Western lifestyles and economies.

In jettisoning the comfortable continuity and safe mediocrity of the Brezhnev era and seeking to modernize and improve Soviet society, Gorbachev (see Figure 21) and his fellow reformers were reacting to profound changes that had taken place within the Soviet population in the four decades since World War II. Most people now enjoyed a relatively sophisticated life in the city, not a brutal existence of isolation and privation in the peasant village and collective farm. People were much better educated than in Stalin's time, and they understood more about the outside world and their own society. They were not so pliable, and many had been chafing under the paternalistic domination and rigid tutelage of a narrow-minded oligarchic leadership and

Figure 21. *Mikhail Gorbachev, General Secretary of the CPSU Central Committee and President of the Presidium of the USSR Supreme Soviet, addresses the UN General Assembly in 1988. (UN photo 172543 by Y. Nagata, courtesy of the United Nations)*

a stultifying bureaucratic party. Some were beginning to want a say in where Soviet society was headed and how it was run. Many were critical of the continuing international tension and the lack of rights at home that accompanied the Brezhnev era. Gorbachev's "revolution" both reflected these changes in Soviet society and was responsive to them.

Gorbachev possessed a general idea of where he wanted to lead the nation, but he certainly did not have a detailed blueprint for reform. He sought a better-off, more efficient, but still socialist society. The new Soviet leader wanted to modify not recast the Soviet system that he inherited.

Gorbachev began by defining problems. As he sought solutions, however, one change led to another. Before he was fully aware of the cumulative impact of the reforms, he had torn apart much of the Soviet socialist edifice and the whole building was tottering. Nevertheless, almost from the beginning Gorbachev recognized that his alterations embraced many aspects of Soviet life and were to some degree interrelated. In 1988 he described his reforms as including:

> not only the economy but all other sides of social life: social relations, the political system, the spiritual and ideological sphere, the style and work methods

of the Party and of all our cadres. Restructuring is a capacious word. I would equate restructuring with revolution . . . a genuine revolution in the minds and hearts of the people.[1]

Gorbachev and his supporters believed in the urgency of sweeping changes in part because they saw clearly how poorly the Soviet system was performing and how rapidly it was being left in the dust by the continually advancing societies of Japan, the United States, and Western Europe. Fundamental changes were necessary to maintain the great power position of the Soviet Union and to protect its security. In analyzing the Soviet system's difficulties, Gorbachev and his supporters focused on three major problems: inefficiency, backwardness, and poor morale. Although these were clearly interrelated, Gorbachev singled each out for special condemnation.

In regard to inefficiency, he faced up to the unpleasant fact that the rate of growth of the Soviet economy had steadily declined since the 1960s and that in the early 1980s it sank to, at best, 2 to 3 percent a year. It was clear, moreover, that the Soviet Union would soon have zero growth. Given the needs of defense and the expanding demands of the Soviet population, this was an unacceptable prospect.

In regard to backwardness, Gorbachev recognized that Soviet technology and techniques were behind the times. Soviet products were costly and shoddy, and the Soviet quality of life was clearly inferior to that of the highly industrialized societies of Japan and the West. Not only was the Soviet Union falling behind its chief competitors; it seemed likely that before long the Soviet Union would sink into the second rank of the world's countries. Gorbachev himself summed up the Soviet Union's bleak circumstances:

Analyzing the situation, we first discovered a slowing economic growth. In the last fifteen years the national income growth rates had declined by more than a half and by the beginning of the eighties had fallen to a level close to economic stagnation. A country that was once quickly closing on the world's advanced nations began to lose one position after another. Moreover, the gap in the efficiency of production, quality of products, scientific and technological development, the production of advanced technology and the use of advanced techniques began to widen, and not to our advantage.[2]

On the issue of poor morale, Gorbachev attacked widespread apathy, sloth, corruption, cynicism, and alienation in Soviet society—a set of attitudes and behavior perhaps best summed up as a collapse of civic virtue:

A gradual erosion of the ideological and moral values of our people began. . . . Eulogizing and servility were encouraged; the needs and opinions of ordinary working people, of the public at large, were ignored. . . .

The presentation of a "problem-free" reality backfired: a breach had formed between word and deed, which bred public passivity and disbelief in the slogans proclaimed. . . . Decay began in public morals. . . .

At some administrative levels there emerged a disrespect for the law and encouragement of eyewash and bribery, servility and glorification.[3]

In Gorbachev's view, all these deficiencies taken together—and he saw them as mutually reinforcing—seriously reduced the military and political power of the Soviet Union in international affairs. Even worse, they made it unlikely that Soviet socialism could achieve the goals Gorbachev believed it should be able to attain. He insisted that a reformed Soviet Union could have a productive, efficient, technologically advanced economy; a rational and relatively humane system; and a peaceful, mutually beneficial relationship with the rest of the world. When these targets were reached, according to Gorbachev, Soviet society would be a shining exemplar of modern socialism and, as such, would soon win over to the socialist cause the majority of other nations. At the same time, Soviet citizens would enjoy a more secure, fruitful, and rewarding life.

EFFORTS TO REJUVENATE THE ECONOMY

Shortly before and immediately after coming to power as the elected general secretary of the Communist party in March 1985, Gorbachev espoused a vague program of change. He urged economic decentralization, more self-government in institutions and society, increased public discussion of vital issues, and greater democracy in the party. He also made clear that he viewed the party as the chief instrument of reform. During his first two years in office, the new Soviet leader appointed a number of reformist advisers, replaced a number of senior and intermediate party leaders, and initiated a few steps to improve economic performance. The last included exhortations to "accelerate" production and to improve efficiency as well as calls to link pay to quality of performance. Mikhail Sergeevich also attacked alcoholism, primarily by restricting the sale of vodka. This effort aroused widespread resentment, did little to ameliorate the problem, and was finally abandoned. In this period Gorbachev also pioneered a new leadership style, mingling with crowds on the street, listening to public complaints, and engaging in spirited exchanges with citizen critics of the existing situation.

When his early measures had little effect, the new Soviet leader called for *perestroika,* or restructuring, in Soviet society. Although the term is often applied to the entire package of Gorbachev's reforms, here we will use it to specify only those measures designed to rejuvenate the economy. Since Stalin's economic revolution of 1928–1929, with its emphasis on centralization and rapid industrialization, the Soviet economy had concentrated on quantity of output as its chief goal and its primary standard of effectiveness. *Perestroika* aimed to replace that criterion with new goals and measures: efficiency, rationality, high quality, and diversity of goods and services. Gorbachev hoped that this shift in goals would lead to a stronger economy that could compete successfully with the leading industrialized nations and provide a much higher standard of living for the Soviet population.

Unfortunately, enthusiastic and superficial accounts in the American media during the early days of restructuring sometimes implied that Gorbachev had abandoned socialism and was urging the wholesale adoption of capitalism. This was not the case. At first Gorbachev insisted that neither central planning of the economy nor state ownership of all major resources and productive capacities—the essentials of socialism—would be changed. By early 1990, however, under the pressures of a faltering economy and widespread popular grumbling, Gorbachev decided to permit private ownership of some enterprises.

Before this radical change of heart Gorbachev had already considerably altered the Soviet economy in a complex set of reforms, of which five key changes will be summarized here. A first area of reform, which had potential long-term benefits, was the effort to decentralize day-to-day economic decision making and to get factories and other individual economic units to be economically self-sufficient and profitable. To oversimplify, the management of each unit was asked to decide for itself what to produce, how to produce it most efficiently and at lowest cost, and where and how to sell it. Each unit was expected to make contracts with other units, including the government, for sales and for acquisition of the machinery and raw materials needed for production. Enterprises could also set wages and hire and fire workers. Each unit would no longer receive financial subsidies from the state and would sink or swim on its own. Most of these changes were embodied in the Law on the State Enterprise, which went into effect on January 1, 1988.

A second area of reform, a corollary to decentralization, was institution of a limited market mechanism through contracts for acquisitions and sales that individual economic units would make. Economic reformers hoped that this change would lead to a rational allocation of goods, a selection of quality products, and a rejection of shoddy merchandise.

Thirdly, the economic changes encouraged jointly owned or cooperative small businesses in services such as restaurants and repair shops and in light industry such as clothing and household articles. Even though these businesses were heavily taxed by the state, remaining profits were divided among the members of the cooperative. Prices the cooperatives charged were not controlled and were consequently considerably higher than state prices for the same goods and services (which, however, were often in short supply or simply unavailable).

A fourth area of economic reform was encouragement of foreign trade and foreign investment in the USSR. Gorbachev hoped both to acquire from abroad needed high-technology products, such as computers and communications equipment, and to upgrade Soviet technology and methods through exposure to more advanced techniques from Japan and the West. The previous state monopoly on foreign trade was broken, and individual economic units were allowed to make their own arrangements with foreign suppliers and purchasers. At the same time the economic reformers invited joint ventures with foreign companies; usually the Soviet government retained at least 51 percent ownership, but in certain cases majority foreign ownership was permitted.

Finally, the reforms included several innovative steps to help the rural economy. The most important was permission given to families or other small groups on a state or collective farm to lease state land and to arrange their agricultural work on the basis of a contract. Thus, they produced food or livestock, a portion of which was sold to the state and the balance of which was sold at free and higher prices on the open market.

During its first few years the results of *perestroika* were mixed at best. Some goods and services of better quality appeared, but the prices were considered too high by many Soviet consumers, and shortages of basic products continued and sometimes worsened. For example, in the fall of 1989 soap powder and detergents were simply not available, even in the two largest cities, Moscow and Leningrad. Soviet economic growth, after a brief spurt, slowed again and by 1989 had not achieved even the levels of the 1970s. Soviet products were not able to compete internationally, and widespread inefficiency and waste continued to characterize the Soviet economy. Moreover, by early 1990 many citizens were highly critical of restructuring. The tangible and quick benefits they had expected had not materialized, and in fact many citizens felt they were worse off than before. This pessimism only exacerbated the economic situation—consumers rushed to hoard scarce items and showed little enthusiasm to work hard, to produce more, and to do a quality job when the rewards in terms of goods and material lifestyle were not apparent.

Although many factors explain the failure of *perestroika*, a few seem primary. First, *perestroika* was only a partial reform. Gorbachev wanted to retain key features of socialism while introducing some capitalist mechanisms. For example, because uncontrolled prices smacked of capitalist exploitation and because higher prices would provoke a strongly negative reaction among a population long accustomed to low, state-subsidized prices, Gorbachev was reluctant to open the market completely and to free most prices. As a result, managers of economic units were trying to make sensible decisions on costs and on profit and loss calculations with prices that were totally unrealistic. Or, to take another example in the same area, Gorbachev and his advisers encouraged units to make their own decisions at the local level but left in place the central economic ministries in Moscow to provide overall plans and guidance. The result was interference from the central planners and ministry managers and inadequate independence and scope for the local managers—in short, a mishmash of a system and, not surprisingly, unsatisfactory results.

A second significant roadblock to the success of the economic reforms was bureaucratic inertia and resistance. Both central planners and local administrators and producers were used to operating in the old ways. They were reluctant to change, and many of them who might lose their positions of power and influence if *perestroika* were to succeed actively opposed the reforms.

Finally, popular attitudes acted to brake restructuring. After years of not working too hard and of enjoying a modest but predictable lifestyle, many Soviet citizens were unwilling to participate actively in the risks of *perestroika*. Doing a good job and working effectively did not seem to promise much of a reward when there was little to buy or do. Moreover, rumors circulated that some might lose their jobs and that higher prices would soon become widespread. Higher and better-quality production depended in part, even under restructuring, on better work habits and different attitudes on the part of Soviet workers at all levels. Yet most people were slow to change, and by 1991 the economic situation was deteriorating and popular dissatisfaction with Gorbachev was mounting.

"NEW THINKING" IN FOREIGN POLICY

Ironically, the area in which Gorbachev's reforms achieved the most, foreign affairs, brought him little credit at home, where Soviet citizens cared more about the worsening condition of their daily lives than diplomatic successes abroad. The Soviet leader's promotion of peace and improved relations with the outside world made him popular in Europe and America but not in the USSR.

When he came to power in 1985, Gorbachev faced a dismal foreign-policy scene. The Soviet Union's powerful position in world affairs was seriously eroding. Bogged down in a wasting war in Afghanistan, deadlocked in a seemingly interminable quarrel with China, burdened with heavy subsidies to prop up Communist economies in North Vietnam and Cuba, and confronted with an increasingly powerful NATO and a nuclear and space arms race with the United States, the Soviet regime was clearly overcommitted and stymied. Mikhail Sergeevich's first concern was to reduce these pressures so that he could concentrate on internal reform. But he also genuinely believed in international cooperation and felt that global peace would benefit everyone. Thus, early in his tenure in office, the new Soviet leader called for fresh approaches and innovative ideas in Soviet foreign policy, a process that he labeled "new thinking." Before long he initiated changes that in the next five years revolutionized Soviet diplomacy and in the process ameliorated international tensions and improved markedly the Soviet Union's image in the world. Gorbachev helped usher in a new era of world history by ending the cold war and shifting the emphasis from the military and ideological struggle between capitalism and socialism to political accommodation and economic and cultural interaction.

Early in his rule Gorbachev changed Soviet national security policy. Beginning near the end of Khrushchev's tenure in office and increasingly in the late 1960s and 1970s under Brezhnev, the Soviet leadership allocated extensive resources to enlarge the USSR's armed forces, both conventional and nuclear. This rearmament forced the nation to spend at least twice as much of gross national product on defense as did the United States, a heavy burden for Soviet citizens and the faltering Soviet economy. The new Soviet leader stopped the military buildup and vigorously advanced arms control proposals. In doing so he argued that Soviet security policy should be based on the idea of "reasonable sufficiency." Though a bit vague, this doctrine seemed to mean that the USSR should maintain only enough armed force to be reasonably sure that it could rebuff any threat to the security of the country. In other words, Gorbachev shifted the emphasis to defense and to limiting the commitments of the Red Army outside Soviet borders.

Implementing this tenet in 1987–1988, he first diplomatically and then militarily disengaged the USSR from Afghanistan, finally bringing home all Soviet forces. After 1988 the Soviet Union supported pro-Communist elements in Afghanistan but did not intervene in the confused political situation there. In addition, the new Soviet leader unilaterally reduced the Soviet armed forces, and by 1988 he had scaled back the Soviet defense budget by several billion rubles. Finally, he cut Soviet military assistance to Vietnam, Ethiopia, Cuba, and Nicaragua and made clear that the USSR was not interested in any new military operations abroad.

The combination of "new thinking" and "reasonable sufficiency" powerfully affected arms control issues between the Soviet Union and the West on three important levels. The first, and most dramatic, result was an agreement signed in December 1987, the Intermediate Nuclear Forces (INF) treaty, to remove from Europe and Asia missiles with a range between 300 and 3,400 miles. Under this pact the Soviet Union eliminated twice as many intermediate-range missiles as the United States did, but both sides kept short-range and battlefield nuclear weapons in Europe. West Germans and other Europeans were nonetheless delighted with the INF agreement because the missiles involved would have landed on them in the event of war between NATO and the Warsaw Pact powers.

A second result was the superpowers' decision in principle in 1988–1989 to cut long-range or strategic nuclear weapons at least 50 percent. Subsequent negotiations resulted in the Strategic Arms Reduction Treaty (START I) embodying this decision. The U.S. Congress and the new states of Russia, Belarus, and Kazakhstan that emerged after the 1991 break-up of the Soviet Union (see Chapter 15) adopted the treaty. Bilateral talks begun in the Gorbachev era resulted in 1992 in a new Russian-American agreement, START II, that further reduced nuclear arms, although the post-Soviet Russian parliament balked at ratifying this follow-on treaty.

A final outcome of the USSR's new security policy emerged in joint efforts among Gorbachev and Western leaders to reduce conventional forces in Europe. These negotiations were well advanced when rejection of socialist rule by the East European nations and dissolution of the Warsaw Pact led to the phased withdrawal of the Red Army from central Europe. Since the 1989 "revolutions" in Eastern Europe belong to the last phase of Gorbachev's rule, we will examine them later in the chapter.

Early in his tenure the new Soviet leader instituted important changes in other areas of Soviet foreign policy, notably the USSR's relations with the Third World, the United Nations, China, and the West. After Stalin's death, Khrushchev and subsequent Soviet leaders had sought to advance socialism in Asia, Africa, and Latin America through arms sales, economic assistance, and support of Marxist-Leninist revolutionary movements. The greatest impact of this endeavor had been to frighten anti-Communists in the West; actual gains for socialism were small. In Cuba, for example, Castro's Communist regime, hobbled by the nation's dependence on a single export, sugar, had mismanaged the economy and required hundreds of millions of dollars annually in Soviet assistance. Similarly, although the Vietnamese socialists had triumphed after a decades-long struggle against the French and then the Americans, their rule had been inefficient, and they, too, depended on massive Soviet aid. A socialist revolution succeeded in Nicaragua in the 1980s, and Marxist governments came to power in Angola and Ethiopia, with Soviet and Cuban assistance, yet these regimes were shaky and the prospects for the advance of socialism elsewhere in the Third World appeared dim indeed in the mid-1980s.

Early in his revaluation of Soviet foreign policy Gorbachev made clear that he was downgrading efforts to export revolution and that he did not expect any immediate victories for socialism in Asia, Africa, and Latin America. Instead of seeking influence or domination, Gorbachev said, the Soviet Union would not interfere in the internal affairs of such countries, it would support their independent foreign policies, and it would do what it could to assist them in development—on their own terms and with no strings attached. Gorbachev expressed hope that Soviet trade with the developing countries would substantially increase, and he forswore any intention of taking sides in regional or local conflicts in the Third World.

Together with this new general approach to the developing countries Gorbachev took specific actions to ease tensions in Asia, Africa, and Latin America. He put pressure on Vietnam to withdraw its troops from Cambodia, which it finally did in late 1989. He cooperated in reaching a settlement designed to end the civil war in Angola and to ensure the independence of Namibia in southern Africa. Finally, he encouraged the revolutionary government of Nicaragua to seek a political rather than a military solution to its struggle against U.S.-backed contra rebels.

At the same time that Gorbachev sought to regularize Soviet relations with Third World states, he initiated a more positive approach to the

United Nations than his predecessors had adopted. He paid up almost all the USSR's obligations to the UN (which left the United States with the dubious distinction of owing more in unpaid obligations to the world organization than any other country) and urged both large and small countries to support more fully both the political and ancillary activities of the UN. In an important speech to the UN on December 7, 1987, Gorbachev called for cooperation on such transnational issues as protection of the environment, management of Third World debts, and exploration of outer space. The Soviet Union also began to participate more fully in various UN agencies and other international organizations.

Before Gorbachev came to power, the Soviet government had begun efforts to improve relations with China, but little progress had been made. Gorbachev intensified the process of accommodation but at first had little success. Chinese leaders insisted that although they were happy to reestablish trade and economic relations with the Soviet Union, close political ties depended on four preconditions: the USSR had to reduce the number of troops and weapons positioned along the Chinese border, progress had to be made on the resolution of long-standing boundary issues, the Soviet Union had to see to it that Vietnam withdrew its troops in Cambodia, and the Red Army had to get out of Afghanistan. By 1989 Gorbachev had managed to fulfill all these conditions, and a major summit meeting was scheduled in Beijing, the Chinese capital, for May 1989. Unfortunately, when Gorbachev arrived, Chinese students and workers were in the midst of noisy public demonstrations and political protests that included occupation of Tiananmen Square (the main square) of Beijing. This made the visit awkward, to say the least, and after Chinese leaders bloodily suppressed the student demonstrations a few weeks later, Gorbachev put the improvement of Sino-Soviet relations on the back burner. After the 1991 collapse of the Soviet Union, Russia quickly established normal relations with Communist China.

Soviet policy in the rest of East Asia in the late 1980s was less successful. Japan remained critical of the Soviet Union, in part on ideological grounds and in part because of the Soviet refusal to return to Japan the Kurile Islands in the north Pacific that Soviet forces occupied at the end of World War II. In Korea Gorbachev urged the reclusive and oppressive socialist regime of North Korea to seek closer relations with South Korea, but this advice was largely ignored.

Some of Gorbachev's greatest successes in applying "new thinking" in foreign policy came in the USSR's relations with Western Europe and the United States. The new Soviet leader determined to reverse the souring of détente that had occurred at the end of the 1970s and in the first half of the 1980s. In the fall of 1985 he held his first summit meeting with Ronald Reagan in Geneva. As Gorbachev hoped, he succeeded in charming the American president and in locking the United States into serious arms control negotiations. Reagan began to support détente, soon agreed to the INF treaty, and endorsed further arms control efforts. A meeting in October 1986 at Reykjavík, Iceland, strengthened the burgeoning cooperation between the superpowers' leaders. After George Bush succeeded Reagan in 1988, Soviet-American relations warmed still further. The new U.S. president signed the START I arms control accords and encouraged greater economic and cultural contacts between the two nations. Moreover, in 1990–1991, Gorbachev threw Soviet support behind the American-organized coalition against Iraq, a former Soviet ally, although the USSR did not contribute troops to the Gulf War that followed. Gorbachev's encouragement of greater freedom of expression and religion within Soviet society and his approval of Jewish emigration largely eliminated the issue of human rights between the two countries and contributed importantly to improving ties between Moscow and Washington.

Europeans were especially enthusiastic in welcoming the new Soviet leader's efforts to cut back arms and to reduce tension. Gorbachev's visits to West European capitals brought forth large crowds chanting, "Gorby, Gorby!" His policies greatly reduced Europeans' fears of Communist aggression and of a possible NATO-Warsaw Pact war in central Europe. For his part, Mikhail Sergeevich called for a future "common European house" stretching from the Atlantic Ocean to the Ural Mountains and espoused substantially increased trade with the more advanced European countries.

GLASNOST'

In reaching out to the rest of the world, Gorbachev strove to be more direct and open and displayed a willingness to listen to the concerns and opinions of others. This stance represented the foreign policy aspect of his domestic policy of *glasnost'*. Although the term is usually translated as "openness," no clear English equivalent exists, and in practice the term has had a more limited connotation. Gorbachev called it "openness in the interests of socialism." During the late 1980s *glasnost'* meant the freedom—in fact the duty—to criticize and to suggest innovations, but *within* certain, if rather vaguely defined, limits. For example, *glasnost'* was not license to condemn Gorbachev, the Communist party as a whole, or the main principles on which the Soviet social and political system operated. What Gorbachev was seeking were fresh ideas, initiative, creativity, originality—all to be applied to solving the country's massive economic and social problems. As a byproduct—one that received much attention in the American press—*glasnost'* supported accountability by encouraging criticism of poor performance, corruption, and "do-nothingness" in the Soviet bureaucracy. *Glasnost'* did not, however, mean complete freedom of the press and of expression in the American sense. Rather, Gorbachev wanted *glasnost'* to serve the positive purpose of encouraging new ideas, stimulating constructive attitudes and action, and raising the morale of the Soviet people as a whole and of the most creative group—scientists, writers, engineers, and other university-educated specialists—in particular.

A frightening disaster at a Soviet nuclear power plant in Chernobyl' in northern Ukraine on April 26, 1986, provided a major stimulus to *glasnost'*. At first government and party officials reacted to the accident in customary Soviet fashion, shrouding the affair in secrecy and displaying incompetence and confusion. Finally, after several weeks Gorbachev acknowledged the seriousness of the meltdown and the resulting radiation, and during the summer of 1986 the Soviet press candidly discussed the Chernobyl' disaster in detail. Moreover, in December 1986 the Soviet leader personally telephoned the noted physicist and dissident Andrei Sakharov to invite him to return to Moscow from KGB-imposed exile in the city of Gorky. Sakharov soon resumed his interrupted career and became an active supporter of democratic reforms until his death in 1990.

Glasnost' had an exhilarating effect on Soviet society in the last half of the 1980s. After sixty years of intellectual repression and conformity, people were astounded and delighted to be able to write and say pretty much what they pleased. Because the outer limits of permissible expression were quite broad, individuals could tackle almost any subject without fear of reprisal. This provided a great psychic lift for the educated elite of the Soviet Union and, as Gorbachev hoped, led to a flood of new ideas and of constructive criticism.

In literature works far removed from the dreary tenets of socialist realism were published, including interesting and revealing fiction and poetry by women writers. Both Soviet and foreign authors had books published that had been banned for many years: for example, Anatoli Rybakov's *Children of the Arbat,* a novel about growing up under Stalinism; Boris Pasternak's *Doctor Zhivago,* a long-prohibited epic of the Russian Revolution; and George Orwell's *Animal Farm,* a satire of the Stalin era.

Radical new themes and approaches emerged in film, theater, and the fine arts. As in literature, both works long suppressed and new pieces appeared. Artists who had painted religious themes and in abstract styles but who had never been able to show such works in public were now honored with exhibitions and brisk sales. Several popular movies attacked aspects of the Stalin era, and plays criticizing the bureaucracy and the problems of daily life were popular.

Newspapers, magazines, and television all expanded and diversified under *glasnost'*. The evening news on television, once the occasion of yawns, was now eagerly watched for the latest revelations. Issues of such radical publications as *Ogonyok* were snapped up at once and passed from hand to hand. In fact, Soviet citizens complained that there was so much fascinating information available in the press that they did not have time to keep up with it all. Social problems such as crime, drugs, prostitution, and deviance that had formerly been treated gingerly if at all were now discussed openly in the media. Even the KGB, the Soviet secret police, invited journalists to visit and to ask questions.

Because under Stalin history had been so greatly distorted and because almost all Soviet citizens knew that what they had been taught about the past did not square with what actually happened, *glasnost'* sparked great interest in revising the historical record. First, existing textbooks and courses in history were scrapped; then, a major commission on historical revision was established. Most historical personages in the Soviet past whom Stalin had purged or had written out of history were rehabilitated (although not Trotsky). Formerly taboo subjects such as the purges, collectivization, and the secret protocol of the Nazi-Soviet pact of 1939 under which Stalin and Hitler divided Poland and Eastern Europe were discussed. Moreover, Western authors whose historical works had previously been heavily criticized and banned were now given a royal welcome, and their books were translated and published in the Soviet Union.

Finally, *glasnost'* stimulated widespread public discourse on a range of topics from political and ethnic issues through social problems such as alcoholism and wife abuse and environmental and ecological questions. In several cases public opposition blocked major projects that critics insisted would have deleterious effects on the environment, such as a plan to divert the waters of some Siberian rivers and an effort to dam the Gulf of Finland near Leningrad. At the same time thousands of public organizations sprang up to advance all sorts of social, recreational, and intellectual concerns. Some organizations were interested in historical preservation, some in enhancing the local environment, and some in health or religious questions. With a few exceptions public meetings and demonstrations were tolerated, including rallies to support the building of a memorial to the victims of Stalin's oppression. Many Orthodox churches reopened, and the number of religious believers increased.

An interesting corollary of *glasnost'* was Gorbachev's decision to reverse his predecessors' policy regarding emigration from the Soviet Union. Earlier, Jews and others who wanted to leave had innumerable obstacles to overcome, but by 1988 Gorbachev had moved to a policy of virtually free emigration, and in 1989 some seventy thousand Jews left for Israel and the United States. This reflected greater openness and removed a major sore point in American-Soviet relations.

DEMOCRATIZATION

Like *perestroika* and *glasnost'*, this term can be misleading. Just as restructuring did not mean total rejection of socialism nor did openness signify complete freedom of expression, so democratization did not mean a fully representative and democratic system. Nevertheless, the new Soviet leader introduced substantial changes in the Soviet political system and paved the way for adoption in early 1990 of a multiparty system. Gorbachev clearly had two chief goals in mind that he hoped democratization would accomplish. First, he wanted to use this set of reforms as a weapon against entrenched officialdom, whether in the party or the government. He saw democratization as a way of getting rid of bureaucrats who had old-fashioned ideas, who were corrupt, or who opposed his reform program. Second, he hoped democratization would unlock popular energies and initiatives and give people a stake in the system. He wanted to stimulate citizen participation in the new course he was setting and to provide individuals with a renewed sense of purpose and direction, attitudes that Stalin had squelched and that had been missing from Soviet society since the heady early days of revolution and the establishment of Soviet power against great odds. But at first Gorbachev retained and stoutly defended the basic Leninist concepts of one-party rule and of the party leadership providing guidance and direction for the citizenry as a whole.

When Gorbachev introduced democratization, he proposed that citizens play a more active role in existing governmental and social organizations. He urged people to demand an accounting from officials, and he contended that directors, managers, and other executives should be elected rather than appointed. In addition to this pressure from below, the Soviet leader acted from above in the traditional way, ousting large numbers of old-line bureaucrats. In his first four years in office he fired, retired, or transferred more than one-half the senior officials in the party and government. Nevertheless, opponents of reform remained in the secret police and the armed forces, and many bureaucrats of the old stripe still existed at middle and lower levels of the administration.

To accelerate democratization, Gorbachev called a special party conference in late June 1988. Over stiff opposition, he pushed through adoption of political reforms in both the party and the government. These changes encouraged (but did not require) multicandidate elections and called for voting to new, representative governmental bodies at all levels. After the Soviet constitution had been amended to reflect the new arrangements, elections were held throughout the USSR in March 1989 to choose two-thirds of the members of Congresses of People's Deputies for the Soviet Union and for each of its republics. The remaining one-third of the deputies were appointed by various organizations, including the Communist party, trade unions, and scientific groups. The national Congress of 2,200 representatives in turn elected a Supreme Soviet of almost five hundred deputies. Later changes eliminated Congresses of People's Deputies except for a congress in Russia and one at the national level.

The elections were freely conducted and occasioned lively public interest and debate. Almost 90 percent of the electorate voted, and in three-quarters of the races they had more than one candidate to choose from (unlike the old-style single-candidate Soviet elections). To the party's chagrin the voters rejected some of its senior leaders, reflecting a popular mandate for change. Still, 87 percent of those elected to the national Congress of People's Deputies were Communists, and 65 percent were party or government officials.

During this period of political reform Gorbachev had continued to insist on the dominant role of the Communist party. During 1988 and 1989, however, the position and prestige of the party rapidly declined. Critics, both within and without the party, strongly attacked its monopoly of political power (enshrined in Article 6 of the Soviet constitution) not only in the media but in debates at the fall 1989 session of the new Supreme Soviet. Scandals of corruption and abuse of authority on the part of prominent party officials were aired in various regions of the country. Dissident party units in the Baltic region declared adoption of multiparty systems in their republics. Confronted with these pressures and with increasingly strident protests against party domination of the reform process, and perhaps discouraged by the ineptness, conservatism, and insensitivity of many upper-level and district party officials, Gorbachev apparently decided in early 1990 to sacrifice the party's unique role in order to try to save the system and the country. He proposed abrogation of Article 6 and toleration of parties other than the Communists, a recommendation that the chief policy-making body of the party, the Central Committee, adopted after intense debate.

GORBACHEV'S DOWNFALL

Although the new Supreme Soviet elected Gorbachev its head, making him president of the USSR, the Soviet leader began to lose ground politically in 1989. Several factors contributed to Mikhail Sergeevich's eclipse and to the disintegration of the Soviet Union. Democratization unleashed political forces that Gorbachev could not control and that increasingly isolated him. Democratic reformers objected to his presidency on the grounds that the new president should be picked in a popular election, not by a limited parliament. They also attacked his ties to the party and to the old guard and insisted that full democracy be instituted. In addition, radical economic reformers castigated the president for hesitancy in moving to privatize the economy and establish a full, free-market system. The most prominent and popular leader of the democratic opposition was Boris Yeltsin, a senior party leader from Sverdlovsk in the Ural Mountains who had rebelled against the central party leadership in the fall of 1987 and who resigned from the party in 1990. A self-declared populist, Yeltsin railed against party privileges and demanded improvements in the average citizen's lot. In popular elections in the spring of 1991, voters chose him as president of the Russian Republic.

At the other end of the political spectrum, party stalwarts, military and police chiefs, Marxist ideologues, Russian nationalists, and conservative bureaucrats chastised Gorbachev for selling out socialism at home and abroad and for undermining the values and institutions that had made the Soviet system powerful and cohesive. As early as March 1988 a letter from a Leningrad educator, Nina Andreeva, which summed up conservative criticism of the Gorbachev reforms, was published in the party press and widely discussed. In response to pressures from both right and left, Gorbachev temporized, sometimes seeming to endorse further reform, sometimes siding with the old guard. Walking a political tightrope, he was unable to find broad centrist support as articulate members of Soviet society became increasingly polarized and as the bulk of the population grew disgusted with the quarreling of the politicians and outraged about their own deteriorating standard of living.

Indeed, the failure of his economic program doomed Gorbachev's efforts to construct a political consensus. According to Western critics of *perestroika*, the Soviet leader made several cardinal errors. Unlike the Chinese economic reforms of the 1980s, which began with agriculture, Gorbachev's proposals left institutional and market arrangements on the farms unchanged. As a good Communist, he did not want to abandon collectivization entirely and shift to private landownership and production. Moreover, Mikhail Sergeevich also resisted all-out privatization of industry and the complete freeing of prices, measures essential to a full conversion to a market system. As a result, under the halfway measures of *perestroika*, confusion reigned; production lagged; the new semimarket worked only fitfully; agricultural output declined; and consumers faced shortages, long lines, and higher prices. Beginning in 1989, miners and other key workers launched a series of strikes and formed independent trade unions. Public complaints about the collapsing economy mushroomed, and the Russian leader's popularity plummeted even as he was being lionized abroad.

Moreover, Gorbachev made little headway in changing the long-ingrained attitudes and behavior of many citizens. Clinging to the egalitarian values of the revolutionary past, they resented that some individuals, viewed as profiteers, benefited financially from *perestroika* and that substantial differences in income and lifestyles between the average citizen and these immediate beneficiaries of reform had emerged. The outlook of many people was not to keep up with the Ivanovs but to make sure that the Ivanovs did not get ahead of them. Few responded to Mikhail Sergeevich's calls for hard work, quality output, and a willingness to sacrifice and to participate. Most citizens preferred the old Brezhnevian "contract" of a guaranteed living and halfhearted work in return for social and political docility.

The revelations of *glasnost'* also undercut Gorbachev's "revolution." As people learned how past Soviet regimes had distorted history, repressed the citizenry, stifled creativity, and consistently lied to everyone, indignation and disgust mounted. Many citizens questioned the legitimacy not only of the government but, more importantly, of the party, Marxism-Leninism, and even the 1917 Revolution. Socialism was discredited, and the values that had upheld the system for seventy years were shown to be false and baleful. Some citizens looked nostalgically to the Orthodox religion or to tsarist times and mores, while many young people uncritically adulated Western customs and culture. Most individuals felt profoundly disillusioned and disoriented and were unsure where to turn. Gorbachev, tainted by his party tie and damned by his economic failures, fell completely out of popular favor.

Developments in Eastern Europe and on the periphery of the USSR sounded the death knell for Gorbachev's vision of reform. In Poland the Communist government installed after the suppression of Solidarity in 1981 had failed to undertake significant social and political reforms. Moreover, the Polish economy floundered, and the populace remained sullen and uncooperative. Harassed by widespread strikes in 1988, the government agreed with representatives of the original Solidarity leadership, including Lech Walesa, and with other opposition groups to hold semifree elections in the spring of 1989. The Communists fared poorly, and a new coalition government headed by Solidarity promised democratic reforms and installation of a market economy.

In response to these developments in Poland, Gorbachev reiterated his assertion on coming to power four years earlier that the East European socialist states must find their own solutions to domestic problems. He also made clear that the Soviet Union would not attempt to impose its reform policies on other systems and that despite the Brezhnev doctrine (discussed in Chapter 13), he would not interfere with or try to influence the changes taking place in Poland. Reassured by this commitment to nonintervention, Polish reformers abandoned socialism in the fall of 1989 and embarked on the road to a privatized economy and a representative political system.

The other states of Eastern Europe soon followed Poland's example. In November 1989 the conservative and seemingly solidly entrenched socialist regime in East Germany collapsed in the face of mass public protests in major East German cities and of the flight to the West of tens of thousands of East German citizens. The Berlin Wall, a symbol of the division of Europe between socialist and nonsocialist countries, was dismantled, and free passage between East Germany and West Germany was permitted for the first time since 1948. During 1990 and 1991 Germany was reunified under predominantly West German leadership. Socialism was forsaken, the new state adopted a democratic and free-market system, and the Western allies admitted the unified German nation to NATO. In Czechoslovakia relatively small public demonstrations led by students in December 1989 forced the resignation of the Communist government. By early 1990 Czechoslovakia, too, had rejected socialism, and Hungary and Bulgaria soon followed. Only in Romania did the collapse of socialism lead to violence. Several days' fighting and some casualties accompanied a popular revolution against the repressive regime headed by Nicolai Ceausescu.

Gorbachev acquiesced in these East European "revolutions," recognizing that he could do little to block them. Under pressure from the new non-socialist governments, he dissolved the Warsaw Pact and initiated the phased withdrawal of all Soviet troops from Eastern Europe. Although Western leaders and public opinion welcomed these developments and praised Gorbachev for his statesmanship and commitment to peace, conservative critics in the USSR were outraged at what they considered the craven surrender of the Soviet domination of Eastern Europe. They argued that accepting the downfall of socialism there gravely threatened Soviet security interests and would permit the encroachment of Western influence and pressure hundred of miles eastward, to the USSR's own borders. Gorbachev attempted to appease such opponents by softening his domestic reform program, but this effort only further undercut his already precarious political position.

Last, and perhaps most significantly, rising nationalism among the non-Russian groups living around the circumference of the country brought the political turmoil in the Soviet Union to a boil and led directly to Gorbachev's downfall. As early as 1986 violent anti-Russian riots had erupted in Kazakhstan. The next year serious ethnic tensions developed in the Caucasus between Armenians and Azerbaijanis over control of a region, Nagorno-Karabakh, inhabited predominantly by Armenians but located in the Republic of Azerbaijan. Troubles also arose in the Baltic area. By the summer of 1989 the Lithuanians, Latvians, and Estonians were demanding full economic independence, with the aim of secession from the Soviet Union clearly the goal of more radical elements among them. Even in the Ukrainian Republic, the second largest in the Soviet Union, some of its inhabitants, although Slavs closely related to the dominant Great Russian population, began to press for greater autonomy and self-determination on the basis of their separate history prior to 1649 and their somewhat different cultural and intellectual traditions.

These nationalist fissures greatly complicated Gorbachev's reform efforts, and in his first four years in office he was unable to develop any program or formula to satisfy the complaints of the non-Russian groups. In addition to their historic, religious, and cultural separateness, many non-Russian nationalities resented what they believed was Great Russian economic exploitation of their territory, and they opposed what they saw as Russian social and political domination of their lives. They took advantage of *glasnost'* and democratization to express their grievances and to assert political and economic autonomy. Gorbachev's reluctance to recognize their claims only heightened their determination to throw off Moscow's yoke.

In the fall of 1988 the Lithuanians formed a nationalist popular front called Sajudis. Soon similar movements sprang up in Latvia, Estonia, Georgia, and Moldavia. As nationalist sentiment mounted, local Communist leaders, in an effort to hang on to their influence, cooperated with, or even joined these fronts, and in December 1989 the Lithuanian Communist party declared its independence from central party headquarters in Moscow. The republican Supreme Soviet of Lithuania declared in March 1990 its intention to seek independence for the nation, and as we saw at the start of this chapter, the reactionary attempt to suppress Lithuanian nationalists in Vilnius in January 1991 only intensified the drive for a complete break from Moscow.

Similarly, police brutality against Georgian nationalists in April 1989 stimulated formation of a Georgian independence movement, the Round Table for a Free Georgia. In the elections of October 1990 the Round Table won 54 percent of the vote. In March 1991 Georgians declared that they would seek independence and elected the nationalist Zviad Gamsakhurdia president. Lithuania moved toward full independence in the spring and summer of 1991, and republican governments in Ukraine and Russia asserted that they, not the central government, would control their resources and economies.

In March 1991, in a futile effort to stem the rising nationalist tide, Gorbachev submitted a proposed new treaty of union to a national referendum. Georgia, Armenia, Moldavia, and the Baltic republics refused to participate. Many of the remaining voters were unsure what they were voting for, but a majority endorsed the treaty. Its provisions, however, did not go far enough toward confederation to satisfy most of the non-Russian nationalists. As a result, Gorbachev made further concessions, and on July 24 he won tentative approval from leaders of the USSR's republics (except those that had abstained in the earlier referendum) for a new arrangement, a "Union of Sovereign Republics." Signing of this treaty was set for August 20. To earlier accusations that he had weakened the party and "lost" Eastern Europe, Gorbachev's opponents added the charge that he was now wrecking the state itself, destroying the unitary structure that had brought the nation power and pride for more than seventy years. Despite ominous signs of discontent from conservative elements in the party, army, and secret police and warnings from liberals and from the U.S. government of a right-wing attempt to seize power, Gorbachev, apparently unperturbed, left Moscow for his customary August vacation in the Crimea. He intended to return briefly to sign the treaty.

THE ATTEMPTED COUP OF AUGUST 1991

Late in the afternoon of Sunday, August 18, his security guards informed Gorbachev that visitors from Moscow had arrived unexpectedly at his opulent dacha on the Black Sea coast and wanted to see him. Surprised and suspicious, the Soviet president tried his phones and found that they were all dead. When he received the delegation, which included representatives of the army, the secret police, and conservative political forces, as well as his formerly trusted personal chief of staff, they asked the Soviet president to endorse an emergency committee that was being formed to deal with the current crisis. Gorbachev refused and pointed out to the conspirators that no legal or constitutional authority had appointed the committee and that they were acting recklessly and treasonously. Leaving him under house arrest, the delegation returned to Moscow.

The next morning, Monday, August 19, radio stations began the day with solemn classical music—usually played on the death of a Soviet leader—followed by an announcement that eight leaders of the Soviet government had established a State Committee on the Emergency Situation to solve the country's urgent problems. They promised to repudiate the union treaty scheduled for signing the next day, to revive the collapsing economy, and to stamp out crime and profiteering. Members of the committee included the vice president, the minister of defense, the head of the KGB, and the minister of interior, all Gorbachev appointees. The committee averred that it was acting in place of President Gorbachev, who was incapacitated by ill health.

As tanks deployed in the streets of Moscow and other parts of the country and civilian leaders not involved in the conspiracy tried to decide what to do, the average person was bewildered and wary. By afternoon, however, citizens had begun to engage troops in conversation, persuading them of the folly of using force against the population. Moreover, several leaders, notably Boris Yeltsin of the Russian Republic, whom the coup leaders had clumsily missed arresting that morning, and Anatoly Sobchak, the mayor of Leningrad, came out strongly against the coup. To dramatize his opposition, Yeltsin climbed on a tank outside the Russian government's headquarters, known as the White House, and harangued a small group of supporters, condemning the seizure of power as illegal and calling for civil disobedience against it. His defiance and the inept performance of the coup leaders at an early evening press conference galvanized opposition in Moscow and throughout the country. By Monday nightfall over fifty thousand citizens had gathered around the White House, building makeshift barricades and forming a human wall against would-be attackers.

During the next twenty-four hours opponents of the putsch managed to persuade army and air force officers designated to take over key installations and government offices, including the White House, that such action would risk thousands of lives and might touch off civil war. On Tuesday, August 20, the crowd around the White House grew to over one hundred thousand. Celebrities, including the poet Yevtushenko and Sakharov's widow, Yelena Bonner, urged on the defenders of Yeltsin's defiant Russian government. Although three young Muscovites were inadvertently killed when an inexperienced tank crew panicked in the act of withdrawing and one person was shot in Lithuania, confrontation between the army and the coup's opponents was avoided. By Wednesday, August 21, the conspirators were in disarray, and their plot collapsed in the face of Yeltsin's courageous resistance, the unwillingness of military forces to fire on civilians, and growing popular opposition to the coup in Moscow and other parts of the country. Two conspirators committed suicide. The others were arrested but were soon freed on bail. (In December 1993 two plotters were elected to the Russian parliamentary Duma, and in March 1994 the Duma amnestied the others awaiting trial). Gorbachev was released on August 22 and flew back to Moscow to take up the reins of government.

But the failed coup had changed everything. What little authority the Soviet president and the central government still retained slipped away from them in the fall of 1991 as the economic crisis deepened and the various republics went their own ways. Latvia, Estonia, Ukraine, Belarus, Azerbaijan, and Moldavia (now called Moldova) all asserted their independence in late August and September. In response Gorbachev set up a state council of presidents of the republics, but other than approving independence for the Baltic states, the council accomplished little. In a referendum on December 1, 1991, Ukrainian voters reaffirmed their republic's separate status. On December 8 the leaders of Russia, Ukraine, and Belarus formed the Commonwealth of Independent States (CIS), ignoring the central Soviet government. The federal administration still existed in Moscow, but republican authorities paid little attention to it. With no country and no government over which to preside, Gorbachev finally resigned as Soviet president on December 25, 1991, and shortly afterward the Soviet Union was formally dissolved. A dramatic era in modern history came to an end.

CONCLUSION

Irony marked Gorbachev's six-year rule. Determined to improve Soviet life, he began with a series of reforms intended to rejuvenate the party, refire the economy, and refurbish the socialist system. But the changes that he introduced disrupted the economy and led to the demise of the party and the discarding of socialism. One step led to another, and before long the changes were snowballing out of Gorbachev's or anyone else's control. Successes in openness and democratization undercut his own and the party's authority, threw into question the values of socialism, and released long-repressed nationalist aspirations that could not be contained within the old federal Soviet structure. At the same time, his inability to revamp the economy demolished potential popular support and made it impossible for Gorbachev to govern or to master the processes that he had unleashed. Both successes and failures were his undoing.

Yet Mikhail Sergeevich accomplished a great deal. He repudiated the Brezhnevian legacy of mediocrity, corruption, and stagnation. He stimulated genuine participation in social and public affairs, thus laying the groundwork for eventual democracy in Russia and the former Soviet states. He uncapped the creativity and energy of the educated and thoughtful elements in Soviet society and enlisted them in the search for a better system. He strengthened the rule of law, permitted Jewish emigration, and guaranteed freedom of religion for the Orthodox faith and other denominations.

Most dramatically, Gorbachev replaced the cold war with cooperative and friendly relations between the USSR and the West. To the world's relief, he capped the arms race and initiated major steps drastically to reduce nuclear stockpiles and conventional forces on both sides. He helped settle several controversies in the Third World, withdrew Soviet forces from Afghanistan, and established normal, businesslike relations with China. He acquiesced in broad popular upheavals to replace socialism in Eastern Europe with democratic, free-market regimes. And he accepted the reunification of Germany and the end of military and diplomatic confrontation in central Europe. For all the world's citizens, the Soviet leader reduced the risk of war and moved the international climate toward calm and cooperation. For these achievements in global affairs, history will certainly remember him as one of the greatest figures of the twentieth century. Paradoxically, these successes earned him little credit at home—and even reproach from those conservative nationalists who chastised the Soviet leader for abnegating Soviet power and endangering Soviet security.

In the end Gorbachev's dream of a more humane, just, and efficient socialist Soviet Union was dashed. He failed to see that the party, his chosen instrument of reform, was a flawed tool increasingly despised by the majority of the population. Too late he accepted the need for a multiparty system. Mikhail Sergeevich also yielded his socialist principles far too slowly. He delayed all-out privatization and a fully free market, hoping against hope that a hybrid socialism could somehow revive the faltering Soviet economy. Again, by the time he was prepared to make broader concessions, the economic deterioration had passed him by. Finally, the Soviet reformer never fully understood the depth and significance of the non-Russian nationalisms that his renovations uncorked. Whether any restructuring of the union would have satisfied the long-persecuted minorities is a moot question. In any case, Gorbachev waited too long to make even modest concessions, and the tidal wave of national independence soon swept him aside and washed away the federal state that the Bolsheviks had erected seventy years earlier. The Soviet Union was dead, and its successor states were left to struggle into an uncertain future.

FURTHER READING

Aslund, Anders. *Gorbachev's Struggle for Economic Reform.* Ithaca, N.Y.: 1989.

Bialer, S., ed. *Politics, Society, and Nationality Inside Gorbachev's Russia.* Boulder, Colo.: 1989.

Brown, Archie. *The Gorbachev Factor.* New York: 1996.

Buckley, Mary. *Women and Ideology in the Soviet Union.* Ann Arbor, Mich.: 1989.

Buckley, Mary, ed. *Perestroika and Soviet Women.* Cambridge, England: 1992.

Campbell, Robert W. *The Failures of Soviet Economic Planning.* Bloomington, Ind.: 1992.

Dallin, Alexander, and Gail Lapidus. *The Soviet System: From Crisis to Collapse.* Boulder, Colo.: 1994.

Desai, P. *Perestroika in Perspective: The Design and Dilemmas of Soviet Reform.* Princeton, N.J.: 1989.

Feshbach, Murray, and Alfred Friendly, Jr. *Ecocide in the USSR: Health and Nature Under Siege.* New York: 1992.

Gill, Graeme J. *Collapse of a Single-Party System.* Cambridge: 1994.

Goldman, Marshall. *What Went Wrong with Perestroika?* New York: 1992.

Gorbachev, Mikhail. *Memoirs.* New York: 1996.

Gorbachev, M. S. *Perestroika: New Thinking for Our Country and the World.* New York: 1987.

Graham, Loren. *The Ghost of the Executed Engineer: Technology and the Fall of the Soviet Union.* Cambridge, Mass.: 1993.

Hosking, Geoffrey. *The Awakening of the Soviet Union.* Cambridge, Mass.: 1991.

Kotkin, Stephen. *Steeltown USSR: Soviet Society in the Gorbachev Era.* Berkeley: 1991.

Lane, David. *Soviet Society Under Perestroika.* Cambridge, Mass.: 1990.

Lieven, Anatol. *The Baltic Revolution.* New Haven, Conn.: 1993.

Matlock, Jack F. *Autopsy on an Empire.* New York: 1995.

Remnick, David. *Lenin's Tomb: The Last Days of the Soviet Empire.* New York: 1993.

Rywkin, Michael. *Moscow's Muslim Challenge: Soviet Central Asia* (2d ed.). Armonk, N.Y.: 1989.

Shneidman, N. N. *Soviet Literature in the 1980s.* Toronto: 1989.

Smith, Hedrick. *The New Russians.* New York: 1991.

Suny, Ronald. *The Revenge of the Past: Nationalism, Revolution and the Collapse of the Soviet Union.* Stanford, Calif.: 1994.

White, Stephen. *Gorbachev and After.* Cambridge, England: 1992.

Yeltsin, Boris. *Against the Grain.* New York: 1990.

15

The "New" Russia in the Post-Soviet Era

As the last hours of December 31, 1999, ticked away, many Russians, disillusioned with their lives in post-Soviet society, expressed little interest in the twentieth century's demise and cherished scant hope for the new millennium ahead. New Year's Eve found them at home apathetically staring at their television screens, a usual nightly recreation. Some beneficiaries of the new order toasted their gains at upscale restaurants, posh night clubs, trendy bars, and private parties, while other, mostly younger citizens unenthusiastically wandered streets in Moscow, St. Petersburg, and other cities, watching fireworks displays mounted by local officials. The stay-at-homes watched disinterestedly as a familiar face appeared on TV to convey New Year's greetings: their president, Boris Yeltsin, chief pallbearer of communism, architect of the new order, and Russia's leader for over seven years (see Figure 22). Heavily criticized at home and abroad, he nevertheless still represented for some citizens the "genuine" Russian person. Yeltsin, frequently in poor health, appeared drawn, depressed, and ashen as he addressed the nation. In a poignant talk he announced his resignation as president, six months before his term's end, and apologized movingly for his failure to bring to the Russian people the good life promised when communism collapsed. Appealing for forgiveness, Yeltsin concluded sadly: "Not all our dreams came to fulfillment . . . we thought we could jump from the grey, stagnant totalitarian past to a light, rich and civilized future in one leap. I believed that myself . . . but it took more than one jump."

Founder of the "new" Russia, Yeltsin had presided over an erratic, messy, still incomplete transition from the failing Soviet system to an entirely different society struggling to implement democratic and free-market reforms. Evaluations of his presidency among both Russians and Western observers diverged sharply. Some charged that bewitched by inappropriate advice from outside specialists and inexperienced Russian economists, he pushed flawed policies of headlong marketization and privatization that produced corruption, crime, and impoverishment, that he introduced a semi-authoritarian political system rampant with cronyism and inefficiency, and that he recklessly initiated a cruel and hopeless war against a small minority in the state, the Chechens of the northern Caucasus. Yeltsin's defend-

Figure 22. *Boris Yeltsin, former Communist Party leader, opponent of Gorbachev, president of the independent Russian republic, 1991. (Courtesy of the Russian Embassy)*

ers pointed to the formidable obstacles he confronted in revamping Russia, to his facing down obstructionists and reactionaries, to his maintenance of democratic forms, and to his success in keeping peace with Russia's near neighbors and strengthening friendly relations with Europe and the United States. The debate over Yeltsin's legacy is certain to keep historians arguing for many years. His handpicked successor, Vladimir Putin, continued many of his predecessor's policies while instituting new reforms. But he also tightened control over the media and failed to stamp out corruption or end the war in Chechnya.

THE QUADRUPLE REVOLUTION

From the ashes of Soviet communism arose one large country, Russia, surrounded on its western and southern borders by fourteen smaller states corresponding to the former constituent republics of the Soviet Union (see Map 1). As these suddenly independent nations struggled to build a reordered life, Russia's size and extensive resources helped it to emerge as the dominant power and bellwether of change in the region. In its new incarnation Russia benefited from several advantages. The young state commanded extensive assets, inheriting 51 percent of the former USSR's population, 76 percent of its territory, and 61 percent of its gross national product. The new Russia also possessed most of the old Soviet Union's petroleum, timber, and mineral resources and boasted a foreign trade surplus. No outside force threatened it; in fact, its former rivals, the Western powers, rushed to provide advice, moral support, and economic assistance. Finally, its people were mainly Russians and, for the most part, well educated and skilled.

Yet the task ahead was overwhelming. Boris Yeltsin and his supporters set in motion one of the swiftest and most sweeping revolutions in modern history, equaling if not surpassing the old regime's destruction in 1789 France, the Bolsheviks' clean sweep of tsarism in 1917, and even the Chinese Communists' Great Leap Forward of the 1950s. For the new Russian leadership sought radically to transform the four most basic aspects of the entrenched Soviet system. Their 180-degree about-face encompassed first and foremost replacing, almost overnight, a centralized, planned, state-owned economy with a free-market system, including unregulated prices and wages, private ownership of factories, businesses, and most resources, and all-out competition for profit. Second, rejecting the oligarchic, tightly controlled Soviet polity, Yeltsin confirmed the democratic changes begun under Gorbachev and extended them to include fully free and broadly representative elections, freedom of speech, press, and assembly, and steps toward a functioning parliament and an impartial judiciary and legal system. Third, the new leaders scrapped Marxist-Leninist ideology for unfamiliar new values of individualism, responsible free choice, consumerism, and self-reliance. Finally, instead of seeking the overthrow of the existing world system and brandishing hostility toward Western and other non-Communist nations, Russian foreign policy now advocated international cooperation, friendly relations with Europe and America, and peaceful intercourse with surrounding states, including former parts of the USSR. A Russian Rip Van Winkle who dozed off in 1982 and woke up in 1992 would have found life and society totally revamped and bewilderingly unrecognizable.

Given the magnitude of what Yeltsin and Putin attempted, the wonder is not that the road was rough and painful nor that they often failed but that the society survived at all and emerged ten years later as a basically democratic if slightly authoritarian polity with a deformed but functioning market economy, an embryonic legal structure, and a recovering social system. Moreover, Russia's progress, however stunted, was achieved in the face of staggering obstacles. The economy inherited by the new leaders was in a state of collapse. The Soviet infrastructure largely built right after World War II was decaying and outmoded. Political and bureaucratic opponents of reform were well placed and intransigent. Regional self-interest often trumped national policy. The people as a whole were bewildered, dispirited, and apathetic. Attitudes and outlooks developed in Soviet times remained entrenched, undermining most reform efforts. Social problems, such as alcoholism, corruption, crime, and worsening health care, multiplied. Finally, although non-Russians made up only about 17 percent of the new state's population, several groups, notably the Volga Tatars and the Chechens, strongly resisted continued Russian hegemony.

ON THE HIGH ROAD TO CAPITALISM

As the Soviet Union fell apart in late 1991, Yeltsin and his advisers gave highest priority to revolutionizing the old, failing socialist economy. In October 1991 they adopted a radical economic program based on "shock therapy," the premise that only rapid conversion to market mechanisms can successfully transform a socialist system. Yeltsin soon appointed a young economist, Yegor Gaidar, to oversee its implementation. The Gaidar team freed almost all prices in January–February 1992, a step that soon succeeded in restocking the empty stores with domestic and imported consumer goods, although often at prices out of reach of most citizens. The reformers also sought to control inflation, to reduce the government's huge budget deficit, and to make the ruble convertible to other currencies. This last goal was eventually achieved, but the other aims proved more elusive.

First results of "shock therapy" were hardly encouraging. During 1992 Russian production, hobbled by deficiencies passed along from the larger Soviet system and floundering under the new ground rules, declined by an estimated 20–25 percent. Inflation reached 30 percent a month, budget deficits mounted, and trade with the former Soviet republics and the rest of the world plummeted. As prices skyrocketed, wage payments were delayed. With the former Soviet social safety net in disarray, the average citizen was forced to work at more than one job, to barter or sell personal possessions, and to rely on garden plots in order to survive. Pensioners, others with fixed incomes, and young women and unskilled workers (who were the first to lose their jobs) suffered especially. By some estimates the poverty rate in Russia reached 40 percent. Yet, despite widespread grumbling and discontent, Russians somehow survived the first two winters of reform, and few signs of social unrest surfaced.

In the following years to 2003 economic reform posted a spotty record, with more downs than ups. Detailed assessment of the Russian economy's performance proved difficult for two reasons. Reform policies were implemented inconsistently and erratically, partly because of leadership failings but chiefly because of old-guard rejection of the new order. Widespread support for change existed, but the many opponents of "shock therapy" reform, primarily ex-Communists, former economic bureaucrats, and factory and farm managers, insisted that markets and free prices be phased in and that the state still operate some sectors of the economy. They wanted to cushion the shock of the changeover by providing subsidies to struggling farms and industries, by controlling wages and consumer prices, and by increasing government spending on social welfare. The radical reformers, though acknowledging some short-term disruption and pain, countered that such costs would be far less than the drawn-out woes that a gradual transition would bring. The political and ideological resistance to economic reform often thwarted Yeltsin and Putin from fully implementing key changes or forced them to make concessions that undercut the efficacy of the transformative program. Also Yeltsin's deteriorating health weakened his determination and ability to advance reform at crucial periods.

In addition, the unreliability and inadequacy of statistics made it difficult to track the Russian economy after 1991. To avoid what were deemed unfair or stifling taxes imposed through an arbitrary and complex tax system that lasted till 2001, most businesses and many individuals did not report their economic activity at all or accounted to the authorities for only part of their work. Moreover, barter underlay many economic transactions at both consumer and industrial levels. Finally, institutes, factories, and other organizations often provided social services that were not tracked by government statistics. Some economists concluded that official data did not cover some 25–40 percent of Russia's total economy.

Whatever the details, the overall pattern of change emerged in bold relief. The Soviet plan-and-command system was scrapped in favor of open markets and private enterprise. The privatization program begun in 1992–1993 transferred ownership of most of the non-agricultural economy from state to private hands. In the process a small elite seized control of many enterprises and natural resources, thus establishing a political-business oligarchy, but by 2002 much of the Russian economy was operating in a competitive, free-market atmosphere. In that year an estimated 97 percent of small-scale businesses (including stores, restaurants, and service institutions) and 75 percent of large factories were privately owned. The state still controlled some defense industries, utilities, and energy companies while state and collective ownership remained dominant in agriculture. Privatization was notably successful in housing: by the turn of the century a majority of Russians owned their own dwelling space, and almost 40 percent of urban dwellers had a country cottage or *dacha*. The reformers believed, probably correctly, that this change in property relationships would transform popular attitudes, giving many Russians a stake in the economy, stimulating individual initiative, and rallying support for the market system. Indeed, by 2002, although most citizens remained politically apathetic, and grumbling about the new economy's inequities was widespread, little sentiment existed for a return to state socialism and many Russians, especially young people, were reconciled to, or even enthusiastic about, their version of capitalism.

Privatization of agriculture proved far more difficult, however. Yeltsin took few initiatives in this area, and less than 10 percent of farms were privately owned by 2001. Putin pushed a land reform law through parliament in that year, but its early results were meager. Collective and state farmers remained reluctant to risk managing individual farmsteads; the government failed to support private farmers with needed credit, agricultural equipment, and technical assistance; and the conservative managers of the existing agricultural system continued to press for substantial state subsidies and to resist reform. Consequently, agricultural output and productivity remained a weak spot in the economy, and rural Russia, in a familiar historical pattern, suffered poverty, backwardness, and despair.

Besides privatization, the reformers could point to other achievements. In 1992 and 1993 inflation had reached peaks of 20 or 30 percent *a month*. By the early 2000s it had been reduced to about 10–15 percent *a year*. The precipitous drop in industrial production dating from the late Soviet era was finally reversed in 1999, and the Russian economy grew modestly in the years 2000–2002. On the other hand productivity improved only slightly and stayed well below European and U.S. levels. Although the number of small businesses remained disappointingly low and bureaucratic regulations and corruption continued to hamper their growth, service industries expanded in number and quality. Putin steadfastly avowed his commitment to economic reform, both as a candidate in 2000 and as president afterward, and the economy improved noticeably during his first years in office. In 2001 he backed a tax reform that simplified the cumbersome system and introduced a 13-percent flat tax on incomes. Tax collections immediately went up, substantially reducing the recurrent danger of government budget deficits. He also urged changes in the banking and legal systems and instituted significant improvements in the judiciary.

Over the first post-Soviet decade the reformers also suffered numerous setbacks. Political pressures and Yeltsin's vacillations often hindered efforts to maintain tight control of the money supply. In the mid-1990s subsidies to regions and to inefficient state enterprises and former collective farms, wage and pension increases, and widespread corruption spawned ballooning deficits and fluctuations in the value of the ruble. Fiscal largesse distributed in the first half of 1996 to help Yeltsin win reelection to the presidency contributed to monetary instability and budget woes. Necessary attempts in 1997 to end chronic wage arrears and smooth out pension payments brought the state close to bankruptcy. The Yeltsin administration bought a temporary reprieve by floating a series of Russian state bonds (GKOs) in 1996–1998, but in August 1998, weakened by a fiscal crisis in the East and Southeast Asian economies, the financial system collapsed. The Russian government defaulted on the bonds and devalued the ruble. Though painful and humiliating at the time, this crisis had some long-term benefits. It much weakened the economic and political power of the "oligarchs" or "tycoons," financiers and manipulators who had profited most in the early days of what some called Russia's "crony capitalism." The August debacle also spurred a restructuring of Russia's substantial external debt. Finally, the cheaper ruble brought favorable terms of trade for Russian exports and made consumer goods produced at home cheaper than imports.

Despite the economy's improved performance after 1998, major problems remained. Entrenched Soviet-era beliefs in state control and government largesse blocked new product development and entrepreneurial initiative. Apathy and disillusionment hampered creativity and productivity. In the late 1990s and particularly under Putin, extortion, at least in its violent and criminal forms, was substantially reduced, but economic activity continued to be crippled by bureaucratic interference and endemic corruption. In 2000 on an educational trip to Novgorod, police stopped the tourist bus I was in three times to demand a payoff from the driver, who explained that the travel company simply built such expenses into the cost of the tour. Inefficient monopolies, remnants of the Soviet era though now in private hands, dominated some industries and blocked innovation and diversification. Russian capital continued to flee abroad, while domestic and foreign investment in Russia remained abysmally low. As a result, the economic infrastructure—factories, equipment, transport, utilities, and buildings—remained outdated and crumbling. Too large a share of the economy depended on energy and other natural resource exploitation, leading some to compare Russia to a Third World country. Oil and natural gas, along with minerals and timber, dominated Russian exports and supplied the bulk of the country's foreign exchange earnings. Although the rise in world petroleum prices after 1999 greatly benefited the Russian exchequer, both Russian and Western specialists pointed out the urgent need for modernization of petroleum exploration and extraction in Russia. In 2002 American and Russian energy sector leaders met to discuss mutually beneficial contracts designed to upgrade Russian energy production.

In his first years in office Putin readily acknowledged the relatively weak position of the Russian economy and the urgent need to rationalize and modernize its operations to be competitive in world markets and particularly to increase its trade with the West. Accepted as a member of the G8 group of the world's largest economic powers, Russia nevertheless had little hope of entering the World Trade Organization before 2005 or later. In the 1990s outside assistance from the International Monetary Fund and the Western powers, particularly Germany, helped Russia move toward fiscal and economic stability, but the amount was relatively small and could not be counted on in the future. President Putin gave high priority to raising substantially the dismal level of foreign investment in Russia, pointing out that China and many Third World countries received far more outside capital than Russia. Foreign investors nevertheless remained wary, citing still incomplete tax reforms, a corrupt interventionist bureaucracy, particularly at local levels, and, most unsettling of all, weakly developed laws protecting property and contracts. Western firms heavily penetrated the consumer market, but few had success establishing production facilities. Some firms such as Weyerhauser wood products and BP Amoco oil suffered major losses, providing a warning beacon to others. Nevertheless, as conditions improve and legal safeguards are introduced and enforced, outside investors will undoubtedly flock to Russia, hoping to meet the pent-up demand of tens of millions of Russian consumers and to benefit from the availability of a highly educated, relatively low-paid Russian workforce.

WHAT IS A "NORMAL" LIFE?

Most Russians, disillusioned with *perestroika*, had looked to the post-1991 reforms as the vehicle to deliver the better life that their leaders had promised since 1985. When some citizens continued to suffer, many people turned against reform or lapsed into apathy. A few, like the talented Russian circus clown Yuri Nikulin, kept their sense of humor: "Where were Adam and Eve born? In Russia, of course. They had no home, were naked and had one apple between them; yet they thought they were in Paradise." A daily struggle to survive, frequent payoffs to get anything done, spreading crime, and fears of unemployment and of an uncertain future became "normal," to use a favorite Russian expression. Intellectuals who were highly honored and well rewarded in Soviet times suffered a depressing decline in status and income. Widows, pensioners, veterans, laid-off state employees, and single parents felt the pinch particularly. The contrast with the security of the Soviet welfare state was stark. As a factory worker commented in 1994, "In the past I took life for granted and wouldn't think about what to do or how to live. Now we have to think about it all the time, just to scrape by."

As the gap between rich and poor widened, some Russians profited from the transition to capitalism. Among those who soon began to amass rubles and dollars were former officials in industry and government; slick traders, including millions of "shuttlers" who bought consumer goods in Turkey, China, and Europe for resale at home; some hardworking entrepreneurs; and assorted shady "wheelers and dealers," extortionists, and criminal elements. These "new Russians" flaunted their wealth by building expensive country houses, spending lavishly on consumer goods, and traveling in grand style to Mediterranean resorts and other "in" destinations. At the same time many young people saw and often seized opportunities in the new economic structure. In a 1997 poll, two-thirds of people under thirty-five years of age thought life was getting better, whereas two-thirds of those over fifty-five concluded that conditions in Russia were getting worse.

In the 1990s both investors and ordinary citizens deplored the spreading influence of organized gangs, dubbed "the Russian mafia." Racketeers seized control of some retail and service operations, gouging consumers, bribing officials, and muscling out or extorting payoffs from competitors. In the early 2000s Putin managed to crack down on these elements, and their impact lessened. Nevertheless, crime rates remained quite high, while prostitution, gambling, and drug use flourished. As a result, many Russians, accustomed to the staid security of the Soviet era, grew increasingly frightened and resentful. In addition, although unemployment rates were officially low, hidden unemployment and wage arrears created job insecurity, which further eroded people's confidence.

Moreover, the physical surroundings in which most Russians lived decayed. Buildings, utilities, and public services were not well maintained. Air and water pollution and other environmental problems, a bitter legacy of Soviet socialism's emphasis on all-out industrial growth, persisted. Neither environmental activists nor the government commanded the resources to enforce conservation measures or to repair earlier devastation.

Health concerns also surfaced as a major social issue after 1991. As the state-supported health care system collapsed, the cash-strapped government struggled to maintain hospitals and other facilities while citizens complained angrily about the shortage of medicines and the inequities of a growing fee-for-service medical practice. The rise in infant mortality that had started in the Soviet era continued, leveling off in 1994 and dropping slightly thereafter. Tuberculosis spread rapidly in the late 1990s, and by the turn of the century Russia was confronting a looming AIDS catastrophe. HIV-positive individuals were estimated at one million in 2002 and were projected to total six or seven million by 2010. The government responded feebly to this crisis, with insufficient treatment and little AIDS-prevention education. Moreover, despite the growing availability of reliable condoms, largely unknown in Soviet times, only a minority of Russians regularly used them. Drug addicts, prostitutes, and soldiers, the most heavily infected groups, increasingly spread the virus throughout the population.

As AIDS-related deaths rise in the mid-2000s, they will only worsen Russia's alarming demographic crisis of a shrinking population. Not only were too many infants dying in post-Soviet times but uncertainty about current and future conditions and a divorce rate approaching 70 percent led many parents not to have children at all. By 2001 the fertility rate sank to 1.17 percent, far below what is needed to maintain a stable population level. Concurrently, the death rate rose, as alcoholism, accidents, cancer, suicide, and cardiovascular disease took their toll, especially among Russian men. By the early 2000s life expectancy had recovered from earlier lows but still remained at 61 for men and 72 for women (compared with 74 and 80 respectively for citizens of the European Union). Although in the 1990s tens of thousands of Russians from former Soviet republics immigrated to Russia each year, the gap between births and deaths meant that the total population shrank, dropping from nearly 150 million in 1991 to below 145 million in 2002. Some experts estimated that Russia might contain as few as 120 million people by 2030, with concomitant shortages of recruits for the army and workers for the economy. No industrialized country ever experienced such a population calamity in peacetime.

The skewed gender and age structure of Russia's population only made this dismal picture bleaker. In 2001 Russia had 9.1 million more women than men. In addition to fewer husbands being available, educated Russian women often decided not to marry because they did not want to be trapped in a traditional patriarchal relationship or because so many men were heavy drinkers. The Russian population was also aging, with 38 percent above working age in 2001. Some continued to work, but the growing number of pensioners will become an increasing burden on the economy.

Despite some European countries' fear in the 1990s that economically destitute Russian migrants would flood across their borders, in fact, except for Jews and Volga Germans, no mass exodus of Russians occurred after 1991. However, a mini-brain drain brought a number of scientists and intellectuals to the West in the 1990s.

The transition from socialism created special obstacles for women. As homemakers, they not only continued to cope with traditional problems of spousal abuse and alcoholism but now faced shrinking family income and skyrocketing prices, at least in the early 1990s, as well as the reduced availability of health and child care facilities. As workers, women were often the first laid off, making up 70 percent of the officially unemployed in 1995. When working, their average wage level reached only 60 percent of what men were paid. Moreover, few women reached senior executive positions in the new free-market enterprises or in the democratized government, whose Duma contained less than 10 percent female deputies. Finally, women in transition Russia felt victimized by the spread of prostitution, pornography and crime.

At the same time several positive signs for the future position of women emerged. Various feminist groups sprang up, some concerned with rape awareness and counseling for rape victims and others focused on helping women in business and the professions. An organization in Moscow even dared to take on the patriarchal Russian custom of sexual harassment in the workplace. Women played active roles in a range of grassroots organizations working on social and environmental issues, and talented women succeeded in retail and other small businesses. They also served as key leaders in some regional administrations, and several women contributed importantly to legislation in the Duma, even though their overall representation in that body was small. With an improving economy, the prospects for women in Russia should brighten, but equal status seems a long way off.

The years after 1991 proved to be a dispiriting time for many Russians. Economic hardship, the repudiation of old values, generational tension between young and old, insecurity, and dismay at the blatant inequities and crudities of "Wild East" capitalism produced cynicism, fatalism, and occasionally despair. Despite considerable disorientation and bewilderment, many citizens seemed relieved to surrender such negative features of Soviet socialism as false and repetitive propaganda, petty party interference in their lives, and repression of individual and civil rights. As one friend told me in 1993 after complaining bitterly about economic conditions and crime, "Still, the important thing is we are free!"

The diminution of Russia's world stature, youngsters' caustic repudiation of the Soviet-era patriotic cult surrounding World War II, and the indifference of many to the heroic achievements of the past proved particularly painful to veterans, military officers, and many ex-Communists. They adapted a stance of injured pride and nationalism that at times bordered on xenophobia and anti-Semitism as some blamed the West and Jews for Russia's plight. Rumors that Western aid and commerce were part of a conspiracy to expropriate the country's resources and to make Russia a vassal state were widely circulated—and believed by many. In addition, drawing on the egalitarian values of Russian and Soviet culture, many citizens found repugnant the materialism and consumerism of the new era with its flashy Western imports, crassly commercial culture, and ostentatious displays of wealth. Finally, an ugly undertone of racism erupted as some Russians denounced "the dark-skinned" or "people from the south"—that is, Tatars, Central Asians, and inhabitants of the Caucasus—for crime, profiteering, and every imaginable ill. The wars against the Chechens on Russia's southern border in the mid-1990s and in the early 2000s (discussed more fully later in the chapter) only intensified this prejudice.

Popular attitudes toward the horrors of the Stalin era became another puzzling and disturbing psychological phenomenon of the post-Soviet era. Unlike Germany, where both government and people struggled successfully to confront and deal with their Nazi past, the vast majority of Russians appeared unwilling even to acknowledge, let alone come to terms with, the murder of millions of their fellow citizens during the 1930s and 1940s. A few farsighted individuals banded together in the human rights organization Memorial, seeking to collect historical data about Stalin's repressions and to honor the victims by identifying them and by erecting monuments and plaques in their memory. But the government most often ignored or hampered these efforts, and the public generally showed no interest or consciously turned a blind eye to Memorial's activities. In 2002, as the organization unearthed an apparent mass grave on a military preserve near St. Petersburg (formerly Leningrad), the local army command harassed the searchers and the government's security service, the FSB (successor to the KGB), denied any knowledge of executions in that area during the 1930s. A local resident whose father, aunt, and uncle were all executed during Stalin's purges pointed to one possible reason for Russians' reluctance to deal with such past horrors: "It's our country's deep wound. You can forget about a wound if you don't touch it, but when you touch it, it bleeds again."

In their bewilderment after 1991 some Russians turned to the Orthodox religion, but the Church suffered from weak leadership and was tarnished by revelations that several high clerics had collaborated with the KGB in the Soviet era. Orthodox prelates struggled to regain control of church lands and properties seized under communism and to reconstruct and refurbish damaged and decaying church buildings. Their interest in material matters alienated some idealistic younger Russians, and church attendance, after an early spurt, fell off. Moreover, Orthodox leaders faced aggressive competition from Protestant, Catholic, and sectarian missionaries. In 1997 Church officials, after hard lobbying, secured a Duma law that imposed numerous requirements on religions other than Orthodoxy, Islam, Judaism, and Buddhism, but they failed to achieve their goal of an outright ban of

Protestant, Catholic and sectarian activity. Afterward, Catholics and some evangelical sects expanded their proselytizing efforts and gained a number of new followers. Conservative in outlook and unresponsive to Russia's socioeconomic ills, the Orthodox leaders did little to provide new directions and inspiration for the country's floundering citizenry.

Some fans of democracy expected a blossoming of Russian cultural life once the yoke of Soviet socialist conformity was lifted. Although a few creative individual artists and writers emerged amid the chaos of the post-1991 transition, most cultural institutions and much artistic activity suffered through the 1990s from diminished budgets, disinterested audiences, and dynamic competition from Western publications, television shows, and movies. The Russian film and publishing industries suffered particularly. Moreover, many "new Russians," with little sense of Russia's artistic tradition, used their ill-gotten rubles and dollars to foster clothing, décor, and architecture in the worst possible taste—a rush to vulgarity, garishness, and banality that blemished the cityscapes and environs of Moscow and St. Petersburg with ugly signs, billboards, and buildings.

Yet by the late 1990s Russian culture began a notable revival. The Russian government's determination to abandon Soviet diktat and to refrain from interfering in artistic and cultural matters helped kick off a renaissance of Russian creativity. Even President Putin, accused by some of seeking to muzzle the press, voiced his support for artistic freedom. Moreover, he personally met with cultural leaders and sought regularly to promote the international reputation of Russia's arts. Although state-supported cultural institutions received miniscule subsidies compared to Soviet times, the government tried to maintain traditional organizations and buildings. The Ministry of Culture's budget grew by 25 percent in the early 2000s. In St. Petersburg the government supported renovation of the Marynsky Theater and the Russian State Museum as well as planning for a new performing arts center. In Moscow funds were set aside for an eventual restoration of the Moscow Conservatory and the Bolshoi Theater, and the mayor and the Russian government supported film festivals and the Third International Theater Olympics in 2000.

Freedom for artists to create also meant freedom for audiences to choose, which some critics argued meant the dominance of lowbrow culture and trash. But the new license also meant diversity, encouraging the founding of two new theaters and three new opera companies in Moscow, as well as the opening of many small theaters, galleries, and clubs there and throughout the country. In the first years after the Soviet collapse nineteenth-century Russian classics were most frequently performed at concerts, opera halls, and theaters, but by 2000, contemporary compositions and new plays had taken center stage. Moreover, traditional cultural giants, like the Kirov Opera and Ballet under the dynamic direction of Valery Gergiev and the Hermitage Museum in a loose partnership with the Guggenheim Museum, survived and grew stronger by revamping their repertoire and presentations. Although they and other major artistic institutions depended in part on foreign sponsorship, tours, and recordings, a small group of Russian philanthropists revived a heritage dating back to the eighteenth century of private support for the arts.

The publishing industry, at first hard hit by the influx of Western books and periodicals, perked up by the end of the 1990s, with a number of Russian authors racking up substantial sales thanks to Russian citizens' continuing passion for reading. Adventure stories, detective fiction, romances, and self-help books dominated the market, but critically acclaimed prose and poetry occupied a growing niche. Almost submerged at first by the tide of American and other imports, the film industry, though still struggling by 2000, turned out some twenty new productions a year, including several internationally recognized films. Some talented visual and performing artists decamped to the West after 1991, but those remaining in Russia continued to seek an authentic Russian voice in their particular medium. On balance, Russian culture entered the twenty-first century more vibrant and flourishing than at any time since the imposition of Stalinist conformity seventy years earlier.

THE ROCKY ROAD TO DEMOCRACY

For the first two years after 1991, discontent over economic conditions, concern over social disintegration, unreformed Communists' ideological aversion to capitalism, and nationalists' resentment at the collapse of the Soviet empire and Russia's weakened world position all fueled mounting opposition to Yeltsin's regime even though most citizens were relieved that Soviet conformity and authoritarianism had been swept away. During fall 1991 Yeltsin concentrated on protecting Russia's interests as the USSR disintegrated. His first priority was to establish Russia's predominant position in whatever different structure emerged among the former components of the Soviet Union. Although declaring his republic's full sovereignty and supporting the symbolic step of adopting a new Russian flag, the Russian president did not encourage independence for everyone. Often cooperating with the desperate Gorbachev, whose position as Soviet president was fast eroding, Yeltsin strove to create a confederation among the former Soviet republics. When Ukrainians voted for independence on December 1, 1991, the Russian president decided to abandon Gorbachev and any hope for a revamped Soviet Union. Asserting the independence of Russia, he cooperated with leaders from several other former republics to set up the Commonwealth of Independent States (CIS), a loose association that ignored the old federal structure (the CIS is discussed more fully later in the chapter). Yeltsin then accepted the demise of the USSR and turned to domestic challenges.

Because of Yeltsin's absorption in the issues surrounding the old state's collapse and because he apparently did not realize how much popular support he had garnered in defeating the August 1991 coup, in the following months he failed to push through the political reforms and constitutional changes needed to underpin genuine democracy in the new Russia. Instead of acting swiftly to rid himself of the old Soviet-era political institutions— the Russian Congress of Deputies elected in March 1989 and the Russian Supreme Soviet chosen by that congress, both of which contained a number of Communist Party holdovers and other conservatives—Yeltsin sought to cooperate with the politicians and structure in place. This effort sputtered along with declining success for the next two years as the president and his opponents in the Soviet tussled over economic policies.

Conflict between the central government in Moscow and the republic's districts and regions generated additional political opposition to Yeltsin. Pressure for autonomy from the almost thirty million non-Russian citizens of the new state exacerbated the struggle for power between Moscow and the periphery. By granting non-Russians some local self-rule and by making extra concessions to the Tatars living along the middle Volga River, the government managed to avert ethnic violence, except for the Chechen region in the north Caucasus, where bitter warfare raged in 1994–1996, flaring up again in 1999–2002 (to be discussed later in this chapter). Elsewhere, local authorities, taking advantage of the political infighting between the president and his conservative opponents in the Supreme Soviet, finagled financial subsidies from each side and resisted Yeltsin's efforts to control regional appointments and policies. Officials outside Moscow husbanded local resources and unilaterally reduced the share of taxes sent to the capital. In the mid-1990s establishment of a Federation Council representing the eighty-nine regions of the Russian Republic and elections at the local level that generally produced popularly controlled governors and other officials helped stabilize relations with the central government. As Yeltsin's grasp on power began to slip in the late 1990s, the regions once again asserted their authority and Moscow-periphery tensions escalated. In 2001 President Putin sought to resolve this issue by dividing Russia into seven large areas or provinces with presidentially appointed "super-governors" charged with establishing firm central government control and with ensuring countrywide implementation of Moscow's directives. This step damped down regional assertiveness, but some critics concluded the move added another layer of bureaucracy and potential corruption without significantly improving coordination and presidential authority.

In Moscow the conflict between Yeltsin and his critics sharpened during 1993. Both sides resorted to tactics of dubious legality. The president often tried to govern by decree, bypassing the legislative process. In turn the Soviet regularly introduced constitutional amendments designed to constrict the president's power and legislation that undercut the government's economic policies. Yeltsin survived threats to impeach him but had to sacrifice his economic reform point man, Gaidar, who was replaced as prime minister by Viktor Chernomyrdin, a Soviet-era industrial manager and a more moderate figure. In a popular referendum in April 1993, 58 percent of voters supported the president and 53 percent backed his economic program, despite its meager results to date.

Taking advantage of this victory, Yeltsin convened a constitutional convention, urging it to adopt the government's draft constitution that provided for a strong presidency. His opponents objected, and by September no agreement had been reached. Moreover, legislative recalcitrance had stalled the president's reform program. Increasingly frustrated, the Russian leader dissolved the Soviet on September 21, 1993, and called for elections to a new and differently structured parliament in December. This decisive action soon led to a major political crisis. The opposition convened a rump session of the Soviet that rejected the president's dissolution decree as unconstitutional, ousted Yeltsin, and installed Alexander Rutskoi, an Afghan war veteran, as acting president. About two hundred Soviet deputies plus assorted hangers-on staged a sit-in at the Soviet's headquarters, the same White House that had been the scene of Yeltsin's bold rebuff to the August 1991 attempted putsch.

The government cut off services to the White House and tried to negotiate with its occupiers during the succeeding week. No solution was found before events spiraled tragically out of control. On Sunday, October 3, several thousand ardent supporters of the Soviet broke through the government forces' cordon around the White House. Opposition leaders, exhausted from the long siege and out of touch with the political reality in Moscow, deluded themselves that this sortie represented the start of a popular uprising against Yeltsin in the city. At their urging, the mob attempted to seize city hall and the main television station, and fighting broke out. Facing armed action against his government, the Russian president, after hesitation, called in local troops, whose units shelled the White House the following morning, causing over a hundred casualties and major damage to the building. The holdouts inside surrendered and were placed under arrest (though most later received amnesty).

Observers inside and outside of Russia were appalled at the violence and loss of life, but no mass support for the rebels materialized. Calm was quickly restored in Moscow while other cities and regions remained quiet. Despite deep resentment of the continuing economic hardships, many citizens were fed up with the political squabbling and cared as little for the oppositionists as for the government. Yeltsin accelerated arrangements for the already announced parliamentary elections in December and ordered that a final draft of the new constitution be submitted to voters at the same time. As electioneering began, the moderates split over the pace of reform and over who should lead the nascent political parties. Yeltsin stood above the electoral fray, sticking by an earlier refusal to form his own political party. One group, Russia's Choice, was clearly pro-Yeltsin, but the others were critical of the government in varying degrees. With the liberals and centrists in disarray and public dismay over economic conditions mounting, extremists on both the left and the right campaigned vigorously against the existing regime.

Despite fears of widespread public apathy, 54.8 percent of 106 million registered voters participated in the December 1993 elections, a reasonably healthy sign for the fledgling Russian democracy. Fifty-eight percent of those voting approved the presidential constitution, which gave Yeltsin the power to appoint the prime minister and cabinet and largely to determine domestic and foreign policy while reserving some fiscal authority to the new parliamentary lower house, the Duma. Under special and not very demanding conditions, the president also had the right to dissolve the Duma, to order popular referenda, and to rule by decree. No clear winner emerged in the parliamentary elections. An extremist nationalist group, misleadingly calling itself the Liberal-Democratic Party, won 15 percent of Duma seats. Its leader, Vladimir Zhirinovsky, a flamboyant personality and effective speaker, campaigned for restoration of Russian pride and dignity, with the slogan, "Raise Russia from her knees!" Subsequently, his idiosyncratic and rude behavior in the Duma and in public undermined his credibility as a national politician. Other conservative and ex-Communist groups garnered 23 percent of the seats, with the result that Yeltsin's opponents outmatched the 36 percent of the deputies elected from the pro-reform parties. But the opposition often failed to act in concert and proved more a hindrance than a complete block to the government's continuing reform efforts.

With free and fair elections behind them and a new constitution and legislature in place, Russians settled into a more stable democratic system. Although the bulk of the population remained politically apathetic or cynical, most citizens valued their right to choose and their ability to criticize the government and other authorities without fear of Soviet-style retribution. Rights of free speech and press were vigorously asserted, particularly as newspaper and television commentators, politicians, and many individual citizens regularly and pointedly lambasted the Yeltsin regime over economic malaise, crime, and "cronyism" (the undue influence of Russia's richest businessmen in government and the economy). The lack of effective political parties proved, however, a major weakness of the fledgling democracy. The Duma parties operated as personal factions, and none, except possibly the ex-Communists, had a broad base in the electorate or a viable national organization. Thus, personalities dominated, programs were shifting and unclear, and voters had no sense of identification with a well-defined political organization or purpose.

Party ineffectiveness only magnified the constitutionally endorsed preponderant power of the presidency in the Russian system. Yeltsin frequently appeared to act erratically and arbitrarily, bypassing the Duma and evoking taunts of "Tsar Boris." At the same time the president had to take account of public opinion and the continuing legislative opposition to much of his program. Often Russia appeared to be at a political stalemate. Yeltsin's deteriorating health further complicated the picture. The president had serious heart attacks in the summer and fall of 1995 and was able to work only intermittently. At times rumors also surfaced of a drinking problem. Nevertheless, the Russian leader pushed ahead with prosecution of a military campaign against Chechen rebels (to be discussed shortly) and with preparations for parliamentary elections in December 1995 and a presidential ballot in June 1996.

As in the first Duma campaign in 1993, the moderates could not coalesce around a single party in preparing for the 1995 elections. They soon split into a number of factions, including the new Our Home Is Russia, led by Prime Minister Chernomyrdin. At the same time the government's opponents were also divided and often at odds with each other. Consequently, although dissatisfaction with the meager results of reform remained widespread, pro-government candidates did not fare as badly as might have been expected. The overall results returned a Duma quite like the 1993–1995 body, with democrats, reformers, and sympathetic independents winning about 30 percent of the seats, the new Communists 33 percent, and the nationalists slipping to about 12 percent. Clearly, many in the electorate had vented their frustration with living conditions by supporting neo-Communists, a familiar party and one that promised better times. But the voters had not swung to the far right, and the decline of nationalist strength reflected the waning influence of chauvinist slogans among a younger body politic. The Communist leader, Gennady Zyuganov, early made clear that he intended to criticize the government heavily but would not use his bloc of votes to obstruct all parliamentary business or to bring the government down. So, for the next four years, the Yeltsin regime and the Duma coexisted in an often tense but not entirely unproductive relationship.

A major milestone for Russian democracy proved to be the presidential elections of June–July 1996. Despite recurring heart troubles and bouts of passivity during the winter and spring of 1996, Yeltsin made clear that he wanted a second term. At first trailing Communist candidate Zyuganov in polls, Yeltsin rallied and stumped energetically in the run-up to the June balloting. In addition, Russia's big businessmen, who had at first shown little interest in the election, began to pour money and media support into the president's campaign once they realized that the alternative to Yeltsin would be Zyuganov. Finally, Western organizations provided experienced electoral strategists and expert campaign organizers to advise the Yeltsin reelection effort.

Despite this assistance, the president barely prevailed in the first round of voting in mid-June 1996, winning 35 percent of the vote to Zyuganov's 32 percent, with recently retired General Alexander Lebed, who had campaigned as a tough-guy maverick, drawing almost 15 percent, and the liberals' hope, Grigory Yavlinsky, garnering just over 7 percent. The electoral share of the nationalists and extreme right dipped even lower than in the 1995 Duma elections, falling to 5.8 percent of the ballots. In the runoff round in July the two top candidates would compete, and even assuming that most of the liberal vote would swing to the president, Yeltsin and his handlers could see that he might have difficulty achieving the majority needed for reelection. Seeking to attract some of Lebed's law-and-order supporters, Yeltsin persuaded the general to support him in return for Lebed's appointment as national security adviser. Although renewed heart trouble sidelined the president for several weeks before the runoff, his final campaign profited from a heavily financed television blitz and openhanded promises of "goodies" for regions, groups, and institutions. In addition, the president wielded the bogey of "communism," insisting that he represented the chief bulwark against a return to the bad old days. Yeltsin won handily, with 53.7 percent of the vote, while Zyuganov lagged at 40.2 percent. Voter turnout neared 70 percent, surpassing the 65 percent of balloters in the 1995 Duma elections. Democratic Russia had thus managed several free and fair national elections, two parliamentary and one presidential, suggesting that the new ideology was well rooted. Critics pointed out obvious flaws in the system: big-money interests possessed too much influence, the president wielded too much power, and parties were weak and disparate. Yet, for a country that had not known open voting since 1917, these three elections indicated that most citizens relished the opportunity for choice at the ballot box.

Yeltsin's performance in his second term was decidedly mixed. In November 1996 the president finally underwent major heart surgery and was unable actively to direct the government for four or five months. In 1997–1999 his health and drinking problems recurred sporadically, and his conduct of public affairs became increasingly erratic. Although Yeltsin managed after some months to fire the outspoken and ambitious Lebed, who went on to fail as governor of the Krasnoyarsk region, and he continued to support the overall reform program, his subordinates, including Prime Minister Chernomyrdin, proved mediocre and ineffective leaders. Critics asserted that the Russian ship of state was without a firm hand at the helm and that Yeltsin's family and a coterie of unsavory behind-the-scenes advisers were in fact the real rulers of the country—and not always in the public interest. Yeltsin responded lethargically to the major financial crisis of August 1998 discussed above, and in 1998 and 1999 he fired and hired prime ministers at will. Nevertheless, he remained on good terms with U.S. President Clinton and with other Western and world leaders. He continued relatively benign relations with Russia's neighbors, including former Soviet republics, and he cooperated with the United States on arms control and denuclearization. By mid-1999, however, many observers concluded Russia was adrift and needed new, strong leadership.

A renewed crisis over Chechnya brought matters to a head. Earlier, in the middle of his first term as president, Yeltsin's stubborn insistence on crushing Chechen rebels by force turned out to be his biggest mistake and the sorriest mark on his record. Some critics of Yeltsin's eight years in office insist that he acted undemocratically, tolerated cronyism and corruption, botched the transition to a market economy, and callously ignored the hardships his policies visited on the Russian people. His defenders point to successful institutionalization of the Duma and local governmental organs, free and fair elections, installation of a free-enterprise system, even if at considerable cost, and a restrained and positive foreign policy. But both detractors and supporters agree that Yeltsin badly mishandled the brewing trouble in Chechnya.

The Chechen ethnic group of the north Caucasus had a long history of opposition to established authorities, dating back to its resistance to imposition of tsarist rule in the first half of the 1800s and including its banishment to Central Asia by Stalin during World War II. Many Chechens returned to their homeland in the Khrushchev era, and in 1991 nationalist leaders declared independence, even though the tiny region of Chechnya, with about one million inhabitants, was isolated and landlocked on the southeastern edge of the Russian Republic. In the fall of 1992 a complicated struggle over land and indigenous rights among Russian Cossacks, Chechens, and other local peoples in Chechnya ended in rioting and pillaging, with several hundred deaths and much property damage before three thousand Russian troops restored order. During 1993 and 1994 Chechen chieftains reaffirmed their earlier claim to separate status and established local rule in some areas. After clumsy Russian attempts to subvert this inchoate and poorly organized breakaway movement, Defense Minister Pavel Grachev and hard-line advisers to Yeltsin persuaded the president to launch a military offensive against the Chechen rebels in December 1994. Following a bungled attack that caused several thousand civilian and military casualties, Russian forces finally occupied the Chechen capital, Grozny, in January 1995. Western leaders as well as Islamic states sympathetic to the Muslim Chechens condemned the government's brutal use of force against a handful of rebels. Nationalists in Moscow mostly backed Yeltsin's actions, while centrist, democratic, and even ex-Communist elements were critical, belittling the president's claim that he had been forced to act to hold the Russian Republic together.

Despite overwhelming superiority in troops and weapons, the Russian army, its largely conscript soldiers demoralized and its generals incompetent, proved incapable during 1995 of quelling the Chechen rebellion in the countryside. Extremist demands from both sides stymied efforts to reach a political settlement of the dispute. The Russian occupiers had little success forming a viable pro-Moscow government in Grozny. Chechens themselves could not agree on what future they sought, opinions running from full independence to limited autonomy. Uniformly anti-Russian, Chechen rebel forces were a ragtag lot of idealistic nationalists, Islamic radicals, and opportunists, including bandits and extortionists, some of whom were former "freedom fighters" trained and equipped by the CIA to undermine Soviet rule in Afghanistan a decade earlier. As tens of thousands of Chechen warriors took to the mountains to launch guerrilla warfare against the Russian army, casualties and criticism mounted. The Chechen war also bled the

Russian exchequer at a time when the government was struggling to control the budget. Despite a nominal cease-fire in July 1995, sporadic fighting and off-and-on peace negotiations continued into mid-1996.

After Chechen rebels retook Grozny in August 1996, General Lebed, newly appointed as Yeltsin's national security adviser, secured a shaky settlement of the conflict. Although the Russian government proclaimed that it had prevented a precedent of unilateral secession, the Chechens could well claim victory. The peace deal provided for withdrawal of almost all Russian forces, establishment of an interim government of moderate Chechen nationalists to have "special status" within the Russian federation, and a referendum on independence after five years. With upwards of ten thousand Russian dead and wounded, plus some one hundred thousand Chechen casualties, military and civilian, Yeltsin reluctantly signed off on these terms and promised a fresh start for Chechnya.

The 1996 settlement lasted only a little over two years, however. Russian officials' reluctance to consider complete independence for Chechnya and political disarray among the Chechens blocked progress toward a permanent resolution of Chechnya's status. In Chechnya the situation deteriorated. Despite Russian promises, reconstruction, relief, and economic development lagged; the Russian-backed government was largely ineffective; and disorder, banditry, and rebel activity predominated in the rural areas. Moreover, Islamic fundamentalism and rebellion appeared to be spreading into other areas of the north Caucasus. During summer 1999 bands of Chechen separatists began operating in Dagestan, a region next door to Chechnya. In September bomb blasts destroyed several apartment houses in Moscow and in the southern town of Volgodonsk, killing several hundred people. Vladimir Putin, unexpectedly named prime minister the preceding month, quickly blamed Chechen rebels for these attacks, though neither at the time nor subsequently did the Russian government present convincing evidence of Chechen complicity. Nevertheless, the Russian public, terrified and angered by this terrorism, responded enthusiastically to Putin's tough stance. In October amid fervent exhortations from Putin and President Yeltsin, whose term would expire in June 2000, the Russian army plunged once more into the Chechen quagmire. Despite claims of better-trained troops, improved equipment, and more reliable intelligence, the Russians again proved incapable of defeating the Chechen insurrection. They succeeded eventually in controlling the main cities and towns, but even after Russian generals had declared victory several times in 2001 and 2002, rebels continued to shoot down Russian helicopters, harass Russian garrisons, and control the Chechen countryside. Moreover, as had been rumored during the first Chechen war, Russian forces were accused of grave human rights violations, including the torture and murder of innocent civilians.

Western governments renewed their criticism of Russian policy in Chechnya while Putin insisted that his troops were simply rooting out bandits and

Figure 23. *President Vladimir Vladimirovich Putin meeting U.S. President Bush in 2001. Source: Russian Cultural Center and the Embassy of the Russian Federation.*

secessionists in order to preserve the territorial integrity of the Russian state. After the September 2001 terrorist attacks in the United States, Putin, now the Russian president (see Figure 23), at once enlisted in the American government's war against terrorism, hastening to link the Chechen rebels with Al-Qaeda and portraying Russian actions in Chechnya as simply another front in that war. Grateful for his prompt and thorough cooperation in their fall 2001 attack on Afghanistan, American and West European leaders muted their criticism of Russia's Chechen policy. During early 2002 Putin accused the government of the neighboring state of Georgia in the Caucasus of harboring Chechen rebels in the Pankisi Gorge border area, but thanks in part to American good offices and assurances, the spat with Georgia blew over finally.

In spite of attempts to use global anti-terrorism to validate suppression of the Chechen independence movement, Putin appeared by fall 2002 to recognize that the festering sore of Chechnya was unlikely to be healed by military poultices. Moreover, polls indicated that public support for the Chechen war, which had helped bring Putin to power, was waning, with almost half the populace leaning toward a peaceful solution. Rumors of secret negotiations between the two sides surfaced. However, in late October 2002, forty-one Chechen commandos seized a Moscow theater and its over 800 patrons, threatening to blow up the building and kill the hostages unless the Russian army withdrew from Chechnya. After several days' hesitation, Putin ordered special forces to end the takeover. Using an opiate-based gas, they immobilized and then killed all the hostage-takers.

At the same time most of the hostages were also gassed, with 120 dying, in part, critics said, because the Russian government refused to tell medical personnel treating the stricken exactly what sort of gas it was. Public opinion in Russia overwhelmingly supported Putin's course of action. The hostage taking and resulting deaths hardened popular and governmental attitudes toward Chechens' demands for independence, but Putin promised a 2003 referendum in Chechnya on its future status and later presidential elections there.

When Yeltsin appointed Vladimir Putin prime minister in August 1999, observers not only in the West but in Russia were surprised and baffled. A newcomer on the political scene, Putin was little known. Born in Leningrad in 1953 of working-class parents, Putin majored in law at Leningrad University and entered the KGB, the Soviet security and intelligence service, in the mid-1970s. Posted to East Germany in the 1980s, he apparently was a competent but not especially remarkable young officer. After 1991 he served as a second-rank official in the government of St. Petersburg (formerly Leningrad), facilitating foreign investment and rising to become one of the city's deputy mayors. Recommended to Yeltsin's staff as a young up-and-comer, Putin was brought to Moscow in 1996 to join the president's administrative team. Capable and self-effacing, Putin endeared himself to Yeltsin before long, and in 1998 was appointed head of domestic counterintelligence. Yeltsin, who was constitutionally required to step down in 2000 after two terms, had run through four different prime ministers during 1998 and the first half of 1999. According to his memoirs, the Russian president decided in August 1999 to make Putin prime minister because the young civil servant had the backbone, ambition, and talent to succeed to the presidency in the scheduled June 2000 elections. If this assertion is true, Yeltsin must have been delighted with his protégé's tough stand against the Chechens a month later and with the public acclaim this brought the new leader. With Yeltsin's health and his ability to govern both deteriorating noticeably during fall 1999, rumors circulated that Yeltsin might step down early to give Putin a better run at the presidency, but most Russians nevertheless were taken by surprise when the president did just that on New Year's Eve 1999.

Although Putin began his prime ministership in Yeltsin's shadow, his firmness, confidence, and considerable competence soon won over Yeltsin's supporters, some moderates, and the broad public. Young, fit, imperturbable, and determined, he presented a reassuring figure in a time of uncertainty. Many Russians vested their hopes for stability, security, and better times in him. By the time Putin became acting president in January 2000, he was immensely popular and the overwhelming favorite for the upcoming presidential elections. His position was bolstered by the government's victory in the December 1999 elections to the Duma, in which almost 62 percent of the electorate voted. A new government-linked party, Unity, won 16.6 percent of the vote, which together with the 15.5 percent of a new center-right grouping, the Fatherland, plus the support of a number of non-party deputies, provided the Yeltsin-Putin regime with a bare but working majority in the new Duma. The ex-Communists slipped slightly to about a quarter of the vote, with the democratic left at 11 percent and the extreme right trailing at 4 percent.

Constitutional provisions for an election within three months after a president's resignation moved the presidential balloting up from June to March 2000. With a bland, all-encompassing platform that promised a continuation of reform and economic improvement and against weak opposition, Putin romped to victory, with 53 percent of the vote. His main opponent, the ex-Communist Zyuganov, lost some ground compared to the 1996 elections but still polled almost 30 percent of the ballots. Yet his supporters, aging, rural, and nostalgic for the good old days, were increasingly marginalized in the new Russia, and by 2001 Putin had weakened the Communist deputies' position in the Duma, which the president now dominated.

During 2000–2002 Putin's domestic policies aimed consistently at a few main goals: prosperity, order, and stability. Abetted by rising world prices for oil and natural gas, he succeeded in growing the Russian economy substantially while admitting candidly that it was still far below the level of most Western economies. Repeatedly stressing his faith in a market system, the new president undertook several steps to make the Russian version work better. He simplified the tax code and customs procedures, improved the pension system, passed land reform laws, and strengthened property rights, all the while stressing the importance of providing a climate that would attract more foreign investment to Russia. Putin also introduced measures to revamp and upgrade the judiciary and moved tentatively toward banking reform. Eschewing direct confrontation, he cleverly circumscribed the economic and political influence of the "tycoons" or "oligarchs," using the threat of investigation and indictment to force two of the most powerful into exile. Though reducing crime and extortion, the president had less success combating widespread corruption and bureaucratic interference in economic activity and daily life. At least he acknowledged these characteristics of transition Russia as a serious problem.

Besides undercutting the parliamentary strength of the ex-Communists and clipping the wings of the oligarchs, Putin over two years succeeded in eroding the powerful position of the regions and reestablishing firmer central government authority throughout the country. He weakened the position of the governors in the upper legislative body, the Federation Council, won authority to remove elected governors if necessary, and established seven large jurisdictions or provinces run by his appointees to supervise activity in Russia's eighty-nine regions.

Politically Putin made only one glaring misstep. In August 2000 when the Russian nuclear submarine *Kursk*, crippled by an accidental explosion, sank with the loss of 180 mariners, Putin, who was on vacation, seemed at first unresponsive to the tragedy. Recovering, he made every effort to assist the surviving families, to investigate and assess blame for the sinking, and to supervise recovery of the *Kursk* and the bodies trapped inside. Learning from this slip, the president subsequently displayed political acumen, and his popularity ratings remained in the 70–80 percent range despite the dragged-out war in Chechnya. He successfully courted a wide range of constituents, ranging from the Orthodox faithful (Putin's mother secretly baptized him at birth) through the military and the nationalist right to the educational establishment and the intelligentsia.

Putin's popularity and success raised questions about democracy in Russia. No other politician had the standing or backing to challenge him. Political parties hardly existed in the Western sense, and Putin's policies prevailed in a Duma that his administration largely controlled. No opposition organization or movement in fact existed. Some critics wondered whether Russia was moving toward authoritarianism. Moreover, the president's own statements raised doubts about his commitment to democracy. Though iterating his support for the concept, Putin also often spoke of wanting to establish "a dictatorship of law," and in his emphasis on law and order for Russia, some observers felt that the president gave greatest weight to the last word in that slogan. Most disturbingly for many doubters, Putin showed little toleration for criticism and on several occasions did not hesitate to use the state's vast authority and apparatus to curtail independent press and television outlets opposing his policies. His government also harassed some foes of the Chechen war, and the president himself rejected all charges of Russian misconduct in that war. On the other hand, under Putin considerable freedom of the press persisted, and individuals retained rights to free speech, assembly, and voting. Clearly, the Russian president sought a more prosperous life for his people and believed firmly that efficiency, order, and stability were needed to move toward that goal, a sentiment shared by most Russians. In the process both leaders and people struggled not to erode their newly found freedom and democracy.

RUSSIA, ITS NEIGHBORS, AND THE WORLD

When the Soviet Union collapsed in 1991, many observers feared that its Russian core would become a destabilizing force in world affairs. Some were concerned that Russian nationalism would impel the new state's untested leaders to reassert control over neighboring nations, formerly USSR republics and before that provinces of the tsarist empire. Others worried that Russia would use its still powerful nuclear arsenal to bully smaller nations in Asia and east central Europe. Yet in the following decade neither fear was realized, and Russian administrations under both Yeltsin and Putin played a largely positive role in the global community.

Amid the debris of Soviet socialism's demise, President Yeltsin of Russia faced two urgent foreign policy issues. First, he had to craft new relationships with the fledgling state's closest neighbors, the fourteen other former republics of the Soviet Union, soon called Russia's "near abroad." These smaller nations surrounded Russia to the west, south, and southeast, leaving only Finland in the northeast and Mongolia and China in the east as previously established states with extensive borders on Russia (see Map 1). Second, Yeltsin needed to maintain and expand the good relations with the West developed by Gorbachev. In particular, the Russian president aimed to enhance Russian security by ensuring that the United States and its European allies would not take advantage of Russia's weakness and by working with these same states, plus USSR successor countries Ukraine, Belarus, and Kazakhstan, to control and reduce the huge arsenal of nuclear weapons left behind by the cold war. Also, Yeltsin desperately sought economic and technical assistance from the capitalist countries as he tried to wrench his society onto the unfamiliar path of open markets and free enterprise.

At the outset it appeared that establishing good relations with the "near abroad" would be the most challenging task. In late fall 1991, despite having worked briefly with Gorbachev to preserve a shell of the Soviet Union, Yeltsin quickly accepted the USSR's demise once Ukrainians voted for independence on December 1. A week later the Russian president cooperated with the leaders of Ukraine and Belarus (formerly Byelorussia) to declare the USSR formally dissolved and to found the Commonwealth of Independent States (CIS), intended as a loose confederation of the former Soviet republics. All these new states except Georgia, embroiled in civil strife, and the Baltic countries, already pursuing an independent path, adhered to the CIS on December 21, 1991. From its birth the CIS encountered major obstacles. The other joiners feared Russian domination of the new body, and agreement on thorny issues of trade, economic cooperation, territory, and minority rights proved elusive among so many disparate members. Individual governments resorted to making bilateral arrangements with their neighbors, often undercutting CIS efforts. Each successor nation acted independently in foreign affairs, and the major global powers soon recognized the new states. The United Nations admitted them all, with Russia assuming the Soviet Union's permanent Security Council seat. Despite several attempts to strengthen the CIS, it never evolved into a working confederation and remained for the next ten years a convenient forum to discuss common issues and a place where lower-level facilitating agreements among the members could be worked out.

Apart from the CIS framework, Russia pursued bilateral relations with its nearest neighbors during the first decade of independence. A number of prickly issues arose, but by 2002 most had been peacefully resolved. During the Soviet era, particularly after World War II, many ethnic Russians had moved to the USSR's non-Russian republics, where they played important economic and political roles. As a result, the demise of the Soviet Union left some twenty-three million Russians stranded in these border countries, with the largest groups in eastern Ukraine, the Baltic states, and northern Kazakhstan. During the 1990s almost four million of these displaced Russians moved to the new Russian Republic. The remainder, however, now a minority in the new non-Russian states, urged the Yeltsin administration to help protect their rights. Particularly in the Baltic states of Estonia, Latvia, and Lithuania, many Russians were aggrieved at citizenship requirements, which often included learning the local, difficult language.

Some also felt discriminated against economically. Under pressure from Russia, Scandinavian countries, the European Union, and the United States, the Baltic governments and their Russian populations gradually worked out compromises on citizenship, language, and minority rights. By 2002 Russian minorities were benefiting from the considerable progress made by the Baltic economies and their discontent became increasingly muted.

Another issue revolved around the removal of military units and bases. In Estonia and Georgia particularly, Yeltsin's government used the presence of Russian (former Soviet) troops to pressure the new states. Only after several years were all Russian forces withdrawn from Estonia, while as late as 2002 some Russian units remained in Georgia, Azerbaijan, and Tajikistan. A related problem was the responsibility and costs of environmentally cleaning former Soviet military sites. A third point of friction centered on adjustments of borders, which Stalin had often set arbitrarily. The most troubling potential dispute arose between Russia and Ukraine. In 1954, to mark the three-hundredth anniversary of Ukraine's accession to Russia, Stalin had transferred control of the Crimean peninsula from the Russian Soviet Republic to the Ukrainian Soviet Republic. Although substantial Ukrainian and Tatar minorities inhabited the Crimea in the 1990s, Russians made up a majority of the population and Russia claimed the former Soviet Black Sea naval fleet and its base port at Sevastopol. Resisting nationalist pressure to recover the Crimea for Russia, Yeltsin managed to reach a settlement in May 1997 that guaranteed the territorial integrity of Ukraine's borders and a Russian lease on Sevastopol for twenty years.

General Russian-Ukrainian relations proved friendlier than expected, given many nationalist Ukrainians' detestation of three centuries of Russian rule. Both sides worked hard to resolve difficult economic issues surrounding trade and Ukrainian arrears in paying for energy imported from Russia. Ukraine found itself in a weak bargaining position as its ex-Communist leaders moved sluggishly to implement reform and its economy floundered during the 1990s and early 2000s. Nevertheless, the two governments cooperated with each other and with the United States on military and security issues, including the transfer to the Ukrainian armed forces of former Soviet troops and the dismantling of all nuclear weapons on Ukrainian soil, the last a crucial task completed in 1996.

The enlargement of NATO, the West European–North Atlantic defensive alliance, emerged as a sticking point in Russia's relations both with the Baltic states and Ukraine and with the West. Arguing that NATO was essentially directed against Russia (as indeed it had been in the Soviet era), Russian administrations criticized the inclusion of Poland, Hungary, and

Czechoslovakia in the alliance during the 1990s and strongly opposed plans to add Ukraine and the Baltic states later. The European powers and the United States countered this hostility first by carving out a special position for Russia within NATO itself, permitting Russia to sit on the NATO Council for most deliberations, though not for decisions regarding future expansion and certain military matters. Second, the Western nations redefined NATO's mission to make the alliance broadly responsible for European security, including that of Russia and Eastern Europe, and for protecting general European interests in nearby regions. Finally, Ukraine and the Baltic states asserted vigorously that their future participation in NATO would not be directed against Russia but would further the overall security of the European continent. Although Russian resistance to NATO expansion continued throughout Yeltsin's presidency, Putin soon took a more pragmatic line, responding positively to the various assurances given. In November 2002 NATO invited the Baltic states to join, without significant Russian protest, and NATO enlargement seemed a dead issue.

Both Yeltsin and Putin found the new failed state of Belarus, just to Russia's west, a minor irritant. Some Russian nationalists and a few Belarusan politicians beat the drums for a merger of Russia and Belarus, but the Russian presidents managed to finesse these efforts by establishing a token union and by making the conditions for genuine union unacceptable to both groups. Russian leaders generally agreed that the disastrous and unreformed Belarusan economy and its political authoritarianism could only be an added burden for reform-minded Russia. Nevertheless, at some point in the future, if prospects for Belarus brighten, these two Slavic states, closely linked historically, economically, and culturally, may well coalesce.

Russia's relations with newly founded states in the Caucasus and Central Asia followed a complicated, sometimes tortuous course. In Kazakhstan, with a Russian population of more than six million, Yeltsin and Kazakh President Nursultan Nazarbayev cooperated to ease emigration for those Russians wishing to leave and to control friction between those remaining and the local population. Elsewhere Russian policy focused on security threats from the south, especially the possible spread of Islamic fundamentalism from Afghanistan and Iran, and on maintaining Russian economic and political influence in the region. In Georgia, Russian military leaders backed anti-Georgian secessionist efforts of the minority Abkhaz people and obtained the right to station troops in Georgia and to maintain bases along Georgia's Turkish frontier. As noted above, Putin also pressured Georgia to block Chechen rebels from taking refuge in its northeastern region. In Armenia and Azerbaijan, Russia asserted its military presence and its commercial interests in development of the latter's extensive oil reserves in and around the Caspian Sea.

In Central Asia, Russian troops intervened in a long-running civil war in Tajikistan, partly for humanitarian reasons and partly to ensure the security of Tajikistan's long border with Afghanistan. In other states, Russia asserted some influence and broadened commercial ties but respected the Central Asian states' independence, including their different Islamic basis and their slow pace of economic and political reform after 1991. Following the Al-Qaeda attacks on the United States in September 2001, President Putin extended wholehearted cooperation in President Bush's war against terrorism, even acquiescing in establishment of American bases in Central Asia to support the offensive against the Taliban in Afghanistan.

Further east, both Yeltsin and Putin successfully bolstered Russia's relations with India, Southeast Asia, China, and Japan. With China, Putin signed a twenty-year treaty of friendship and cooperation on July 16, 2001. In addition, minor border disputes were resolved, trade and arms sales expanded, and scientific and technical exchanges broadened. In Southeast Asia, Russia received high marks for promising to turn over the former Soviet base at Cam Ranh Bay to the Vietnamese government. Regarding Japan, issues of fishing rights in nearby seas were clarified, and the Japanese promised support for Russian development of a new natural gas field in Siberia and construction of a pipeline to Russia's Pacific coast. No agreement could be found, however, on the festering dispute over ownership of the Kurile Islands seized by the Soviet Union after World War II (see Chapter 14).

Apart from stabilizing ties with the "near abroad," the main focus of Russian foreign policy during the first post-Soviet decade remained relations with the West, particularly the United States. Though marked by ups and downs, this relationship proved remarkably positive and cooperative, given the intense Soviet-Western rivalry during the cold war. To be sure, Russia, weak economically and militarily, had little choice. The new state urgently needed Western support and friendship as it ventured into a new era. Yet both Yeltsin and Putin had to fend off chauvinist critics at home who blamed the United States and especially the CIA for Russia's loss of great-power status and who demanded Russia reassert its dominance in Eastern Europe and surrounding regions. Yeltsin's presidency coincided with that of Bill Clinton, and the two soon established a congenial and effective working relationship. Their most impressive achievement came from a joint commitment to continue the process of nuclear disarmament begun under Gorbachev. Going beyond the START I treaty of July 1991, the United States and Russia agreed in START II to reduce nuclear arms on each side to a level of 3,000–3,500 weapons. Presidents Bush and Putin signed a pact on May 25, 2002, setting an even lower figure of no more than 2,200 warheads by 2012, with the Russians hoping for 1,500 and U.S. military specialists targeting about 1,750. While certainly desirable and a cost-saving measure for both sides, the treaty still left each country with weapons totals that could vaporize the whole world.

Earlier, the two countries succeeded in enhancing nuclear security by persuading Kazakhstan, Belarus, and Ukraine to surrender former Soviet nuclear missiles on their territory, whose dismantling was completed by the end of 1996. The United States also provided funds for the inspection, supervision, and defusing of weapons on both sides, for much improved security at remaining Russian nuclear sites, and for the employment of Russian atomic scientists who might otherwise have been tempted to go to work for aspiring nuclear states such as Iraq, Iran, and North Korea. Although unverified rumors of leakage abroad of Russian fissionable materials continued, the cooperative effort to reduce and control nuclear weapons marked a major success of Russian-American relations after 1991.

Western aid proved to be quite a different story. Although emergency relief assistance was effectively delivered to Russia in the difficult winters of 1991–1992 and 1992–1993, Russian leaders clearly hoped that substantial economic help would reward their cooperative attitude. Indeed, the Western powers plus Japan earmarked some $40 billion for assistance to Russia in the first half of the 1990s. But only a small portion of this sum was actually delivered because of delays in setting specific targets for the aid. Moreover, according to critics, the help that did arrive was often misspent, was siphoned into the pockets of rich tycoons, or simply disappeared. Much Western economic assistance was channeled through the International Monetary Fund, whose strict budgetary and fiscal requirements the Russians greatly resented. Unilateral American aid, both governmental and private, amounted to some $5 billion in the 1990s. Its effect was disputed, critics claiming that most of it was wasted, defenders arguing that it successfully targeted specific needs, including technical assistance and support for key civic and grassroots organizations. By the early 2000s, with the Russian budget and economy healthy, Western aid tapered off. Despite the Western powers' willingness to help, their inclusion of Russia in key economic summits, and their support of eventual Russian entry into the World Trade Organization, many Russians complained that the West had not only done too little but had in fact used aid to undermine or control the Russian economy. Even some Western observers concluded that the United States and its allies had risked Russia's future stability by not providing massive economic assistance along the lines of the post–World War II Marshall Plan for Europe.

Several nettlesome issues rippled the smooth surface of Russo-American harmony in the first post-Soviet decade. As described above, Russia at first vehemently opposed NATO's spread eastward, but after Western assurances and Russia's accepting a role in NATO the issue faded away. Similarly, when the new Bush administration determined in 2001 that it must create a defensive shield to protect the United States against future missile attacks from such rogue states as North Korea and Iran, Putin objected strongly, insisting that America had to abide by the Anti-Ballistic Missile (ABM) Treaty of 1972. Yet months later, after Russian leaders realized the enormous costs of missile defense and its uncertain reliability, after U.S. promises to share new defensive technological breakthroughs with Russia, and after Putin had been among the first to enlist in the American war against terrorism, the Russian president barely whimpered when Bush unilaterally withdrew from the ABM Treaty in June 2002.

In a parallel fashion, Russia and the United States at first disagreed over developments in Yugoslavia, but eventually these differences were resolved and Russia became a supporter of and participant in Western policy toward the Balkans. When the Yugoslav state first began to dissolve in chaos and anarchy in the late 1980s and early 1990s, Russian diplomacy frequently supported the position of the Serbs (fellow Slavs and former allies of the tsarist government), criticizing Western interference in the region. In 1994, however, Russian leaders helped broker a compromise with the Bosnian Serbs and sent Russian units to participate in peacekeeping efforts in Bosnia and later in Kosovo.

Russo-American friction over policy toward Iran and Iraq proved harder to overcome. Russia opposed American efforts to isolate and impose an embargo on Iran, its southern neighbor. The Russians continued a lively commercial intercourse with Iran, including sales of arms and non-military nuclear technology, and stood ready to participate in further development of the Iranian petroleum industry. Both the Clinton and Bush administrations complained intermittently that Russia's exports in fact supported the buildup of Iran's military strength and might be facilitating its effort to acquire nuclear weapons. Russian leaders retorted that everything it sold was for peaceful uses only and that trade helped promote moderation and responsibility in Iran. Parallel disagreements erupted over Iraq. Although Russia backed the U.S.-led Gulf War against Iraq in 1992, it objected to later American air strikes. In the late 1990s, Russian diplomats ignored Iraq's ousting of UN weapons inspectors and flouting of UN resolutions. At times Russia seemed to be supporting Iraqi leader Saddam Hussein's efforts to secure a lifting of UN sanctions against Iraq, perhaps because the Russian government hoped to collect part of Iraq's $7 billion debt to Russia and to develop a strong commercial presence in post-sanctions Iraq. Nevertheless, after initial hesitation and publicly expressed concerns about unilateral American action, Russia eventually supported the UN decision in November 2002 to return arms inspectors to Iraq with broadened powers.

CONCLUSION

In reviewing the record of new Russia's first decade, observers divided, some seeing the glass half full, others depicting the glass as half empty. Certainly, the cataclysmic transition from a doctrinaire, authoritarian, totally regulated system to a free, democratic, individualized society proved far from easy. Many Russians suffered economically, socially, and psychologically. Yet no other large nation had ever attempted such a monumental leap, and by 2002 fewer and fewer Russians wanted to turn back. As President Putin said in a public radio interview on his November 2001 visit to the United States: "The choice was made, and I am absolutely, 100 percent confident that it is an irreversible process. . . . And the basics of democracy, the foundation of democracy, will continue to be strengthened and the market economy will again continue to progress. . . . The point of no return is way in the past."

In the process of reform, mistakes were certainly made and negative features surfaced. At times the economy appeared near meltdown, and a small elite profited unjustifiably from the chaos and the sale of state assets. Environmental damage from the Soviet era remained unrepaired. Political conflict between reformers and conservatives led to a brief but violent confrontation in October 1993 and to later periods of near paralysis of the government. Under the new constitution the president possessed too much power, which after 2000 Putin exercised, according to his critics, to override any potential opposition and to muzzle the mass media. Crime, corruption, deteriorating public health and other social services, a growing drug and AIDS problem, and skyrocketing divorce rates created social conditions that made life difficult for many. Materialism, selfishness, apathy, and despair all flourished.

On the other hand, by 2002, the economy was growing, markedly in output and slowly in productivity, and the percentage of the population living in poverty dropped. Although rural life remained bleak, an increasing number of city dwellers began to taste the benefits of reform. Elections, a responsible legislature, an improving judiciary, and a partially free press undergirded Russian democracy. Revamped educational institutions opened a number of opportunities, particularly for younger Russians. Despite the flood of cheap Western imports, cultural life and creativity rebounded. Russia's stature in the world, though clearly diminished from the days of the Soviet superpower, had solidified. Despite outsiders' fear of a renewed Russian imperialism, Yeltsin and Putin established good relations with the newly independent states on Russia's borders, exerting influence but not domination there, and with Russia's neighbors in Asia. Both the United States and the European powers allotted Russia a significant role in European security and international affairs, and relations with the West remained friendly and cooperative.

Into the twenty-first century Russia faces considerable challenges: the need to diversify its economy, to replace a decaying industrial, transportation, and communications infrastructure, to reduce bureaucratic interference and corruption, and to revive a lagging agricultural sector; the establishment of a clearer and fairer legal system, the creation of viable political parties, the buildup of grassroots organizations, and the nurturing of a sense of civic responsibility; and the protection of freedom of expression. Yet the progress made since 1991 provides grounds for optimism about Russia's future. Outside observers can only sympathize with the Russians' stoic struggle, after a thousand years of tortured history, to find prosperity, stability, freedom, and their own unique destiny in the modern world.

FURTHER READING

Aslund, Anders. *Russia's Economic Transformation in the 1990s.* Herndon, Va.: 1997.

Blasi, Joseph R., Maya Kroumira, and Douglas Kruse. *Kremlin Capitalism: Privatizing the Russian Economy.* Ithaca, N.Y.: 1999.

Dawisha, Karen, and Bruce Parrott. *Russia and the New States of Eurasia: The Politics of Upheaval.* New York: 1994.

Davis, Nathaniel. *A Long Walk to Church: A Contemporary History of Russian Orthodoxy.* Boulder, Colo.: 1994.

Gustafson, Thane. *Capitalism Russian-Style.* Cambridge: 1999.

Lloyd, John. *Rebirth of a Nation: An Anatomy of Russia.* London: 1998.

McFaul, Michael, and Sergei Markov. *The Troubled Birth of Russian Democracy.* Stanford, Calif.: 1993.

Millar, James R., and Sharon L. Wolchik, eds. *The Social Legacy of Communism.* Cambridge, England: 1994.

Remnick, David. *Resurrection.* New York: 1997.

Shevtsova, Lilia. *Yeltsin's Russia: Myth and Reality.* Washington, D.C.: 1999.

Steele, Jonathan. *Eternal Russia: Yeltsin, Gorbachev, and the Mirage of Democracy.* Cambridge, Mass.: 1994.

Yeltsin, Boris. *The Struggle for Russia.* New York: 1994.

Notes

CHAPTER 1

1. B. D. Grekov, *The Culture of Kiev Rus* (Moscow: 1947), 9.
2. From *Medieval Russia: A Source Book, 900–1700* (p. 74) by Basil Dmytryshyn. Copyright © 1967 by Holt, Rinehart and Winston, Inc. Reprinted by permission of the publisher.
3. Samuel H. Cross and Olgerd P. Sherbowitz-Wetzer, trans. and eds., *The Russian Primary Chronicle, Laurentian Text* (Cambridge, Mass.: 1953), 84.

CHAPTER 2

1. From *Medieval Russia: A Source Book, 900–1700* (p. 129) by Basil Dmytryshyn. Copyright © 1967 by Holt, Rinehart and Winston, Inc. Reprinted by permission of the publisher.
2. Cited from a compilation by Sir Robert Kennaway Douglas in Frank Trippet, *The Emergence of Man: The First Horsemen* (New York: 1974), 139.
3. In Russia the Mongols were known as Tartars or Tatars, but *Tatar* is more accurately used to designate Turkic groups allied with the Mongols who subsequently settled in southeastern Russia and the Crimea.
4. In L. S. Stavrianos, ed., *The Epic of Man to 1500* (Englewood Cliffs, N.J.: 1970), 241.

CHAPTER 3

1. From *Medieval Russia: A Source Book, 900–1700* (pp. 134–135) by Basil Dmytryshyn. Copyright © 1967 by Holt, Rinehart and Winston, Inc. Reprinted by permission of the publisher.
2. Ibid., 155–156.

CHAPTER 4

1. From *The Correspondence Between Prince A. M. Kurbsky and Tsar Ivan IV of Russia, 1564–1579*, trans. and ed., J.L.I. Fennell (Cambridge, England: 1955), 73–75.
2. A Soviet scholar, R. G. Skrynnikov, contends that this incident was largely a myth concocted later by Ivan himself to justify his policies.

3. From *Medieval Russia: A Source Book, 900–1700* (p. 224) by Basil Dmytryshyn. Copyright © 1967 by Holt, Rinehart and Winston, Inc. Reprinted by permission of the publisher.

CHAPTER 5

1. Joseph T. Fuhrmann, *Tsar Alexis: His Reign and His Russia* (Gulf Breeze, Fla.: Academic International Press, 1981), 149.

2. Cited in Mark C. Lapham's review of E. V. Chistiakova, "Gorodskie vosstaniia v Rossii v pervoi polovine XVII veka (30–40-e gody) [City rebellions in Russia in the first half of the 17th century (1630s–40s)]," *Kritika*, vol. XII, no. 2 (Spring 1977), p. 87.

3. In Paul Miliukov, *Outlines of Russian Culture*, Part I, *Religion and the Church* (Philadelphia: University of Pennsylvania Press, 1942), 38.

CHAPTER 6

1. Robert K. Massie, *Peter the Great* (New York: 1980), 142.

2. From the published diary of Johann Georg Korb, an Austrian diplomat at Peter's court, cited in Basil Dmytryshyn, ed., *Imperial Russia: A Source Book 1700–1917* (New York: 1967), 11–12.

3. R. M. Hatton, *Charles XII of Sweden* (New York: 1968), 299–300.

4. George Vernadsky, ed., *A Source Book for Russian History From Early Times to 1917* (Vol. 2) (New Haven, Conn.: 1972), 349.

CHAPTER 7

1. Isabel de Madariaga, *Russia in the Age of Catherine the Great* (New Haven, Conn.: 1982), 1.

2. Warren B. Walsh, comp. and ed., *Readings in Russian History* (4th ed., vol. 1) (Syracuse, N.Y.: 1963), 225–226.

CHAPTER 8

1. This vignette of the Decembrist uprising is based largely on material in George Vernadsky, ed., *A Source Book for Russian History from Early Times to 1917,* vol. 2, *Peter the Great to Nicholas I* (New Haven: 1971), 524–530.

2. Ibid., 552.

3. Cited in W.G.F. Jackson, *Seven Roads to Moscow* (New York: 1958), 160.

CHAPTER 9

1. This account of the assassination is based on information in W. Bruce Lincoln, *The Romanovs: Autocrats of All the Russias* (New York: 1981), 443–447.

2. Cited in Thomas Riha, ed., *Readings in Russian Civilization*, vol. 2, *Imperial Russia, 1700–1917* (2d ed., Chicago: 1969), 375.

3. In George Vernadsky, ed., *A Source Book for Russian History from Early Times to 1917*, vol. 3, *Alexander II to the February Revolution* (New Haven, Conn.: 1972), 664.

4. Riha, *Readings*, 410, 413.

CHAPTER 10

1. Based on the account in Howard D. Mehlinger and John M. Thompson, *Count Witte and the Tsarist Government in the 1905 Revolution* (Bloomington, Ind.: 1972), 40–45.

2. Sir John Maynard, *Russia in Flux* (London: 1941), 42–43.

3. Adapted from the version in Basil Dmytryshyn, ed., *Imperial Russia: A Source Book, 1700–1917* (New York: 1967), 309–313.

4. Mehlinger and Thompson, *Count Witte and the Tsarist Government in the 1905 Revolution*, 336.

5. Vladimir Mayakovsky, *The Bedbug and Selected Poetry*, ed. Patricia Blake (Cleveland: 1960), 75.

6. Allan K. Wildman, *The End of the Russian Imperial Army: The Old Army and the Soldiers' Revolt, March–April 1917* (Princeton, N.J.: 1979), 89.

CHAPTER 11

1. This description of events on March 10 and 11 is based on W. Bruce Lincoln, *The Romanovs: Autocrats of All the Russias* (New York: 1981), 717–722, and on other accounts.

2. Warren B. Walsh, ed., *Readings in Russian History* (Syracuse: 1963), 3, 727.

3. Leonard Schapiro, *The Origins of the Communist Autocracy, 1917–22* (Cambridge, Mass.: 1955), 301.

4. Quoted in Robert C. Tucker, *Stalin as Revolutionary, 1879–1929* (New York: 1973), 270–271.

CHAPTER 12

1. Quoted in Warren B. Walsh, ed., *Readings in Russian History*, vol. 3, 4th ed. rev. (Syracuse: 1963), 761. By permission of the publisher.

2. Joseph V. Stalin, *Works*, vol. 13, *July 1930–January 1934* (Moscow: 1955), 40–41.

3. F. V. Gladkov, *Cement* (London: 1929), 302–304.

4. Bukharin's initial plea is found in Stephen F. Cohen, *Bukharin and the Bolshevik Revolution: A Political Biography, 1888–1938* (New York: 1973), 377; his final statement is in Walsh, *Readings in Russian History*, vol. 3, 770–771.

CHAPTER 13

1. Fedor Burlatskii, "A Political Portrait of Khrushchev," in Donald J. Raleigh, ed., *Soviet Historians and Perestroika: The First Phase* (Armonk, N.Y., and London: 1989), 232–233.

2. Basil Dmytryshyn, *USSR: A Concise History*, 4th ed. (New York: 1984), 544.

CHAPTER 14

1. Quoted in Seweryn Bialer, ed., *Politics, Society and Nationality Inside Gorbachev's Russia* (Boulder, Colo.: 1989), 122.

2. Mikhail Gorbachev, *Perestroika: New Thinking for Our Country and the World* (New York: 1987), 19.

3. Ibid., 21–23.

Index